The Emergence of Liberation Theology

The Emergence of Liberation Theology

Radical Religion and Social Movement Theory

Christian Smith

The University of Chicago Press
Chicago and London

CHRISTIAN SMITH is assistant professor of sociology at Gordon College.

The University of Chicago Press, Chicago 60637
The University of Chicago Press, Ltd., London
© 1991 by The University of Chicago
All rights reserved. Published 1991
Printed in the United States of America
00 99 98 97 96 95 94 93 92 91   5 4 3 2 1

Library of Congress Cataloging in Publication Data

Smith, Christian (Christian Stephen), 1960–
    The emergence of liberation theology : radical religion and social
movement theory / Christian Smith.
        p. cm.
    Includes bibliographical references and index.
    ISBN 0-226-76409-5 (alk. paper). — 0-226-76410-9 (pbk.; alk. paper)
    1. Liberation theology.   2. Sociology, Christian (Catholic)
I. Title.
BT83.57.S64m1991
306.6'3028—DC20   90-26575
                                                                    CIP

For Robert and Helen Smith,
who taught me,
in word and in deed,
the value of
education, learning, and understanding

and

for Emily,
whose love and sacrifice
made this work possible

Contents

Tables and Figures

Tables

Figures

Acknowledgments

It goes without saying that research and writing projects like this are possible only with the help and support of many people, some of whom I wish to recognize and thank here.

First, I must thank three advisors from Harvard University for their tremendously helpful guidance: Donald Warwick, Steve Rytina, and Harvey Cox. Their support, suggestions, and criticisms strengthened this work considerably. They deserve much credit for positively shaping this work.

Second, for emotional support in trying times, I honor my comrades in misery, Monique Taylor and Debra Minkoff. I could have never survived the terrors and agonies of graduate school without them. Thanks to both of you.

I also wish to thank all who spent the time and effort to give me the interviews which brought this investigation alive. Thanks especially to those who went well out of their way to help me in my research: Archbishop Marcos McGrath, Tom Quigley, Richard Schall, Phillip Berryman, José Míguez Bonino, Francis O'Gorman, Sergio Torres, Julio de Santa Ana, Edward Cleary, Marina Bandeira, Marc Ellis, various administrators and secretaries of CELAM, and the Princeton Speer Library staff.

I am grateful for the financial support for research travel generously granted by Judson Carlberg of the Academic Dean's Office of Gordon College and by the Committee for Higher Degrees of the Sociology department of Harvard University.

For help with translations, thanks to Royce Miller, Bryan and Doris-Ann Vosseler, and Luis Lugo. Thanks, also, to Joyce Spaulding, Michele Csaki, and Bethany Maggs for their careful statistical and bibliographical assistance. For helpful and supportive feedback on early drafts of the manuscript, thanks to Stan Gaede and Hal Miller. And, for miscellaneous help and encouragement, thanks to Roderick

xi

Harrison, Merilee Grindle, Ivy George, Stephen Smith, Jan Youga, Tony Castro, and David Sherwood.

For his consistent, heartening faith in this project, I must express my appreciation to Douglas Mitchell of the University of Chicago Press.

And, finally, for her ever-present love, encouragement, and belief in me and my work, I thank my wife, Emily.

Acronyms

BEC	Base Ecclesial Community (Comunidade Eclesial de Base)
CEDI	Ecumenical Center of Documentation and Information (Centro Ecumenico de Documentação e Informação. Rio de Janeiro, Brazil)
CEDIAL	Research Center for Development and Integration of Latin America (Centro de Estudios para el Desarrollo y la Integración de América Latina. Bogotá, Colombia)
CEHILA	Commission on Historical Studies of the Church in Latin America (Centro de Estudios de la Historia de la Iglesia en América Latina. Mexico City)
CELAM	Latin American Episcopal Conference (Consejo Episcopal Latinoamericano. Bogotá, Columbia)
CEP	Study and Publication Center (Centro de Estudios y Publicaciones. Lima, Peru)
CERIS	Center for Religious Research and Statistics (Centro de Estatistíca Religiósa e Investigações. Brazil)
CESEP	Ecumenical Center of Service for Evangelization and Popular Education (Centro Ecumenico de Servicos a Evangelização e Educação Popular. São Paulo, Brazil)
CIAS	Center for Social Investigation and Action (Centro de Investigaciones y Acción Social)
CICOP	Catholic Inter-American Cooperation Program (U.S.A.)
CLAR	Latin American Conference of Religious Orders (Confederación Latinoamericana de Religiosos)
CLASC	Latin American Conference of Christian Unions (Confederación Latinoamericana de Sindicatos Cristianos)
CNBB	National Conference of Brazilian Bishops (Conferência Nacional dos Bispos do Brasil)
DEI	Ecumenical Research Department (Departamento Ecuménico de Investigaciones. San José, Costa Rica)
DESAL	Center of Economic and Social Development in Latin America

	(Centro de Desarrollo Económico y Social en América Latina. Santiago, Chile)
ECLA	United Nations Economic Commission for Latin America
FERES	Federation of Religious and Social Studies (Federación de Estudios Religiosos y Sociales. Bogotá, Colombia; Rio de Janeiro, Brazil)
IDES	Institute of Social and Economic Development (Instituto para el Desarrollo Económico y Social. Colombia)
ILADES	Latin American Institute of Doctrine and Social Studies (Instituto Latinamericano de Doctrina y Estudios Sociales. Santiago, Chile)
IPLA	Pastoral Institute of Latin America (Instituto Pastoral Latinoamericano. Quito, Ecuador)
ISAL	Church and Society in Latin America (Iglesia y Sociedad en América Latina. Brazil; Bolivia)
JAC	Young Catholic Farmers (Juventude Agrária Católica)
JEC	Young Catholic Secondary School Students (Juventude Estudantil Católica)
JIC	Young Catholic Independent Movement (Juventude Independente Católica)
JOC	Young Catholic Factory Workers (Juventude Operária Católica)
JUC	Young Catholic University Students (Juventude Universitária Católica)
LADOC	Latin American Documentation Service (Peru)
MAPU	Movement of Unitary Popular Action (Movimiento para la Acción Popular Unitária, Chile)
MEB	Movement for Basic Education (Movimento de Educação de Base. Northeast Brazil)
NIEO	New International Economic Order
ONIS	National Office of Social Information (Oficina Nacional de Información Social. Lima, Peru)
OSORE	Office of Religious Sociology (Oficina de Sociología Religiosa. Santiago, Chile)
SAL	Priests of Latin America (Sacerdotes de América Latina. Colombia)
SNI	National Information Service (Servicio Nacional de Informacion. Brazil)
SODEPAX	Committee on Society, Development, and Peace (Campine, Switzerland)
UNEC	National Union of Catholic University Students (Unión Nacional de Estudiantes Católicos. Lima, Peru)
USCC	United States Catholic Conference (Washington, D.C.)
WCC	The World Council of Churches (Geneva, Switzerland)

Introduction

March 24, 1980, Archbishop Oscar Romero of San Salvador, El Salvador, was gunned down before his congregation while celebrating mass. At the conclusion of his homily, in the Basilica of the Sacred Heart, a single bullet pierced his chest and fragmented, causing heavy internal bleeding. Within minutes, after choking on his own blood, he was dead (Martin-Baro 1985: 1).

Romero was executed by a right-wing assassin, probably a member of the White Warrior Union. Many on the political right had come to hate Romero for his outspoken social and political views. In the months before his assassination, the archbishop had received constant death threats, threats that were authenticated by the murders of many of his priests, close friends, and co-workers (Martin-Baro 1985). Yet, despite cautions from his fellow bishops and the Roman hierarchy, Romero persisted in denouncing violence, oppression, and injustice.[1]

Two weeks before his death, Romero told a reporter,

> I have often been threatened with death. Nevertheless, as a Christian, I do not believe in death without resurrection. If they kill me, I shall arise in the Salvadoran people. Martyrdom is a grace of God that I do not believe I deserve. But if God accepts the sacrifice of my life, let my blood be a seed of freedom. Let my death be for the liberation of my people. (Brockman 1982: 223)

No one would have predicted Oscar Romero's fate. In 1977, when the Vatican chose him as the new archbishop of San Salvador, he was a traditional bishop who spoke of the "eminently religious and transcendent" mission of priests, and who criticized political theologies.[2] His appointment rankled the progressive clergy of his archdiocese. They favored auxiliary bishop Arturo Rivera y Damas, whose pastoral philosophy stressed social justice and liberation in a way that chal-

1

lenged the wealthy class and government of El Salvador (Quigley 1984: 366; Brockman 1982: 3–4; Martin-Baro 1985: 1). However, Rome chose to appoint Romero.[3]

Three years later, on March 23, 1980, in the midst of great violence, Romero proclaimed in his Sunday homily at the basilica (broadcast on international radio):

> Let no one take it ill that in the light of God's words that we read in our mass we enlighten social, political, and economic realities. If we did not, it would not be Christianity for us. . . .
>
> Every solution that we want to give, to a better distribution of land, to a better administration of money in El Salvador, to a political organization fitted to the common good of Salvadorans, will have to be sought always in the totality of the definitive liberation. . . .
>
> Now, I would like to make an appeal in a special way to the men of the army, and in particular to the ranks of the National Guard. Brothers, you are part of our own people. You kill your own campesino brothers and sisters. And before an order that a man may give to kill, the law of God must prevail that says: Thou shalt not kill! No soldier is obliged to obey an order against the law of God. No one has to fulfill an immoral law. It is time to recover your consciences and obey your consciences rather than the orders of sin. The Church, defender of the rights of God, of the law of God, of human dignity, the dignity of the person, cannot remain silent before such an abomination. In the name of God, and in the name of this suffering people whose laments rise to heaven each day more tumultuously, I beg you, I ask you, I order you in the name of God: Stop the repression!

Romero concluded his homily, which was interrupted five times by prolonged applause:

> The Church preaches its liberation just as we have studied it today in the Holy Bible—a liberation that has, above all, respect for the dignity of the person, the saving of the common good of the people, and a transcendence that looks before all to God, and from God derives its hope and its force. (Brockman 1982: 216–17)

The next evening, Romero was murdered.

Romero's experience—his life and death—is provocative and revealing. It evokes questions such as, How could a man who was a stable supporter of traditional, conservative Catholicism for thirty-five years be so quickly transformed into a forceful voice of social and political opposition? What could have transpired in those few years to turn the acceptable choice of El Salvador's rich and powerful into one of their greatest enemies?

More importantly, Romero's ordeal prompts us to ask, does this particular event reveal something about the experience of the Church in Latin America as a whole? Was Oscar Romero's experience an isolated, exceptional incident or does it somehow represent the experience of the Catholic Church all over Central and South America?

The Transformation of the Latin American Church

One need not be a theological expert or a Latin American specialist to have reason to suspect that Oscar Romero's life and death was not simply an isolated event. A casual observation of the news media in recent years would easily lead one to surmise that Romero's experience is somehow indicative of a broad, profound movement for change in the Roman Catholic Church in Latin America. And this suspicion would be entirely accurate. This study is an investigation of that change. However, my goal here is to move beyond the news media accounts of this movement, to penetrate into the deepest motivating impulses and dynamics of this profound transformation of the Latin American Church.

The stereotypic image of the Roman Catholic Church in Latin America long was of a tradition-bound, inflexible, conservative, elite-allied institution. Although this image is, to a certain degree, a caricature, it does have some basis in fact, and, historically, has been more often true than false. But in the last two decades, things have been changing. Oscar Romero was a sign of that change.

Romero did not live out his life in a social or ideological vacuum. Instead, he was shaped by and helped to shape the social world that he inhabited. To understand the outcome of Romero's life, one must understand the influence of that social world.

In particular, Romero was influenced by the ideas of a new, peculiarly Latin American way of understanding the meaning of the Christian faith, commonly known as "liberation theology." Although not a leading liberation theologian himself, Romero's *lived experience* in a violent, oppressive, and unjust situation made many of the *ideas* of liberation theology very real to him, transforming his perception and evaluation of the world.

Similarly, yet in their own distinct ways, many Roman Catholic Christians and Churches all over Latin America are being transformed by liberation theology.

Unlike most classical theologies, which remain in university discussions and seminary classrooms, liberation theology is gripping the imaginations and directing the actions of many academics, bishops, clergy, religious, and laity alike. "Liberation theology," says Radomiro Tomic, Chile's 1970 Christian Democrat presidential candidate, "has spread like wildfire in dry prairie grass across the breadth of Latin America, from Mexico to Chile, among clerics and religious women, the poor and the young, and among lay people of varied social conditions" (LADOC 1986: 56). Liberation theology has transformed and is transforming the organization of the Church, the spiritualities of the masses, and the alliances of Latin American social institutions. In light of this transformation we can accurately speak of this as a liberation theology *movement.*

In its earliest years, liberation theology was thought by many to be a passing fad. But, far from being an interesting but peripheral religious novelty, the movement has had and portends to have a long-term impact on the religious and political experience of Latin America. Furthermore, the influence of liberation theology is spreading to certain sectors of Christianity in India, the Philippines, Africa, North America, and Europe.[4] Indeed, some of the works of liberation theology have been translated into twelve languages, and can be found in Bible school and Marxist bookstores alike.

Representing a significant shift in institutional allegiances, the liberation theology movement has produced in many places a commitment of the institutional Church to the poor and the creation of a new model of Church participation and pastoral work. Often in Latin America, it has helped to generate opposition to political regimes, sometimes resulting in the arrests, exile, torture, and murder of lay leaders, clergy, nuns, and bishops (Beeson and Pearce 1984; Lernoux 1982; Lange and Iblacker 1981; Brockman 1982). And, the movement has helped produce progressive and revolutionary laity and clergy who have often played key roles in Latin American popular movements, insurrections, and revolutions (Berryman 1984b; Montgomery 1982; Quigley 1982; Williams 1985; Bonpane 1985; Cabestrero 1983; Jerez 1984; Cardenal 1982; Belli 1988).

This transforming movement has been likened in socioreligious profundity to the sixteeth-century Protestant Reformation and the eighteenth-century Great Awakening. Because of the actual and potential consequences of the liberation theology movement for Latin America and beyond, it has, on the one hand, evoked distress from the U.S. State Department: for example, the "Santa Fe" document, published by the Committee of Santa Fe for the Council for Inter-American Security, considers liberation theology to be a "political weapon" of "Marxist-Leninist forces" for the purpose of "infiltrating the religious community" and spreading ideas "against private ownership and productive capitalism," declaring finally that "American foreign policy should begin to mount a counterattack on (and not merely react against) liberation theology" (quoted in Boff and Boff 1986: 8).[5] On the other hand, it caused Fidel Castro to change Cuban policy to acknowledge the value of religion for socialism (Reding 1987; Crahan 1985; David 1985; Betto 1987).[6]

The Question of Origins

Clearly, a movement of this importance deserves and has received the attention of social scientists (for example, Adriance 1986; Bruneau 1974, 1985; Berryman 1984b; Levine 1981, 1984, 1985, 1986; Levine, ed., 1979; Levine and Wilde 1977; Sanders 1969, 1972; Landsberger 1970; Littwin 1974; Dodson 1984, 1986; Johnson and Figa 1988; Maduro 1982; Langton and Rapoport 1976; Mainwaring 1984; Smith 1982; and Neuhouser 1989). Many of these analyses are high-quality works that provide valuable insight into the political dynamics of a changing Church in Latin America.

One important question, however, has not, as yet, been explored in a focused, systematic manner: *How and why did the liberation theology movement emerge and survive when and where it did?* Harvey Cox (1988: 11) has observed: "the story of liberation theology is about how in less than twenty years, a quiet conversation among a few out-of-the-way Latin Americans became a worldwide theological movement." Exactly how and why this movement emerged and spread is the problem that I will explore, the question that I seek to answer in this study.

I will limit my substantive scope to the Roman Catholic Church, although some Protestants played a vital role in bringing the movement to birth and some of the liberation theology movement's most important leaders are Protestant. I focus here on the Catholic Church, since it is within that institution that liberation theology has had its most profound expression. I will pay attention to the role of Protestants in the emergence of the liberation theology movement only insofar as it relates to understanding that emergence within the Catholic Church.

Most works on liberation theology spend a few pages reviewing a standard list of events to indicate how and why it was born—the influences of Vatican II, Base Ecclesial Communities, Camilo Torres, and so on. But this kind of list simply catalogues events without seriously specifying the historical relationships among those factors.

A few basically sound historical accounts of events related to the emergence of liberation theology have been written (Prada 1975; Oliveros, 1977; CELAM 1982; Gotay, 1983; Dussel, 1976, 1979, 1981; Richard, 1976, 1987a; Lernoux, 1982). None of them, however, fully addresses the question I have posed. They either focus on background facts (such as colonial precursors to liberation theology), focus on only one event (such as Medellín), focus on only one institution (such as CELAM), or employ an historical framework to make an essentially future-oriented, normative argument, for example, that the model of New Christendom is no longer a viable option for the Latin American Church. Most of these works are excellent resources, but none takes as its central task a thorough sociological explanation of the emergence of liberation theology. And so the question of how and why the movement emerged remains unanswered.

A Sociological Approach

Sociologists seek to explain events by moving from the particular to the general and back to the particular. The sociologist continually keeps an eye on both the empirical data at hand and general analytical models which seek to interpret and illuminate that and other empirical data. In this sense, sociologists are not only interested in understanding particular social events, but also in constructing general theoretical models that make sense of *whole classes* of social events. As Max Weber (1978: 19) noted, "Sociology seeks to formulate type concepts and generalized uniformities of empirical process. This distinguishes it from history, which is oriented to the causal analysis and explanation of individual actions, structures, and personalities."

The approach of this study is sociological and, as such, reflects a twofold interest. First, I endeavor to answer the empirically oriented question, How and why did the liberation theology movement emerge and survive when and where it did? In this way, I hope to contribute to a more comprehensive understanding of the movement than has yet appeared in the literature. The general methodological approach I employ for this task is historical sociology, that is, the reconstruction of past events, through the use of interviews, texts, historical documents, and statistics, guided and illuminated by analytical, theoretical models of explanation.

My second interest is theoretical. The emergence of liberation theology belongs to the class of phenomena known as "social movements" (see chapter 3). I will make use of a theoretical model which has sought to explain social movement emergence and development, the political process model, to assist and illuminate this investigation of the liberation theology movement. But I also expect—and will argue—that the case of the liberation theology movement can contribute to the advancement of social movement theory. In this way, the general theoretical model and the specific historical case will amplify each other.

Plan of the Study

This study is organized into two sections. Part 1 seeks to describe the basic outlines of the liberation theology movement. In chapter 1, I give a brief, historical overview of the emergence and growth of the liberation theology movement, for the purpose of providing a framework within which the rest of the study can fit. Chapter 2 focuses specifically on the movement's ideology and tries to show its basic meaning and intentions. Chapter 3 explains the theoretical model of social movements, the political process model, that I will use to analyze the liberation theology movement.

Part 2 constitutes the heart of this study, the place where the empirical facts of the liberation theology movement are interpreted through the political process model of social movements. In chapter 4 I explore the historical background out of which the liberation theology movement grew from 1930 to 1955, up to the year in which the Latin American Episcopal Conference (CELAM) was formed. Chapter 5 considers relevant changes during the decade after that, including the Second Vatican Council, 1955 to 1965. In chapter 6 I focus on the crucial years after the Second Vatican Council which led to the 1968 CELAM conference in Medellín, Colombia. Chapter 7 is concerned with the making of the Medellín conference itself. In chapter 8 I investigate the "honeymoon" years of liberation theology, from the 1968 Medellín conference to the 1972 meeting of CELAM in Sucre, Bolivia, where an organized conservative backlash against liberation theology was begun. Chapter 9 explores the years between the Sucre meeting and the 1979 CELAM conference in Puebla, Mexico, where liberation theology was established as a valid expression of Christian life in the Church. Finally, chapter 10 reviews briefly the experience of the liberation theology movement since Puebla.

Part One

Understanding the
Liberation Theology
Movement

1

A Brief History of the Liberation Theology Movement

Christianity arrived in Latin America through the Spanish and Portuguese conquest. Along with the musket and cannon came the Roman Catholic faith; behind the marching soldier walked the zealous missionary. Columbus reached America in the same year that the Spaniards succeeded in crushing the last Muslim stronghold in Spain. Having achieved victory over the Moors, the Spaniards (and Portuguese) turned their attention to the New World. And they came "in a conquest spirit already well developed at home" (Skidmore and Smith 1984, 17).

Latin America was conquered and colonized, then, with mixed motives. On the one hand, the Iberians came to acquire wealth and noble rank . On the other, they came to save the souls of the heathen natives, by the sword if necessary. As Hernán Cortés, conquistador of Mexico, said, "We came here to serve God and the King, and also to get gold" (Skidmore and Smith 1984: 18). Hugo Latorre Cabal (1978: 3) notes, "After land had been sighted from the *Pinta,* the chief of the expedition in his admiral's array, with Christ's standard in one hand and the insignia of the Catholic Monarchs in the other, took possession of the new territory with Portuguese pomp in the name of the Church and State made one by theology and law. He proclaimed, 'Our Redeemer gave this victory to our own most illustrious King and Queen and to their Kingdoms famous for such a noble cause, therefore all Christianity should rejoice and celebrate . . . for an achievement which will join so many people to our Holy Faith.'"

Thus, the conquest introduced a social order in which the crusade of Spain and the mission of Jesus Christ were identical. From the very beginning, the Church was closely allied with the military and governmental powers of colonial Latin America. As the years went on, the Church endorsed the Crown's authority and legitimated the colonial social system. In return, the Church was granted status as a cultural authority, was allowed to control education, and occupied a privileged economic position (Medhurst 1987: 17; Bauer 1983; Bouvier 1983: 7–8; Vekemans 1976, 18–20).

Early Voices of Protest

The conquest resulted in the destruction of the Mayan, Aztec, and Incan civilizations. These civilizations—whose people once numbered between 90 and 112 million—were overwhelmed by Spanish military operations, subjection to slavery, a smallpox epidemic, and other diseases. In some areas these native Americans were forced into a harsh, humiliating subjugation; in others, entire native populations were eliminated. This behavior was generally sanctioned by the Church, which sometimes doubted that the natives actually possessed souls, but never doubted that—in cases of resistance to the Catholic faith—death was better than life without Christ (Carroll 1987: 9; see also Bouvier 1983: 4).

Not all Catholics adopted this practice concerning the treatment of natives. Indeed, in the sixteenth century, many bishops and priests fiercely protested their subjugation and extermination. Among those who actively resisted this treatment of natives are Bartolomé de Las Casas, bishop of Chiapas, Mexico; Diego Medellín, bishop of Santiago, Chile; Antonio de Valdivieso, bishop of Nicaragua; Antonio San Miguel, bishop of La Imperial, Peru; Juan del Valle, bishop of Popayan; Luis Beltran; Antonio de Vieyra; and Antonio Montesinos (Richard 1987a: 28; Cabal 1978: 5–8). They preached against the inhuman treatment of natives, protested in writing to the Crown and to Rome, took legal actions to defend the local peoples, promoted resistance to oppressive governmental policies, and absolved the sins of natives. In 1511, for example, Antonio de Montesinos preached this sermon to the settlers of Española:

Tell me by what right and under what law do you hold these Indians in such cruel and horrible servitude? By what authority do you make such detestable war against these people who were dwelling gently and peacefully in their lands? . . . You kill them everyday to gain wealth! . . . Are they not men? Do they not have souls? Are you not commanded to love them as yourselves? Don't you understand this? Why are you so sunk in lethargy, so fast asleep? It is certain that in your present state you have no more hope of salvation than the Moors or Turks. (Cabal 1978: 7)

Some of these Catholic protesters even led open revolts (Cabal 1978: 6).

Contemporary liberation theologians claim that these early acts of resistance to the oppression of colonial Christendom foreshadowed the present-day movement of liberation theology in the Church. Indeed, they praise these early voices of religious opposition to domination and exploitation, elevate these people as true heroes of the faith, and name their research institutes after them.[1]

Independence

In the nineteenth century, partly as a result of Napoleon Bonaparte's 1807 occupation of Iberia, most Latin American countries gained political independence from Spain and Portugal. This forced the Church to adjust the basis of its position in Latin American society, since it could no longer rely on the protection of the Iberian Crown.

Some of the new republics, such as Colombia, continued the traditional, mutually beneficial alliances of legitimation and protection between Church and state. However, many of the protagonists for independence who became the ruling elite of the new republics were of a liberal persuasion, and saw little social value in the Catholic Church (Burns 1980). Furthermore, most Church hierarchies had generally opposed the independence movements, siding with the Spanish Crown. Consequently, many liberal elites sought to reduce the social power of the Church by legislating against its privileged position in society (Berryman 1987a: 11; Bouvier 1983: 9–12; see also Vekemans 1976: 21–23).

Church leaders reacted to these liberal, anti-clerical attacks by strengthening their ties with those groups who were sympathetic to the traditional alliance: conservative parties, landowners, and the old aristocracy (Bouvier 1983: 13). The Church thus tended, in many cases, to become further estranged from the liberal intelligentsia and progressive political leaders. The net effect of these struggles and realignments was "to confirm the Church as a socially conservative but economically diminished institution, whose leaders were inclined to regard challenges to the social or political status quo as inimical to the interests of the Catholic religion" (Medhurst 1987: 17).

A New Christendom

Throughout the nineteenth century and into the early twentieth century, in addition to placing its confidence in the conservative sectors of society, the Church generally assumed that its influence among the peasants and workers was strong, that the masses were supportive of and attached to official Catholic institutions and teachings. As the process of modernization and urbanization progressed, however, it became clear in many countries that the Church had overestimated its popular influence. The Catholic Church increasingly found itself, in the first decades of the twentieth century, unsuccessfully competing for the allegiances of the people against secular unions, left-wing political groups, African-derived spiritualist cults, and newly arrived Protestant churches.

In the face of these threats to the Church's social and religious influence and in light of an emerging nationalist, developmental populism, beginning in the 1930s the Latin American Church in many countries undertook the project of building a "new Christendom" (Dussel 1976: 106; Carroll 1987: 10; Vekemans 1976: 23–26). This was, essentially, a strategy to establish Catholicism as a major institutional and cultural influence in Latin America's modernizing society (Shaull 1970). This new strategy was largely encouraged and guided by European influences, especially Jacques Maritain's philosophy of "integral humanism."[2]

The New Christendom project, in the decades after 1930, but especially in the early 1960s, dismantled the Church's conservative, anti-liberal alliances, placing it on the side of—rather than against—"progress," "science," "modernity," and "development" (Richard 1987a: 76–77). It imported European models of Catholic Action, which organized Catholic laity for religiously informed participation in the spheres of education, politics, the economy, culture, and the family. Christian Democratic parties, with Catholic laypersons as political candidates, were created in many countries, with notable successes in Chile, Venezuela, and Brazil. And the Church built new schools and seminaries to increase educational efforts among lay, religious, and clerical pastoral workers.

By the 1950s and early 1960s, Catholic Churches in many countries were heavily invested in increasing their influence among the laity, and committed to aiding the process of socioeconomic development (Vekemans 1976: 26–28). Many worked to sponsor programs and courses to develop lay leadership, to encourage an increase of foreign missionary aid, to utilize radio technology to broadcast Church teachings, to fund social research and documentation institutes to collect socioeconomic data, to write theological reflections on socioeconomic development, and so on.

Until the end of the Second Vatican Council in 1965, despite some conflicts within the Church over the new strategy, this project of "new Christendom" was accomplished with "relative ease, security, optimism, and even some triumphalism" (Richard 1987a: 77). New Christendom reached its apex in 1964 when the Christian Democrat candidate Eduardo Frei won the presidency of Chile.

Signs of a New Time

In the early 1960s, however, a number of events transpired that began to cast a shadow over the whole New Christendom strategy (Pastene 1986; Vekemans 1976: 29). Projects failed, and prophets in the church raised their voices.

In 1959, the Cuban government was overthrown by the socialist Fidel Castro. In 1964, a military coup in Brazil ended democracy for what was to be twenty years. In time, it became evident that the Christian Democratic parties could not deliver the reforms they campaigned for. Eduardo Frei's "revolution in freedom" gradually began to curb opposition (Richard 1988). Only a few years after its inauguration, John F. Kennedy's Alliance for Progress began showing signs of inadequacy. The activities of police and security forces, trained in counterinsurgency and torture, increased. Events like these cast doubt in the minds of some on the promise of democratic capitalism and, by extension, on the Church's strategy of a "new Christendom." Many university students began questioning the Church's relevance and effectiveness. Young people, it seemed, were becoming more and more attracted to Marxism (Torres 1988; Santa Ana 1988).

Within the Church the voices of new critics and visionaries began to be heard. In Brazil, for example, Dom Hélder Camera, a charismatic bishop from Rio de Janeiro, began to criticize the capitalist economic system (Nuñez 1985: 105–9). Hélder Camera had been the national chaplain of Catholic Action since 1947, had initiated the formation of the National Conference of Brazilian Bishops in 1952 and of the Latin American Episcopal Conference (CELAM) in 1955, and was influential in the 1961–67 Basic Education Movement

(MEB) which sought to conscientize the masses through church radio programs (Adriance 1986). He denounced the poverty and violence of capitalism, called for the conscientization, or "consciousness-raising," of the poor (based on Paulo Freire's literacy training method), and raised the possibility of a move toward socialism.

At the end of the Second Vatican Council, Hélder Camera organized a group of fifteen bishops from Africa, Latin America, and Asia who wrote and publicized a document titled "A Message to the People of the Third World." Hélder Camera's name led the list of signatures, which included those of seven other Latin American bishops. The message declared that "the peoples of the Third World are the proletariat of today's humanity," that "the gospel demands the first, radical revolution," and that "wealth must be shared by all." The letter charges that the wealthy wage a "class warfare" against the workers, "massacring entire peoples throughout the whole world," and that "true socialism is Christianity integrally lived."[3]

In Colombia, an even more radical prophet arose in the person of Camilo Torres. Torres was a European-educated priest and sociologist who spent years conducting research on poverty in Colombia. In May 1965, in the midst of disputes with University and Church authorities, Torres organized a "United Front" to link together peasants, slum dwellers, workers, and professionals to work for social change. Immediately, his cardinal denounced his work, accusing Torres of separating himself from the doctrines and directives of the Church. In June, after an escalation of differences between Torres and his superiors, Torres renounced his priesthood (Ramirez 1971: 31). By October, he had joined the guerrilla Army of National Liberation, believing that "armed struggle is the only means that remains [for social change]" (C. Torres 1969: 201; see also Nuñez 1985: 103–5). On February 16, 1966, in an army ambush and counterattack, Torres was shot and killed.

Torres had proclaimed: "I took off my cassock to be more truly a priest," "The duty of every Catholic is to be a revolutionary, the duty of every revolutionary is to make the revolution," and "The Catholic who is not a revolutionary is living in mortal sin" (Gerassi 1971: xiii). Many Catholics considered Torres to be naive and foolish, anything but a faithful Christian. Even his friend, the theologian Gustavo Gutiérrez, "did not believe that the decision of Camilo to join the guerrilla movement was a wise one" (Nuñez 1985: 116). Others, especially young Latin Americans, were inspired by Torres' life, and his death elevated him, in the eyes of many, to the status of martyred sainthood. Torres' writings and speeches were published and the newspaper he founded, *Frente Unido,* was continued and expanded. Hundreds of "Camilista groups" sprang up in Colombia, Venezuela, Ecuador, Peru, and Bolivia. Most importantly, Torres had forced to the center of Christian debates questions about the futility of reformist strategies and the justification of violent revolution.

Elsewhere, the debates among mainline Protestant denominations echoed Torres' concerns. Since the early 1960s, the Latin American organization Church and Society in Latin America (Iglesia y Sociedad en América Latina—ISAL), led by Presbyterian missionary to Brazil Richard Shaull and sponsored by the World Council of Churches (WCC), had been developing a "theology of revolution." Shaull and his followers became convinced over the years that moderate reform in Latin America was inadequate. They therefore set themselves to work on a Christian justification for radical social-structural transformation—what they called "revolution"—not necessarily meaning violent insurrection.[4] The influence of this "theology of revolution" was felt as far away as the Geneva headquarters of the WCC, and close to home among Latin American Catholic theologians, who were becoming more and more ecumenically oriented.

Finally, the changes set in motion by the Second Vatican Council (1961–65) profoundly undermined the strategy of New Christendom. Under the leadership of popes John XXIII and Paul VI, and progressive European theologians, Vatican II altered the official Church teachings on the nature of the Church and the value of secular historical progress, opening the door for a fundamental rethinking of the Christian faith and its place in the modern world. Whereas the New Christendom strategy tried to "christianize" and control society, Vatican II affirmed the more humble "pilgrim" status of the Church, journeying alongside the rest of humankind. Furthermore, Vatican II recognized evidence of God's work in—and therefore the value of—"secular historical progress" (Berryman 1987a: 16).[5]

By the second half of the 1960s, the Roman Catholic Church in Latin America was experiencing enormous ferment and unrest. Uncertainties and debates abounded concerning the role of the clergy, Christian involvement in politics, the justification of violent revolution, the celibacy of priests, the nature of ecclesiastical authority, the Church's role in socioeconomic development, and the possibility of dialogue and cooperation with Marxists.

Clearly the Church was changing. The question to be answered was, what direction should that change take? At the time, an aggressive group of leaders in the Church began to articulate a very progressive, seemingly promising answer to that question. In 1968 the Church chose to adopt that answer as its official position in Latin America. Things began to change rapidly.

An Alternative Vision

From August 24 to September 6, 1968, 130 bishops, representing the more than 600 bishops of every country in Latin America, met in the Colombian city of Medellín for the second plenary session of CELAM.[6] The purpose of the meeting, entitled "The Church in the Present-Day Transformation of Latin America in the Light of the Council," was to apply Vatican II to Latin America. The actual outcome of the meeting was to throw the weight of the Roman Catholic Church's authority into controversial programs for social change. The final documents of Medellín—which the bishops adopted and endorsed—became the Magna Carta of a whole new approach to the mission of the Church.

The Medellín document on poverty begins:

> The Latin American bishops cannot remain indifferent in the face of the tremendous social injustices existent in Latin America, which keep the majority of our peoples in dismal poverty, which in many cases becomes inhuman wretchedness. A deafening cry pours from the throats of millions of men, asking their pastors for a liberation that reaches them from nowhere else. (Gremillion 1976: 471)

The Medellín documents are an answer to that cry.[7]

The documents begin with an analysis of the Latin American social situation. They charge that Latin America suffers under "neocolonialism," "internal colonialism," "external colonialism," "the international imperialism of money," "a dependence on a center of economic power," and "a marked bi-classism." These exploitative structures constitute "serious sins," "a sinful situation," and "a situation of injustice that can be called institutionalized violence." The documents claim that poverty "is in itself evil," that the "growing distortion of international commerce [is] . . . a permanent menace against peace," and that "those who have the greater share of wealth, culture, and power [by retaining their privilege] are responsible to history for provoking explosive revolutions of despair." In response, the Medellín conclusions call for "all-embracing, courageous, urgent, and profoundly renovating transformations."

Claiming that "to create a just social order . . . is an eminently Christian task," the documents commit the Church to a project of radical social change toward "authentic liberation." Condemning both "liberal capitalism" and "the Marxist system" as "militating against the dignity of the human person," the Medellín conclusions devote the Church to a "solidarity with the poor" which "gives preference to the poorest and most needy sectors." What is necessary, claims the text, is "a global organization, where all of the peoples, but more especially the lower classes, have, by means of territorial and functional structures, an active and receptive, creative and decisive participation in the construction of a new society" in which man is "an agent of his own history." This will require the "task of 'conscientizacion' and social education" which "ought to be integrated into joint Pastoral Action at various levels." "The Church—the People of God—will lend its support to the downtrodden," states the document on justice, "so that they might come to know their rights and how to make use of them." Reflecting a commitment to the development of Base Ecclesial Communities (BECs) and to ecumenism, the documents encourage the formation of "small communities," "grass-roots organizations," and "collaboration . . . with non-Catholic Christian Churches and institutions dedicated to the task of restoring justice in human relations."[8]

Though relatively mild compared with the theologies that would be written in succeeding years, the Medellín documents marked a radical departure from the rhetoric and strategy of an institution which, for centuries, had justified the killing of native peoples, provided a religious legitimation for an authoritarian, hierarchical social system, and aligned itself with conservative power elites. The hierarchies of Colombia and Argentina objected to the Medellín conclusions. Despite this, because of the ratifying vote of the representing bishops, Medellín was made the official statement and position of the Latin American Church. Three months later, at the twelfth regular CELAM assembly, Medellín was reaffirmed as "the norm for inspiration and action in the coming years" (Dussel 1981: 147).

Medellín provided direction to many in the Church who were confused and searching. More importantly, it provided—or was interpreted as providing—open approval of Catholics who were already working for progressive or radical social change. The next years, especially the next four years, witnessed an explosion of controversial activities organized by Catholics to achieve "authentic and integral liberation" along the lines stated at Medellín.

The number of BECs—which were to become the prime organizational channel for popular participation in the liberation theology movement—increased dramatically. BECs had their origins in the late 1950s and the 1960s in the Northeast of Brazil and in the San

Miguelito slum of Panama. By 1978, only ten years after Medellín, there were an estimated 150,000 to 200,000 BECs in Latin America (Cox 1984: 108; Cook 1985: 7; Libby 1983: 80; Carroll 1987: 12).

"Priest groups" became common as priests organized themselves to take progressive and radical stands on ecclesiastical, social, economic, and political issues. Sometimes they sought the support of their bishops; sometimes they denounced their bishops. The most famous of these priest groups were Priests for the Third World (Argentina); ONIS (Peru); Golconda (Colombia); Priests for the People (Mexico); and The Eighty (Chile).

Participation by clergy and members of religious orders in protests increased. One of the first incidents was the August 11, 1968 occupation of Santiago Cathedral by a group of 250 priests and parishioners, protesting the elitism of the Church, its indifference to the poor, and the visit of Pope Paul VI to Colombia (Donoso Loero 1975: 65–82; Gheerbrandt 1974: 61–64; Cabal 1978: 36). After Medellín such protests became increasingly common.

Furthermore, in December of 1971 the group Christians for Socialism was organized. In April 1972, over four hundred priests, nuns, and lay people (and one bishop) met in Santiago, Chile, for the controversial organization's first international meeting, entitled "The First Latin American Meeting of Christians for Socialism." Committees were formed, national councils were organized, and documents were published. The goal was to promote socialism in and beyond Latin America in the name of the Christian gospel (Richard 1976).

After Medellín, ugly clashes between priests and bishops erupted everywhere over issues of authority and politics. Penny Lernoux recounts, for example:

> Thirty diocesan priests in Mexico demanded the resignation of Bishop Leoinardo Viera Contreras, and in Maracaibo, Venezuela, twenty-two pastors called on Archbishop Domingo Roa to resign. Several hundred priests and laymen petitioned the Guatemalan Congress to expel Archbishop Mario Casariego, cardinal of Guatemala City; in Argentina a group of priests from Cordoba and Rosario demanded the dismissal of Bishop Victorio Bonamin, chief military chaplain. Similarly, activist priests in Rio de Janeiro and Peru insisted on their right to elect the local archbishop. Chile's left-wing religious movement, Christians for Socialism, attacked Santaigo's Cardinal Raul Silva, while in Rosario, Argentina, Archbishop Guillermo Bolatti and thirty priests engaged in a mudslinging match that lasted three months. Dissident priests also

demanded the removal of the papal nuncio in Bolivia; in Peru they actually prevailed on the hierarchy to blackball Papal Nuncio Romulo Carboni. (1982: 44)

Finally, a most important phenomenon after Medellín was the emergence of a new theology—"the theology of liberation." What Medellín introduced, liberation theology cultivated, elaborated, and systematized.

A turning point in this regard occurred at a 1969 World Council of Churches meeting in Campine, Switzerland. In the 1960s many of Latin America's most creative theologians—still working within the New Christendom framework—had been developing a "theology of development." Along these lines, the WCC sponsored a program called the Committee on Society, Development, and Peace (SODEPAX) which brought together theologians to develop a theological understanding of the role of the Church in socioeconomic development. On his transatlantic flight to a November 1969 SODEPAX meeting, the Peruvian theologian Gustavo Gutiérrez, while reviewing his notes on what was to be a talk entitled "The Meaning of Development," asked himself, "Why 'development'? Why not 'liberation'?" He decided then to change the title of his presentation to "Notes on Theology of Liberation." Thus the project of liberation theology was publicly inaugurated (Richard 1988; Motessi 1985: 87).

In 1971, Gutiérrez published his ideas in a ground-breaking book, *A Theology of Liberation.* Immediately, a wave of works on liberation theology was published.[9] These writings began to overturn traditional theology and to reformulate Christian theology from the viewpoint of the liberation of the poor. This new body of theological work provided a reasoned justification for the liberation theology movement.

Enduring the Storm

Not everyone was pleased with these events. Military and government officials began to accuse the Church of tolerating "Marxist infiltration" and "red priests." A number of bishops—even ones who had personally signed the Medellín documents—began to back away from their results, stating that they didn't realize at the time how radical the consequences would be.

The conservative element of the Church regrouped and organized. In 1972, the Latin American bishops elected a new, more conservative CELAM leadership, headed by its general secretary, Alfonso

López Trujillo. López proceeded to dismiss from the CELAM organization most who belonged to the liberation theology movement, replacing them with more conservative officials (Cleary 1985: 45, 121–22; Carroll 1987: 18–19).

Meanwhile, the political climate of Latin America was changing. In 1973, Chile's Marxist Salvador Allende was overthrown and replaced by the military government of Augusto Pinochet. A severe repression of leftist forces followed. The central headquarters of Christians for Socialism moved to Canada; many liberation theologians left or were expelled from the country.

In addition to the military coups in Brazil in 1964 and Chile in 1973, moderate governments were replaced by military bureaucratic authoritarian regimes in Bolivia in 1971, Uruguay in 1973, Peru in 1975, and Ecuador and Argentina in 1976 (O'Donnell 1973; Collier 1979; Dussel 1981). Such military regimes did not hesitate to control Church activities which they considered subversive. The Church had abandoned its alliances with power elites and was no longer thought to deserve special protection. In the next years, more than a thousand bishops, priests, and religious were threatened, arrested, kidnapped, tortured, killed, raped, and exiled (Lernoux 1982, 466). Oscar Romero was only one of many. The number of Catholic lay leaders who were imprisoned or killed is inestimable.

Times were difficult for the liberation theology movement. Leonardo Boff, one of its major theologians, suggested that perhaps it was time to start writing a more sober "theology of captivity." Nevertheless, while many in the movement, in the face of setbacks and opposition, abandoned their early optimism, few abandoned the movement itself, which had established a solid enough foundation by 1972 to be able to survive the attacks of the 1970s and 1980s. While to its opponents, the liberation theology movement's leaders appeared intractable and obscurantist, the leaders viewed themselves as resolute and steadfast. And for most of them, the prospect of martyrdom only made the project more serious. In any case, for most there was, it seemed, no turning back.

But the liberation theology movement did more than stand its ground; at times it advanced its position. In Central America, for example, participants in the movement played instrumental roles in the 1979 overthrow of the Somoza regime in Nicaragua and in the 1980 insurrection in El Salvador. In both instances, Christian participation was vital; indeed, the insurrections were strongest in areas where Church pastoral workers had organized BECs and promoted conscientization (Montgomery 1982). In Nicaragua, three Catholic priests who had fought with the FSLN—Ernesto Cardenal, Fernando

Cardenal, and Miguel D'Escoto—were appointed, much to the consternation of Rome, to Sandinista cabinet posts.

Furthermore, by the mid-1970s the theology of liberation was receiving international recognition. Theological conferences held in North America, Europe, Africa, and Asia provided opportunities for the Latin Americans to communicate their new theology. Works of liberation theology began to be translated into other languages and published abroad. Seminaries and divinity schools began offering courses in liberation theology. Whether it was criticized or lauded, liberation theology received great attention as a major theological innovation.

However, by the end of the 1970s there was not yet a decisive outcome in the Latin American Church. The liberation theology movement had experienced setbacks and defeats. It no longer had access to CELAM institutions, and was experiencing heavy persecution outside and strong opposition inside the Church. Nevertheless, the movement was surviving and, in some places, thriving. Although many originally supportive bishops withdrew support, others continued their backing, and new bishops became converted to the liberationist strategy. Liberation theology itself was expanding, maturing, and producing a second generation of theological innovators. BECs were proliferating and Christians were participating in (sometimes successful) socialist revolutions.

The Showdown at Puebla

In 1977 CELAM began planning its third plenary session, marking the tenth anniversary of Medellín, to take place in Puebla, Mexico, in January 1979.[10] While conservatives, led by López Trujillo, saw Puebla as an opportunity to reverse the effects of Medellín and put an end to the movement, the leaders of the liberation theology movement viewed Puebla as an important opportunity officially to reaffirm the principles of liberation theology and continue on the path charted at Medellín. Both sides knew that they must establish their positions at Puebla; both sides perceived that the battle at Puebla could be decisive in determining the long-term fate of the liberation theology movement. This sense of importance and expectation was heightened by the announced participation of the Pope.

As secretary general of CELAM, López Trujillo was the authority who organized CELAM III, and he used his position to do everything possible to outmaneuver his opponents. Conservative bishops were strategically placed to control committees, conservative staff members wrote the preparatory documents; none of the theologians of liberation were invited. López even arranged to have the Vatican appoint extra conservative delegates at Puebla (Eagleson and Scharper 1979: 30).

The final result of Puebla, however, was ambiguous. In the end, neither side was obviously triumphant or obviously defeated (Carroll 1987: 20–21). On one hand, the final document was not one that liberation theologians would have written; López's influence was evident. On the other hand, the majority of bishops refused to endorse López's original document. It was changed significantly before it was approved, and the final version contained numerous statements reflecting the language and philosophy of liberation theology. The necessity of "integral liberation," the use of BECs as a pastoral strategy, and "the preferential option for the poor" were all explicitly affirmed.

In this sense, from the point of view of the liberation theology movement, although Puebla was not a resounding victory, it was a success nonetheless. Despite his access to institutional resources and his best efforts, López Trujillo and his colleagues were unable to stop the movement. Indeed, his original intentions were largely overruled by the majority of bishops. Furthermore, after ten years of mixed implementation and opposition, many of the central ideas and strategies of liberation theology were officially affirmed by the Latin American episcopate. In this way, Puebla represented, if not an absolute victory for control over the future shape of the Church, at least the tolerance and partial acceptance of liberation theology as a feature of the Latin American Catholic landscape.

In the years that followed, as in the previous ten years, liberation theology continued to face opposition from within and outside of the Church. For example, in 1985, in a case that drew international attention, the Brazilian liberation theologian Leonardo Boff was officially silenced for ten months by Cardinal Joseph Ratzinger, prefect of the Sacred Congregation for the Doctrine of the Faith, for the ideas about ecclesial authority in his book, *Church, Charism and Power* (Cox 1988). Nevertheless, in part because of the outcome of Puebla and in part because of the established popular support for this movement, liberation theology continued to struggle and survive.

2

What Is Liberation Theology?

A Theology and a Movement

To begin, it is important to make a distinction between "liberation theology" and the movement for which it is named. Liberation theology is simply a coherent set of religious ideas, about and for liberation.

The liberation theology movement, however, is not only a set of theological ideas or beliefs, but an attempt to mobilize a previously unmobilized constituency for collective action against an antagonist to promote social change. The movement does articulate a specific set of ideas: liberation theology. But, as a movement, it consists of more than ideas. It is organization. It is action. It is social change.[1]

Liberation theologians are themselves explicit about the distinction between the theology and the movement. Their theologies, they insist, are not synonymous with the active social movement of liberation, but are rather reflections of that movement. For liberation theologians, action aimed at achieving human liberation comes first—chronologically and in importance—and theological reflection on that action comes second.

Gutiérrez (1973: 11, 307) makes the distinction and connection clearly:

> Theology is reflection, a critical attitude. Theology *follows;* it is the second step. What Hegel used to say about philosophy can likewise be applied to theology: it rises only at sundown. The pastoral activity of the church does not flow as a conclusion from theological premises. Theology does not produce pastoral activity; rather it reflects upon it. . . . The theology of liberation attempts to reflect

25

on the experience and meaning of the faith based on the commitment to abolish injustice and to build a new society; this theology
must be verified by the practice of that commitment, by active,
effective participation in the struggle which the exploited social
classes have undertaken against their oppressors.[2]

This relationship between action and thought explains why many
liberation theologians are not merely academics, but also pastoral
agents working with the poor. Gutiérrez himself, for example, lives
and works in a slum in the Rimac neighborhood of Lima. Clodovis
Boff, a Brazilian theologian, is known for spending six months a year
doing pastoral work in the Acre region of the Amazon jungle and the
other six months in a university writing and teaching what he calls
"feet-on-the-ground theology" (C. Boff 1987).[3]

The primary subject of this study is not the body of theological
ideas known as liberation theology. Rather, it is the faith-based social
movement about which liberation theology is a theological reflection. Nevertheless, to truly understand the movement, it is necessary
to understand the basic elements of its teachings.

Approaching Liberation Theology

The diversity that characterizes liberation theology makes it difficult
to describe in a coherent, systematic way. It is written by a host of
authors with diverse experiences, burdens, educations, and religious
traditions, out of disparate social situations. They write, from the
Amazon jungles of Northern Brazil to the industrial sprawl of São
Paulo; from the relatively open political environment of Costa Rica
to the torturously repressive situation of El Salvador; from the quiet
shores of Nicaragua's Solentiname archipelago to the bustling streets
of Santiago and Buenos Aires. Liberation theology has typically been
written "on the run," so to speak—in the midst of the urgency and
confusion of challenging and changing social and political events,
rather than in the relaxed, contemplative ease of politically stable
situations. Finally, the burdens and themes of the liberation theology
project have shifted over time, as the movement has faced changing
external political and economic, as well as internal ecclesiastical,
circumstances.

Technically speaking, there is no single liberation theology; there
are liberation theolog*ies*. Nevertheless, these works of theological
reflection make similar assumptions, articulate like themes, and
work toward a common purpose. Therefore, Leonardo Boff is correct in arguing that "A purely academic and didactic interest will

discern various accents within the one, single theology of liberation. I must insist that there is one, and only one, theology of liberation. There is only one point of departure—a reality of social misery—and one goal—the liberation of the oppressed" (Boff and Boff 1984: 24). Juan Luis Segundo (1979: 247) writes similarly: "We can disregard the differences between various theologians who are included under that head [liberation theology]. . . . There is something basic shared by all of them. They all maintain that human beings are already building up the kingdom of God here and now in history" (see also Segundo 1976: 3). For these reasons, and for matters of convenience, I will refer to these theologies in the singular, as liberation theology.

What, then, is liberation theology? How can it be described? To begin, liberation theology essentially is an attempt to reconceptualize the Christian faith from the perspective of the poor and oppressed.[4] At heart, it contends that the Christian gospel, the "good news," is that God is working—and that God's people should therefore be working—in history to combat and eradicate all forms of oppression and domination, whether social, cultural, political, economic, or spiritual. All of the vastness and diversity of the literature reflect the enormous task of, and the divergent approaches to, reconstructing the whole of theology from this perspective.[5]

In the following pages I will explore what this reconstructed theology looks like, focusing on eight central themes in liberation theology. These themes roughly approximate the subject divisions of traditional Catholic systematic theology—Revelation and Faith; Scripture and Tradition; God; Creation; Original Sin; Jesus Christ; Grace; the Church; the Sacraments; and the Last Things. Nevertheless, it would misrepresent liberation theology to present it in these exact catagories, since liberation theology is a self-professed, self-conscious break from this European method of theological reflection (Kirk 1980: 116–17). This exploration will draw largely from the works of Gustavo Gutiérrez, Juan Luis Segundo, José Míguez Bonino, and Leonardo and Clodovis Boff.[6]

Eight Central Themes

Methodology: Theory, Praxis, and the Hermeneutical Circle

"The novelty of liberation theology does not lie only in the historical challenge [of liberation]," states Clodovis Boff,

> The novelty of the theology of liberation also, and especially, resides in its manner of developing this modern thematic. The key to the new approach is the praxis of liberation. In the theology of

liberation we have a bond—intimate but not rigid—between theory and practice, between theology and the life of faith. The
method practiced by the theology of liberation, we observe, is
neither exclusively inductive nor deductive. It is both of these at
once: it is *dialectical*. (Boff and Boff 1986: 15)

Most traditional theology works deductively, beginning with the
universal and eternal truths of the Bible and Church teachings and
applying them, as a second step, to life. Theory, in other words,
shapes praxis. However, liberation theology has a different understanding of the relationship between theory and practice. Here, people work for liberation first, then theology is formed as a reflection
on that praxis. Liberating praxis then continues, strengthened and
directed by the new theological reflection. Theory is shaped by
praxis as much as it shapes it.

Liberation theologians take this approach because they believe
"there is no truth outside or beyond the concrete historical events in
which men are involved as agents. There is, therefore, no knowledge
except in action itself, in the process of transforming the world
through participation in history" (Bonino 1975: 88). What is needed
methodologically, then, in the words of Juan Luis Segundo, is a "hermeneutical circle," which from liberating praxis constructs a theology which, in turn, informs and strengthens liberating praxis.
Segundo (1976: 8) defines the hermeneutical circle as "the continuing change in our interpretation of the Bible which is dictated by the
continuing changes in our present-day reality, both individual and
societal." In the words of the Boffs:

> Before we can do theology we have to "do" liberation. The first
> step for liberation theology is pre-theological. . . . Links with spe-
> cific practice are *at the root* of liberation theology. It operates
> within the great dialectic of theory (faith) and practice (love). In
> fact, it is *only* this effective connection with liberating practice that
> can give theologians a "new spirit," a new style, or a new way of
> doing theology. (Boff and Boff 1987: 22)

Sociology, Marxism, and the Reality of Class Struggle
Liberation theology does not restrict itself to the personal or spiritual realms of life. It also engages with economic, political, and cultural matters. It must deal not only with the concerns, questions, and
issues of the discipline of theology, traditionally conceived, but also
understand the workings of the larger social world (Lacy 1985: 238).
Liberation theologians, therefore, insist on utilizing the tools and
data of the social sciences in the theological process.[7] Gutiérrez

(1973: 136) notes: "Medellín marks the beginning of a new relationship between theological and pastoral language on the one hand and
the social sciences which seek to interpret this reality on the other."

However, liberation theologians do not employ any and every social science perspective. They explicitly reject, for example, the struc-
tural-functionalist framework of social analysis (Boff and Boff 1987:
26; Bonino 1975: 26, 34, 97).[8] Instead, liberation theologians, for the
most part, stand within the neo-Marxist tradition, and employ what
they call "dialectical" or "historico-structural" analysis. This analysis
views poverty as a collective and conflictive result of oppression
which can only be overcome through the establishment of an alternative social system through social-structural transformation (Boff
and Boff 1987: 26–27).

Liberation theologians use neo-Marxist analysis simply because, as
a tool, it seems to them to explain their social world best (Gutiérrez
1990: 421). Bonino (1975: 97–98) declares:

> [Marxism] seems to many of us that it has proved, and still proves
> to be, the best instrument available for an effective and rational
> realization of human possibilities in historical life. . . . When we
> speak of assuming Marxist analysis and ideology at this point,
> there is therefore no sacralization of an ideology, no desire to
> "theologize" sociological, economic, or political catagories. We
> move totally and solely in the area of human rationality—in the
> realm where God has invited man to be *on his own*. The only legit-
> imate question is therefore whether this analysis and this projec-
> tion do in fact correspond to the facts of human history.

Theoretically, any sociologically analytic tool is eligible and would
be employed according to its usefulness. The Boff brothers explain:

> Whatever truth there is in Marxism—always a merely "approx-
> imate" truth, of course—Christian faith will always consider that
> truth to be something it must assimilate. In this, the attitude of
> faith toward Marxism is no different from its attitude toward any
> other system of thought. (Boff and Boff 1986: 70)

Marxism, liberation theologians claim, is simply used as a tool, not
embraced as a comprehensive worldview (Aman 1984). "The Christian communities and the bishops of Latin America," the Boff brothers contend, "do use 'elements' borrowed from Marxism—without,
for all that, being bounded by its ideology or having to wear the
Marxist label and tip their hats to Karl Marx" (1986: 71). Clodovis
Boff argues:

By no means is Marxism the moving force, basis, or inspiration of the theology of liberation. Christian faith is. . . . Marxism is a secondary, peripheral issue. When Marxism is used at all, it is used only *partially* and *instrumentally*. (Boff and Boff 1986: 22)

Elsewhere the Boffs explain:

In liberation theology, Marxism is never treated as a subject on its own but always *from and in relation to the poor*. Placing themselves firmly on the side of the poor, liberation theologians ask Marx: "What can you tell us about the situation of poverty and ways of overcoming it?" Here Marxists are submitted to the judgement of the poor and their cause, and not the other way around. Therefore, liberation theology uses Marxism purely as an *instrument*. It does not venerate it as it venerates the gospel. And it feels no obligation to account to social scientists for any use it may make— correct or otherwise—of Marxist terminology and ideas. . . . To put it in more specific terms, liberation theology freely borrows from Marxism certain 'methodological pointers' that have proved fruitful in understanding the world of the oppressed. (Boff and Boff 1987: 28)

This use of Marxism demands a serious Christian-Marxist dialogue. Liberation theologians encourage such a dialogue and are prepared to allow Marxism to challenge and change them.[9] José Miranda, a liberation theologian who specializes in Christian-Marxist encounter, argues:

At one time Marx's contributions . . . were disdainfully considered as less than irrelevant; now there is an overwhelming need to study his theses with great dedication. But institutions have always demonstrated a conspicuous inability to repent. . . . Thus we must realize that it is not enough merely to take seriously today the Marx whom we scorned yesterday. . . . If we are to abandon yesterday's positions, we must also revise the whole system of ideas and values which make such a position necessary. (1974: xv; see also Miranda 1980)

Perhaps Marxism's most important influence on liberation theology is in the acceptance of the reality of class struggle. Critics of liberation theology accuse it of inciting class struggle; liberation theologians, however, claim that they are only recognizing and acknowledging a class struggle that already exists and that must be overcome. Gutiérrez (1973: 273–74) claims:

Any consideration of this subject must start from two elemental points: class struggle is a fact, and neutrality in this matter is impossible. The class struggle is part of our economic, social, political, cultural, and religious reality. . . . Those who speak of class struggle do not "advocate" it—as some would say—in the sense of creating it out of nothing by an act of (bad) will. What they do is to recognize a fact and contribute to an awareness of that fact. And there is nothing more certain than a fact.

Liberation theology's certainty about many of Marx's concepts, including class struggle, however, does not translate into an uncritical endorsement of Marxism generally. Liberation theologians are aware of Marxism's deficiencies. Hugo Assman (1984: 133), for example, acknowledges: "The scientific instruments for 'reading reality' are still highly imperfect. This has to be said, against every type of systematized, schematized Marxism—and indeed for the benefit of Marxism." Bonino (1975: 35) underscores this thought: "A rigid Marxist orthodoxy or dogmatism is immediately rejected. . . . The Marxist scheme cannot be taken as a dogma but rather as a method which has to be applied to our own reality in terms of this reality."

Segundo states two main problems liberation theologians have with Marx: his consistently negative view of religion and his methodological rejection of the relative autonomy of the "superstructure." Because of these problems, Segundo goes so far as to say that direct collaboration between orthodox Marxist sociology and liberation theology is improbable (1976: 58–62).

Liberation theologians always insist on waging the struggle for justice from the point of departure of faith, and are critical of everything, including Marxism, that is incompatible with the faith. Thus, the Boff brothers warn:

> Liberation, for Christians, draws its inspiration from the Gospel, in the "truth about Christ, the Church, and human being." Marxism may never be allowed to become a determinative reference point and principle. If Marxism is understood as a closed, monolithic system, denying God, the dignity of the person, and human freedom and rights . . . then obviously a theologian may not utilize it as a conceptual tool for understanding history and the conflicts of history, as such a system would stand in diametrical opposition to Christianity. This . . . obliges Christians to redouble their critical vigilance vis-à-vis Marxism, whose devouring mystical seduction is totalitarian here, and extremely difficult for incautious, uncritical minds to resist. (Boff and Boff 1986: 66)

God of the Poor

According to liberation theologians, because of secularization the critical problem that orients most European and North American Christianity is the *nonbeliever.* The relevant theological question, therefore, is: how can modern people still believe in God? However, the critical problem of Latin American Christianity is not the nonbeliever, but the *non-person:* the one who has been dehumanized through poverty, oppression, and domination (see Gutiérrez 1983: 92, 193, 213). The relevant question for Latin American theology, is not how can we believe? but,

> How are we to talk about a God who is revealed as love in a situation characterized by poverty and oppression? How are we to proclaim the God of life to men and women who die prematurely and unjustly? How are we to acknowledge that God makes us a free gift of love and justice when we have before us the suffering of the innocent? What words are we to use in telling those who are not even regarded as persons that they are daughters and sons of God? (Gutiérrez 1987: xiv)

Liberation theology, then, struggles not with God's existence but with God's character. It answers the question of God's character, in part, by portraying a God who consistently imparts life and opposes death, who faithfully takes sides with the poor against the rich and powerful, and who acts in history to liberate the oppressed.

The God of liberation theology is not an impassive, detached Other but is instead intimately involved with and totally invested in human history, especially the experience and destiny of the poor and suffering. Segundo writes (1974: 169, 175): "God does not dictate from outside of history. . . . Man will encounter the living God only *in* man, *in* his history. He will not encounter him in the skies or in the beyond." Gutiérrez (1973: 190) reiterates this theme: "The biblical God is close to man; he is a God of communion with and commitment to man. The active presence of God in the midst of his people is a part of the oldest and most enduring Biblical promises."

Liberation theology emphasizes God as the continual giver of life and opponent of death. "The biblical God," observe the Boff brothers, "is fundamentally a living God, the author and sustainer of all life. Whenever persons see their lives threatened, they can count on the presence and power of God who comes to their aid" (Boff and Boff 1987: 44). Clodovis Boff argues:

> Liberation theology recovers the image of *God as creator of life,* a God whose glory is the "human being alive." Among a people for

whom death is not a simple figure of speech but a daily reality thrust upon their attention in infant mortality, violent conflict, kidnappings, and torture, a theology of God as creator and sustainer of life acquires a piercing relevancy. (Boff and Boff 1986: 25).

God, however, is not a benign, neutral dispenser of life to all. The God of liberation theology is partisan—he takes sides. God has a preferential love for the poor and suffering. The Boffs write:

God is especially close to those who are oppressed; God hears their cry and resolves to set them free. God is father of all, but most particularly father and defender of those who are oppressed and treated unjustly. Out of love for them, God takes sides, takes *their* side against the repressive measures of all pharaohs. (Boff and Boff 1987: 50–51)

And, Gutiérrez (1983: 7–8) argues:

The God of the Bible is a God who not only governs history, but who orients it in the direction of establishment of justice and right. He is more than a provident God. He is a God who takes sides with the poor and liberates them from slavery and oppression. . . . The reciprocal relationship between God and the poor person is the very heart of biblical faith.

Gutiérrez claims elsewhere (1983: 209): "The God we believe and hope in comes to us as the God of the poor, the God of the oppressed. This is why he reveals himself only to the person who does justice to the poor."

God taking sides with the poor means that he takes sides *against* the rich, against "the pharaohs of this world" (Boff and Boff 1987: 50). God, says Gutiérrez (1983: 19), "considers the rich blasphemers because they speak of God in order to better oppress the poor."

Why is God partisan? Why does he take sides? "God loves the poor," Gutiérrez explains, "just because they are poor, and not necessarily, or even primarily, because they are better believers than others, or morally firmer than others. God loves them simply because they are poor, because they are hungry, because they are persecuted" (1983: 95; see also 116).

But God does more than simply take sides with the poor. God acts decisively on their behalf. "God does not," argue the Boffs, "stand by impassively watching the drama of human history, in which, generally speaking, the strong impose their laws and their will on the weak. The biblical authors often present Yahweh as *Go'el*, which means: he who does justice to the weak, father of orphans, and comforter of widows" (Boff and Boff 1987: 51). There is no question, then, but that God's will is for human liberation. Franz Hinkelammert (1986: 231) contends that,

> God's will and human liberation coincide completely. Because human liberation is the will of God, the imperatives of human liberation indicate what God's will is. The point is not to compare these imperatives with God's will to see if they agree. They are God's will and the covenant is God's promise to bring liberation to complete fulfillment.

Therefore, to be one of God's own, "to know God as liberator *is* to liberate, *is* to do justice" (Gutiérrez, 1983: 8). Gutiérrez explains:

> To know God is to do justice, is to be in solidarity with the poor person . . . as he or she actually exists today—as someone who is oppressed, as a member of an exploited class, or ethnic group, or culture, or nation. . . . Thus, in order to know or love God, one must come to grips with the concrete life situation of the poor today, and undertake the radical transformation of a society that makes them poor. (1983: 51, 96)

Again, Gutiérrez argues (1973: 195), "To know Yahweh, which in Biblical language is equivalent to saying to love Yahweh, *is* to establish just relationships among men, it *is* to recognize the rights of the poor. The God of biblical revelation is known through interhuman justice. When justice does not exist, God is not known; he is absent."

The picture of God in liberation theology, then, is not that of an impartial, detached being. Neither, however, is it of an ever-triumphant God. God suffers with the poor; still, liberation theology avoids the picture of the defeated God portrayed in some recent works by European theologians (e.g., Moltmann 1974). As Cox (1984: 147) writes, "The God of liberation theology . . . is neither all-powerful nor a powerless sufferer. Rather, God is portrayed as one who must contend with strong and stubborn evil. God suffers, but in confrontation, not in acquiescence. God is *el Dios pobre*."

Sin, Domination, and Oppression

Why do people suffer? Why does God suffer? What is the cause, ask liberation theologians, of the proliferation of poverty, domination, and oppression in the world? Their answer is the traditional Christian one: because of sin. Sin, they argue, is the ultimate root, the fundamental cause of all that is wrong with the world, of all evil in history. Says Gutiérrez, "The existence of poverty represents a sundering both of solidarity among men and also of communion with God. Poverty is an expression of sin. Sin [is] the ultimate root of all injustice, all exploitation, all dissidence among men" (1973: 295, 237).[10]

Breaking with those post-Enlightenment theologies of Europe and North America that minimize or demythologize the concept of sin, liberation theologians identify sin as the key to understanding society and history. "In this approach," writes Gutiérrez, "we are far from that naive optimism which denies the role of sin in the historical development of humanity" (1973: 175). Indeed, sin in liberation theology is a profound, personal malady. Segundo (1974: 73) echoes Saint Paul when he argues, "'Sin' is different from the 'sins' that come from freely made choices. Sin is a condition that subdues and enslaves me against my own will. It is part of my being, the most basic and low-level part if not the most profound and authentic part." In essence, sin is "the breach of friendship with God and with the human community" (Gutiérrez 1983: 18). In these ways, liberation theology is quite traditional in its view of sin.

Liberation theologians move beyond many traditional theological treatments of sin by also insisting on its suprapersonal nature. "In the liberation approach" argues Gutiérrez (1973: 175), "sin is not considered as an individual, private, or merely interior reality. . . . Sin is regarded as a social, historical fact. . . . When it is considered in this way, the collective dimensions of sin are rediscovered."

It is this understanding of sin as a "personal and social intrahistorical reality"[11] which enables liberation theologians to speak of "social sinfulness," "institutionalized violence," and "structural sin." Gutiérrez argues (1983: 147):

> Sin, the breach with God, is not something that occurs only within some intimate sanctuary of the heart. It always translates into interpersonal relationships . . . and hence is the ultimate root of all injustice and oppression—as well as of the social confrontations and conflicts of concrete history.

For this reason, discussions of sin need not and must not remain at an individual or theoretical level, but must always identify sin's concrete, historical manifestations. Gutiérrez states (1983: 22):

> Faith . . . strikes at the very root of social injustice: sin. . . . But it will not tear up that root without coming to grips with the historical mediations and with a socio-political analysis of these concrete historical realities. . . . Sin is the basic alienation. For that very

reason, sin cannot be touched in itself, in the abstract. It can be attacked only in concrete historical situations—in particular instances of alienation. Apart from particular, concrete alienation, sin is meaningless and incomprehensible.[12]

However, this emphasis on the suprapersonal nature of sin does not negate the personal dimension of sin. Indeed, personal sin is taken as that which ultimately generates socially sinful reality, which then takes on a life of its own. Gutiérrez (1973: 175) affirms: "An unjust situation does not happen by chance; it is not something branded by a fatal destiny: there is human responsibility behind it."

So, liberation theologians argue, we must understand sin—the breach with God and humanity—both as personal and social:

> In describing sin as the ultimate cause [of poverty, injustice, and oppression] we do not in any way negate the structural reasons and the objective determinants leading to these situations. It does, however, emphasize the fact that things do not happen by chance and that behind an unjust structure there is a personal or collective will responsible—a willingness to reject God and neighbor. It suggests, likewise, that a social transformation, no matter how radical it may be, does not automatically achieve the suppression of all evils. (Gutiérrez 1973: 35)

Jesus Christ Liberator

The historical pivot on which the Christian gospel turns is the life, death, and resurrection of Jesus Christ. Christology—the theology of the person and work of Christ—therefore, is a key determinant in shaping the meaning of the Christian faith as a whole. Throughout history, Christ has been variously interpreted as a great spiritual teacher, as the final propitiatory sacrifice for sin, as a brilliant but failed political revolutionary, and in other ways. Liberation theology interprets Jesus Christ as the inaugurator of the kingdom of God and, therefore, as the great liberator of the poor and oppressed.

The Christ of liberation theology is spiritual—but he is not spiritualized, in the sense of being other-worldly. The Christ of liberation theology is political—but he is not politicized, in that he is not a revolutionary political leader. The Christ of liberation theology is the historical incarnation—"God-made-flesh"—of *el Dios pobre*. Jesus is the concrete sign and agent of God's commitment to liberate the dominated and oppressed. Thus, the character of God is revealed most clearly in the person and work of Jesus the Messiah.

God's preferential love for the poor, for example, is authenticated by the incarnation. Gutiérrez (1983: 13) writes:

The nub, the nucleus, of the biblical message, we have said, is in the relationship between God and the poor. Jesus Christ is precisely *God become poor.* This was the human life he took—a poor life. And this is the life in and by which we recognize him as Son of his Father. He was poor indeed. He was born into a social milieu characterized by poverty. He chose to live with the poor. He addressed his gospel by preference to the poor. He lashed out with invective against the rich who oppressed the poor and despised them. And before the Father, he was poor in spirit.

But Jesus did more than just live in solidarity with the poor: he established the kingdom of God. Leonardo Boff (1978: 53) notes: "Christ understands himself as Liberator because he preaches, presides over, and is already inaugurating the kingdom of God." What is the kingdom of God? Boff goes on to explain:

> The kingdom of God is a total, global, and structural transfiguration and revolution of the reality of human beings; it is the cosmos purified of all evils and full of the reality of God. The kingdom of God is not to be in another world but is the old world transformed into a new one. . . . The kingdom of God does not simply signify the annihilation of sin but the annihilation of all that sin means for human beings, society, and the cosmos. In the kingdom of God, pain, blindness, hunger, tempests, sin, and death will not have their turn.

The kingdom of God is not a future event; it is here and now, though not in fullness, still in reality. At the heart of this kingdom is justice. Gutiérrez (1983: 14) claims that Jesus proclaimed "a kingdom of justice and liberation, to be established in favor of the poor, the oppressed, and the marginalized of history. . . . The only justice is the definitive justice that builds, starting right now, in our conflict-filled history, a kingdom in which God's love will be present and exploitation abolished."

According to Segundo Galilea (1984: 98):

> [Jesus] preached to his disciples a new orientation, a new vision of humankind, new values—values that contrast with the society of his time and with the values promoted by political power, for he preaches love of neighbor, poverty, humility, detachment from prestige and power, forgiveness, and the like. . . . To the extent that these values penetrate the heart of men and women and society, they pass a death sentence on every socio-political structure at variance with them—the Roman Empire, to begin with—and they take root as the permanent seed of freedom.[13]

Few sociopolitical structures take kindly to being sentenced to death—and the one Jesus inhabited was no exception. In reaction it sentenced Jesus to death. "Jesus' death," argues Gutiérrez (1983: 15), "is the consequence of his struggle for justice, his proclamation of the kingdom, and his identification with the poor." Elsewhere, Gutiérrez observes: "During all his public life, Jesus confronted the *groups in power* of the Jewish people. . . . When Jesus struck against the very foundation of their machinations, he unmasked the falsity of their position and appeared in the eyes of the Pharisees as a dangerous traitor" (1973: 228–29). Jesus' death is, therefore, a religious— but also an eminently political—event. Gutiérrez (1973: 229), echoing Oscar Cullmann, observes: "Jesus *died at the hands of the political authorities,* the oppressors of the Jewish people. According to the Roman custom, the title on the cross indicated the reason for the sentence; in the case of Jesus this title denoted political guilt: King of the Jews. . . . We see clearly that the trial of Jesus was a political trial and that he was condemned for being a Zealot."

Leonardo Boff (1978: 289) writes:

> The motives behind the assassination of Jesus are two-fold. Both have something to do with the structural level. First of all, Jesus was condemned as a *blasphemer.* He presents a God who is different from the God of the status quo. As Jon Sobrino points out, Jesus unmasked the religious hypocrisy of the standing order and its use of God to justify injustice. . . . Secondly, his whole attitude and approach was eminently liberative, as we have already noted. Thus the political authorities accuse him of being a *guerrilla fighter* and executed him for that.

However, the story of Jesus does not end with his death, for as Boff says (1978: 122), "the grass did not grow on the sepulcher of Jesus. A few days after Jesus' death an unheard-of event, unique in the history of humankind, occurred: God raised him up." What is the meaning of the resurrection? According to Boff (1978: 122, 191):

> The resurrection is the realization of his [Jesus'] announcement of total liberation, especially from the reign of death. The resurrection signifies a concretization of the kingdom of God in the life of Jesus. . . . The resurrection points to the goal and fulfillment sought by every liberation process: arrival at complete freedom. . . . The import of the total liberation to be found in the resurrection appears only when we tie it in with Jesus' struggle to establish God's kingdom in the world.

Liberation theology's understanding of the nature of the person, life, death, and resurrection of Jesus, finally, determines what it means to be a follower, a disciple of Jesus. As in knowledge of *el Dios pobre,* to follow Jesus is to seek justice. "A Christology that proclaims Jesus Christ as the Liberator," writes Leonardo Boff (1968: 266), "seeks to be committed to the economic, social, and political liberation of those groups that are oppressed and dominated." Gutiérrez (1983: 96), likewise, contends,

> To be a disciple of Jesus is to make his messianic practice our own. Our discipleship is our appropriation of his message of life, his love for the poor, his denunciation of injustice, his sharing of bread, his hope for resurrection. The Christian community, the *ecclesia,* is made up of those who take up that messianic practice of Jesus and use it to create social relationships of a community of brothers and sisters. . . . Messianic practice is the proclamation of the kingdom of God and the transformation of the historical conditions of the poor.

The Unity of History

An important task of Christian theology is specifying the exact relationship between world history and the history of salvation. Clearly they are not identical—but neither are they absolutely separate. How, then, are they related?

One answer to this question—the answer that has dominated Christian theology since Augustine's separation of "the city of God" and "the city of man"—is that salvation history occurs within and beyond secular history. This historical dualism assumes two distinct histories which operate on separate but intersecting planes (Gutiérrez 1971). Sacred history is played out on the stage of world history, so to speak. But sacred history ultimately surpasses secular history, destroying it at the Parousia and replacing it with a radically distinct heavenly kingdom.

Liberation theology rejects this solution. Gutiérrez (1973: 72) comments: "The distinction of planes appears as a burnt-out model with nothing to say to the advances in theological thinking." Instead, liberation theology insists on collapsing the distinction between sacred salvation history and secular earthly history, while simultaneously insisting that the two are not synonymous. Though salvation history is not identical to world history, the argument goes, there is no salvation history apart from world history (Bandera 1975: 297–303). Gutiérrez (1973: 153) contends:

> There are not two histories, one profane and one sacred, "juxtaposed" or "closely linked." Rather, there is only one human des-

tiny, irreversibly assumed by Christ, the Lord of history. . . . The history of salvation is the very heart of human history. . . . The salvific action of God underlies all human existence. The historical destiny of humanity must be placed definitively in the salvific horizon. . . . There is only one history—a "Christo-finalized" history.

And, Bonino (1975: 137–38) writes:

Theologians of liberation have decidedly rejected the "dualistic" position. . . . They strive to maintain the integrity of "one single God-fulfilled history". . . . God builds his Kingdom from and within human history in its entirety; his action is a constant call and challenge to man. Man's response is realized in the concrete arena of history with its economic, political, and ideological options. Faith is not a different history.

Exactly specifying the nature of this identified but not identical relationship between salvation and earthly history requires the making of fine distinctions. Leonardo Boff explains:

Once again, there are not two histories and two realities . . . there are plural dimensions of one and the same reality. . . . The kingdom takes flesh in justice—though it is not simply synonymous with a just society, for it is also realized in dimensions other than the social. Kingdom of God and just society are not totally coextensive. But they overlap. Hence, we can speak of an identification of the one *in* the other, though not an identity of the one *with* the other. . . . In historical liberation is the whole of salvation; but this salvation is not more shaped by the confines of an historical liberation than spirit is shaped by the body. Salvation always transcends liberation, just as spirit always transcends body. Without coinciding totally, then, salvation and historical liberation nonetheless constitute the unity-in-duality of one single history. (Boff and Boff 1984: 57–58, 64)

The lack of historical dualism in the Bible serves as one basis for this orientation. As Bonino points out (1975: 134, 137):

There is scarcely a question of "two histories" in relation to the Old Testament. There, God's action takes place in history and as history. . . . Any separation between the brute facts of history and their prophetic interpretation is alien to the Bible and originates in the Greek epistemological split between brute facts and *logos*. . . . It is difficult to read the Bible and go on saying that general history is a mere episode, unrelated to the Kingdom, and without eschatological significance.[14]

Furthermore, liberation theologians argue, the incarnation of Christ—Emmanuel (God-with-us)—dissolves the distinction between the two histories. Segundo (1974: 26) writes:

> In Jesus "the Word became flesh; he came to dwell among us." It is precisely when this interiorization within human history reaches its acme, in total self-giving even unto death, that the veil of the temple is rent in a symbolic way. That which seemed to separate the sacred from history disappears; all that remains is history, which is simultaneously human history and divine history.

The unity of history has profound consequences, theologically and politically. For one thing, divine salvation must find its realization through historical salvation, "the salvation of history" (Segundo 1974: 37). Ignacio Ellacuría (1986: 18) writes:

> Action in and on history, the salvation of social man in history, is the real pathway whereby God will ultimately deify man. It is not just that salvation history entails salvation in history as a corollary. Rather, the salvation of man in history is the one and only way in which salvation history can reach its culmination.

Similarly, Gutiérrez (1973: 160) writes:

> Building the temporal city is not simply a stage of "humanization" or "pre-evangelization" as was held in theology up until a few years ago. Rather it is to become part of a saving process which embraces the whole of man and all human history.

If this is so, then, any and all liberating experiences—whether they appear sacred or secular—represent God's kingdom, in the view of faith. Leonardo Boff writes:

> This [salvation] process, which gradually actualizes salvation within the limits of history, especially within the space of the church, can be understood as a process of liberation *from* situations that contradict God's salvific design, *for* situations that gradually conform to that design. Historical liberations are thus anticipations and concretizations, ever limited, but real, of the salvation that will be full and complete only in eternity. . . . In proportion as economic and social structures foster a greater participation by all in the economy and in society and create a greater symmetry among groups of persons, in that same proportion they

signify, to the eyes of faith, the presence of grace and the realization, in seed, of the kingdom of God. . . . In a nutshell, we could say: Liberation in Jesus Christ is not identified *with* political, economic, and social liberation, but it is historically identified *in* political, economic, and social liberation. (Boff and Boff 1984: 18–19, 32[15]

Logically, then, this relationship imputes a special salvific significance to all earthly, liberative action—"sacred" or "secular." According to Gutiérrez (1973: 72),

[Liberative action] gives religious value in a completely new way to the action of man in history, Christian and non-Christian alike. The building of a just society has worth in terms of the Kingdom. . . . To participate in the process of liberation is already, in a certain sense, a salvific work.

Later, he states:

Any effort to build a just society is liberating. And it has an indirect but effective impact on the fundamental alienation [sin]. It is a salvific work, although it is not all of salvation. . . . The growth of the kingdom is a process which occurs historically *in* liberation, insofar as liberation means a greater fulfillment of man. (Gutiérrez 1973: 177)

This infusion of the mundane with ultimate religious significance has the very practical consequence of motivating fervent this-worldly action. Bonino (1975: 142–43) concludes:

When this perspective is adopted, the main question which recent theology has been asking must also be shifted. Instead of asking, where is the Kingdom present or visible in today's history? we are moved to ask, how can I participate—not only individually but in a community of faith and in history—in the coming world? The main problem is not noetic but, so to say, empirical. It has to do with an active response. . . . History, in relation to the Kingdom, is not a riddle to be solved but a mission to be fulfilled.

Finally, all of this implies that the Parousia, the Second Coming of Christ, constitutes not the destruction of history, but the fulfillment of history. History is not moving toward its own termination but—through concrete liberative action—toward its completion (Gutiérrez 1973: 165–68). Bonino (1975: 142) writes: "The Kingdom is not the denial of history but the elimination of its corruptibility, its frustrations, weaknesses, ambiguities—more deeply, its sin—in order to bring to full realization the true meaning of the communal life of man."

The Church—A Preferential Option for the Poor

In his controversial book, *Church: Charism and Power,* Leonardo Boff writes, "The Church is not doomed to carry out a purely preservative mission, contrary to the view held by orthodox Marxism." He then continues (1985: 115):

> Rather, because of its ideals and origins (the dangerous and subversive memory of Jesus of Nazareth crucified under Pontius Pilate), its mission is revolutionary. But this is dependent upon certain social conditions as well as the Church's own internal structure. Given a certain break with the ruling class(es), the Church may find itself allied with the lower classes in their struggles against domination, especially with those groups possessing a religious vision of the world. These groups . . . tend to create a *strategy of liberation.*

The Church, says liberation theology, traditionally has been "closely linked to the established order" (Gutiérrez 1973: 133). "But for some time now," observes Gutiérrez (1973: 101), "we have been witnessing a great effort by the Church to rise up out of this ghetto power and mentality and to shake off the ambiguous protection provided by the beneficiaries of the unjust order." He continues (1973: 138):

> For the Latin American church, it is becoming increasingly clearer that to be in the world without being of the world means concretely to be in the system without being of the system. It is evident that only a break with the unjust order and a frank commitment to a new society can make the message of love . . . credible to Latin Americans. . . . In Latin America, the Church must place itself squarely within the process of revolution, amid the violence which is present in different ways. The Church's mission is defined . . . in relation to this revolutionary process.[16]

Furthermore, Gutiérrez argues, the Church cannot occupy neutral ground in the exercise of its influence: it must act either for or against the unjust social order (1973: 267). Neither can it ignore the reality of class division and conflict, both in the world and within the Church. Church unity, so highly valued in Roman Catholicism, must be achieved, not simply by asserting a lack of division, but by rallying around the cause of the oppressed (ibid., 276–78).[17]

In effect, the Church must live in solidarity with the poor and so become a "Church of the poor":

> If the church wishes to be faithful to the God of Jesus Christ, it must become aware of itself from underneath, from among the poor of this world, the exploited classes, despised ethnic groups, and marginalized cultures. It must descend into the hell of this world, into communion with the misery, injustice, struggle, and hopes of the wretched of the earth—for "of such is the kingdom of heaven." At bottom it is a matter of living, as church, what the majority of its own members live every day. To be born, to be reborn, as church, from below, from among them, today means to die, in a concrete history of oppression and complicity with oppression. (Gutiérrez 1983: 211)

Ronaldo Muñoz (1981: 153) contends that the Church must "incarnate itself among the common people, *among the poor* and marginalized of the earth; for that is where Jesus Christ himself once became incarnate and fulfilled his ministry."[18]

This requires that the Church be "converted" by the poor. Gutiérrez (1983: 156) observes: "The demands made on Christians in solidarity with the poor and oppressed are so serious that they are leading the whole Church to a radical change in its way of life—to a conversion." According to Muñoz (1981: 154):

> Today the church is being summoned to undergo a *conversion to the poor* of the land. It is being called upon to let itself be "domesticated" by the poor. . . . This means that the church must thoroughly revise its structures, its viewpoints, its practices, and the concrete life of its members. . . . The aim of all this is to ensure that the poor will be able to find in the church *their own true home* as an oppressed, believing people, *the expression of their own faith* and hope, and the anticipation of their own yearnings for liberty, community, and participation.

And, Alvaro Barreiro (1982: 68) asserts: "A church that fails to evangelize the poor, and that is not evangelized by the poor . . . would not be the Church of Jesus Christ."

Central to the Church's mission, then, are the two tasks of symbolizing and struggling for liberation. Muñoz observes (1979: 158):

> The church, through its message and life, once again becomes a "sign" or "sacrament" injecting the gospel as a leavening agent into human life and placing Christ on the lampstand for all hu-

manity to see. It becomes the sign and saving instrument of a God who has revealed himself to us as the God of life.

First, through its preaching, celebration, ritualization, and popular dramatization, the Church must be *a sign* of liberation (Boff and Boff 1987: 60). Comments Barreiro (1982: 49–50): "If it wants to remain faithful to the mission entrusted to it, the Church must preach the good news of liberation of the poor as what it is: the focal point of its message. To fail in this preaching is to betray its mission." Bonino (1975: 169) argues: "The Church . . . cannot exist except as it concretely celebrates this freedom, reflects on it, and proclaims it."[19]

Second, the Church itself must be *an instrument* of liberation. Gutiérrez says (1973: 268):

This critical function of the Church runs the risk of remaining on a purely verbal and external level. . . . It should be backed up with clear action and commitments. Prophetic denunciation can be made validly and truly only from within the heart of the struggle for a more human world.

Barreiro (1982: 52) also affirms:

The Church cannot, however, confine itself to a merely verbal proclamation. . . . In addition to the announcement and denunciation, which are always necessary, the Church must perform deeds and acts of liberation like Jesus [did] . . . actions which were "signs" and "proof" of the presence of God's justice and mercy among human beings.[20]

The New Man, the New Society

What kind of world does liberation theology envision? What kind of society does it seek to realize? What, in short, is its ultimate goal? Gutiérrez (1973: 28, 307) calls for "liberation from exploitation," "a more human and dignified life," "the creation of a new man," "the abolition of injustice," "a new society," "a truly human existence," "a free life," and "a dynamic liberty." The Boff brothers aim for "a society of freed men and women," for a society whose members are "comradely, prophetic, committed, free, joyful, contemplative, and utopian" (Boff and Boff 1987: 93–94) and Frances O'Gorman (1983: 36) dreams of "a world without miserable poverty, selfishness, corruption, a world of loving forgiveness." But can the goal of liberation theology be specified more precisely than this? Can it be put in more concrete terms?

To begin, the aims of liberation theology go beyond reform of the present system to the construction of a "qualitatively different" society.[21] Leonardo Boff states: "Liberation, by definition, involves a qualitatively new society. Reformist measures are only tactical steps, not strategic goals" (Boff and Boff 1984: 12).[22] And, Gutiérrez (1973: 48) writes: "To support the social revolution means to abolish the present status quo and to attempt to replace it with a qualitatively different one."

In order for this to happen, however, in addition to structural change, the inner human will have to be transformed (Morelli 1971: 90–92). Leonardo Boff (1978: 64) argues: "In order that such a liberation . . . be realized, Christ makes two fundamental demands: He demands personal conversion and postulates a restructuring of the human world." Gutiérrez, too, contends:

> The liberation of our continent means more than overcoming economic, social, and political dependence. It means, in a deeper sense, to see the becoming of mankind as a process of the emancipation of man in history. It is to see man in search of a qualitatively different society in which he will be free from all servitude, in which he will be an artisan of his own destiny. (1973: 91)

This, then, demands the emergence of a "new man" (Damico 1987). "The goal," Gutiérrez argues (1973: 32), "is not only better living conditions, a radical change of structures, a social revolution; it is much more: the continuous creation, never ending, of a new way to be a man, a *permanent cultural revolution*."[23]

Still, the discussion thus far has remained in the realm of abstract values and visions. How, more specifically, does liberation theology articulate its vision of the world it wants to create?

Liberation theologians refuse to answer this question when they are pressed on it. They believe it is inappropriate and impossible to specify the end result too concretely. O'Gorman (1983: 41) writes: "There is no blueprint for the building of a new society; no map for the journey toward justness. Inspiration from faith and from the reality of daily living are the sign-posts but the way has to be forged as people move along together." Segundo (1979: 249) comments, "Some might ask here: Why not spell out the socialist model more fully? Or why not talk about the possibility of a moderated, renovated capitalism? For a very simple reason, I would reply. We are not seers, nor are we capable of controlling the world of the future." According to Segundo, "The only real and possible option open to us lies within our own countries. Right now today the only thing we can do is to decide whether or not we are going to give individuals or private groups the right to own the means of production that exist in our countries. And that decision is what I call the option between capitalism and socialism" (ibid., 249–50).

Instead of drawing-up precise blueprints, liberation theologians prefer to pursue a "historical project." Bonino (1975: 38–39) explains:

"Historical project" is an expression frequently used in our discussions as a midway term between a utopia, a vision which makes no attempt to connect itself historically to the present, and a program, a technically developed model for the organization of society. A historical project is defined enough to force options in terms of the basic structures of society. It points in a given direction. But frequently its contents are expressed in symbolical and elusive forms rather than in terms of precise language. . . . It is in this general sense that we speak of *a Latin American socialist project of liberation.*

What are the general characteristics of this historical project of liberation theology?

First, it rejects capitalist "developmentalism." Bonino (1975: 31) charges:

Capitalism creates in the dependent countries (perhaps not only in them) a form of human existence characterized by artificiality, selfishness, the inhuman and dehumanizing pursuit of success measured in terms of prestige and money, and the resignation of responsibility for the world and for one's neighbor. . . . This sham culture kills in the people even the awareness of their own condition of dependence and exploitation, it destroys the very core of their humanity.

Because of this, Gutiérrez (1979: 17–18) argues,

Only by getting beyond a society divided into classes, only by establishing a form of political power designed to serve the vast majority of our people, and only by eliminating private ownership of wealth created by human labor will we be able to lay the foundations of a more just society.

Second, it believes that exploitative capitalism should be replaced by an indigenously-created brand of socialism. Gutiérrez writes: "The history of the private ownership of the means of production makes evident the necessity of its reduction or suppression for the welfare of society. We must hence *opt for social ownership of the means of production* (1973: 111–12; on socialism, see also Gutiérrez 1973: 26–27, 30, 274; Buhle and Fiehrer 1985). And, the Boff brothers state,

> The Christian ideal is closer to socialism than to capitalism. It is not a matter of creating a Christian socialism. It is a matter of being able to say that the social system, when actually carried out in reality, enables Christians better to live the humanitarian and divine ideals of their faith. (Boff and Boff 1984: 10)[24]

This new socialism, liberation theologians insist, must be an indigenously developed, uniquely Latin American version of socialism:

> The socialist system which will finally emerge in the Latin American countries will not be a copy of existing ones, but a creation related to our reality. . . . There is a strong sense of freedom to find an authentic Latin American socialism, forged in a realistic understanding of our situation, true to our own history and to the characteristics of the Latin American people. (Bonino 1975: 35, 40)

Segundo (1979: 241) also argues:

> For us in Latin America it is not a matter of choosing between the society existing in the United States and that existing in the Soviet Union. Our option must be made from the oppressed periphery of the great economic empires. We must choose some socio-political scheme from our own context as an underdeveloped continent.[25]

Third, whatever form the sociopolitical system takes, liberation theologians maintain that it must be constructed by the local people: "The agent of social transformation should be the people itself, in conjunction with strata organically associated with the people, and not the dominant elite" (Boff and Boff 1984: 15). In this sense, the process is as important as the outcome. Gutiérrez (1983: x, 113) demands that people be "the agents of their own destiny," the "protagonists of their own liberation." He says, "In order for this liberation to be authentic and complete, it has to be undertaken by the oppressed people themselves and so must stem from the values proper to these people. Only in this context can a true cultural revolution come about" (ibid., 91; see also 114).

Fourth, according to the historical project, constructing the new society is an essentially *human* project; it will not be handed down from God: "The Gospel does not provide utopia for us; this is a human work" (ibid., 238). Bonino (1975: 98) maintains that in our liberating activities, we work "totally and solely in the area of human rationality—in the realm where God has invited man to be *on his own."* Says Bonino (1975: 124): "Christians are called to use for this struggle the same rational tools that are at the disposal of all human beings."

Fifth, liberation theology's historical project envisions a new society in which power and wealth are shared equitably, in a spirit of participation and cooperation. That society must, according to the Boffs, "foster a greater participation by all in the economy and in society and create a greater symmetry among groups of persons" (Boff and Boff 1984: 19).[26] According to Gutiérrez (1979: 1–2), the historical project

> insists that the people must come to power if such a society is to be truly free and egalitarian. . . . In such a reordered society the social takeover of the means of production will be accompanied by a social takeover of the reins of political power that will ensure people's liberty. Thus, the way will be open to a new social awareness.

In this way, the new society, argue the Boffs, should be modeled after the inner being of the Holy Trinity:

> The Christian God is a trinity of persons, Father, Son, and Holy Spirit. Each distinct from the other, they coexist eternally in a relationship of absolute equality and reciprocity. In the beginning there was not merely the oneness of a divine nature, but the full and perfect communion of three divine persons. This mystery provides the prototype for what society should be according to the plan of the triune God: by affirming and respecting personal individuality, it should enable persons to live in such communion and collaboration with each other as to constitute a unified society of equals and fellow citizens. (Boff and Boff 1987: 52)

They continue, "The society we commonly find today, full of divisions, antagonism, and discriminations, does not offer an environment in which we can experience the mystery of the Holy Trinity. It has to be transformed if it is to become the image and likeness of the communion of the divine persons."

Finally, the historical project envisions a society in which the quality of human relationships moves beyond mere justice to the realization of solidarity and, even, love among all (Gutiérrez 1973: 47). Leonardo Boff (1978: 71) explains:

> The love demanded by Christ is superior by far to justice. Justice, in the classical definition, consists of giving to each his own. Evidently, this "his own" presupposes a given social system. In slave

society, giving to each his own consists in giving to the slaves what is theirs and to the masters what is theirs. . . . In neocapitalist systems it means giving to the magnates what is theirs and to the proletariat what is theirs. In the Sermon on the Mount Christ breaks this circle. He does not preach any such system of justice that signifies the consecration and legitimation of a social status quo that has as its starting point discrimination between people. He announces a fundamental equality: All are worthy of love. Who is my neighbor? This question is fallacious and ought not to be asked. All are neighbors to each person.

Here, then, are the central themes of liberation theology. They constitute a reconceptualization of the Christian faith from the perspective of the poor and oppressed, and provide an ideology for the liberation theology movement.

3

Theoretical Tools for Analysis

Why and how did the liberation theology movement emerge when and where it did? Answering this question requires employing theoretic tools which can help to explain the sources and outcomes of social movements. To this end, this chapter defines different types of actors in Latin American Catholicism, explores the movement's strategy and tactics, and explains a political process model of social movements. These conceptual tools will be used in this study to interpret the forces and events that generated the liberation theology movement.

Types of Latin American Catholics

Following the practice of previous analysts (Vallier 1967; Sanders 1969; F. Turner 1971; Dodson 1979; Berryman 1979; Levine 1981; Cleary 1985; Kselman 1986; Fleet 1988; Mainwaring and Wilde 1989), this study categorizes Latin American Catholics into a number of ideal types: radicals (also called liberationists), progressives, moderates, and conservatives.[1] These types are differentiated by their general orientation to the Church's involvement in sociopolitical change. The terms are chosen for their common use in the literature and imply no value judgments; "progressive," for example, does not imply intellectual or moral advancement, progress, or superiority.

Radicals advocate the direct and open use of the Church's human and material resources to promote social change toward some form of democratic socialism. They view the gospel as an active liberation from all forms of oppression: spiritual, social, racial, cultural, economic, and political. Radicals employ Marxist social analysis; reject reformist capitalist development; favor participation with non-Christians, including secular leftists, in popular movements; and are sometimes open to some forms of violent, revolutionary struggle.

Progressives promote active Church support for social, political, and economic reforms toward democracy and economic modernization to improve the general welfare of Latin Americans. In general, progressives accept reformist, capitalist development, but are also apt to view social problems in structural terms and to engage in social criticism. They are open to the radicals' view of liberation, to selective use of Marxist analytical concepts, and to dialogue and discerning cooperation with leftists. Progressives are inclined to experiment with new Church programs and strategies to help achieve their religious and social goals. However, unlike radicals, in keeping with the views of Vatican II and Catholic social teachings, progressives maintain the distinction between the appropriate political involvement of clergy and laity: clergy should inspire and activate laity who themselves should be the actual agents of social change.

Moderates largely accept existing social and political arrangements. Their central desire, as a means to fulfilling the Church's mission, is to increase the Church's institutional strength and moral influence on society. Moderates are not opposed in principle to social and ecclesiastical reforms, nor to the radicals' perspective of liberation. Indeed, they view many social problems in structural terms. But they generally are not active advocates of reform or structural change. Being more pragmatic than ideological in style, moderates are very concerned to maintain Church unity and social stability, and are willing to support either progressives or conservatives who, in a given situation, seem able to promote that. Moderates reject Marxist social analysis, but are likely to criticize extreme poverty and to condemn serious abuses of human rights.

Conservatives also accept existing social and political arrangements but generally resist religious or social change. Conservatives are most concerned with maintaining Church tradition, hierarchical authority, and doctrinal orthodoxy. They tend to view social ills in personal, not structural, terms and view the appropriate social role of Catholicism as providing conventional charity and moral guidelines for society and challenging individuals to personal conversion. Conservatives reject Marxist social analysis as dangerous and incompatible with Christian faith and actively oppose Catholic radicals and their understanding of liberation. However, they do accept the language of liberation when understood as spiritual liberation from the bondage of sin.

Throughout the following analysis, these types will be used to label the various actors in the emergence of liberation theology.

Liberation Theology's Strategy and Tactics

A social movement, broadly defined, is an attempt to mobilize a previously unmobilized constituency for collective action against an antagonist to promote or resist social change (Gamson 1990: 14–16). In forming and guiding their movement, liberation theology leaders have had to develop an appropriate strategy and effective tactics. A *strategy* is a broad plan for the long-range employment of forces and resources to achieve one's overall goals. *Tactics* are the specific techniques, maneuvers, or procedures used to implement one's strategy.

The strategy of the liberation theology movement has been simple and consistent since its inception. It has been to mobilize Latin American Christians to participate as Christians in popular campaigns, organizations, and movements toward the fundamental restructuring and transformation of their own societies and cultures in a way that facilitates human liberation (Richard n.d.: 20–23).[2] The idea has not been to create specifically "Christian" campaigns, organizations, and movements, such as Catholic Action, and Christian Democracy. Rather, for the most part, the idea has been to build coalitions with other militants—labor unions, peasant leagues, Marxist organizations, student groups, guerrilla movements, and so on— to produce popular campaigns, organizations, and movements that achieve commonly held goals. Christians in the liberation theology movement contribute a specifically Christian motivation, presence, and energy to these movements, but they do not try to make the movements themselves "Christian" (Richard n.d.: 20–23). It is inappropriate, therefore, from the liberation theology perspective, to speak of these organizations as either "Christian," "secular," "Catholic," "religious," or "non-Christian," for they typically represent alliances of a broad spectrum of participants—Christians and atheists, Marxists and Catholics, and others.

Mobilizing Latin American Catholics to participate as Christians in popular movements toward radical social change has required support from the Catholic Church. A necessary component of the movement's mobilization strategy, therefore, has been to gain control over the Church's institutional authority and resources. This was a task logically akin to an organizational takeover, since the Church's resources and authority would not otherwise have been used for such a purpose.

Once sufficiently secured, however, the second component of the strategy has been to employ the Church's resources and authority to mobilize participation in popular movements. In this sense, the first component has been a movement of Catholic activists within the Church, the second a movement of a newly designated activist institution (or, more accurately, a sector of that institution) in society.

While the liberation theology movement's strategy has been simple and consistent since its inception, the movement's *tactics* have been numerous and changing through the years, responding to the opportunities and constraints of different situations. Briefly, movement tactics for clergy and laity have, at various times and places, included organizing and participating in strikes, protests, rallies, and marches; organizing consciousness-raising programs for the poor; working for socialist political candidates; issuing official Church pastoral letters and documents that oppose poverty, repression, and injustice and call for liberating structural change; working to restructure the Church into small, decentralized neighborhood churches, called Base Ecclesial Communities (BECs), which are politically active; diffusing liberation theology to ground-level pastoral workers who, in turn, diffuse it to Catholic laity through a process of conscientization; offering the Church as a sanctuary for repressed progressive and leftist political militants; organizing peasant occupations of land owned by speculators; collecting and publicizing information about abuses of human rights in order to damage rightist military and governmental powers; and agitating for improved neighborhood services. In a few cases, mostly limited to Central America, tactics also included aiding guerrilla insurgents; participating in popular, armed insurrections and revolutions; and advising or serving in revolutionary government administrations.

While specific movement tactics have been adjusted to fit individual situations, a general trend in tactical change over the years can be observed in the liberation theology movement: the older it grew, the more the liberation theology movement emphasized long-term, quiet, steady education and organization at the grass-roots level (Sigmund 1988: 22).

In its earliest years—the late 1960s and early 1970s—liberation theologians were very optimistic about the possibilities of political and economic change. Therefore, they adopted—perhaps not consciously—what was essentially a Leninist approach, seeking a revolutionary process spearheaded by a "vanguard," consisting of the leftist intelligentsia . The 1973 military coup in Chile and a backlash within the Church, however, tempered their optimism, forcing them to reassess their tactics (Berryman 1984b: 30).

In the mid- and late 1970s, movement leaders gave increased

attention to the importance of the actual participation of the common people in the movement for liberation. Rejecting whatever notions they had assumed about the importance of the "vanguard," liberation theologians spoke more and more of *popular* movements. This change necessitated less attention to activities like convincing university students and academics of the relevance of the Christian faith for Latin America's problems and more attention to activities like organizing BECs in slums, promoting literacy programs, conscientization, food cooperatives, and mass protests (Segundo 1990: 353–66; Berryman 1984b: 30).[3] These tactical changes also necessitated adjusting expectations about achieving radical social change. As movement leaders came to see that revolutionary liberation would be a long-term process, not a short-term accomplishment, they focused increasingly on extended, quiet, persistent education and organization at the grass-roots level (Sigmund 1988: 22). The people, they came to understand, would, indeed, have to become the agents and makers of their own destiny.

The Importance of Insurgent Consciousness

For analytical purposes, it is useful to understand the emergence and growth of liberation theology in Latin America as a social movement. Still, liberation theology appears to be unlike many other social movements, such as labor, civil rights, environmental, and anti-war movements. Exactly how is it different? It is a religious movement. It is a diffuse movement spanning an entire continent. It is a Third World movement.

Yet none of these aspects gets to the heart of the matter. The crucial fact that sets the liberation theology movement apart from many other social movements is that its first task and goal was the institutionalization of novel symbolic and ideological forms in a relatively inhospitable, self-reproducing institutional structure.

What most social movements have in common is that they work to influence the state on behalf of a defined group of beneficiaries. Within a given set of political arrangements, they construct new organizations and mobilize latent constituencies to contest state policy by either electoral means or, failing that, by disruption.

However, this kind of activity was a second step for the liberation theology movement. Before it could mobilize its members to exert pressure to transform society, it faced the problem of diffusing and institutionalizing its action strategy in the Church.[4] In other words, before the liberation theology movement could become a movement *of* the Church, it first had to succeed as a movement *within* the Church.

Unlike people's relationship to the state, membership in and submission to the Church is voluntary, and withdrawal is a readily available option. One of the Church's ongoing tasks, therefore, in its effort to effectively carry out its mission, is maintaining the active commitment of its pastoral workers and parishioners. Its theological worldview serves as a major integrative force to accomplish this. But the Church's theological system also entails action commitments that place demands on its members.

Liberation theology is an alternative theological worldview demanding a distinctive set of action commitments. It was first established in the Church, in part, as a means of revitalizing an institution seemingly losing its struggle to maintain the commitment of its members. Later, it survived opposition by successfully controlling valuable organizational resources that Church leaders were loath to cut off.

The first analytic problem faced by the liberation theology activists, therefore, was not the mobilization of a powerless, excluded group for noninstitutionalized methods of political action. Rather, the first problem was essentially that of organizational takeover and validation of a new worldview. The original problem was not how, as excluded ones, to constrain the state, but how to develop, diffuse, and institutionalize a new form of consciousness in the Church. Only having successfully accomplished that aim could the movement leaders work to carry out the new action commitments by mobilizing the excluded and powerless for collective action.

This peculiar feature of the liberation theology movement provides an opening to an issue that is relevant to understanding most other social movements but which is, nevertheless, typically neglected in discussions of those movements. The present case of liberation theology illuminates, by necessity, the social-psychological factor addressed but misunderstood by breakdown-deprivation theories and all but ignored by resource mobilization theories: the development and establishment of "insurgent consciousness."[5]

Grievances and discontent were critical factors in the emergence of liberation theology. Its prime movers were not simply those who found themselves, by a stroke of historical luck or external benevolence, with access to an abundance of potential resources which they then put to use. Rather, they were a group of people who were so grieved by hunger and poverty, so incensed by what they perceived as oppression and imperialism, and so gripped by the possibility of change that they themselves actively mobilized the resources necessary to begin a movement. Thus, the emergence of liberation theology required more than a shift in the supply of resources. It also required a motivation, a reason powerful enough to compel activists to take the initiative to organize and appropriate resources in the first place.

Furthermore, these grievances were not constant and stable. Only years before, most of those who were the prime movers of the liberation theology movement were content with the reformist, developmentalist strategy of New Christendom. The formation of their grievances can only be attributed to a change in their perception of the situation that provoked a common sense of frustration and a resolve to change their reality. The emergence of the movement required, in short, the development of a grievance-motivated insurgent consciousness.

Breakdown-deprivation theories rightly identify changes in consciousness, such as rising discontent and grievances, as key factors in social movement emergence. However, they wrongly characterize these experiences as irrational, reactive, pathological, or anomic. Resource mobilization theorists, on the other hand, largely ignore changed consciousness, claiming that discontent is ubiquitous and stable, and, therefore, unproblematic.

The case of the liberation theology movement does not lend itself to analysis by either of these theoretical approaches, for it is, at heart, a movement concerned with the deliberate development, diffusion, and institutionalization of a change in consciousness. Consciousness, it turns out, cannot simply be brushed aside or treated as a stable or residual category. In the liberation theology movement, then, we have the opportunity and necessity to focus on insurgent consciousness, an issue too long underplayed or misplayed by most treatments of social movements.

Of the available theoretical approaches to social movements, the one which, in addition to its other strengths, best takes into account the importance of the critical social-psychological factor of insurgent consciousness is Doug McAdam's political process model. In this study, I will use this model as the key analytical tool to interpret the forces and events which generated the liberation theology movement. Therefore, a review of the political process model is appropriate here.

The Political Process Model

The theoretical groundwork for the Political Process model was laid by Charles Tilly in his historical and theoretical works on collective action (Tilly et. al 1975; Rule and Tilly 1975).[6] But it was Doug McAdam who first systematically articulated the political process model in his 1982 work on black insurgency. The following exposition of this model will closely follow McAdam's insightful presentation and logic.

As the name indicates, the political process model assumes that a social movement is primarily a *political* phenomenon, in that it concerns the exercise of power among competing interests, and "represents a continuous *process,* from generation to decline, rather than a discrete series of developmental stages" (McAdam 1982: 36). The model attempts to account for the external, environmental constraints and opportunities shaping the actions of mobilizing groups. It also seeks to do justice to variables internal to the movement, such as organization, commitment, responsibility, beliefs, and values, which also influence the endeavors of mobilizing groups.

The political process model specifies three key variables in the emergence and life course of social movements, (1) the relative availability of political opportunities in the broad, political environment; (2) the relative strength of related organizations that can help facilitate a social movement; and (3) the collective realization that social change is both imperative and viable. What follows will first explore these components individually, and then discuss the relationships among them.

Political Opportunities

The structure of the political milieu within which the institutionalized political decision-making process takes place is not rigid or static. The political environment is continually subject to alteration by forces from within and without (McAdam 1982: 40–41). Shifts in the structure of the larger political milieu often have the effect of enhancing or diminishing the opportunities of potential movement groups to use their limited resources to pursue their interests effectively (ibid., 42–3; Goldstone 1979: 1037). These changes in political opportunities are an important influence on the emergence and life course of social movements.

What exactly causes these alterations in the political environment? McAdam (1982: 41) suggests that,

> *Any* event or broad social process that serves to undermine the calculations and assumptions on which the political establishment is structured occasions a shift in political opportunities. Among the events and processes likely to prove disruptive of the political status quo are wars, industrialization, international political realignments, prolonged unemployment, and widespread demographic changes.[7]

The resulting increased political opportunities can take three forms: general political instability, enhanced political positions for movement groups, and ideological openness (ibid., 42).

General political instability—through such events as wars, insurrections, and stock-market crashes—weakens the control of dominant groups over the political process. They must spend increasing amounts of resources simply to maintain their positions (ibid.). Instability also shakes confidence in the structure of the political process and raises the possibility of a partial or total restructuring of political institutions, with a resulting redistribution of political rewards.

The second form of increased political opportunity is enhanced political position: an absolute increase in political resources resulting in a relative increase in power vis-à-vis established political groups (ibid.). Enhanced political position is typically realized through long-term economic trends and political realignments rather than short-term events that generate instability. Consequently, the increase in political opportunity through enhanced political positions for movement groups is usually achieved more gradually than through political instability.

Ideological openness is a third form of increased political opportunity resulting from shifts in the broader cultural environment. Ideological openness denotes a social atmosphere which tolerates or encourages the serious consideration of new, alternative, or critical—perhaps even subversive—ideas and worldviews. Since the exercise of power is often closely linked to the manipulation of ideas, the expansion of freedom of thought and expression combined with an influx of creative, critical ideas may result in a marked increase in political opportunity for potential movement groups.

Each of these three forms of increased political opportunity translates into a relative increase in power. This, in turn, increases the probability of insurgent actions in the form of social movements (McAdam 1982: 43).

Organizational Strength

McAdam (1982: 43) writes, "A conducive political environment only affords the aggrieved population the opportunity for successful insurgent action. It is the resources of the minority community that enable insurgent groups to exploit these opportunities." The crucial resource, in this regard, is organizational strength. Therefore, the second component of the political process model is the relative strength of organizations, especially indigenous organizations, which are potential facilitators of social movement.[8]

Strong organizations contribute five key resources to a social movement: members, leaders, a communication network, solidary incentives, and "enterprise tools," such as meeting places, mimeograph machines, lawyers, office supplies, telephones, secretarial help (McAdam 1982: 44–48).[9]

MEMBERS. Social movements do not spring from masses of disorganized, isolated individuals. They typically emerge out of situations of strong integration through relational networks and organizations (Snow et al. 1980). Increasing solidarity, and not breakdown, is, in fact, the force which helps to generate social movements (McAdam 1982: 44).[10] This is true, in part, because social movements recruit new participants most successfully from existing organizations with related interests. Whether that means recruiting individuals or small clusters of people or "block recruitment" (Oberschall 1973: 125), drawing from related, existent organizations is a more efficient means of building organizational membership than recruiting random, unorganized individuals (McAdam 1982: 45).

LEADERS. Social movements need people who take initiative to organize activities, make strategic decisions, and articulate the movement's interests (McAdam 1982: 47). Since leadership skills are typically cultivated over time through experience, existing organizations often serve the function of a training ground for social movement leaders. And, as McAdam notes (ibid.), "it may well be that established leaders are among the first to join a new movement by virtue of their central position in the community." As a consequence, the social movement benefits from both the leader's skills and prestige and the organization's rank-and-file members who follow the leader in joining the movement.

COMMUNICATION NETWORK. Since "a social movement is a new cultural item subject to the same pattern of diffusion and adoption as other innovations" (McAdam 1982: 47), the rate and efficiency of communication with potential movement participants is a key variable in determining the growth of social movements (ibid., 46). Furthermore, efficient intra-group communication is an organizational capability which social movements need to acquire. Preexistent organizations possess intact, functioning communication infrastructures (ibid.). When social movements break into those networks, their message is more efficiently propagated. And when they successfully recruit enough members from existent organizations, they automatically acquire the communication networks of those organizations (ibid.; Freeman 1973).

SOLIDARY INCENTIVES. Marcus Olson's "selective incentive" answer to the "free-rider problem"—that is, the problem of eliciting focused individual sacrifice to achieve broadly enjoyed collective goods—assumes an overly rational and self-interested view of human beings (Olson 1965). Motivation for action can be based on value commitments, responsibility to others, and a sense of group solidarity, in addition to self-interest. One of these, group solidarity—the sense of belonging, participation, and group accomplishment—is a property which existing organizations offer (McAdam 1982: 45).[11] McAdam writes (ibid., 46):

> These organizations already rest on a solid structure of solidary incentives which insurgents have, in effect, appropriated by defining movement participation as synonymous with organizational membership. Accordingly, the myriad of incentives that have heretofore served as the motive force for participation in the group are now simply transferred to the movement. Thus, insurgents have been spared the difficult task of inducing participation through the provision of new incentives of either a solidary or material nature.

ENTERPRISE TOOLS. Finally, existing organizations can provide social movements with the use of practical tools and services necessary for basic organizational operations. Instead of spending their own limited resources to acquire telephones, typewriters, meeting places, copying and mimeograph machines, lawyers, computers, office supplies, secretarial help, and other facilities, social movements can borrow or inherit these items from existing, sympathetic organizations.

Insurgent Consciousness

Relative openness of political opportunities—the first component of the political process model—concerns the structure of the political environment in which all groups operate. Relative strength of indigenous organizations—the second factor—concerns the degree of organizational capacity for action on the part of mobilizing populations (McAdam 1982: 40). Propitious conditions in both of these areas encourage the emergence of social movements.

Nevertheless, expanded political opportunity and increased indigenous organizational strength are *insufficient*—even if necessary—conditions for the generation of social movements (ibid., 48, 51). Together they constitute a kind of "structural conductivity" for social movement emergence, but by themselves fail to generate insurgent action (ibid., 48). A third, social-psychological factor is necessary for that to happen: insurgent consciousness.[12]

Insurgent consciousness is a collective state of understanding which stems from the subjective interpretation of the objective social situation in which a potential movement group finds itself.[13] It is a state of being which perceives, interprets, and explains a social situation in such a way that compels people to collectively organize and act to change that social situation (McAdam 1982: 51).

Essentially, insurgent consciousness is *a collective state of understanding which recognizes that social change is both imperative and viable*. It combines the pressing necessity for social change with the real possibility of social change to produce decisive actions to effect change.[14] Important aspects of insurgent consciousness are the recognition that the felt grief is actually structurally or intentionally caused; that the cause is identifiable; that the grief is undeserved and unjust; that unless organized action is taken the grief will continue; that if organized action is taken there is a reasonable chance that the grief will end.[15]

Insurgent consciousness is not simply a rational, self-interested calculation, but an experience that involves the human mind, will, and emotion. Insurgent consciousness entails a mental awareness and reasoned evaluation; it involves a choice, a decision, a commitment; and it entails an emotional involvement, a sense of anger or moral outrage.

The concept of insurgent consciousness recognizes the central role of deprivations and grievances in generating social movements without falling into two traps in breakdown-deprivation theories. First, it does not assume that society is "normally" stable and harmonious, thereby treating grievances and conflict as anomalous, irrational, pathological, or anomic. Neither does it assume that grievances automatically and directly cause social movements. Other key factors, such as the political environment and availability of resources also come into play.

In addition, with insurgent consciousness, the political process model parts company with resource mobilization's treatment of grievances. Far from treating grievances as unproblematic and unimportant, the political process model recognizes in them a key explanatory variable. While conceding that real, socially rooted injustices are ubiquitous, this model contends that to generate social movements they must be perceived as such (Snow et al. 1986). The objective grounds for discontent may be universal but people's accurate interpretations of them are not (Klandermans 1984).[16]

It is not adequate to assume an unproblematic, ubiquitous supply of grievances that serve as a readily available reserve for social movements, for, as Anthony Oberschall (1973: 35) points out, "Interests and dissatisfactions are experienced and interpreted by way of moral ideas about right and wrong, justice and injustice, of conceptions of the social order as they are expressed in ideals and highly regarded principles." It is helpful to distinguish between passive grievances and active grievances. The grievances which result from structural injustices can be, and often are, interpreted as deserved, fated, meaningless, God's will, unchangeable, or self-changing. These interpretations produce passive grievances: real, felt injuries, but the kind that will not generate social movements. It is only when such grievances are transformed into active grievances, through a change in situation-interpretation leading to an insurgent consciousness, that the potential for social movement generation exists (McAdam 1982: 51).[17]

Developing an insurgent consciousness through a change in interpretation of the situation involves a redefinition of reality. It is a process analogous to Marx's theory of the shift from false consciousness to class consciousness. Both require a more accurate understanding of the objective reality. (The difference between the two is that Marx insists on restricting the fault lines of structural grievances and the boundary lines of movement constituents to a social class dimension alone, whereas the political process model does not.) In this sense, the possibility of the realization of a successful social movement presupposes a mental and emotional realization that throws grievances into a new perspective, requiring social movement action. Ferree and Miller (1985: 39) correctly point out that, "Although movement organizations do need to establish control over inert resources, they also need to mobilize the active support of individual human beings. Costs and benefits certainly play a role in generating movement support, but the translation of objective social relationships into subjectively experienced group interests is also critical in building movements, as in political activity generally."

Some recent social movement theorists (e.g., Gamson and Modigliani 1989; Gamson 1990; Snow et al. 1986; Snow and Benford 1988) have employed Erving Goffman's term *frame* to illuminate the social psychological variable in social movements. A frame, thus conceived, is an interpretive scheme that individuals use to order reality, make events meaningful, organize experience, and guide action. Frames often come as predefined "packages" or "clusters" of interests, values, beliefs, and understandings which individuals adopt as interpretive perspectives to make sense of their environments (Gamson and Modigliani 1989: 2). Insurgent consciousness erupts when a group of people adopt an "injustice frame," and they are mobilized for social movement participation when their frame becomes aligned with the frame of a social movement organization (Snow et al. 1986).

Insurgent consciousness, then, is one of many possible responses to the common recognition that things in this world are not the way they should be. It responds not by accepting or ignoring wrongs in the world, but, instead, by struggling to make the world, or an aspect of it, what it thinks it should be.

For the liberation theology movement specifically, insurgent consciousness came with the perception by some Catholic bishops, theologians, pastoral workers, and laity that the Christian faith demands a fundamentally just society, that the majority of Latin Americans were being exploited and oppressed, that Church allegiances with the wealthy and powerful were a betrayal of the Christian gospel, that a gradualist strategy of social reform was entirely inadequate, and that God himself desires, in history, to replace social systems of injustice with fundamentally just, humane social systems.

The Political Process Model in Action

Just as it takes the right proportion of different substances—potassium nitrite, sulfur, and charcoal—to make gunpowder, it takes a propitious mix of complex social conditions to produce and sustain a social movement. If that mix is incomplete, the social movement will either never begin or will abort.

None of the factors in the political process model is alone sufficient to generate social movements. Expanding political opportunities may go unexploited because of organizational weaknesses. Indigenous organizations may fail to capitalize on their strengths because of escapist or defeatist attitudes among their members. And, activists with a passionate insurgent consciousness may be crushed by hostile political environments. However, when the right social forces do converge, social movements emerge. According to McAdam (1982: 51), movement generation requires that all three components of the model develop together:

> The generation of insurgency is expected to reflect the favorable confluence of three sets of factors. Expanding political opportunities combine with [strong] indigenous organizations . . . to afford insurgents the "structural potential" for collective action. That potential is, in turn, transformed into actual insurgency by means of the crucial intervening process of cognitive liberation [insurgent consciousness]. All three factors, then, are regarded as necessary, but insufficient, causes of social insurgency.[18]

Under what conditions do these three factors converge? Broad, long-term social and cultural changes—such as urbanization, industrialization, revolutions, mass migrations, the rise of new social and political ideologies, shifting national and international political alliances, wars, the rise or decline of religious hegemony, prolonged

FIGURE 3.1

THE POLITICAL PROCESS MODEL OF SOCIAL MOVEMENTS

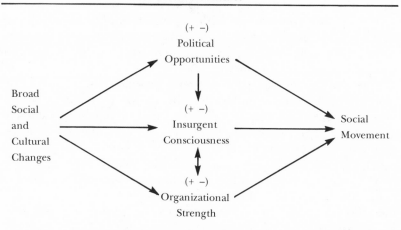

unemployment, technological developments, widespread demographic changes, and the effects of other social movements—often alter the general political environment, the strength of relevant indigenous organizations, and people's interpretation of reality (McAdam 1982: 60).

When these broad social changes open up new political opportunities and strengthen indigenous organizations, potential movement groups are more likely to perceive that beneficial social change is viable. This change in perception is all the more likely when broad cultural changes alter those groups' interpretations of reality in ways compatible with an insurgent consciousness (ibid., 49). If this increasing awareness of *viability* becomes linked with a collective conviction that social change is *imperative,* an insurgent consciousness appears.

Once insurgent consciousness is born, it becomes an independent variable that effects organizational strength. The increasing awareness of group power and responsibility to affect social change infuses the members of associate organizations with a sense of importance and anticipation. This may stimulate the recruitment of new members, participation, and commitment to the group. As such, increased insurgent consciousness and organizational strength have an escalating effect on each other.[19]

Social movements thus emerge when favorable political opportunities become available, when their facilitating organizations are strong, and when they develop an insurgent consciousness (ibid., 51).[20] This process is depicted in figure 3.1.

Social Control and Movement Dynamics

The political process model emphasizes the importance of the inter-action of social movements with other actors and groups in the broader political environment. Social movements do not take place in a vacuum. In this respect the political process model concurs with resource mobilization theory (Aveni 1978).

However, the political process model maintains, in contrast to the resource mobilization model, that the response of members and elites to social movement actions is typically—though not always—re-actionary and repressive, since it is not in their interest for move-ments to succeed (McAdam 1982: 25–29).[21] Another factor, then, which must be added to the model, is social control.

The means of social control can include making negative remarks about the movement in the media; inhibiting supplies of money and facilities; harassing movement participants; infiltrating organiza-tions; gathering information on the movement; inhibiting freedom of movement, expression, and action; encouraging internal conflict; sabotaging specific actions; derecruitment; supporting competitors; creating an unfavorable public image and counter-ideology; apply-ing legal sanctions; intimidating through false surveillance; and kid-napping, torturing, or killing movement leaders (Marx 1979).

Social control can have a direct effect on political opportunities, organizational strength, and insurgent consciousness. Through re-pressive social control, the social situation which generated the movement can be altered in a way that crushes the movement (Mc-Adam 1982: 58). However, Gary Marx has noted that social control can also backfire and strengthen the social movement by intensify-ing the insurgent consciousness, which can, in turn, strengthen in-digenous organizations. Excessive social control measures, if publi-cized, can shift the weight of moderate public opinion against elites.[22] Furthermore, repression may elicit increased resource sup-port from movement constituencies and sympathetic audiences. Fi-nally, social control can convince activists that their movement is a genuine threat and, therefore, that their actions are exceedingly important (Marx 1979: 117–23).

The political process model views the emergence and life course of social movements as a process, the outcome of which is largely determined by shifts in the political environment, in organizational strength, and in insurgent consciousness. Once a movement has emerged, however, the repression or facilitation effects of social con-trol must be accounted for as well, for they play a critical role in directing those shifts in the first three variables (McAdam 1982: 56).

Broadening the Application of the Political Process Model

There is considerable disagreement in the literature about what social movements exactly are. McAdam (1982: 24) observes:

> There is, in fact, no widely accepted typology, within the field, to differentiate the diverse phenomena encountered in the empirical literature. To theorize about social movements, then, is to address activities ranging from peyote cults on the one hand to revolutions on the other, with all manner of variations arrayed in between. Obviously, no theory—save perhaps the most general and therefore least useful—can adequately account for such a diverse range of phenomena. The failure to distinguish between these various behavioral forms has, in the view of one critic, "produced a field of study loosely joining phenomena so diverse as to defy explanation by any single theoretical framework. The desire for inclusiveness has had a high but hidden cost in theoretical specificity."

In response, McAdam concludes: "What is needed are several theories specifically tailored to particular categories of action."

In his work, McAdam focused on the particular action of a relatively powerless, politically excluded category of people: American blacks of the early- and mid-twentieth century. In his analysis, McAdam (ibid.) distinguished between "members" and "challengers." He defined members as those groups which possess the political and economic resources necessary to influence institutionalized political decision making and who therefore can work to realize their interests through standard political channels. Challengers, in contrast, are groups that lack those resources and whose interests are, consequently, left out of the conventional political decision-making process. Because of their weakness in resources, in order to realize their interests through institutionalized political channels, challengers must pursue their interest through nonstandard, noninstitutional means (ibid., 25).

While liberation theology and black insurgency do share some features in common, it is clear that in more important ways the two are dissimilar. As mentioned above, before the liberation theology movement was able to become a mass-based movement of excluded peasants and workers, the movement's leaders had to gain control over the Church's institutional authority and resources through a task logically akin to an organizational takeover. Before it could mobilize its members to exert pressure to transform society, it faced the problem of institutionalizing its ideology and action strategy in the Church. This first and crucial step of the movement was carried out not by powerless, excluded masses using nonconventional means, but by theological elites in the context of a powerful, well-established organization using largely institutionalized means. With liberation theology, then, we are dealing with a fundamentally different kind of social movement than that of McAdam's black insurgency.

However, despite these differences, McAdam's political process model still offers the most useful theoretical tool for analyzing the liberation theology movement. In other words, the usefulness of the model extends far beyond the specific type of social movement McAdam studied. The political process model provides a useful explanatory account not only of the often-studied grass-roots movements of the powerless and excluded, but also of another type of social movement largely unexamined in the literature: elite-initiated revitalization movements which aim drastically to redirect the strategies and resources of established institutions.[23] Other examples of revitalization movements include Jesse Jackson's Rainbow Coalition within the Democratic party, the collective political action of scientists in groups such as the Union of Concerned Scientists and the Education Foundation for Nuclear Science, Mikhail Gorbachev's program of *perestroika* and *glasnost* within the Communist party of the Soviet Union, the hospice movement within the medical establishment, feminist and gay theology and ordination rights movements within established religious denominations, and "school choice" movements within the American public education establishment.

For this reason and because, as argued above, McAdam's model best accounts for the factor of insurgent consciousness so important to understanding this movement, in this work I broaden the application of the political process model by employing a somewhat modified version of McAdam's model to help understand the emergence of liberation theology. Although originally conceived with a different kind of movement in mind, the political process model proves, in the case of liberation theology, to be quite useful and illuminating.

Part Two

The Emergence of a
Movement

4

The Historical Context, 1930–1955

Social movements do not develop overnight, but are the products of diverse, long-term social and cultural developments. The political process model used in this analysis assumes that many of the preconditions and causes of social movements have roots that go back for decades before the actual birth of the movement. Therefore, it is necessary to explore the broad, historical context out of which any social movement emerges. In the case of the liberation theology movement, we must begin as far back as the 1930s.

According to the political process model, one should expect social movements to emerge in conditions of expanding political opportunity, increasing organizational strength, and growing insurgent consciousness. Consequently, this and the following chapters will examine social conditions as they relate to critical moments and turning points in the emergence of the liberation theology movement.

The decades of the 1930s, '40s, and '50s, lacked the right combination of forces to bring such a movement into being. In many countries, lower-class interests and aspirations found a sympathetic response in populist political regimes. The Church was often fragmented organizationally, due to diocese-centered ecclesiastical structures. Poor national and international communication and transportation systems served to isolate Church personnel, hindering the possibility of extensive intra-church communication. Furthermore, Marxism was typically considered anathema in both Catholic culture and the Church's official social teachings. For all of these reasons, a movement such as liberation theology was, during these years, impossible. It is possible, nevertheless, to identify the gradual development of certain forces and events—both within and outside

71

the church—that would eventually generate the liberation theology movement.

The Background of Expanding Political Opportunity

Expanded political opportunity consists of an increase in the possibility of realizing one's own will in the face of opposition. This expansion of opportunity is typically caused by an increase in one's resources, power, or authority relative to those who would obstruct their realization. Such a situation could be the result of either an absolute increase in one's own resources, power, or authority *or* an absolute decline in the resources, power, or authority of one's opponent,[1] or both. During this period, a number of major social changes worked to expand political opportunity for progressive Catholics.

Urbanization

In the final decades of the nineteenth century, many Latin American nations experienced significant urban growth, as a result of both European immigration and internal migration prompted by economic opportunities resulting from these nations' entry into the world market as primary product exporters (Hardoy 1975: 44–50; Boyer and Davies 1973; Balan 1983: 153–66). Urbanization increased rapidly in the 1930s and continued to accelerate in the decades thereafter, as millions of Latin Americans left rural areas to settle in major cities (Hardoy 1975: 52–53; Germani 1981: 236; Beyer 1967: 95) (see tables 4.1 and 4.2).

The urbanization process had various causes and took distinct forms in different countries (Balan 1983: 152). Nevertheless, scholars agree on a number of factors, common to much of the Latin American experience during and after the 1930s, that worked to "push" rural populations from the country and "pull" them to the cities. In general, Latin Americans were pushed out of rural areas by poverty, lack of educational opportunities, insufficient land, the absence of sanitation and medical services, and, in some cases, drought, violence, natural disasters, civil war, or the deterioration of soil fertility. It was the prospect of well-paid employment, educational opportunities, health facilities, and the presence of relatives in the city that drew Latin Americans to urban centers. And this migration was facilitated by transportation and communication systems, which were improving greatly after 1930 (Germani 1981: 236; Butterworth and Chance 1981: 40–49; Beyer 1967: 97; Solberg 1978: 153; Castro et al. 1978: 5–6; Balan 1983: 166–70).[2]

A major factor in the push of peasants out of rural areas in a num-

TABLE 4.1

RATES OF URBANIZATION FOR CAPITAL CITIES, 1930–1960

City	Percent of National Population in City		Total Population of City (thousands)		Change in City Population (%)
	1930	1960	1930	1960	1930–60
Buenos Aires	20	32	476	6,706	+1,409
Bogotá	2	8	146	1,237	+847
Mexico City	5	15	829	5,403	+651
Caracas	7	18	207	1,320	+637
Managua	5	15	35	222	+634
Lima	5	19	283	1,449	+512
Guatemala	5	10	89	377	+423
La Paz	5	12	108	444	+411
Rio de Janeiro	4	7	1,343	4,922	+366
Panama City	16	25	84	264	+314
Quito	5	7	101	302	+299
Santiago	13	22	567	1,678	+296
Asunción	14	18	123	318	+258
Montevideo	28	31	486	772	+158

Sources: *Statistical Abstract of Latin America* (1968); *Statistical Bulletin for Latin America*, vol. 1, no. 1 (1964).

ber of countries, such as Brazil, Colombia, Argentina, and Mexico, was the mechanization of rural agriculture (Balan 1983: 169; Butterworth and Chance 1981: 42; Adriance 1986: 11–13). Prior to the 1930s, agricultural production was quite labor intensive. In Brazil, for example, rural agriculture was often organized neo-feudally, with landless peasants trading their manual labor to plantation owners for a place to live and access to small plots of land for subsistence farming (Adriance 1984: 501; 1986: 11–13). Similar conditions existed in Peru through the early 1960s (Butterworth and Chance 1981: 45). With the development of new, more capital-intensive technologies of agricultural production and processing, large landowners in many Latin American countries—sometimes aided by government supports—increasingly mechanized production or switched to less labor-intensive crops or products, such as cattle ranching (Butterworth and Chance 1981: 42; Balan 1983: 169, 174–76). This greatly reduced the need for manual labor in rural areas, and sometimes required that small plots of land previously used by peasants for subsistence farming be converted to commercial production (Adriance 1984: 501; 1986: 11–13). The net effect was to push *campesinos* out of rural areas.

In addition, a major force pulling *campesinos* to cities was the pros-

74 The Emergence of a Movement

TABLE 4.2
INCREASE IN URBAN POPULATION, 1930–1960

Decade	Percent of Population
1930–40	39
1940–50	61
1950–60	67

Source: Beyer 1967, 95.
Note: Table includes cities of 20,000 or more inhabitants.

TABLE 4.3
REAL GROWTH INDICES OF AGRICULTURE AND INDUSTRY

	1947	1951	1956	1960	1961
Agriculture	100	114	142	172	187
Industry	100	146	213	327	362

Source: Bruneau 1974, 56.

pect of finding a job in urban industry (Quijano 1975: 132; Lattes 1981; Roberts 1981). The Great Depression of the 1930s initially had devastating effects on Latin American economies (Solberg 1978: 152; Hauser 1961: 37). Latin American exports for the years 1930–34 dropped 48 percent below 1925–29 levels, and imported manufactured goods became scarce (Skidmore and Smith 1984: 56–59). In Argentina, Brazil, Chile, Mexico, and Uruguay, economic elites responded by investing in domestic manufacturing for national consumption; import-substitution industries expanded rapidly, creating many new jobs for wage laborers (Quijano 1975: 130–31; Solberg 1978: 152; Castro et al. 1978: 5).[3] In Brazil, for example, the number of industrial workers almost tripled between 1920 and 1940 (Adriance 1986: 10) and during the 1950s, industry continued to expand twice as fast as agriculture (see table 4.3).

These factors helped spawn a mass migration to Latin American cities, leading to an expanded urban working class and the rapid growth of shantytowns on the outskirts of cities (Hardoy 1975: 53).

These changes posed new problems to a Church grappling with how best to minister to and maintain the religious commitment of the urban poor (Bouvier 1983: 14).[4] For many Catholics, a deep reevaluation of the Church's social position, organizational goals, and strategies in the light of this changing social reality was the beginning of a long process of institutional soul searching that would act as an opening of political opportunity. And, for some, this soul searching, combined with other factors, would lead to the development of liberation theology.

Otto Maduro, a Venezuelan sociologist with a liberation theology orientation, underscores the importance of urbanization for liberation theology: "The concentration of migrant populations in the cities is always a factor of social transformation, of movements of mass protest and dissent; and it helped give birth to liberation theology. In fact, without the process of urbanization, we would probably not have seen liberation theology, even given all of the other contributing conditions" (interview, 1987).

Protestantism, Syncretism, and Secular Movements

Urbanization was itself the partial cause of another social trend that posed problems for the Roman Catholic Church in Latin America: the astounding growth of competitive religious and secular organizations. Since the conquest, Catholicism had enjoyed cultural hegemony over Latin American peoples. But this dominance began to erode in the mid-twentieth century.

The growth of Protestant and Pentecostal denominations[5] in Latin America was remarkable (Bouvier 1983: 14) (see table 4.4). The average growth rate of Protestant churches for the years 1925 to 1961 was 10.11 percent annually (Damboriena 1963). This growth was the fruit of well-financed missionary efforts of Protestant churches in North America and of a large influx of Protestant missionaries expelled from China (Adriance 1984: 501; 1986: 15). In 1949, there were 3,821 foreign and 7,150 national Protestant missionaries in Latin America. Three years later, the number had risen to 5,708 foreign and 10,515 national. By 1961, 6,541 foreign and 34,547 national Protestant missionaries were working in Latin America, an average increase in Protestant missionary personnel of more than 6.8 percent annually from 1949 to 1961 (Damboriena 1963).

Protestant missionaries were very successful among the new urban populations, especially in Brazil (Read et al. 1968: 245). The Assembly of God churches had an especially rapid rate of growth, increasing in size sevenfold between 1930 and 1950. And, between 1950 and 1967, they accelerated to an average annual growth rate of 15.7 percent (ibid., 290). Of Pentecostals, Kenneth Latourette (1962: 169) writes: "A striking characteristic was the fashion in which they quickly took root, spread, developed an indigenous leadership, and became independent of financial aid or any direction from abroad. They drew especially from elements on a low economic and educational level."

Syncretistic cults, which combine beliefs and rituals from various traditions—indigenous native religions, folk Catholicism, African spiritism—have existed in Latin America for centuries (O'Gorman 1977). Whether due to an actual increase in syncretistic cult mem-

TABLE 4.4
GROWTH OF PROTESTANT CHURCHES, 1925–1961

	Total Church Members (thousands)[a]			
Country	1925	1938	1949	1961
Argentina	11	38	229	414
Bolivia	0.1	4	14	47
Brazil	101	241	1658	4072
Chile	12	99	265	835
Colombia	3	3	26	93
Costa Rica	1	2	8	23
Ecuador	0.1	0.5	3	11
El Salvador	1	3	22	58
Guatemala	10	21	76	149
Honduras	2	2	17	34
Nicaragua	11	17	30	38[b]
Panama	5	17	32	42
Peru	5	12	27	94
Mexico	32	56	265	897
Uruguay	1	2	21	43
Venezuela	2	5	14	26
Totals	240	633	3,172	7,710

Average Annual Growth	(1925–38)	(1938–49)	(1949–61)
	7.7%	15.8%	7.7%

Source: Prudencio Damboriena 1963.   [a]Rounded to nearest thousand.
                                                [b]1957 data used for Nicaragua here.

bers or to a mere increased visibility through a concentration of cult practices with urbanization, Catholic pastoral workers in the 1940s and 1950s became alarmed at the extent of participation in these cults (Adriance 1984: 501; 1986: 15).[6] Such concern is evident in a letter written by Belgian priest-sociologist François Houtart from São Paulo to friends in Chicago, dated July 30, 1954:

> In Rio there are already more than six hundred spiritist temples officially registered. In São Paulo, there are one hundred and eighty. . . . The bishops are very worried about this situation, since it affects mostly Catholics. . . . Because of the shortage of priests, there is no one to teach the people to do better. (Quoted in Adriance 1986: 15–16)

Secular working class movements, such as labor unions, socialist organizations, and communist parties, were also gaining adherents during this period (Medhurst 1987: 17; Bouvier 1983: 15). Union movements appealed to the working class; socialism appealed especially to middle-class university students, drawing them away from commitment to the Catholic church (Cleary 1985: 128). These changes, too, evoked a deep concern on the part of Catholic pastoral workers.

Thus, according to Thomas C. Bruneau (1985: 284), "the Church was confronted by threats to its religious monopoly and influence not only at the religious level by Protestants and Spiritists (the later mainly in Brazil) but also by urban and rural unions, radical political movements on the Right and Left, and political demagogues." These threats, like the threat of urbanization, provoked in many sectors of the clergy and hierarchy a strong sense of institutional insecurity that would play an important role in the emergence of liberation theology (Vallier 1970: 12; Neuhouser 1989: 234).

Growing Awareness of Institutional Weakness

One 1965 study of the diocese of Ribeirão Preto, Brazil showed that the coming of urbanization and advanced industrial technology resulted in a 52 percent to 64 percent reduction in attendance at Catholic mass (Bruneau 1974: 62). José Míguez Bonino recalls:

> There was a crisis in the church over the failing of the old alliances of influence and the problem of urbanization and the working masses. For the bishops, that didn't begin until the late 1950s. But for some of the priests and theologians, it began in the late 1940s.

It was then that a number of Catholics began to realize that they lacked the institutional resources to deal with these new challenges (Vallier 1967: 194).

Perhaps the Church's most significant problem was a dearth of Catholic pastoral workers (Ramirez and Labelle 1964; Poblete 1966; Bouvier 1983: 14). Edward L. Cleary (1985: 9) explains:

> The expulsion of Spanish priests from most Latin American countries in the nineteenth century and the hardships and limitations imposed on the church by newly formed republican governments caused a precipitous decline in the number of priests and religious brothers, a decline from which the Latin American church has never fully recovered. Before the wars of independence in the 1880s, there was one priest or brother for about every 1,000 persons; by 1890 there was one priest or brother for every 3,000 persons; and by 1930 and thereafter, one for every 5,000 persons.[7]

Studies in the mid-1940s showed that two-thirds of Brazilians were without organized parish life, and that over half of Peruvians were without clergy. It was estimated then that for the Church to have only one priest for every two thousand people, forty thousand more priests would be needed (Latourette 1962: 162).

The lack of clergy was made all the more painful by studies conducted by sociologist-priests which confirmed the weakness of religious commitment among most of the laity. In 1941, for example, Alberto Hurtado, S.J., published a widely read book, *Is Chile a Catholic Country?*[8] In it, he argued the negative, that the religious beliefs and commitments of the majority of Catholics were very shallow, that few Chileans were aware of the Church's social teachings, that the Church was extremely understaffed, and that it was institutionally absent in many regions of the country.[9] The book also stressed the church's overcommitment of personnel and programs to upper-class concerns, to the serious neglect of the needs of the majority of lower-class Chileans. A similar book, reemphasizing these themes, was published by the priest Alberto Muñoz in 1956 (Smith 1982: 98; Poblete 1986: 66).[10]

Efforts to deal with these problems by recruiting and training indigenous clergy were entirely inadequate. Church historian Kenneth Latourette (1962: 166) reports:

> Late in the 1950s, Latin America had 216 major seminaries and scholasticates with a combined enrollment of 8,808 students taking courses in philosophy and theology. But this was estimated to be 9 percent less than was required to fill the annual vacancies. Moreover, of the seminary students, 82 percent were in Mexico, Colombia, Brazil, and Argentina. In Brazil and Argentina the number graduated were insufficient for the needed replacements. In other countries in Latin America only about half enough were being graduated to make good the attrition brought by death.

Thomas Quigley recalls the effects of these works:

> There is no question, there was a sense of crisis and weakness in the Catholic Church coming from the realization that the masses had never really internalized the teachings and values of the church. Sociological research proved that the Church was really, in effect, a sect: that it had the adherence of a minority but that the majority had no adherence, no clear sense of the church in their lives or of being Catholic. This pushed the Church into a more activist role. (Interview, 1987)

José Míguez Bonino describes the situation:

> Urbanization made the poor visible—they were concentrated in

the slums around the cities. That began in the 1930s and grew into the '40s and '50s. As an Argentine bishop said, "The invisible of Argentina became visible." It was a threat to the Catholic authorities when they realized that these people were only nominally Catholic and were beginning to be lost for the Church. The Church realized then that it could no longer merely conserve its position, but needed to become an evangelizing, missionary church. There was a conscious feeling that what had happened in Europe—the secularization of the urban, working class—could not be allowed to happen in Latin America. The sense of a need to create a new approach for a new situation was felt—more or less—all over Latin America. (Interview, 1987)

In 1953, deep concern over the Church's predicament was expressed at the Second International Study Week of Catholic Action in Chimbote, Peru, where delegates from twenty Latin American countries convened for a self-evaluation. This conference has been called "the turning point in Latin American Catholicism" (Vitalis 1968), an event that "anticipated a new era" (Cleary 1985: 5). There, reflecting on their socioeconomic, political, and cultural situations, the delegates, in their final document, officially declared the weakness and vulnerability of the Catholic Church and the need for a profound revitalization.[11] Cleary (1987) recalls:

> People woke up one day and said, "You know, we're really a weak church." They saw other parts of the world that were much more Christian; they saw 60 percent attendance rates at North American Catholic churches and said, "These people are Catholics, we're not Catholics; we're a sinful Church in a sinful society." That gives you a whole new perspective. After the Chimbote conference, there was a feeling of weakness, of truth-telling. There was a conscious sense of, "We're in trouble if we don't come up with something better."

But recognition of the problem did not solve the problem. Many made efforts to address this institutional weakness, including actively supporting Catholic Action groups, promoting laity-training seminars (most notably, the *Cursillos de Cristiandad,* in which millions of laity participated),[12] establishing new theological schools,[13] and recruiting new pastoral workers. However, many of these solutions either focused attention primarily on middle- and upper-class sectors, where Catholic allegiances were already relatively strong, or they were simply unsuccessful.[14]

The problem of ministry to and loyalty of the masses remained unsolved. Uncertainties about the Church's ability to compete for the commitment of the people continued. Eventually, those uncertainties grew into a shared sense of profound crisis (Ramirez and Labelle 1964). It was that crisis that would provide the political opportunity to help open the door for the emergence of liberation theology.

The Genesis of Organizational Strength

Catholic Action

Organizational strength concerns the number of capable leaders, committed members, useful communication channels, and enterprise tools that can be coordinated to facilitate and sustain a social movement. Increased organizational strength can result from the conversion or emergence of new members and leaders and the creation of new institutions, from the takeover of preexisting institutions and memberships, or both. Important ecclesiological developments taking place between 1930 and 1955 laid the foundation of organizational strength for the liberation theology movement.

Beginning in the 1930s, and increasingly after World War II, Latin American Catholics began to experience the influence of a French theological and philosophical current called "integral humanism," or "Social Christianity," whose founder was the Catholic lay philosopher Jacques Maritain, and whose major institutional incarnation was the organization "Catholic Action" (Mottesi 1985: 28–29).[15] The original impetus behind the development of Social Christianity and Catholic Action in Europe was concern about the decline of Church influence over the majority of French and Belgian people and about the spread of socialism among factory workers (Adriance 1986: 20). With similar concerns in mind, Catholic Action was imported to and promoted in Latin America through the efforts of Rome, Latin American bishops, and religious orders.

The essential purpose of Catholic Action was to exert a strong Catholic influence on the secular society, shaping the social milieu according to Catholic ideals.[16] However, since the Church made a strong distinction between the role of clergy and laity in society, limiting the sociopolitical activities of clergy, Catholic Action focused on training lay people to carry out the mission of exerting Catholic influence (Dussel 1978: 177). The strategy was "to develop cadres of lay men and women imbued with a knowledge of the Church's social teaching and committed to finding adequate strategies to carry out these principles in the secular world" (Smith 1982: 25).

To this end, a number of specialized Catholic Action groups were promoted, including Young Catholic Factory Workers (Juventude Operária Católica—JOC), Young Catholic University Students (Juventude Universitária Católica—JUC), Young Catholic Farmers (Juventude Agrária Católica—JAC), Young Catholic Secondary School Students (Juventude Estudiantil Católica—JEC), and Young Catholic Independent Movement (Juventude Independente Católica—JIC), and the Latin American Confederation of Christian Unions (Confederación Latino Americana de Sindicados Cristianos—CLASC). The method of Catholic Action groups was "See-Judge-Act": to "see and describe the situation in which they worked or lived, to judge the situation in light of Christian principles (such as justice and charity), and then to act realistically to correct or enhance their milieu" (Cleary 1985: 4).

Catholic Action became a major factor in the life of the Catholic Church in Latin America, especially in Brazil, Argentina, Chile, Venezuela, and Uruguay.[17] It laid the groundwork for the later success of Christian Democratic parties (Smith 1982: 105) and nurtured a whole generation of Catholic leaders who would eventually rise to positions of national political and intellectual leadership (Cleary 1985: 3–4).[18] Indeed, many who became important liberation theologians in the 1970s were involved in—and often, especially in Brazil, became radicalized through—Catholic Action in the 1950s and 1960s (Ramalho 1988; Bonino 1987).

More generally, Catholic Action was important in that it validated Catholic lay people as Church members with a unique, vital mission and motivated them to actively reform society to better reflect the values of Catholic social teachings (Adriance 1986: 22). In these and other ways, Catholic Action helped set the stage for the coming of liberation theology.

The Formation of the CNBB and CELAM

Until the 1950s, the Catholic church in Latin America was organized around the diocese, a geographical unit whose pastoral administrator, the bishop, related directly to Rome (Levine 1981: 9). In this way, the continent was simply divided into approximately 267 organizational units,[19] each administered by a bishop or the equivalent, and each formally separate from the others (Cleary 1985: 11). The structural effects of this arrangement were institutional fragmentation, organizational isolation, and uncoordinated policy. Bishops in different dioceses, and their staffs, were relatively cut off from one another. Consequently, it was not uncommon for a bishop in one diocese to issue statements or initiate programs that contradicted or undermined those of a bishop of a neighboring diocese (Bandeira 1988). This structure focused power in Rome but diminished the overall effectiveness of the Church.

Recognizing this problem, Dom Hélder Camera, an energetic, charismatic, Brazilian bishop, expressed the need for a national conference of bishops to the Vatican secretary of state, Cardinal Montini, who later became Pope Paul VI (Adriance 1984: 502). Rome responded sympathetically,[20] and at the World Congress of Lay Apostolate, held in Rome in October 1951, the basic goals and structure of the National Conference of Brazilian Bishops (CNBB) were organized. The CNBB was officially instituted in 1952 (Adriance 1986: 24).[21] Dom Hélder Camera was elected secretary general, a post he would hold for twelve years.

The effects of this organizational innovation were many. The CNBB enabled bishops to address problems more comprehensively, systematically, and effectively (Cloin 1966). It facilitated the rapid dissemination of theological and pastoral innovations through national offices of education and pastoral planning (Bastos 1966). Furthermore, the CNBB gave individual bishops more social influence by providing them with the support of a nationally organized Church (Cleary 1985: 12).[22] The CNBB facilitated a progressive orientation: "Through its official documents, the CNBB would take stands that were more progressive than many of the bishops might have taken individually" (Adriance 1984: 502-3). Also, the national council provided "inspiration and ecclesial approval for the work of nuns, priests, and lay church workers whose own local bishops might not be very supportive of their efforts at pastoral renewal" (Adriance 1986: 25). Finally, the CNBB made the bishops' decisions more public, so that "when the bishops as a body began taking positions that would lead to the loss of their alliances with the upper class, it would become virtually impossible for the Church as a whole to turn back to the past" (ibid.).

In sum, the CNBB became "a means of facilitating a dynamic of permanent renovation and effective coordination of pastoral action for all the dioceses in Brazil. . . . Under the leadership of some of the most progressive bishops, the national conference would adopt positions and directives far more daring than many of the bishops would have taken on their own" (ibid.).

The CNBB represented a major institutional innovation for the Catholic Church.[23] And, the example of the CNBB was later followed by bishops of many other Latin American nations, who organized their own national councils.[24] More importantly, the CNBB became the model for a *transnational* organization of bishops, the Latin American Episcopal Council (CELAM).

Again, Dom Hélder Camera of Brazil, together with the bishop of Talca, Chile, Manuel Larraín, took the initiative in forming CELAM. Their idea was to create an international bishops' conference to strengthen the mission of the Latin American church and to increase its social influence. Marina Bandeira (1988) explains:

> Hélder Camera's vision was a Latin American forum that would be equivalent to the CNBB. The CNBB coordinated the Brazilian church; why not reproduce it on a continental scale? Especially, he wanted a way to discuss social problems and come out with a unified view. Hélder Camera and Larraín were great friends and were both very concerned about the extensive misery of our Catholic continent. They thought it was a disgrace, and wanted to know what the Church could do to help change that situation.[25]

With the approval of Rome, the first meeting of CELAM was held in Rio de Janeiro, Brazil, from July 25, to August 4, 1955. Five departments were created,[26] and officers were elected. Dom Jaime de Barros Camara—archbishop of Rio de Janeiro, for whom Hélder Camera was auxiliary bishop—was elected president and Manuel Larrain was elected second vice-president (CELAM 1982: 365). The Colombian Church offered to fund and house the new organization, so Bogotá was the location chosen for CELAM headquarters (Bandeira 1988).[27]

In its first years, CELAM was a relatively weak instrument for change (Cleary 1985: 20). But with the changes of Vatican II, CELAM was to grow into a very important institution, taking the strengths of the national conferences of bishops and making them felt across the continent. This enabled the Latin American bishops to speak with a more unified, coordinated voice.

In time, CELAM also became a major organizational facilitator of the emergence and growth of liberation theology. For four years, movement leaders used the resources and authority of CELAM to promote the liberation theology agenda. Conflict was inevitable in this arrangement, however, since the liberationist perspective did not truly represent the views of the majority of Latin American bishops that CELAM was supposed to represent. Eventually, a backlash was organized, movement leaders were dismissed, and CELAM took a more oppositional stance toward liberation theology.

The Background to Insurgent Consciousness

Developments in Roman Catholic Social Teachings

Insurgent consciousness is a collective state of being in which the members of a group think, feel, and believe that social change is both possible and necessary. It typically involves moral outrage and passionate rejection of what exists, combined with a genuine belief both that conditions could be made better and that the cost of doing so would be worth it.

During the 1930s, '40s, and '50s, no such insurgent consciousness existed. Nevertheless, a number of doctrinal and theoretical developments were happening inside and outside of the Church that would, in time, help to form liberation theology's insurgent consciousness.

For decades before liberation theology, the Roman Catholic church had been developing an official body of teachings on social, political, and economic issues, known as "Catholic social teachings," consisting primarily of papal encyclicals and discourses. These teachings had, over an eighty-year period, taken progressively broader and stronger stands on social and political issues, especially on distributive justice.

Pope Leo XIII initiated modern Catholic social doctrine when he issued *Rerum Novarum* ("Of New Things," also known as "The Condition of the Working Classes") in 1891. This encyclical laid the foundation on which later social teachings were built (Dorr 1983: 11–18). Concerned with the harsh living conditions of Europe's urban poor, and possibly about a mass working-class exodus from the Church , Leo XIII (1903: 209) took a clear stand against the exploitations of laissez-faire capitalism, protesting against the "misery and wretchedness pressing so heavily and unjustly . . . on the vast majority of the working classes."

Leo XIII opposed both liberal economics and socialism. He challenged many of the laws of liberal economics, including the treatment of labor as a commodity and the determination of fair labor wages through the market mechanism of supply and demand (ibid., 234, 236–37). Leo also advocated a minimum wage (ibid.) and affirmed the right to form unions (238–44). And, while explicitly affirming private property and rejecting socialism (209–16, 221), Leo called on the state to protect the interests of the poor:

> The poor and helpless have a claim to special consideration. The richer classes have many ways of shielding themselves . . . whereas those who are badly off have no resources of their own to fall back upon, and must chiefly depend on assistance from the State. And,

it is for this reason that wage earners . . . should be specially cared for and protected by the government. (231)

In 1931, Pius XI issued *Quadragesimo Anno* ("On the Fortieth Year"), commemorating the fortieth anniversary of *Rerum Novarum*.[28] As in *Rerum Novarum*, Pius spoke with moral outrage at economic exploitation and criticized the deficiencies of liberal capitalism, but his teaching was stronger and more concrete than that of Leo (Cleary 1985: 57). Pius viewed sin as potentially collective, arguing that injustice and fraud take place under the common name of a corporate firm so that no one need take individual responsibility (Pius XI 1957: 265). Whereas Leo, who focused on personal sin, had mainly called for reform of individual conduct, Pius advocated social-structural, as well as moral, changes (ibid., 247).

Furthermore, *Quadragesimo Anno* marked the beginning of a shift in the official Church attitude toward socialism. Although Pius XI, like Leo, rejected socialism (261), he nevertheless recognized that certain forms of moderate socialism might have some affinity with Christianity:

> Socialism inclines toward and in a certain measure approaches the truths which Christian tradition has always held sacred; for it cannot be denied that its demands at times come very near those that Christian reformers of society justly insist upon. . . . It can even come to the point that imperceptibly these ideas of the more moderate Socialism will no longer differ from the desires and demands of those who are striving to remold human society on the basis of Christian principles. For certain kinds of property . . . ought to be reserved to the State since they carry with them a dominating power so great that they cannot without danger to the general welfare be entrusted to private individuals. (258–59)[29]

Pius XII, the last Pope before John XXIII, likewise contributed to the Church's social teachings on distributive justice. Specifically, he argued that any healthy, moral economy must have an equitable distribution of wealth, even if that results in a decrease in the total wealth to be distributed (Pius XII 1949: 200–201). Second, while embracing the right to private ownership of property, Pius XII insisted that this limited right must be subordinate to the interests of the common welfare and the broad right of all people to benefit from the wealth of the earth (ibid., 198–99; see also Dorr 1983: 83–84).

Catholic social doctrine through the 1950s served as preparation for the social teachings of Popes John XXIII and Paul VI that were later used by liberation theologians to defend their movement. Furthermore, many of the themes that developed progressively in early Catholic social doctrine—the immorality of economic exploitation, the right to fair compensation for labor, the need for structural analysis, the reality of collectivized sin, affinities between socialist and Christian values, the demand for an equitable distribution of a society's wealth, and the priority of the common welfare over the right to private property—are basic themes in liberation theology.

In these ways, the development of liberation theology would be as much an extension of, as it would be a break from, the traditional social teachings of the Catholic Church. In extending them, liberation theologians understood these social doctrines as supporting their more radical theology. However, in that they also significantly departed from the original intent of Catholic social teachings, liberation theologians eventually had to face opposition from more conservative wings of the Church.

The "New Theology" in Europe

In the years after World War II, a ferment of new ideas and approaches to theology emerged in various European theology schools. This would have an important effect on the Second Vatican Council of 1962–65 and on Latin American graduate students who came to Europe to study (Novak 1979: 62).

The most important theological ferment was in France, among a group of Jesuit and Dominican professors at the Fourviere Theological Seminary at Lyons and the Dominican House of Studies at Le Saulchoir, who wrote and taught what was know as the "theologie nouvelle"—the New Theology. Well known among them were Jean Danielou, Henri de Lubac, Yves Congar, Father Chenu, and Henri Bouillard. In the course of time, they developed contacts with Swiss theologians Hans Kung and H. Urs von Balthasar, Karl Rahner of Germany, and Dutch theologians Edward Schillebeeckx and P. Schoonenberg (Praamsma 1981: 187). Other theologians who later played important roles were Johannes Metz of the Netherlands and the French Jesuit Pierre Teilhard de Chardin.

Influenced by their experience in the French resistance[30] and by liberal Protestant theologians, these men wanted a theological renewal that would put the Church into contact with and make it relevant to the concerns of the modern world. They "were convinced that theology still had a great role to play in the contemporary world, on condition that it was able to set stereotyped formulas aside and face modern-day problems with courage" (Martina 1988: 34). "The New Theology tried to reach out to the common man again by speaking his language, by listening to what he had to say, and by making an effort to share with him" (Praamsma 1981: 188). In this way, for example, the New Theology was the primary inspiration for the controversial "worker-priest" movement of the 1950s.

The theologians of Lyons were opposed to the rigid Roman Catholic hierarchy, favoring instead an emphasis on the importance of the Catholic laity. Their scholarly work was characterized by a return to the Bible and the Church Fathers of the first five centuries. Many in Rome interpreted this emphasis as a lack of respect for Vatican authority. Also, "the New Theology radically denounced the old Roman Catholic exclusivism; the reformers found sparks of the knowledge of God everywhere, even in non-Christian religions, as a saving revelation of God" (Praamsma 1981: 190).[31]

This New Theology was controversial, though it later would become influential in European Catholicism. The 1950 papal encyclical *Humani Generis* was written largely to refute and warn against the New Theology (Martina 1988: 32). Many of the books and articles of Bouillard, Danielou, de Lubac, Chenu, and Congar were banned by the Church, and most of these theologians were forbidden to teach, at one time or another, during the late 1940s and the 1950s (Martina 1988: 33–38).

However, these restrictions broadened their exposure and influence. During the 1950s, the theology schools at Paris and Louvain, Belgium—where many Latin Americans attended—developed a version of the New Theology which emphasized the use of sociology in the process of theological reflection (Lernoux 1982: 29). Even the Biblical Institute of Rome was influenced by developments in modern hermeneutics through German and Dutch Jesuit professors sympathetic to the New Theology (Martina 1988: 39). Finally, many French Catholics, influenced by the New Theology—including Paul Blanquart and Ignas Lepp—began exploring the compatibilities between Christianity and Marxism.

The authors of this New Theology had an impact on those who eventually became the leaders of the liberation theology movement, many of whom studied with these European theologians. And, eventually, those liberation theologians generated and encountered as much conflict and opposition as did their older, European teachers.

Economics from a Latin American Perspective

After World War II, and with the success of the Marshall Plan in Europe, much energy was devoted to the socioeconomic development of Latin America. To this end, the United Nations declared the first "decade of development" in 1950. A number of international organizations were likewise created: the Inter-American Development Bank (IDB), The World Bank, and the International Monetary Fund (IMF) (Bonino 1975: 24–25).

In 1948, the United Nations created a regional agency called the Economic Commission for Latin America (ECLA), whose job was to analyze the economic problems of Latin America. The executive secretary of ECLA for many years was Raul Prebisch, an Argentine economist (Skidmore and Smith 1984: 340).

ECLA produced an economic analysis known as "the Prebisch-ECLA thesis," which argued that, "the world economy since the 1880s had been working systematically to the disadvantage of the countries that relied on the export of primary products, . . . [such that] developing countries found themselves in a steady deteriorating position vis-à-vis the industrial countries" (Skidmore and Smith 1984: 341). This analysis became, beginning in the early 1950s, "the most influential theory in Latin American social sciences" (Cardoso and Faletto 1979: viii).

However, more important than the Prebisch-ECLA thesis, ECLA provided an institutional base for the training of a whole generation of Latin American economists who learned to analyze their countries' problems on a continental and international level, and from a distinctively Latin American perspective (Skidmore and Smith 1984: 341). Many of this generation of economists later developed economic analyses much more critical of the international economic system than was the original Prebisch-ECLA thesis. One of these critical analytical perspectives which evolved from the work and approach of ECLA was dependency theory (Kahl 1976: 139).[32] This theory played a critical role during the late 1960s in the emergence of liberation theology (see chapter 6), and skepticism of dependency theory represented one of the bases for much of the later criticism of liberation theology.

5

From the Creation of CELAM to
Vatican II, 1955–1965

Between 1930 and 1955, many Latin American Cath-
olics gradually became aware of threats to the position of the Church
and of its internal institutional weaknesses. This awareness caused
many of the leaders in the Church to make efforts to counteract
these threats and to strengthen the Church's ability to carry out its
mission. The years 1955 to 1965 saw a continuation and intensification of the processes that worked to threaten the Church. Rapid
urbanization and the decline of agriculture, for example, continued
(see tables 5.1 and 5.2). Protestant churches also continued to expand, with an average annual growth rate of 10 percent (see table
5.3). In the seven years between 1961 and 1968, the number of Protestant foreign missionaries in Latin America rose from 6,541 to
7,139, an increase of 9.1 percent. The number of Protestant seminaries and Bible schools in Latin America grew to 248 (UCLA 1969:
1109). Thus, during these years, challenges to the Church continued
and increased, the sense of institutional weakness became more
acute,[1] and, in seeking to respond to these and other problems, the
Church became more active, open, and experimental.

I have argued that social movements emerge in situations of significant increase in political opportunity, organizational strength, and
"insurgent consciousness." Between 1955 and 1965, events were tran-
spiring—in Latin America and beyond—that would begin to produce exactly that situation in Latin American Catholicism. Although
liberation theology was nowhere on the horizon during this period,
the complicated set of conditions which would later bring it to birth
were developing.

TABLE 5.1
INCREASE IN URBAN POPULATION, 1950–1960

| Country | Percent of total population urban | | % increase |
	1950	1960	1950–60
Colombia	39	53	+14
Venezuela	54	67	+13
Argentina	63	74	+11
Peru	36	47	+11
Brazil	36	46	+10
Guatemala	25	34	+9
Chile	60	68	+8
Mexico	43	51	+8
Ecuador	29	36	+7
Panama	38	44	+6
Nicaragua	35	41	+6
Honduras	17	23	+6

Source: *Statistical Bulletin of Latin America,* vol. 8, no. 1 (New York: United Nations, March 1971).

Expansion of Political Opportunity

For the liberation theology movement, expansion of political opportunity during this period would mean a growth in the perceived legitimacy of their strategy, the neutralization of parties inside and outside the church who would oppose them, and access to institutional resources useful for carrying out their program. From 1955 to 1965, three events facilitated such an increase in political opportunity: the Cuban Revolution, the Second Vatican Council, and the emergence of a cadre of progressive Catholic bishops.

The Cuban Revolution

In January 1959, Fidel Castro, having defeated the army of Fulgencio Batista, marched into Havana, Cuba, to take power. This event sent shock waves through the Latin American Catholic Church. The worst fears of many Catholics had been realized: a Catholic nation had fallen to a communist regime, one declared atheist and hostile to the Church (Bouvier 1983: 16).[2] Furthermore, Castro's success and early export of revolution inspired other socialist guerrilla movements in Venezuela, Guatemala, Peru, and elsewhere (Berryman 1987a: 14). No one knew where socialism would stop.

It is hard to overestimate the impact that the Cuban Revolution had on Latin American Catholics. David Mutchler (1971: 63) called

TABLE 5.2
EMPLOYMENT IN THE AGRICULTURAL SECTOR

Country	1950	1960	1970
Argentina	26.7	19.9	16.2
Bolivia	72.5	—	46.9
Brazil	60.1	54.5	45.3
Colombia	55.9	48.7	43.5
Costa Rica	56.5	49.8	38.3
Chile	31.5	30.5	23.1
Ecuador	65.5	56.2	48.4
El Salvador	64.6	60.6	56.1
Guatemala	68.4	65.7	58.1
Honduras	80.5	68.4	61.4
Mexico	58.3	49.4	40.9
Nicaragua	67.7	57.4	47.7
Panama	55.5	53.1	42.0
Paraguay	55.4	55.9	51.4
Peru	59.7	51.3	42.9
Uruguay	21.3	19.4	17.5
Venezuela	44.0	32.2	24.2
Averages	56.7	48.3	41.9
Change (%)	—	−8.4	−6.4

Source: *Statistical Yearbook for Latin America* (New York: United Nations, 1981).
Note: Table shows economically active population in agricultural activities as a percentage of the total economically active population.

it "the decisive event in the development of Latin American Catholicism in the 1960s." Thomas Quigley (1987) reported that the Cuban Revolution had "a major effect, it was the backdrop throughout Latin America," against which the Church subsequently acted and reacted. Many Catholics who previously experienced apprehension about the changing world now felt outright fear; many who previously felt insecure about the position of the Church, now became desperate.[3]

The Cuban Revolution confirmed, for many who previously doubted, that the status quo was unacceptable, that some kind of significant changes were necessary if the Church was to survive and prosper in Latin America. The question for many ceased to be, "Might we be in danger if things don't change?" and became, "We are in serious danger, so how *must* we change?"

This shift in attitude had a number of effects. First, it fostered a sense of unity and cooperation among Catholics—both internationally and in Latin America—as attention shifted from various internal

TABLE 5.3
GROWTH OF PROTESTANT CHURCHES, 1960–1968

Country	Protestant Population, 1968 (thousands)	Annual Rate of Growth, 1960–67 (%)
Argentina	530	5.0
Bolivia	67	11.5
Brazil	7,923	11.0
Chile	880	8.5
Colombia	111	12.0
Costa Rica	39	7.0
Ecuador	19	15.0
El Salvador	75	5.5
Guatemala	131	9.0
Honduras	57	8.5
Mexico	702	11.0
Nicaragua	54	3.0
Panama	57	5.5
Paraguay	19	11.0
Peru	128	6.5
Uruguay	40	7.0
Venezuela	52	14.0
Total	16,102	10.0 (Average)

Source: *Statistical Abstract of Latin America,* vol. 20 (1969); Read et al. 1968.

differences to a common external threat. People realized that they needed to put aside their dissimilarities and disagreements, pull together, and prepare to make changes. "Latin American–North American cooperation was strongest and Latin Catholics were most supportive of one another," argues Mutchler, "when the threat of a Castro-style revolution seemed imminent" (1971: 63).

Second, the Cuban Revolution boosted efforts of social reform aimed at demonstrating that democratic capitalism was, indeed, workable in Latin America.[4] It roused the Church to expand its commitment to political and economic reforms, especially through the political programs of Christian Democratic parties. After Cuba, the Church was decisively committed, by necessity, to socioeconomic and political development. Many in the church began writing a "theology of development" (Urresti 1973: 24). "Five years later," Pablo Richard (1988) recounts, "Christian Democracy's [Chilean presidential candidate] Eduardo Frei's 'revolution in liberty' was exactly against the

Cuban Revolution. It was the alternative. The Church wanted to prove that it was possible to do revolution without Marxism."

In 1961, United States President John F. Kennedy, prompted by the Cuban Revolution, announced The Alliance for Progress, a major economic development program modeled after the Marshall Plan of post–World War II Europe. The Alliance for Progress was intended, in part, to preempt and neutralize communist appeals to the impoverished masses through extensive economic development that would increase their standard of living (Bouvier 1983: 17).

The Cuban Revolution also disturbed Rome and drew greater attention to Latin America. "The Vatican was very concerned about the Cuban Revolution because the Church in Cuba was mostly shut down" (Quigley 1987). In 1961, the pope himself wrote a letter to the Latin American bishops imploring them to take action in response to the Church's pastoral weakness and to work on deepening the faith of their people (Torres 1988; Adriance 1984: 504). Most importantly, the Vatican, recognizing the critical problem of the lack of priests in Latin America, extended appeals to North American and European Catholics to send large numbers of missionaries to Latin America. In 1961, Pope John XXIII requested that religious orders send *10 percent* of their members to Latin America. Though they were less than that 10 percent, thousands of priests, sisters, and brothers responded (Cleary 1985: 9).

Finally, and very importantly, "the Cuban Revolution propelled the anticommunist Latin American Church to go to the poor" (Richard 1988). Maduro (1987) explains:

> The Cuban Revolution . . . produced a lot of fear in the hierarchy of the Church and in most of the clergy and lay leadership. Part of the reaction to this was precisely in going to the poor. . . . The solution to the problem seemed to be not so much fighting directly against communism, but in fighting the roots of communism: poverty, misery, exploitation, malnutrition, and so on.

Many pastoral workers all over Latin America left their positions in wealthy parishes and elite schools and went to work among the masses. This shift had a major impact on the social and political perspectives of these pastoral workers.

In sum, the Cuban Revolution posed to many Catholics a concrete case of the loss of a country to "the enemy," thus significantly raising the stakes of further loss through continued inaction. It confirmed the necessity of devising and implementing a new strategy for an effective presence in society. Many Catholic pastoral workers decided to work with the poor. The net effect was loss of credibility for conservative and traditionalist strategies and a growth in confidence in progressive ideas.

Latin American Catholics were in need of a new vision, but they were not quite sure what that vision should consist of. Vatican II was to begin to provide them with the substance of a new vision.

Vatican II

The Second Vatican Council (1962–1965)[5] has been called "The greatest event in twentieth-century church history," an event which caused a "Copernican shift" in Catholic thought (Berryman 1984b: 26).[6] Hugo Cabal (1978: 11–12) writes:

> On October 28, 1958 the conclave of cardinals which met to elect a successor to Pius XII chose Angelo Roncalli, son of a humble working-class family of Bergamo, who became John XXIII. With him the Church inaugurated a new era in its long history. . . . He let fresh air into the Church; he opened windows to our world, even doors and floodgates. "John's revolution" found expression in Vatican Council II which he conceived and prepared for the liberation of the dormant energies of the Church.

The First Vatican Council (1869–1870) had been concerned primarily with protecting the Church's authority and property against the forces of modernity sweeping through Europe at the time. But by the mid-twentieth century the world had changed considerably; the Second Vatican Council met in a very different atmosphere. No longer needing to be on the defensive, the Church "now had to relate her mission to a world not openly hostile to religion but less convinced of its public importance. . . . The pronouncements of Vatican II were an attempt to recoup some of the loss of credibility the Church was experiencing in the modern world" (Smith 1982: 16, 155). Vatican II produced a major "rethinking [of] the nature of the Church, the world, and the proper relation between the two" (Levine 1981: 35).[7]

This major shift did not take place without struggle and conflict (F. Turner 1971: 216; Rynne 1964: 223–41). Indeed, Nichols (1968: 294, 296) states: "The years of the Council were marked by sharp practice, by bitterness and by intrigue. . . . This antagonism [between the bishops and the Curia] resulted in unnecessary strife during the Council and in shameless, if understandable, attempts by members of the Curia to slow down the application of the Council's work once the bishops had departed."

One of the major struggles was between the assembled bishops and the Roman Curia over the composition of the various conciliar committees. The bishops, led by the German and French, "flexed their intellectual and spiritual muscles at the very opening of the first session, by challenging the Curia's attempt to dominate the proceedings. . . . [They] refused to have their minds made up for them about whom they should elect to the various conciliar committees" (Nichols 1968, 294–95). Thus, according to Berryman (1987a: 16), "in the opening days of the Council in the Fall of 1962, a group of European bishops thwarted efforts at control by Vatican officials and established an open atmosphere" (see also Mutchler 1971: 28). Consequently, "in the Council's plenary sessions and working groups, ideas and proposals that had been cautiously advanced only in progressive theological circles were legitimized" (Berryman, ibid.). Indeed, the first completed document, the decree on worship (1963), terminated the Latin mass which had been the norm for fifteen centuries (ibid.).

Another conflict between the bishops and the Curia centered on the writing of the document drafts. According to Nichols (1968: 298):

> The first severe clash on a conciliar document came over the subject of Divine Revelation. This immediately brought out the essence of the quarrel with the Curia: the juxtaposition of a traditional, official view, desperately trying to insist on teaching the ways of truth from the old textbooks, with the fresher view from the outside, which wanted new thinking on the presentation of the Church's teaching.

The bishops were bitter and angry after failing to secure the two-thirds vote necessary to force the withdrawal of the Curia's document. The next day, Pope John, overriding the procedural rules, intervened and ordered the Curia's draft to be withdrawn and a new draft to be written by an appointed committee (ibid., 299–301). This heartened the bishops, "giving encouragement to moderate reform while curbing the pretensions of the Curia" (ibid., 301).

Despite the conflicts along the way, the Council was decisive and momentous in its outcomes. Led, as we've seen, by the spirit of John XXIII and dominated for the most part by progressive European bishops and theologians—many of whom, including Yves Congar, Henri de Lubac, and Jean Danielou, were the "New Theologians" of the 1940s and '50s[8]—the conclusions of Vatican II were marked by a sense of new possibilities for the future (Carroll 1987: 7).

Vatican II established a number of new principles for the Church (Nuñez 1985: 83–90). One key principle was a more positive, accepting attitude of the Church toward the world. "[Pope] John made clear in his address at the opening ceremony on 11 October 1962 that condemnations were not to be the order of the day. The Church had always opposed errors, he said, but nowadays it preferred to make use of the 'medicine of mercy rather than of severity'" (Nichols 1968: 293). Consequently, the general demeanor of Vatican II toward the world was friendly:

> Condemnation of modern secular values and movements, such as freedom of conscience, religious toleration, liberalism, communism, socialism, articulated by the nineteenth-century Church were conspicuously absent in Vatican II's treatment of the mission of the Church in the world today. (Smith 1982: 17)

Robert McAfee Brown (1966: 310) likewise noted: "In the past, there has been much Protestant negativism toward the world and the flesh, and until very recently 'secularism' was the favorite whipping boy of Catholic apologists—all of which was a denial of the goodness of creation. . . . But 'The Church in the Modern World' adopts an affirmative stance from the beginning." This positive attitude included "a willingness on the part of the Church to learn from the world, as well as to speak to the world [and] has the further corollary that all men must work together for the betterment of the human lot" (ibid., 310–11). Working together even included cooperation with atheists (Abbott 1966: 218–20).

Another major new principle established by Vatican II was the idea of the Church as the People of God (Abbot 1966: 24–37). Callahan (1966: 99) explains this view:

> The whole Church is the People of God. That means the Church is a community, made up of people each with different gifts, vocations, and functions, but each sharing a common humanity, equality, and destiny in the eyes of God. Some will have the power of orders (priests); some will have the power of jurisdiction (bishops and popes); some will have neither of these powers (the laity). Nonetheless, these different functions do not disturb the Christian equality of each person.

This vision of the Church, as well as Vatican II's vision of the Church as a mystery and as a community (Abbott 1966: 14–24), "taken together . . . succeed in decisively shifting an emphasis from the Church as a structured hierarchical society to the Church as a living community of men, each bound to the service of the other and all committed to the service of God" (Callahan 1966: 109). In viewing the Church as a community of equals instead of a hierarchy, "the Second Vatican Council . . . tried to revive some of the communitarian aspects of the early Church, open up once again greater local initiative and pluralism, and encourage less authoritarian methods in exercising authority" (Smith 1982: 37).

Finally, Vatican II also rejected the idea of a mighty Church aligned with the powerful, in favor of a more humble, servant image of the Church. Important in Vatican II, "are the twin recognitions that the Church, along with all Christians, must bear a large measure of responsibility for the present plight of the world, and that rather than striving to rule the affairs of men, the Church must offer herself as a servant to men" (Brown 1966: 311–12). For this reason, Brian Smith (1982: 4–5) remarks, "Vatican II officially set aside the longstanding Catholic tradition of the desirability of the union between Church and state, stating that the Church 'does not lodge her hope in privileges conferred by civil authority.'"

This did not mean, however, that the Church withdrew from political matters (Abbott 1966: 285–89). Rather, this view of the Church in the world focused even more attention on the need for social and political activism (Levine 1981: 146–47).

In the view of Vatican II, the Christian Church needs to exert a powerful, direct influence on politics through the activity of the laity (Abbott 1966: 56–65, 285–89). Furthermore, the Council declared that the Church itself "has the right to pass moral judgments, even on matters touching the political order, whenever basic personal rights or the salvation of souls make such judgments necessary" (ibid., 289). According to Vatican II, "the role, therefore, of the Church in modern society is to act as a catalytic and prophetic force, using moral rather than temporal power to promote justice at national and international levels" (Smith 1982: 4–5, 18).

As important as the substance of Vatican II was the impact the experience of Vatican II had on Latin American Catholics (Bonino 1985).[9] What the Latin Americans contributed to the Council— which was relatively little, since it was dominated by European interests—was not nearly as important as what they took away from it:

> The Latin American Church did not go to the Council as a pacesetter. It went rather as a learner. The Council was a vast learning experience for the Latin American Church. The learning began with the bishops and their advisors and spread to grassroots levels throughout the ensuing years. (Cleary 1985: 19)

Vatican II thrust the Latin American bishops into an environment of intellectual ferment and challenging ideas. "The Council brought Latin Americans into daily contact with church leaders from all over

the world and it forced submerged issues to the surface" (Cleary
1985: 18). Latin American bishops were forced to reevaluate their
own situations in light of the Council:

> You take a bishop who had spent his whole life in nothing but his
> own diocese and send him off for four years to Vatican II and he
> comes back a very changed person. There was a lot of wringing of
> hands and saying, "What do I do now?" (Cleary 1987)

This "culture shock" of Vatican II for many Latin American bishops
had the consequence of solidifying a sense of common identity
among them. Archbishop Marcos McGrath (1988) recalls:

> During the Council, the Latin American bishops became con-
> scious of one another and we became conscious of Latin America
> as our own entity. The six hundred Latin American bishops pres-
> ent discovered that we were all from the same place. That was very
> important. The Council was an educational process for the bish-
> ops and an integrational process as well.

This integration and identity-formation among Latin American
bishops resulted in new lines of communication and new relationships:

> The Council was important, too, for the formation of informal
> networks of the new ecclesial leadership groups. Ties were made
> or strengthened across continental . . . [and] denominational
> lines. . . . But the ties that proved to be the most telling . . . were
> those forged among the Latin American bishops themselves. The
> four year experience of the Council brought them together in a
> way that no other experience had. (Cleary 1985: 19–29)[10]

Vatican II also exposed the Latin American bishops to the potential usefulness of staff advisers and experts *(periti)*. This exposure
came through the example of European bishops, many of whom
used staff advisers extensively for support and advice in an effort to
influence the outcome of the Council. Bonino (1987) describes the
prominent role of staff advisers:

> At Vatican II the advisers really did most of the work, with some of
> the bishops. Johannes Metz was there; Hans Kung was running all
> over the place, giving lectures every day and talking with the bish-
> ops. The advisers also did much of the writing—people like
> Schillebeeckx and the whole Dutch contingent. It was mostly the
> Dutch, the Germans, and the French. Sometimes a bishop would
> be speaking and you knew exactly who had written the speech.[11]

The Latin American bishops had already begun using *periti* themselves,[12] but the experience of Vatican II convinced them to increase the number of staff advisers. Maduro (1987) recalls, "It was exactly after Vatican II that we started to hear about advisers to bishops."[13]

This rise in the number and importance of staff advisers to Latin American bishops had the effect of coupling the authority of bishops with the inventive ideas of a new generation of progressive theologians and social scientists. This combination would, in time, play an important role in the emergence of liberation theology.[14]

Another important outcome of Vatican II for the Latin American church was its effect on the Catholic laity. "The thousands of active members of Catholic Action and other lay movements became an instant audience for the teaching of Vatican II and for the theology that undergirded the conciliar deliberations" (Cleary 1985: 25). Vatican II made the practice and doctrines of the faith more accessible and relevant to Latin American Catholics. It also encouraged laity to study the Bible for themselves, further stimulating their participation in Church issues and activities:

> Because of the example of Vatican II, its exploratory attitude, and its use of sacred scripture in a 'new' way, [in Latin America] many biblical study groups came into existence. Popular and inexpensive Spanish versions of the Bible appeared as part of this biblical movement. Millions of copies of the Bible were sold or distributed in the years after Vatican II. (Ibid.)

For Latin American Catholics who were already experimenting with progressive pastoral strategies and social activities, Vatican II came as an unequivocal endorsement. Marina Bandeira, who was working with education among the poor in Northeast Brazil, recalls (1988):

> We had been criticized by some bishops that the laity were getting too involved in social problems. Suddenly, the bishops of Vatican II voted that this was exactly what the Church wanted. It certainly was an encouragement. Vatican II made official what was already happening in Brazil; we were living it.

Perhaps most important, at the end of Vatican II the Latin American bishops were forced to work out the implications of the Council for their own particular situation. They had come to understand themselves as a distinct group, with distinct problems, and now knew they needed to apply the changes of Vatican II to Latin America. It was bishop Manuel Larraín who had the idea of using the CELAM organization as the forum to do just that.

At the heart of the Latin American groups [at Vatican II] was bishop Manuel Larraín of Chile. A consummate integrator, he worked during the Council to pull the Latin American church together and to project it into the future. . . . Larraín formed the idea of having a Latin American conference apply what was being expressed at Vatican II to the Latin American situation. At the psychologically appropriate moment, Larraín proposed this to the other Latin American bishops at the last session of the Council (1965). The idea was enthusiastically received by the other bishops and Pope Paul VI. (Cleary 1985: 20)[15]

The bishops decided to hold this CELAM meeting in 1967. Larraín (who was by then president of CELAM) and Hélder Camera (who was first vice-president) soon began to organize a conference that would itself produce a "Copernican shift" in the life of Latin American Catholicism: the Second General Conference of the Latin American Episcopate, the Medellín Conference.

In sum, Vatican II officially sanctioned an atmosphere of openness, creativity, change, and participation in the Church and in the world. It shook up the Latin American bishops, forcing them to rethink their mission and strategy and stimulated them to increase their communication with each other. Vatican II substantially augmented the influence that staff advisers had on bishops. And it injected vitality into interested laity in Latin America, generating small groups to study both the teachings of the Council and the Bible. Furthermore, Vatican II officially affirmed the activities of progressive pastoral workers.

The Catholic Church worldwide was undergoing a profound renovation (Hebblethwaithe 1975). The Latin American bishops had scheduled a conference to reconstruct their Church in the light of the Council. Legitimacy was now with those who had new and creative ideas (Considine 1966). Traditionalists and conservatives found themselves, for the moment, at least, moving against the current. Momentum was now with those who wanted to experiment, to implement progressive innovations. And those people wasted no time in taking advantage of this momentum.

Progressive Bishops Emerge
Vatican II provided Latin American Catholics with the beginnings of a new vision. To have any social impact, however, that vision needed capable leaders to develop and implement it in Latin America. When that need presented itself, a group of dynamic, capable bishops emerged to do just that.

Representing an expansion of political opportunity, these bishops pushed hard for change, facilitating the implementation of progressive ideas. They moved into key institutional positions and opened up the organizational doors for a new generation of theologians to institute an inventive Church strategy. As things progressed, they would use their authority to protect liberation theologians against countermovement actions, providing support for liberation movement activities.

This was important in an organization such as the Roman Catholic Church which—even after Vatican II—operated through authority and hierarchy. Thomas Quigley, a staff member in the U.S. Catholic Conference, explains (1987):

> Don't underestimate the importance of structure and the hierarchy in the emergence of liberation theology. Even Gutiérrez had a sense that the Church was not just a force for evil that should be sloughed off, but that it had the potential for something good. The progressive bishops were very much within the "company structure." That helped to facilitate some things. People don't walk on water, they needed those structures to enable them to carry out their work.

We have already noted two important bishops who facilitated, in the early years, a vision for a new strategy for the Latin American Church: Manuel Larraín of Chile and Dom Hélder Camera of Brazil. They were very good friends and had for years both been deeply concerned by and vocal about the social problems of Latin America. Vatican II gave them the final impetus to take action on a continental level. Cleary (1987) explains:

> Hélder Camera was pushing the Church toward some kind of reform, saying, "Let's make the Church adequate to the twentieth century!" When Vatican II came, it was like a catalyst for these people, it gave them a Magna Carta to say, "Look here, let's go in this direction."

A number of other bishops were important in the early years as well: Marcos McGrath of Panama (who like many of Latin American Catholic progressives had studied theology in Europe at the Institut Catholique of Paris), Avalar Brandão, Cándido Padim, and Eugenio Sales of Brazil, Eduardo Pironio and Enrique Angelelli of Argentina, Lionidas Proaño of Ecuador, Landázuri Ricketts of Peru, Raul Silva of Chile, Méndez Arceo of Mexico, and Muñoz Vega of Ecuador.[16]

Clearly, out of more than six hundred Latin American bishops, these were only a handful. But, it turned out, that was all that was needed. What this group lacked in numbers, they made up in ability and determination. Indeed, what is striking is the high caliber of these progressive bishops. Most of them were intelligent, aggressive, and organized. They knew what they wanted and how to get it. Descriptions of a few of them make this clear:

> Manuel Larraín was a pioneer of social action. He was very much an intellectual man, well educated, up to date on European movements—French and Belgian. He had been trained in Rome, had traveled in Europe, and was one of the first to travel to the United States, contacting USCC bishops in Washington, becoming good friends with them. He was very internationally minded and had many personal relationships with other bishops. He spoke French and English very well and could move with bishops from the United States and Europe. Larraín was the most intelligent bishop we had in Chile. He had the sensitivity to pick up all of the ideas that were in the air. And, since he was young, he was very much concerned with social issues. (Poblete 1988)[17]

> Dom Hélder was reelected every three years to secretary general of the CNBB. He was dynamic, charismatic—the bishops trusted him. He was an indisputable leader. Hélder Camera organized the 1955 meeting [of CELAM] for two and a half years. It was amazing what he organized and managed, without a hitch. This made Dom Hélder more famous than he was already; people wanted to see this bishop who had created some order in Brazil. (Bandeira 1988)

> Hélder Camera has the reputation for being a little saint, two inches tall, talking to the birds, saying "love one another." But Hélder was an organizer. . . . He just had a way of importuning people until they did things. (Quigley 1987)[18]

> Marcos McGrath was very big at the time of the Council. He was one of the most organized bishops. Even by 1972, he was the candidate for secretary general of CELAM against López Trujillo [the candidate staging a conservative backlash], so strong he was. (Dussel 1988)

> Cardinal Silva was very important at Vatican II. Cardinals could speak, not just raise their hands. Silva was a very good friend of Larraín, who had organized the Latin American bishops. Silva was willing to be outspoken. They organized a meeting at his house, attended by many good theologians and hundreds of bishops. Silva became the voice of others at Vatican II, especially of Larraín. (Poblete 1988)

Cardinal Arns is a strong bishop in Latin America against Rome; he is the most powerful bishop against the Catholic Curia. Rome is furious against the things he does, but he protects all these things in São Paulo. (Dussel 1988)

Landázuri Ricketts protected Gutiérrez, keeping him out of the Vatican's hands. He was also a prime mover at Medellin, where he had Gustavo as his adviser. He allowed Gustavo to push his ideas there, the option for the poor. (Anonymous interviewee, 1988)

In sum, by the end of Vatican II, there existed a kind of power vacuum among the Latin America bishops at a continental level. Momentum and legitimacy were with the progressives, and it was precisely they who stepped in and took control of the situation, effectively blocking, for the time being, potential opposition.[19] Cleary (1987) argues:

The people who would later become opponents of liberation theology simply didn't realize what was happening, the enormity of what was taking place. The progressives were able to take a leadership role because the roles were vacant. The more traditional, conservative people just were not taking the lead. The reforms that Vatican II proposed were pushed by open-minded bishops and activist priests; progressives had a lot of room to operate after 1965. What could the conservatives say against this tide? They didn't have at that time a very well-articulated philosophy; their opposition was basically emotional. So, Vatican II opened the doors for these people to go and run as best they could.

The progressive bishops possessed great skills, energy, and personal connections—in fact, Hélder Camera was a close friend of Pope Paul VI (Quigley 1987). These they directed in the next years, through CELAM, toward the task of renovating the Latin American Church. In doing so, they would, for a period of time, open doors and create institutional positions for those who would lead the Church for a few years to officially embrace liberation theology.

Increase in Organizational Strength

Leadership

For the liberation theology movement, increase in organizational strength during this period meant the institutional protection and support of Catholic Church authorities, the emergence of charismatic, articulate leaders and ideologists, access to institutional channels of communication, the committed dedication of a sufficient

number of ground-level pastoral workers, widespread acceptance of
the ideology among active laity, and the development of creative
organizational structures for the propagation and maintenance of
the movement.

Social movements emerge successfully when, among other things,
capable leaders are on hand to organize and defend them. We have
already seen that a handful of progressive bishops emerged after
Vatican II to take the initiative in renovating the Latin American
Church. However, for the most part, bishops did not constitute the
core of what would become the liberation theology movement's leadership, per se. Rather, they helped to support, authorize, and protect
those who became the movement's leaders.

The real leaders of the liberation theology movement were a
group of young theologians and staff advisers to bishops. They did
not form as a self-conscious leadership group until the late 1960s and
early 1970s. Nevertheless, their preparation to become such a group
was well underway between 1955 and 1965.

Up through the 1960s, Latin American Catholicism was Eu-
rocentered in its theology, organizational forms, and social strategy.
The ideas and organizations of scholastic theology, integral humanism, Catholic Action, New Christendom, and Christian Democratic
parties all originated in Europe. It was only natural, therefore, for
priests who wanted to receive top-quality graduate educations to go
to Europe to study.[20] Quigley (1987) explains:

> After World War II, Latin American bishops began sending bright,
> young priests overseas to study theology and social sciences. They
> went to Paris, Louvain, Strasbourg, Innsbruck, even Iowa and
> Princeton. They were sent and funded by their bishops.[21]

The cohort of bright, young Latin American priests sent to Europe
for graduate education in the 1950s and early 1960s were particularly
important, for many of them found themselves at the center of
Europe's intense theological ferment, provoked by the New Theology. Often, Latin American foreign students studied not under classical scholastic scholars, but under or in dialogue with theological
innovators: Congar, de Lubac, Schillebeeckx, Kung, Rahner, Metz,
and Pannenburg (Bonino 1987). Such innovators had a major impact on the thinking of these Latin Americans (Bandera 1975: 285ff.;
Nuñez 1985: 46).

Not only was this cohort immersed in the theological ferment of
academia; many of them were also present at Vatican II as *periti* of
Latin American bishops (Bonino 1987). At Vatican II, Latin American graduate students watched their European theological mentors,

with the support of certain European bishops, radically transform the self-understanding and mission of the Roman Catholic Church. This experience deeply impressed them. In less than five years after the close of Vatican II, that very cohort of students would be accomplishing the same thing in their own Church in Latin America, and moving on to become the leaders of the liberation theology movement.[22]

Members

In addition to leaders, successful social movements require members to carry out the program of the movement. Once again, during the years 1955 to 1965, no body of people constituting the membership of the liberation theology movement existed; indeed, the movement itself did not exist. However, a number of events were occurring that would eventually play major roles in providing a substantial membership for the movement.

First, Latin America experienced a large influx of foreign pastoral workers. Protestants were not the only ones expanding missionary efforts in Latin America after World War II; the number of Catholic missionaries increased as well. This was due in part to the closing or restricting of mission fields in Asia (especially China) and Africa, which diverted missionaries to Latin America (Della Cava 1976: 23), and, in part to the efforts of Latin Americans and the Vatican to bolster the number of Catholic pastoral workers (Verhoeven 1966). Latin America was becoming the major destination of missionaries from the United States. Of the 6,120 priests, brothers, sisters, and lay missionaries from the United States who were serving overseas in 1958, 2,127—more than a third—were in Latin America, an increase from 489 in 1940 (Latourette 1962: 167). They were joined by lay men and women who served through PAVLA (Papal Volunteers for Latin America), initiated by Pope John XXIII in 1960, and similar organizations (Cleary 1985: 9–10).

Foreign pastoral workers proved to be much more likely than Latin American priests to participate in and promote the liberation theology movement. Their influx into Latin America represented a significant contribution to building the organizational strength necessary for the emergence of liberation theology. One popular misconception about the emergence of the liberation theology movement is that it represents a simple, spontaneous eruption of Latin America's poor, unaided by other classes or institutions. Adriance (1984) refutes this theory, demonstrating the critical role played by middle-class pastoral workers acting as "organic intellectuals" (Gramsci) in the conscientization of the poor.

A second factor which would, in the 1970s, provide a substantial membership for the liberation theology movement was the birth of a radical innovation in ecclesiology, the Base Ecclesial Communities (BECs). BECs are essentially Catholic neighborhood churches that meet in homes or community centers. They range in size from ten to seventy members. In contrast to traditional parish churches, BECs typically emphasize participation, equality, small group Bible study, lay leadership, consciousness raising, and sociopolitical activism (Pomerleau 1983; Fragoso 1987). BECs offered an excellent ecclesial structure for the introduction, propagation, facilitation, and survival of the liberation theology movement (Berryman 1984a).[23]

BECs were born in Brazil and Panama.[24] In 1956, in the neighborhood of Barra do Piai in Northeast Brazil, a woman complained to her bishop, Agnelo Rossi: "At Christmas, the three Protestant churches were lighted and crowded, we could hear their hymns. But our Catholic church was closed and dark. Why don't we get any priests?" Bishop Rossi, stung by the complaint, decided to train "popular catechists" to keep parishes alive when priests were absent, to conduct "Mass without a priest" (Adriance 1986: 53; Cook 1985: 64). Within a year, 372 lay catechists had been trained, and by 1960, 475 BECs had formed in the area (LADOC 14:4).

In November 1960, the National Conference of Brazilian Bishops drew up a proposal to organize a network of radio schools for large-scale, grass-roots education.[25] In March 1961, Brazil's newly elected president, Janio Quadros, signed a decree to fund the project, called the Basic Education Movement (MEB), with four hundred million cruzeiros (equivalent to U.S.$1,481,000 in 1961). By 1963, MEB had 1,400 radio schools operating in the archdiocese of Natal alone, and was spreading out to the rest of Northeast and Center-West Brazil. It reached groups of isolated villagers with a program of literacy classes, health education, and religious instruction (Bruneau 1974: 79–83).[26] MEB was operated almost entirely by Catholic Action militants, who employed the pedagogical method of conscientization.[27] Eventually, the Sunday morning radio programs began broadcasting Mass, and "the community (without a priest) would assemble around its radio set to answer the Mass prayers while the bishop celebrated. . . . Out of this came the creation of small, human ecclesial communities" (LADOC 14:4; see also Adriance 1986: 46–52).

Finally, in 1963, BECs were organized in the San Miguelito slum of Panama City, under the authority of Bishop Marcos McGrath, through the work of a team of priests and sisters led by Father Leo Mahon of Chicago. Mahon devised adult conscientization courses for the BECs that utilized the Socratic method of dialogue and could be taught by trained lay people themselves, creating a multiplier effect. Mahon's experiment was successful and the San Miguelito BECs flourished (Berryman 1984b: 60).

By the mid-1960s, people began to realize that BECs might represent a solution to the severe shortage of clergy in Latin America. Word of Leo Mahon's experiment had spread, and hundreds of interested pastoral workers visited San Miguelito to learn how to organize BECs (Cleary 1985: 107). At the same time, in Brazil, the CNBB had commissioned a team of fifteen experienced priests, religious, and lay people to give seminars on grass-roots pastoral structures throughout Brazil; over a period of five years, 1,800 courses were given to members of religious congregations (LADOC 14:4; Cook 1984: 65). "In those years, the BECs spread like wildfire, not only in Brazil, but in Bolivia, Chile, Colombia, the Dominican Republic, Ecuador, El Salvador, Honduras, Nicaragua, Panama, and Paraguay" (LADOC 14:5).

BECs offered not only a solution to the lack of clergy but also, for the liberation theology movement, a means of educating the masses at the grass roots. Pastoral workers, utilizing Paulo Freire's method of conscientization, taught community members how to do critical social analysis (see, for example, Bonpan 1985: 23–32). This had a powerful effect on the social awareness of BEC members. In one BEC, for example, *new* members, when asked "Why is the situation— poverty, lack of land, drought, hunger, etc.—as it is?" gave these answers:

"The will of God."
"Because of our sins."
"Because we have to pray more."
"Suffering is the test of our faith."
"Those who suffer are close to God."

Older, more experienced, members of the *same* BEC, however, answered:

"There is no rain because the rich people are destroying the forests—the drought is caused by the lack of trees."
"The landowners do not provide the necessary services for the workers."
"There are two classes—the rich and the poor. The poor are exploited, humiliated, forgotten; the rich create this situation; the landowners care only for themselves."
"When there are people who try to help the poor, some end up in prison, and others dead." (Adriance 1986: 109–10)

By the late 1970s, the number of BECs in Latin America had grown to between 150,000 and 200,000 (Cox 1984: 108; idem. 1985: 7; Libby 1983: 80), with approximately 90,000 in Brazil alone (Barbé 1987: 89; O'Gorman 1983: 33).[28] Such numbers of conscientized people[29] able to be mobilized represented a significant, though diffuse, potential membership for the liberation theology movement, and brought a major increase in organizational strength.

Communication Networks

Access to channels of communication was critical to the emergence and success of the liberation theology movement, since it took place in and through an institution spread out over a continent. Between 1955 and 1965 the well-developed communication network necessary to sustain such a movement in Latin America was in the initial stages of formation. Cleary (1987) explains: "In the 1950s, a new idea took years to travel to other parts of the continent. But by the mid-1960s, we had jet planes, which meant that mail could get everywhere in one week, enabling us to hear almost instantaneously from all around Latin America." In this and other ways, the jet airplane proved to be a necessary precondition for the generation of liberation theology.

Second, the young priests from different Latin American countries who were sent to the key European schools for graduate education were meeting and getting to know one another, thereby creating a set of interconnected relationships that would in the future constitute the heart of the leadership of the liberation theology movement. For example, the early leaders of liberation theology included Gustavo Gutiérrez from Peru, Juan Luis Segundo from Uruguay, Enrique Dussel from Argentina, Rubem Alves, and Hugo Assman, both Brazilian, and José Comblin, a Belgian-turned-Brazilian. Gutiérrez first met Segundo in Louvain in 1952; Dussel first encountered Gutiérrez in Milan in 1962 (Gutiérrez 1988).[30] Comblin met Dussel in 1959, when Dussel read Comblin's critique of Catholic Action *(L'echec de l'Action Catholique);* Segundo first got to know Dussel in Paris in 1963 (Dussel 1988). Gutiérrez, Comblin, and Dussel all attended Vatican II—along with many others who became liberation theologians (Dussel 1988).[31]

Third, CELAM—which was to become *the* institutional facilitator of the liberation theology movement—was beginning to expand rapidly. From 1959 to 1964, under the presidency of Miguel Dario Miranda, CELAM had only two sub-departments: Catechetics and the Committee on Faith. In 1964, Manuel Larraín became president of

CELAM and Hélder Camera first vice-president. They immediately expanded the number of sub-departments—by adding and subdividing—to nine: Vocations and Ministries, Education, University Pastoral, Pastoral of CELAM, Public Opinion, Lay Apostolates, Liturgy, Seminaries, and Social Action (F. Turner 1971: 181).[32] In addition, CELAM, under Larraín and Hélder Camera, created four new institutes: the Institute of Pastoral Liturgy and the Pastoral Institute for Latin American, in Quito, the Institute on Latin American Catechetics, in Santiago, and the Institute on Latin American Catechetics, in Manizales.

Positions for officers in CELAM, most of which were newly created, were then filled in the next years by persons such as Marcos McGrath, Leonidas Proaño, Eugenio Araujo Sales, Cándido Padin, Pablo Muñoz Vega, Eduardo Pironio, Samuel Ruiz, Luciano Metzinger, Segundo Galilea, Cecilio de Lora, Gonzalo Arroyo, Pierre Bigo, and Edgar Beltran—in short, by the membership of the cadre of progressive bishops and their staff (CELAM 1982: 365–73). In the following years this growth of CELAM would provide an increase in organizational strength through an expansion of political opportunity in a key institution.

Incipient Insurgent Consciousness

From 1955 to 1965, the insurgent consciousness that sparked the liberation theology movement was virtually nonexistent in the Latin American Catholic Church. Nevertheless, during this period, diverse events were occurring, inside and outside of the Church, that would help to lead many Catholics to an insurgent consciousness.

The Cuban Revolution

Not all Latin Americans—even Catholics—were threatened by Fidel Castro's victory. For political leftists, including a small group of Catholic radicals (a number of whom would later become liberation theologians), the Cuban Revolution was a signal of hope and inspiration. "The Cuban Revolution," Bonino (1987) recounts, "had a great impact. It was evidence to many in Latin America that there was another way, not only revolution, but of socialism." Otto Maduro, who was at that time involved in the radical wing of Venezuela's Christian Democratic party, likewise recalls (1987):

The Cuban Revolution stirred a lot of hopes and re-posed the question of the possibility and methods of social revolution in

Latin America. It contributed to a continental consciousness of the need and possibility of social transformation toward a redistribution of wealth.

Cuba dispelled for many the idea that a successful socialist revolution was a noble but unrealizable aspiration, and presented, for that time, at least, the possibility of a specifically indigenous Latin American socialism. Pablo Richard (1988) echoes these sentiments: "Cuba was a concrete demonstration that an alternative was possible, that socialism is possible in Latin America." The event that for many Catholics represented a terrible loss, inspired a minority with renewed hope for the future. Ironically, however, whether the Cuban Revolution evoked fear or admiration from Catholics, the practical consequence, was identical: a move to work with the poor. Bonino (1987) explains:

> The Cuban Revolution produced two motivations which were channeled into one effect. In some it evoked hope and in others it provoked terror. Some people wanted to renew the church against socialism and others wanted to find a socialist alternative. But the practical effect of both reactions was to go and work with the poor.

Later, as the liberation theology movement was emerging, these antithetical perspectives on socialist revolution erupted into major conflict between traditionalists, moderate reformers, and liberationists.

Developments in the Social Teachings of the Church

Pope John XXIII continued and expanded the social teachings of the Church with two important encyclicals: *Mater et Magistra* (1961) and *Pacem in Terris* (1963). Although John XXIII was fundamentally optimistic about the modern, capitalist world—believing that the social system could be readily humanized—he nevertheless emphasized certain teachings that represented a decisive move away from the right and an opening to the left (Dorr 1983: 113–14; Nuñez 1985: 90–93).

First, in *Mater et Magistra*, John XXIII placed a greater stress than any of his predecessors on the social obligations of private property. John was not satisfied with simply encouraging property owners to act responsibly. He argued that they should be compelled by the law and public agencies to do so (John XXIII 1961: 167–68; see also Dorr 1983; 113). Furthermore, John (1961: 154–55, 168) defended the right of the State to own the means of production and to intervene to promote the common welfare.

Second, in *Mater et Magistra,* Pope John warned against new forms of colonialism through economic, cultural, and political domination (180). Instead, he argued, wealthy nations have a moral responsibility to give "disinterested aid" to poor nations, that is, aid which is not used as a tool for political domination (178).

Third, John XXIII (1963: 235–36) opened the door for Catholics, guided by the virtue of prudence, to work together and cooperate with non-Christians to achieve "economic, social, cultural, and political ends which are honorable and useful." This collaboration is possible even with unbelievers living in moral and religious error and motivated by false philosophies.

This opening was later interpreted by Latin American Catholic progressives to include cooperation with socialists, for two reasons. First, socialism was not explicitly condemned in *Pacem in Terris.* Second, John XXIII explicitly distinguished between "false philosophical teachings," such as Marxism, and "historical movements" inspired by those teachings, which John XXIII recognized are subject to positive influence and profound change by "evolving historical situations" (1963: 236; see also Cleary 1985: 60). "Besides," argued John XXIII, "who can deny that those movements, insofar as they conform to the dictates of right reason and are interpreters of the lawful aspirations of the human person, contain elements that are positive and deserving of approval?" (1963: 236).

In this fashion, Catholic social doctrine developed in a way that caused many Catholics to become more critical of specific social systems that did not live up to the ideals of these teachings. Pope John XXIII's encyclicals presented an authoritative basis on which many Latin American Catholics came later to judge their socioeconomic system to be morally unacceptable and to devise new ways to try to transform them. But it first took a major disappointment with the promise of capitalist development to stimulate such a critical social judgement.

The Failure of the Alliance for Progress

In 1961, John F. Kennedy announced a massive development program, called the Alliance for Progress. The program's objectives, stated in the Alliance's Charter of Punta del Este, were to achieve the following in Latin America within a decade (Dreier 1962: 120–122):

1. An economic growth rate of not less than 2.5 percent per capita per year;

2. A more equitable distribution of national income;
3. A diversification of national economic structures;
4. Increased industrialization and employment;
5. Greater agricultural productivity;
6. Comprehensive agrarian reform;
7. 100 percent adult literacy and universal child education through the sixth grade;
8. A five-year increase in life expectancy and a 50 percent reduction of the infant mortality rate;
9. Increased construction of low-cost housing;
10. Stable price levels, avoiding inflation and deflation;
11. Economic integration through a common market;
12. Stabilization of foreign exchange earnings.

The Alliance for Progress did make partial progress toward some of its goals. Between 1961 and 1967, economic growth averaged 1.5 percent per year, and in 1968 met the target of 2.5 percent. Industrialization advanced significantly in most countries. Food production increased 4 percent annually, 1 percent ahead of population growth. Enrollment in primary schools increased 9 percent. Some progress was made in life expectancy and infant mortality. And, in countries such as Brazil, Colombia, and Chile, inflation was curbed (Levinson and Onis 1970: 8–11; see also Perloff 1969).

Nevertheless, it is commonly acknowledged that the Alliance for Progress was, on balance, a failure, falling short of achieving most of its own objectives (Levinson and Onis 1970: 8–16, 307–310). In some cases where advances were made, stated targets weren't met; in most other cases, the Alliance had very little impact. For example, income distribution patterns were hardly altered. Unemployment rose from 18 million persons in 1960 to 25 million in 1969. Little significant land reform was accomplished. The decade saw only a slight increase in adult literacy. And demand for new low-income housing outstripped the supply (Levinson and Onis 1970: 8–11).

In 1969, an evaluative study concluded: "The accomplishments of the Alliance since 1961 have been poor indeed. . . . It had been hoped that the launching of the Alliance would be a significant turning point. . . . But the bright promises of Punta del Este were not to be realized" (Perloff 1969: xv, 65). One can note the administrators' early optimism giving way to concern in a similar study's report evaluating the situation in 1965: "In short, the unquestionable progress attained is not yet a satisfactorily generalized trend, and it appears to be threatened by undermining forces" (DEASAPAU 1967: 5; see also Gordon 1963: 98–99).

U.S. Congressman Dante B. Fascell, chairman of the Subcommittee on Inter-American Affairs, opened a Congressional hearing in March 1969 on the Alliance's achievements with the observation that "the consensus seems to have developed that most of the [Alliance's] goals remain substantially unfulfilled" (U.S. House Committee on Foreign Affairs 1969: 1). The acting assistant secretary of state for Inter-American Affairs, Mr. Viron P. Vakey, was the first to testify at that hearing. He reported (ibid., 3–4): "We have learned that the development process is highly complex, long term, and we know very little about it. . . . What the original framers hoped for was a mystique of peaceful democratic revolution which would sweep societies on a tide sufficient to overcome vested interests and political problems. A sweeping mystique of this nature has not occurred." Consequently, "at the end of the 1960s U.S. policy in Latin America had virtually abandoned the Alliance principle" (Levinson and Onis 1970: 308).[33]

The causes of the Alliance's failure are many and complex. The most important basis of failure was built in from the start: the Alliance's designers set the program's goals so high that almost any realistic outcome would have been considered a failure. To what extent that was due to unrealistic expectations genuinely held by the planners and to what extent the benefits of the program were simply overstated for promotional reasons is uncertain.[34] What is certain, is that vast numbers of Americans and Latin Americans, including Catholic progressives, accepted the Alliance's lofty goals at face value, and raised their expectations to that standard. And what they, however naively, believed to be real, for them became real in its consequences.

Other, more substantive reasons for the failure of the Alliance include the termination within one year of the Alliance's kickoff of the political regimes in Brazil, Argentina, and Peru that originally entered into the Alliance; conflict within the U.S. government over the Alliance's administration; the use of much of the U.S. foreign aid to service previous debts rather than to finance new productive investments; the failure of Latin American governments to make agreed-to structural changes, such as land and tax reforms; the failure of Latin Americans to raise sufficient domestic investment capital; the high Latin American birthrate; and a general shift in U.S. foreign policy attention to Vietnam (Levinson and Onis 1970).

Whatever the extent and causes of the Alliance's failure to achieve its goals, many Latin Americans had come as early as 1965 to perceived the Alliance as a major failure (Costas 1976). Consequently, their high hopes for Latin American reformist development crashed in disappointment. It was a severe disappointment, too, for the Alliance for Progress had been announced with, and had the effect of promoting, great optimism and confidence. Because of the Alliance, President Kennedy had become a hero in much of Latin America: "In backland villages of Columbia, Peace Corp volunteers had found photographs of Jesus and Kennedy as the only adornments in humble homes" (Levinson and Onis 1970: 87). Bonino (1987) recounts:

> The modernization model culminated in the conscience of Latin America in the great hope of Kennedy's Alliance for Progress. People placed a lot of hope in this, a lot of hope. Kennedy was seen as a great hope. Then there was a crisis. The populist regimes had failed and now the Alliance came tumbling down. It was a fact: they had failed. It was clearly seen [then] that it was an alliance with the same power elites that had always controlled the economic life of Latin America, that there was a lot of corruption on both sides.

Assimilating in their thinking the Alliance's economic failure had an important impact on many Latin American Catholics committed to social development (Bandera 1975: 96–101). Míguez Bonino (1987) recalls: "The failure challenged us to find out more precisely what went wrong."

For many Catholic progressives, the greatest disappointment and shock was not economic but political. The event which for many crushed any hope about the Alliance for Progress and confirmed its failure was Johnson's invasion of the Dominican Republic on April 28, 1965. Berryman recalls (1987b):

> For me, it was reflecting on the invasion of the Dominican Republic that signaled the hoax of the Alliance for Progress. I recognized later what it meant: that Johnson sent in the Marines to frustrate a movement trying to restore the supposedly elected government. That had an impact on Latin Americans. The invasion became a symbol of what the gringos were really up to.

According to Pablo Richard (1988), the invasion of Santo Domingo also had the effect of introducing Christians to Marxists: "In the demonstrations against the 1965 invasion, Marxists and [progressive] Christians were protesting together in the streets. Marxists started to discover Christians and Christians, Marxists. By 1970, we were dialoguing with Fidel Castro."

Johnson's invasion left many Latin American Catholic progressives feeling betrayed. Some began to consider the possibility that the Alliance was less a good idea that failed than a self-serving strategy of North American imperialism that succeeded. Julio de Santa Ana (1988) remembers:

Kennedy's Alliance—its implementation and failure—was very important in changing our thinking. [We realized] it was a developmentalist project that changed no structures, that the Alliance for Progress was really an alliance to *stop* progress.[35]

By 1965, then, the capitalist, modernization model of socioeconomic development was judged, in the minds of many concerned Catholics, to be a failure, even a hoax.[36] The next step for them was to find a new economic model to explain that failure.

The 1964 Brazilian Coup

Another political event of the mid-1960s which worked to generate insurgent consciousness among Catholics was the 1964 military coup in Brazil.[37] The Brazilian Church was, by far, the most progressive in all of Latin America, ten or more years ahead of the other national Churches in its thinking and social activities.[38] But Brazil was somewhat isolated by language—even within the Church—from the Spanish-speaking countries of Latin America (Torres 1988).

When the Brazilian military took power in 1964, they expelled many of the most radical people from various sectors of society, including the Church. Many radical Brazilian Catholics—such as the leaders of MEB—were exiled. And because, naturally, these exiles took their radical ideas with them, this action on the part of the Brazilian military forced the spread of radical ideas and programs, originally developed in the Brazilian Church, to other Catholics in Latin America. Sergio Torres (1988) recalls the impact of Brazilian exiles on Chilean Catholics:

My early thought was influenced by the social teachings of the Church. Then Paulo Freire had an influence in Chile. He had to leave Brazil in 1964 because of the military coup. Freire came to Santiago with four other people from his MEB team and got a position in the university. They introduced us to the concept of conscientization, which was an important step in the Chilean social mind about what was necessary. The Brazilian military thought they were stomping things out. In reality they were only spreading it further—outside of Brazil.

In this way, the Brazilian military fostered a "cross-pollination" process of radical ideas throughout Latin America.

ISAL

Years before Latin American Catholics began to articulate a theology of liberation, a group of Latin American Protestants from an organization called Church and Society in Latin America (ISAL) were aggressively promoting a theological justification for socialist revolution, called the "theology of revolution."[39] Though not identical with liberation theology, this theology played an important role in the emergence of liberation theology (Ptacek 1986).[40] The leader of ISAL and creator of the "theology of revolution" was Richard Shaull.[41]

Shaull, a North American Presbyterian, came to Colombia as a missionary in 1942 and, in 1952, moved to Brazil. Until the mid-1950s, Shaull primarily concerned himself with combating communism through church evangelism. In 1955, however, he published *Encounter With Revolution,* which revealed that his thinking had shifted toward a greater concern with social justice. He became more and more interested in getting Protestants of the pietistic tradition to be socially active and responsible, especially in political change.

During that period, Shaull became involved in conferences and publications of the World Council of Churches. In 1955, the WCC sponsored a ten-year series of conferences entitled "Christian Responsibility Toward Areas of Rapid Social Change," and invited Shaull to participate. Shaull organized a group of talented, committed Brazilian students—most of whom were involved in the Student Christian Movement (SCM) with which he was involved—to make presentations (Shaull 1987). These included José Míguez Bonino, Julio de Santa Ana, Gonzalo Castillo Cardenas, Rubem Alves, Valdo Ceasar, Dick Schatier, Jether Ramalho, and Hiber Conteris (Santa Ana 1988).[42] After the July 1961 conference, in Huampani, Peru, ISAL was formally created. Over the next years, ISAL groups spread from Brazil to Uruguay, Chile, Bolivia, Argentina. In 1963, ISAL began publishing the journal, *Cristianismo y Sociedad,* edited by Julio de Santa Ana (Neely 1977: 187).

In its first years, ISAL explored how Christians could contribute positively to economic and political development according to the modernization model. However, the "leaders of ISAL became increasingly disenchanted with the development model and programs, and they were soon convinced that the structures of Latin American society would have to be eradicated before any genuine development would be possible" (ibid., 189). By early 1964, ISAL was arguing that social change in Latin America demanded participation in revolution (Santa Ana 1988; Nuñez 1985: 71–77). "By late 1964 . . . revolution had become almost a monochord in ISAL publications" (Neely 1977: 189). By 1966, Shaull was arguing—at the WCC headquarters in Geneva, Switzerland, and at Princeton Theological Seminary, where he held a teaching position—that, in a revolutionary world,

Christians should adopt the tactics of guerrilla warfare (Santa Ana 1988).[43]

In 1967 and 1968, Shaull's followers began to feel that the language of "revolution" was not entirely appropriate for Latin America, but was more oriented toward impressing a North American audience. They began searching for a new language. It was then that they began to talk about "liberation" (Santa Ana 1988). Within a few years, most of the ISAL leaders—notably Bonino, Alves, and Santa Ana—became publishing theologians of liberation.[44]

ISAL and the theology of revolution contributed to the emergence of liberation theology in two ways. First, Between 1961 and 1968, while Latin American Catholics were trying to assimilate Vatican II and construct a new social strategy, radical Protestants of ISAL were promoting for adoption by Christians such themes as the futility of capitalist development, the imperialism of the United States, and the need for structural revolution, all of which influenced groups of Catholic progressives.[45] ISAL and the theology of revolution, then, acted as a "trial run" for Christians in first expressing and championing—in a way that did not threaten Catholics cognitively or emotionally—some of the concepts that liberation theology would later draw on and reformulate (Nuñez 1985: 81).

Second, the theology of revolution represented an intellectual school that, after 1968, propelled an organized body of Protestant theologians—soon joined by Catholic theologians—into the leadership of the liberation theology movement.[46] It would be wrong to overestimate ISAL's influence on liberation theology. Still, in these two ways, ISAL contributed to a foundation on which insurgent consciousness was later built, and produced a group of radical theologians who helped increase organizational strength.

The Bishops of Northeast Brazil

Many Catholics were also challenged by pastoral letters issued by the bishops from the Northeast of Brazil. If Brazil's was the most progressive Church in Latin America in the early 1960s, the most progressive bishops of Brazil were those from the Northeast region. This was because Brazil's socioeconomic problems were most obvious and pressing in the Northeast.

With the twentieth century's mechanization of agriculture in Northeast Brazil and rapid industrialization of the South of Brazil (São Paulo and Rio de Janeiro), Brazil's Northeast was a region in relative decline. Its major cities—Natal, Recife, Salvador—were becoming overcrowded and impoverished, the final stop of landless, jobless peasants. Massive poverty was exacerbated by severe droughts

that hit the Northeast in the 1950s. "This made clear the socioeconomic problems of the Northeast. The bishops from there then
began to clamor, to cry out, saying something must be done"
(Bandeira 1988). Thomas Bruneau (1974, 71) notes that the Northeast is the poorest area of Brazil, where Francisco Julião successfully
organized secular "peasant leagues," and where communist organizing became most active; these, too, constituted threats to the
Church, prodding the bishops of the Northeast to action. Led by
Eugenio Sales and Dom Hélder Camera,[47] the bishops of the Northeast worked to organize themselves as a regional conference within
the CNBB.[48]

These bishops were among the first in Latin America to issue joint
pastoral letters, which, even as early as the 1950s, reflected a critical
consciousness:

> If you read the documents signed by the bishops in the 1950s, you
> can see a change in the attitude of bishops toward the realization
> that many social problems were *structural* problems. In 1951, for
> example, one document was written, entitled, "With Us, Without
> Us, or Against Us Land Reform Will Come."[49] By the late 1950s,
> the bishops of the Northeast were really clamoring for land re-
> form. (Bandeira 1988)

They were also the first publicly and officially to criticize the military
regime after the coup in 1964 (Adriance 1986: 150).

Ivan Illich

We have noted above that foreign pastoral workers proved to be
highly susceptible to supporting the liberation theology movement.
One reason for this was the training they received during their transition to Latin America. Many foreign pastoral workers passed
through an orientation program operated by Ivan Illich (himself a
foreign priest from New York, born and educated in Europe), who
headed the Center for Intercultural Formation in Cuernavaca, Mexico. Illich's basic goal in this program was to break down what he
considered to be these foreigners' unrealistic expectations about the
value of their contribution to the Latin American Church by overwhelming them with information about Latin American reality.
David Mitchell (1981: 295) calls the Cuernavaca Center for Intercultural Formation Illich's "de-Yankification center."

Renato Poblete (1988) recounts:

> I worked with Illich as a teacher, from 1962 to 1965, in Cuerna-
> vaca. We were preparing foreign priests and some laity, giving

them a sort of "shock treatment." It was very effective. They were coming with an attitude of the North Americans to conquer the world. I used to teach them to be realistic, to think about social and economic problems.

Teachers at Cuernavaca included Illich, Poblete, Juan Luis Segundo, and Gustavo Gutiérrez. Over a period of eight years, more than 1,200 foreign priests passed through Illich's Center (Poblete 1988), many of whom were profoundly affected by his program. According to Berryman (1987b):

Illich was very much a presence for foreign clergy in the 1960s. Large numbers of priests went through Cuernavaca—Canadians, Americans, Irish, Australians. Under the guise of language and cultural training, Illich tried to jolt these foreigners into questioning what they were doing.

"As the 1960s progressed, Illich himself began questioning whether these foreigners had any business coming here at all" (Berryman, 1987b). Cuernavaca became more and more oriented toward sending foreign priests home. In 1967, Illich published an article in *America* entitled, "The Seamy Side of Charity," declaring that Latin America did not need or want the help of foreigners.[50] Quigley (1987) explains that by the mid- to late-1960s,

Cuernavaca was a tight grid and Illich's main goal was to send as many foreign priests back home as possible. So, many foreign priests on their way to working in Latin America were forced to confront his ideas and challenges.

It would be wrong to overstate Illich's influence. He did not make an impact on everyone. Indeed, he was quite controversial among clergy. Nevertheless, because of Illich, many of the foreign pastoral workers who were spreading out all over Latin America were challenged to abandon their preconceived notions about their mission, forced to study the economic, cultural, and political situation of Latin America, and provoked to consider carefully their role in the Latin American Church . This made some of them more flexible and openminded and, thus, in time, more willing to support and promote the new strategy of liberation theology, even if it appeared somewhat novel and possibly dangerous (Berryman, 1987b).

Search for a Latin American Theology

The first half of the 1960s saw the beginning of a search among Latin American theologians for a genuinely Latin American theology to replace the imported theologies of Europe. This search was initiated by Larraín and Hélder Camera:

> In 1961, when the Council was coming, Larraín and Hélder Camera called an informal meeting in Rio de Janeiro where they tried to present the first Latin American pastoral program of the Church. It was attended by Illich, Poblete, Vekemans, Houtart, Larraín, Dom Hélder, and others. We were preparing for the Council. (Poblete 1988)

It was, however, Ivan Illich, whom Cleary calls "the consummate leadership figure in Latin America" in 1964, who pressed to continue this search, organizing a series of informal meetings of Latin American theologians. "Illich functioned well at bringing together 'idea' persons, especially those with ideas similar to his own, which at the time ran along the lines of radical latinamericanization of Latin American churches" (Cleary 1985: 35). Dussel (1988) observes, in retrospect, "Ivan Illich is someone we need to be very thankful for. He helped very much at the beginning, especially with his sense of organization. He would move around Latin America and organize many pastoral meetings."

The first of these meetings was held in Petrópolis, Brazil, in March, 1964. There, a select group of intellectuals, whom Illich had invited—including Gustavo Gutiérrez, Juan Luis Segundo, Segundo Galilea, and Lucio Gera—"pledged themselves to the search for the meaning of the Christian message in the context of poverty and oppression in Latin America" (Kirby, 1981: 61; Mottesi 1985: 33). Gutiérrez (1988) recalls, "Illich's Petrópolis meeting, where we spoke about theology in Latin America, was rather informal. It was at this meeting that I first presented my thoughts on the methodology of theology."

Gutiérrez's paper presented theology as "critical reflection on praxis." As such it was the first articulation of the theological methodology that would undergird and produce liberation theology. The basis for a new theology had been formulated and, though still unnamed, the formation of liberation theology had begun.

Illich's group expanded and continued to meet:

> The inner circle that began at Petrópolis expanded through a series of informal meetings over the next four years. In 1965 alone, the group (which had flexible boundaries) met in June at Bogotá, and in July at Cuernavaca and Havana. Another pioneering network was being solidly established. (Cleary 1985: 35)[51]

Summary

At the end of 1965, few Latin American Catholics could have foreseen the radical transformation their Church was about to undergo. The dynamics of what was to come were only just beginning to reveal themselves. True, Vatican II promised to renovate the Church, but the meaning of that for Latin America was still undefined. And, the strategy of Christian political reformism appeared to be thriving—indeed, the Christian Democratic party had reached its zenith with the 1964 election of Eduardo Frei to the Chilean presidency. The capitalist model of economic development was only beginning to be seriously criticized, and the outlines of what was to become the liberation theology movement had only been conceived among a small group of theologians. Nevertheless, though few in the Church could have known it, the logic of the past was rapidly disintegrating and the conditions for a new movement were falling into place.

Vatican II, the Cuban Revolution, and the emergence of progressive bishops all worked to expand political opportunity for the liberation theology movement. The coming of age of a new generation of Latin American theologians, an influx of foreign pastoral workers, the creation of BECs, the rapid improvement of international communication and transportation infrastructures, and the expansion of CELAM all contributed to an increase in what would constitute the movement's organizational strength. The Cuban Revolution, developments in Catholic Social Teachings, the perceived failure of the Alliance for Progress, the Brazilian Coup of 1964, the theology of ISAL, the public statements of the bishops of Northeast Brazil, and the work of Ivan Illich all contributed to the beginnings of an insurgent consciousness. Some Latin American theologians were beginning to search, with some success, for a new kind of theology, one particularly appropriate for the Latin American reality. The Catholic Church in Latin America was at the edge of a new era.

6

From Vatican II to Medellín, 1965–1968

        In the Latin American Church, the three years after Vatican II were dominated by progressives who were preparing for the Second General Conference of the Latin American Bishops. It was clear to most that the Catholic Church in Latin America needed renovation. Furthermore, the pressures continued to build concerning the Church's own institutional weakness and inability to counter effectively the competition from Protestants, communists, labor unions, and spiritist groups.

    In the face of these realities, progressive bishops, theologians, and social scientists took the lead in deciding how the Church's renovation should proceed and just what the renovated Church should look like. These progressives were organized. They enjoyed the momentum of Vatican II, the continued approval of Rome, and the support of pastoral workers who were becoming increasingly radicalized. They also enjoyed an almost free reign in CELAM, the most important Catholic organization in Latin America.

    By September 1968, the Latin American Catholic progressives—who themselves were also becoming more radical—had accomplished an achievement of landmark proportions. They had persuaded the bishops of every Latin American country to endorse a radically innovative Church strategy that involved breaking traditional power allegiances, opting to champion the cause of the poor, and putting the weight of the Church institution into work for social-structural changes.

    This chapter explores the events and forces of the years 1966 through 1968. The focus is again on the opening of political opportunities, increases in organizational strength, and the development of insurgent consciousness. The culmination was the historic conference at Medellín.

Political Opportunity

Since the 1930s, diverse social processes had gradually worked to expand political opportunity for the liberation theology movement. These processes intensified between 1955 and 1965. From 1966 to 1968, the political opportunities for progressives in the Latin American Church were almost wide open. Progressive ideas were not only considered legitimate, but the keys to the future life of the Church. And, for the time being, organized opposition to progressives was virtually nonexistent. Quigley (1987) notes:

> The progressives were able to carry out their program without opposition. There were people opposed to their agenda, but there was no organized opposition and the progressives were organized. They weren't so organized that they had every step planned out ahead; the progressives just happened to be with the current of the way things were going at the time.

Momentum of Vatican II

The most important current of the way things were going at that time, which served as a political opportunity for progressives, was the momentum of Vatican II. Latin American bishops and staff advisers returned from Rome prepared to renovate their own Church. In the year and a half before Medellín, bishops of various Latin American nations met to discuss ways to apply Vatican II to the Latin American context. Some, including those of Uruguay, Argentina, Ecuador, and Peru, met during the summer of 1966. Others met later, such as the Bolivians, who met in January 1968 (Dussel 1981: 141).

Applying Vatican II to Latin America involved a process of translating an essentially European program into a new social context. Effectively executing this translation required not only familiarity with the intentions of Vatican II, but a thorough knowledge of the social context into which Vatican II had to be translated. With a new openness and readiness to change, the Latin American bishops turned their attention to the realities of *their* territory (Bastos 1966). What they confronted was a world very different from the one which had engendered Vatican II. Berryman (1987a: 20) explains:

> Vatican II encouraged people to enter into dialogue with "the world." Viewed optimistically from Europe, that world seemed to

be one of rapid technological and social change. A Third World angle of vision, however, revealed a world of vast poverty and oppression that seemed to call for revolution.

As the bishops and theologians began to wrestle with the question of how best to apply Vatican II to Latin America, it became clear that the relevant social facts, the "signs of the times," to which the renovation of the Church had to respond, were not modernity, science, and secularization, but underdevelopment, massive poverty, and oppression. The progressive Catholics were especially aware of this fact, and made it the starting point of their entire approach to renovating the Church (Muñoz 1973: 4).

Populorum Progressio

The heavy emphasis of Latin American progressives on the problems of underdevelopment, poverty, and oppression was reinforced and legitimated by further developments in Catholic social teachings. Latin American progressives received nothing but positive signals from Rome.

On June 3, 1963, Pope John XXIII died, and on June 21 was succeeded by Paul VI. Paul continued John XXIII's work of reforming the Church, overseeing the last half of Vatican II.

On 26 March 1967—a little more than one year before Medellín—Paul VI issued the social encyclical, *Populorum Progressio* (On the Progress of Peoples), which took a stronger stand on social issues than any encyclical before it (Nuñez 1985: 93–97). *Populorum Progressio* had an immense impact on Latin American Catholics. It was quoted extensively as an authority in national bishops' letters, priest groups' statements, the Medellín documents, and in early works of liberation theology. For example, "the Chilean bishops quoted extensively from *Populorum Progressio* in 1968, reiterating their staunch support for continued efforts to transform economic and social structures" (Smith 1982: 148). Gustavo Gutiérrez cited *Populorum Progressio* eight times in his ground-breaking work, *A Theology of Liberation* (1973).

Paul's substantive focus in *Populorum Progressio* was international poverty and development, continuing the emphasis of Catholic social teaching on the need for both moral and structural changes (Dorr 1983: 141; Marzani 1982). The encyclical opened: "The development of peoples has the Church's close attention, particularly the development of those peoples who are striving to escape from hunger, misery, endemic diseases and ignorance; of those who are looking for a wider share in the benefits of civilization" (Paul VI 1967: 387).

Anticipating key tenets of liberation theology, Paul argued that the causes of poverty and injustice are the evils of past colonialism, new forms of neocolonialism, and vast inequities of power between nations. The encyclical asserted that,

> colonizing powers have often furthered their own interests, power, or glory, and . . . their departure has sometimes left a precarious economy, bound up for instance with the production of one kind of crop whose market prices are subject to sudden and considerable variation. (389)

The Pope suggested the possibility that

> under the cloak of financial aid or technical assistance, there lurk certain manifestations of what has come to be called neo-colonialism, in the form of political pressures and economic suzerainty aimed at maintaining or acquiring complete dominance. (403)

As a result,

> while a small restricted group enjoys a refined civilization in certain regions, the remainder of the population, poor and scattered, is deprived of nearly all possibility of personal initiative and of responsibility, and oftentimes even its living and working conditions are unworthy of the human person. (390)

In a later section of the encyclical, Paul charges that, "the poor nations remain ever poor while the rich ones become still richer" (405).

Echoing Pius XI, Paul VI argued that a just economic order could not be built on the principles and ideology of liberal capitalism, on "profit as the key motive for economic progress, competition as the supreme law of economics, and private ownership of the means of production as an absolute right that has no limits and carries no corresponding social obligation" (395). Pope Paul was explicit in his disapproval of the free market of liberal capitalism: "One must recognize that it is the fundamental principle of liberalism, as the rule for commercial exchange, which is in question here" (405).

Paul VI observed that poverty and oppression constitute serious threats to peace: "excessive economic, social, and cultural inequalities among peoples arouse tensions and conflicts, and are a danger to peace," and,

> When whole populations destitute of necessities live in a state of dependence barring them from all initiative and responsibility and all opportunity to advance culturally and share in social and

political life, recourse to violence, as a means to right these wrongs to human dignity, is a grave temptation. (410, 396)

While strongly discouraging violent revolution, the encyclical does leave open the possibility that revolutionary uprising is justified in situations of "manifest, long-standing tyranny which would do great damage to fundamental personal rights and dangerous harm to the common good" (396).

Pope Paul VI argued that a better solution is just development, that "development is a new name for peace" (410). The principles of just development would include increased aid to poor nations, equitable trade relations, and solidarity of rich and poor, with dialogue between them leading to planning on a global scale (Dorr 1983: 143; Paul VI 1967: 400). Paul VI stated clearly that "the superfluous wealth of rich countries should be placed at the service of poor nations" (1967: 402).

Furthermore, anticipating again a key theme in liberation theology, *Populorum Progressio* argued that people are entitled to be the shapers of their own futures: "the peoples themselves have the prime responsibility to work for their own development," to "become the artisans of their destiny" (410, 407). The encyclical conveyed a strong sense of urgency:

We must make haste: too many are suffering, and the distance is growing that separates the progress of some and the . . . regression, of others. . . . Development demands bold transformations, innovations that go deep. Urgent reforms should be undertaken without delay. (396)

The responsibility for these bold, deep transformations lies with Catholic laity: "it belongs to laymen, without waiting passively for orders and directives, to take the initiative freely" (411). The document closes with an intense appeal: "We ask you, all of you, to heed Our cry of anguish, in the name of the Lord" (413).

Latin American progressives—who also felt a sense of urgency, of desperation, of anguish—took seriously *Populorum Progressio*'s appeal for "free initiative" toward "bold transformations and deep innovations" (Hennelly 1990: 58–61). They received this encyclical as a resounding endorsement—from the highest authority in the Church—of their emerging strategy. Had they had doubts about the increasingly radical road down which they were beginning to lead the Latin American Church, *Populorum Progressio* dispelled them. Whether intentionally or not, Rome itself was opening the doors of political opportunity for the liberation theology movement.[1]

Crisis of Religious Vocations

In the meantime, in the midst of the preparations to apply Vatican II to Latin America, there emerged a new, even more threatening variation of an old Latin American Catholic problem: the lack of clergy. This time not only was the per person number of pastoral workers declining, but in the late 1960s large numbers of clergy began leaving the priesthood. In Brazil, one thousand priests (8.3 percent of the total clergy) left the priesthood between 1965 and 1970 (LADOC 5:17). Thomas Quigley (1987) recalls, "1968 was the year when the bottom fell out on the Roman Catholic priesthood. The worst hemorrhaging of people leaving the priesthood was precisely in 1968."

The statistics for religious women were even more dramatic. In this same period, almost one-third of all new religious women renounced their vows:

> While 12,906 women pronounced their vows in religious life between 1965 and 1968, during those same years 4,200 abandoned religious life after vows. In the three year period since then, the rate of departures has clearly accelerated. . . . At the same time, the number of new candidates has kept dwindling away. (LADOC 4:31)

With priests, the overall *absolute* number was not declining. Indeed, in eight different years between 1965 and 1979 there was gradual growth in the number of priests. However, after 1965, the gap between the number of priests and the number of Latin American Catholics began to widen (see figure 6.1).

Furthermore, the only reason that the absolute number of priests did not decline as a result of the massive exodus of priests from the priesthood was because missionary and newly ordained priests were able to replace them. However, this meant that the only two sources of new priests—foreigners and new ordinations—were being spent to fight a battle against attrition rather than to increase the Church's pastoral manpower. And, even so, the absolute number of priests actually declined in 1968, 1971, 1975, 1976, and 1978. On numbers of clergy, the Church was under more pressure than ever.

Some priests had become cynical about the Church; a handful were attracted to revolutionary movements. Ironically, however, it was the reforms of Vatican II themselves that caused most to leave the priesthood. Phillip Berryman recalled, in a 1987 interview:

> There was a sense of crisis and inadequacy with pastoral workers, partially because the traditional role of the priest was changing. Vatican II brought a radical shift in thinking about many things,

FIGURE 6.1

GROWTH OF CATHOLIC PRIESTS AND POPULATION, 1956–1978

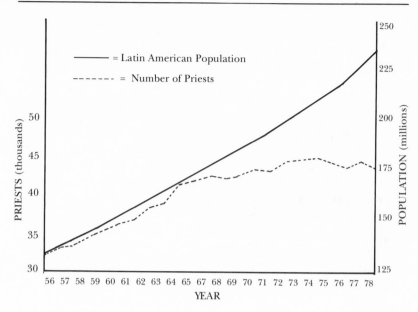

Note: For valid comparison, the relative scale for doubling the number of priests and population are equivilant.

Source: *Statistical Abstract of Latin America,* Vol. 20, 1981.

including pastoral work. This all cast a profound doubt, for clergy, on the meaning of their mission, forcing them to question and reformulate their concept of what their mission was. The sense of security among priests was undermined.[2]

The Church was changing faster than some pastoral workers could handle:

> They were asking, "what does it mean to be a Dominican in 1968?" For some people there was a clear sense that all bets were off, that everything was up for grabs, that there was no sure guidance. There was an awful lot of scrambling around at every level of the Church, and a feeling of permissiveness, if you will, while trying to assimilate all of the reforms and changes. (Quigley 1987)

One issue that especially troubled priests was religious celibacy: "Priests were dealing with questions of celibacy in a new way after Vatican II. Celibacy was becoming more of an insistent issue, more of a problem" (Quigley 1987).[3] Foreign priests, too, were effected by this unrest:

> There was a strong feeling on the part of many foreign priests: "let's get out of here." So, a lot of people started to leave; they felt they had gone as far as they could. Some wanted their own life. In many cases priests wanted to get married. There was a lot of dissatisfaction. (Cleary 1987)

This exodus from the clergy fueled the sense of insecurity about the Church's ability to carry out its mission that many in the Church had developed over the previous two decades (Sabatte 1973). It reminded Church authorities that, although the Church was committed to renovation, its problems were far from solved; indeed, in some ways, they appeared to be getting worse. This continued to increase the pressure—on progressives and conservatives alike—to find a new strategy that would save the Church from what appeared to be the real possibility of disintegration. Quigley (1987) remembers:

> There was an apocalyptic style that was characteristic then, that the Church would fall apart and be extinct in twenty years. Remember, this was 1968 and around the world there were many crises going on. . . . 1968 was a year when everything was open. There was a theme of radical discontinuity: that the past was absolutely past, having nothing to say today, a bad thing. The feeling was that we're in a new era and we'll build history from now, that everything is moving into a new dispensation. That view was held by quite a few people in the Church.

In 1967, a number of Latin American and North American bishops met in Miami to discuss the Latin American Church's situation. The outcome of their meeting conveys a sense of the perspective of leaders of the Church at the time:

> The Miami meeting ended with episcopal consensus concerning a state of crisis in the Latin American church. The bishops accepted the dictum of Cardinal Silva that, "in Latin America, every day the Church loses to its enemies as many souls as are won in the rest of the world combined." (Mutchler 1971: 46)

The bishops agreed that the CELAM apparatus was the solution to the Church's problems.

Looking to CELAM to save the Church from falling apart bode well for the progressives, since they had, for the moment, taken control of that organization. The opportunity to realize their will was, by 1968, almost completely open.

Organizational Strength

In the decade before and including Vatican II, events transpired that increased the number and quality of leaders, members, and communication channels that would facilitate and sustain the liberation theology movement organizationally. By 1968, the organizational capacity of what was to become that movement was strong and growing stronger.

BECs Multiply

Base Ecclesial Communities—the grass-roots innovation that would prove to be an excellent structure for the introduction, propagation, and survival of the liberation theology movement— multiplied and flourished between 1965 and 1968, promoted all over Latin America through seminars and courses. This trend was bolstered after 1965 in large measure by a massive shift of pastoral workers from ministry to elites to work with the poor. Not only did some Church authorities begin to realize that BECs represented a solution to the shortage of clergy and the lack of a religious presence among the poor, but many of the clergy themselves began to realize that they belonged among the poor. When pastoral workers did go to the poor, often one of their major pastoral ministries was starting and supporting BECs.

A related trend was the diffusion of Bibles in the vernacular to millions of Catholic laity during the years surrounding Vatican II (see table 6.1). BECs, we have seen, emphasize lay participation in Bible study. Vatican II helped make the Bible and the rituals of Catholicism accessible to the masses by putting them in Spanish and Portuguese.

Having the Bible in the vernacular was a key element in the process of conscientization through BECs. Through participatory, inductive studies of certain biblical passages—typically from Exodus, the Prophets, the Gospels, and selected Epistles—poor Catholics came to see and believe for themselves that the Bible taught that God was on the side of the poor and wanted their liberation. Frances O'Gorman, in a 1988 interview, offered some examples:

> The sons of Israel sighed because of their bondage and they cried out; their cry for help because of their bondage rose up to God. So God heard their groaning and God remembered his covenant. . . . And the Lord said, "I have surely seen the affliction of my people who are in Egypt, and have given heed to their cry because of their taskmasters, for I am aware of their sufferings. So I have come down to deliver them from the power of the Egyptians and

TABLE 6.1
ORGANIZED BIBLE DISTRIBUTION, 1900–1975

	Free and Subsidized Bibles				
Country	1900	1950	1960	1970	1975
Argentina	13,000	37,579	73,640	67,191	44,159
Bolivia	0	8,016	10,434	15,894	39,401
Brazil	17,782	77,387	297,546	205,203	189,005
Chile	500	13,934	31,338	34,964	28,736
Colombia	0	2,721	25,736	47,660	37,964
Costa Rica	400	832	3,695	8,886	14,222
Cuba	1,360	12,206	40,532	0	2,000
Dom. Republic	300	5,510	5,396	17,362	22,324
Ecuador	10	2,868	4,052	15,972	21,878
El Salvador	400	2,274	6,103	9,328	16,513
Guatemala	100	4,661	11,096	24,944	31,925
Haiti	200	7,944	3,846	24,776	35,475
Honduras	50	1,606	3,666	9,054	22,807
Mexico	6,544	27,130	38,579	93,501	159,164
Nicaragua	200	992	3,540	6,761	13,709
Panama	400	3,884	4,310	12,827	14,419
Paraguay	50	3,177	3,676	3,117	7,027
Peru	49	13,344	22,117	46,557	79,390
Uruguay	50	4,547	8,736	14,974	10,490
Venezuela	0	5,835	20,998	45,663	45,233
TOTALS:	41,595	236,347	617,036	704,634	835,842

Source: *Statistical Abstract of Latin America,* vol. 25 (1987).

to bring them up from that land to a good and spacious land, to a land flowing with milk and honey." (Exodus 2:23–24; 3:7–8)

Hear this word, you cows of Bashan who are on the mountain of Samaria, who oppress the poor, who crush the needy. . . . The Lord God has sworn by his holiness, "Behold, the days are coming upon you, when they will take you away with meat hooks and the last of you with fish hooks. You will go through breaches in the wall." (Amos 4:1–2)

And Jesus opened the book and found the prophesy where it was written, "The Spirit of the Lord is upon me, because he has anointed me to preach the gospel to the poor. He has sent me to proclaim release to the captives, and recovery of sight to the blind, to liberate those who are downtrodden, to proclaim the favorable year of our Lord." And he closed the book, gave it back to the attendant, and sat down; and the eyes of all in the synagogue were upon him. And he said to them, "Today, this scripture has been fulfilled in your hearing." (Luke 4:17–21)

Come now, you rich, weep and howl for your miseries which are coming upon you. Your riches have rotted and your garments have become moth-eaten; and their rust will be a witness against you and will consume your flesh like fire. It is in the last days that you have stored up your treasure! Behold, the pay of the laborers who mowed your fields, and which has been withheld by you, cries out against you. The outcry of those who did the harvesting has reached the ears of the Lord. You have lived luxuriously on the earth and led a life of wanton pleasure; you have fattened your hearts in the day of slaughter. You have condemned and put to death the righteous man. (James 5:1–6)

Such passages were amazing to *campesinos* and laborers who had always been taught that their poverty and suffering was God's will, that they needed to be accepting and patient. Such passages were heartening and conscientizing. As a result, the ranks of con-scientized Catholic laity who would join the struggle for liberation was rapidly expanding.

Connections with Protestants

Between 1965 and 1968, progressive Protestant theologians began establishing more ties with progressive Catholic theologians, through informal, personal links (Gutiérrez 1988). For example, Julio de Santa Ana (1988) recalls:

Little by little, in Brazil, small conversations emerged between some Catholic theologians and our group [ISAL]. We started to have contacts with the Pax Romana group. In dialogues with Gustavo Gutiérrez, Juan Luis Segundo, and Luis Alberto de Souza, we discovered that, despite our different backgrounds, we were talking the same language. Even before 1967, then, we were collaborating.

Thus, the relational network of progressive theologians that would eventually constitute the heart of the leadership of the liberation theology movement was becoming stronger and more ecumenical.

Jesuit Reforms

In 1965, Jesuit General Johan Baptist Janssens died, after serving eighteen years as Superior General of the order. Pedro Arrupe was elected as his successor.

Arrupe's life experience had given him a sensitivity to social and political issues. He was a Spanish Basque—the first Basque Jesuit General since Ignatius—and had suffered under the Franco regime of Spain.[4] During his novitiate and his studies, the Jesuits were expelled from Spain for political reasons (Hollis 1968: 252).[5] As a consequence, he studied philosophy in Belgium and theology in Holland, both places of theological ferment (Barthel 1984: 272). Arrupe spent most of his life doing missionary work in Japan, and was in Hiroshima when the atom bomb was dropped (Hollis 1968: 252).

Arrupe brought to his office a social awareness and progressive agenda; he wanted to reform and energize the Order.[6] Proclaiming at his first General Congregation that the Jesuits were undergoing a "crisis of confidence," he stated that "the Order should be completely pervaded by the spirit of Vatican II" (Barthel 1984: 272–73). Like the pope, Arrupe rejected the "ghetto attitude" and the "judgmental attitude" toward society, advocating instead an attitude of "dialogue," in order to work to improve the world (Hollis 1968: 256).

With an eye to the future, Arrupe declared in 1967 that "the voice of the young Jesuit is the voice of the modern world within the order." He argued that "we must start to prepare our novices for the twenty-first century" (Mitchell 1981: 287). Arrupe called all Jesuits to embrace "a life of poverty, simplicity, relentless activity, a life spent among the poor, a life of obedience, austerity, and chastity" (Barthel 1984: 285).

General Arrupe was particularly concerned with the problem of poverty, declaring that "the battle against atheism is identical in part with the battle against poverty which was one of the causes of mass exodus of the working class from the Church" (Hollis 1968: 256). Concerning Jesuit credibility, Arrupe asked: "How will the people be convinced that we believe what we preach if they see us enjoying a standard of living superior to many of our fellow citizens, if all we do smacks of privilege?" In a speech given in Montreal, on November 21, 1977, he recommended going to the poor, "working directly among them, often alone, in pastoral, auxiliary, or social works . . . sharing their life, their needs, and their hopes" (Mitchell 1981: 297).

In Latin America, Arrupe worked for a profound revision of the mission of the Jesuits, stating that "daring transformations that will radically renew the structures are the only means of promoting social peace" (Dussel 1981: 210). "In 1966 Arrupe wrote to the Latin American Jesuit provinces criticizing a tendency to put too much effort into educating a Christian elite which had failed to produce Christian leaders who challenged social injustice" (Mitchell 1981: 290). And, Latin American Jesuits responded, for example, "[Jesuit] Instituto Patria, probably the best private school in Mexico, was closed and the provincial explained that 'the education we provide is meaningless if it does not include a determined effort to resolve social problems and overcome the egoistical attitudes of liberal capitalism.'" Right-wing journalists responded by calling the Jesuits "Communists, confederates of a Mao, Castro, Moscow-inspired subversion" (ibid.).

Jesuits began to abandon educational work with elites en masse, to develop ministries with the poor. Latin American Jesuits also increased dialogue with Marxists.[7] In an essay entitled "On the Marxist Analysis of Society," Order General Pedro Arrupe wrote that "there can be no doubt that an inequitable distribution of wealth . . . creates or facilitates exploitation," a reality that has been "analyzed by Karl Marx as well as denounced by the Church"; and that "there is very little that is inherently 'socialistic' in denouncing a social evil, in the same way that certain forms of anticommunism often consist of nothing more than an attempt to conceal the evidence of injustice" (Barthel 1984: 295).

In 1964, there were 36,000 Jesuits in the world, a large proportion of whom worked in Latin America (Mitchell 1981: 272). The renovations established by General Pedro Arrupe resulted in an increased sensitivity to poverty, the abandonment of many projects of pastoral work with elites, a large shift of Jesuit pastoral workers to the poor, and an increased interest in Marxism. Many in a very large and powerful Catholic order were becoming actively interested and involved in the liberation theology movement (Maduro 1987; Hennelly 1990: 77–83). Indeed, of those who later became liberation theologians, so many were themselves Jesuits that Mitchell (1981: 295) rightly comments that "Jesuits contributed substantially to a theology of liberation."

CELAM

Of all of the organizations that helped the development of liberation theology, the most important was CELAM. At the end of Vatican II, CELAM was essentially taken over by the progressive bishops of Latin America, expanded, and filled with the most progressive theologians, social scientists, and pastoral workers in Latin America. CELAM became the major think tank that first formulated liberation theology, and the major organizational base from which it was propagated (Cleary 1987). From 1966 to 1968, the most important factor in this regard was the preparation for the Medellín conference, to be explored in the next chapter.

Insurgent Consciousness

The sense among Latin American Catholics that things needed to change was, by the late 1960s, growing stronger each year. Catholics were becoming more and more aware of their problems, and many were beginning to speak out for fundamental change in the Church and in society.[8]

Insurgent consciousness was not only growing stronger, but was becoming more focused. What for years were generalized perceptions of insecurity and crisis—disjointed feelings of uneasiness and discontent—had by 1968 converged and been synthesized into a single, widespread, simple explanation of what exactly was wrong and what kinds of things needed to change. Here we examine the forces and events that caused this intensification and focusing of insurgent consciousness.

The Death of Camilo Torres

In life and in death, Camilo Torres acted as a catalyst in focusing the attention of Catholics on the issues of injustice and structural change.[9] Although many, perhaps the majority of clergy, viewed Torres' strategy as naively un-Christian and counterproductive, still Torres represented a challenge that shook the Church. Maduro (1987) recalls:

> Camilo Torres was a very important turning point. The first major news fact that made most progressive Catholics aware that there was something going on *everywhere,* and not only in their own parish or diocese, was the assassination of Camilo Torres.

For many Catholics, Camilo Torres forced a new set of issues. For others, however, Torres symbolized a dynamic that already existed. Berryman (1987b) explains:

> Camilo Torres' plodding logic, his way of reasoning and reading the Scriptures which led him to action—that love demands structural changes—represented a common insight or intuition that was going around Latin America in the 1960s.

Finally, Torres' last years and death certainly had a tremendous impact on the Peruvian theologian Gustavo Gutiérrez, who would later be the first to articulate liberation theology. Gutiérrez had become a close friend of Torres when, for two years, they studied together at the Catholic University of Louvain, experiencing a direct, intense interchange of ideas (Mottesi 1985: 74).

Priest Groups

During this period, a new and controversial phenomenon—sometimes related to the life experience of Camilo Torres—emerged in the Latin American Church: independent priest groups that agitated for changes in the Church and society. Phillip Berryman, in a 1987 interview, observed, "A key crystallizing element from 1965 to 1968 were the priest groups and manifestos. There were many. As priests became aware of Vatican II and the poor, they formed these groups." It was Vatican II that sparked many of these groups:

> Although poverty was not a major theme in the documents of Vatican II, the self-criticism unleashed by the Council began to raise questions about world poverty and about the church's attitude toward wealth and poverty. (Berryman 1987a: 31)

Priests across Latin America began to discuss these issues, organize, and issue manifestos. Priest groups were often highly critical of the Church.[10] A constant theme in the manifestos was the inflexibility and sluggishness of national hierarchies in dealing with the pressing problems of poverty and injustice. These priests took it upon themselves to push their bishops into action.[11]

The best known of these groups were "Priests for the Third World" of Argentina, "ONIS" of Peru,[12] "Priests for the People" and "Costegua" of the Central American nations, "Golconda" of Colombia, the *"Populorum Progressio* Movement" of Panama, the so-called Camilista groups of Colombia and Venezuela, "Movement for Priestly Reflection" of Ecuador, and "The Eighty" of Chile. Less well known were SAL of Columbia, "Exodo" of Costa Rica, and MNCL of Ecuador (Richard 1979). In Brazil, the hierarchy was already so progressive that priests did not feel the need to organize independent groups to press for change.

The first of these priest groups to emerge was Priests for the Third World, formed in Argentina. On June 28, 1965, nineteen days after Camilo Torres officially renounced the priesthood, a group of eighty Argentine clergy met with two bishops in Buenos Aires to discuss their priestly role in the light of Vatican II. They asked: Who is God for us? What are we in the Church? What are we in the world? In their final document, they questioned the lack of support from the Argentine hierarchy, the purpose of celibacy, their separation from the world and the people, and the bourgeois lifestyle of seminarians (Dussel 1981: 194–95).

Argentine priests met again on May 11, 1967, to discuss the theme, "The Church and the World," and on May 25–26 to discuss "The Third World, Socialism, and the Gospel" (Dussel 1979). Two months later, an event occurred which prompted these priests to officially form the group Priests for the Third World.

At the end of Vatican II, fifteen bishops from the Third World—of whom seven were Brazilian, including Dom Hélder Camera, and one was Colombian—had got together to write a pastoral letter to their peoples.[13] On August 15, 1967, they published, in the French weekly *Témoignage Chrétien*, the document, "A Message to the People of the Third World."

Citing *Populorum Progressio,* the bishops' "Message" claimed that, "the people of the Third World are the proletariat of today's humanity," and that "true socialism is Christianity integrally lived, with a just distribution of property and a basic equality." Condemning the "international imperialism of money," the bishops charged that "it is a subversive war that money has slyly been carrying on for a long, long time, massacring entire peoples throughout the whole world." The bishops argued for a redistribution of wealth, saying that, "if anyone tries to keep for himself what others need, government leaders must distribute the wealth despite them," and that "governments should take steps to halt that class warfare which . . . the wealthy wage against the workers." While acknowledging that not every violent revolution has been good, the bishops observed that, nevertheless, "history has shown . . . that some revolutions were necessary." As for the Church, they argued that, "the moment a system fails to provide for the common good and shows favoritism to a particular few, the Church has the duty not only to denounce the injustice, but also to cut free from that unjust system, seeking to collaborate with some other system."[14]

The bishops' "message" was quickly diffused throughout the Latin American Church. On November 11–12, Argentine priests and laity met in Santa Fe, and wrote a supportive addendum to the bishops' message (Dussel 1981: 197). A middle-aged priest, Miguel Ramondetti, then traveled the country collecting endorsing signatures from priests (LADOC 5:45). In January 1968, the Argentine addendum was published, with 320 signatures representing about 6 percent of Argentina's priests (Dussel 1981: 197). Plans then began for a national meeting of Priests for the Third World (Dussel 1981: 197). They met in Cordoba in May 1968 (25 participants), in Cordoba in May 1969 (90 participants), and in Santa Fe in 1970 (113 participants), and continued into the early 1970s (Deiner 1975; LADOC 5:48, 49, 51, 61). At the height of the movement, eight hundred of Argentina's five thousand priests (16 percent) were members of Priests for the Third World (Berryman 1987a: 21).

Declaring themselves a "sacerdotal, hence Christian organization," the Priests for the Third World claimed that they were "resolutely determined to belong to the Catholic Church," arguing, "our membership in the Church of Argentina and of Latin America is not an obstacle to, but rather a stimulus for, our priestly, Christian insertion in the revolutionary process" (LADOC 5:43).

In their "Basic Agreements," the Priests for the Third World declared:

> As human beings, Christians, and priests of that Christ who came to liberate the people from all bondage and bade His Church to carry on His work, we feel ourselves one with the Third World...
>
> This inescapably obliges us to join in the revolutionary process for *urgent, radical change* of existing structures and to reject formally the capitalistic system we see around us and every kind of economic, political, and cultural imperialism. We shall go forward in search of a Latin American brand of socialism that will hasten the coming of the New Man. . . . [This] will necessarily mean a socialization of the means of production, of economic and political power, and of culture (LADOC 5:42)

The Colombian priest group, Golconda, began in July 1968 when 60 priests met in the hamlet of Golconda to study the encyclical *Populorum Progressio* (LADOC 5:13, 40; see also Bronx 1978). They met again on December 13, in Buenaventura, and issued a statement, "The Golconda Declaration,"[15] which argued that Colombia's "tragic underdevelopment results from our dependence . . . on foreign centers of power, who maintain it in collusion with our own dominant class" (Gotay 1983: 65). They declared that, "we irrevocably commit ourselves to every manner of revolutionary action against imperialism and the neo-colonial bourgeoisie. . . . We vigorously repudiate neo-colonial capitalism . . . and . . . direct ourselves toward setting up a socialistic society. . . . We call upon all popular and revolutionary groups . . . [to] forge a revolutionary alliance that will break our chains" (LADOC 5:19–24).[16]

Most of the other priest groups mentioned above organized for similar reasons and issued manifestos which articulated like concerns.[17] Berryman (1987b) argues that,

> the emergence of different priest groups wasn't entirely spontaneous because the idea was easily transferable. For example, I remember at IPLA a group of Maryknoll priests who came for one night who were traveling around selling the idea of priest groups. It wasn't conspiratorial—they had simply found something and wanted to share their experience. It was not unusual at that time for people to spend a few weeks traveling around spreading ideas.

Priest groups—by agitating and issuing such radical manifestos—played important roles as forerunners of liberation theology. "These priest groups," argues Maduro (1987), "which were before the actual emergence of liberation theology, were part of the earth in which liberation theology took root." According to Berryman (1987b),

> priest group manifestos contained most of the ideas of liberation theology in a nutshell. Indeed, in part, it was the questions of these pastoral workers at the local level that liberation theology was trying to answer.

Many who eventually became important Catholic liberation theologians were, during this time, leaders of priest groups.[18]

Radicalized Brazilian Bishops

We saw in the previous chapter that the Brazilian military coup of 1964, through expulsions, spread progressive and radical ideas to Catholics of other nations. But the coup also had a radicalizing effect on the Brazilian Church itself: Brazilian pastoral workers and bishops became aware of the concerns of the poor through government repression (Lima 1979: 145–266; Adriance 1984: 505; Floridi 1973).

Brazil's National Security Law, which took effect on March 17, 1967, provided a legal basis for a repressive police state, while the National Information Service (SNI) operated as a "Brazilian Gestapo" (Adriance 1986: 127–28). By the late 1960s, political arrests, torture, expulsions, and murder were common.

Dom Hélder Camera led in criticizing the government. On March 31, 1966, he refused to celebrate a mass commemorating the military coup of 1964. He also helped create the "Manifesto of the Bishops of the Northeast," which claimed that "the ambitions and uncontrolled egoism of some has created the current situation in which the poor are sacrificed for the benefit of the privileged." The army responded with defamation campaigns against Hélder Camera (Dussel 1981: 151).[19]

Eventually, however, many of the Brazilian bishops became involved in conflicts with the state. Marina Bandeira, then general secretary of MEB, explained in a 1988 interview:

> The military coup of 1964 radicalized the Church. Early on, many thought that it was just a transition. But the military government became more radical and repressive. In 1964, most bishops were anticommunists and supported the coup; they thought that the military had liberated Brazil from communism, that it was the savior of the nation. Later, because of repression, they changed

their minds. It was difficult at first for the majority of bishops to really believe that people were being tortured and persecuted. But censorship forced the bishops to go down to the common people of their diocese to find out what was going on. Then they got direct contact with poor people. An enormous concern developed.[20]

One example of the situations provoking the conversion of bishops is the experience of Archbishop Aloisio Lorscheider:

Lorscheider . . . was middle-of-the-road, although respected by all. One day he was giving a talk at the Catholic University in Rio. The federal troops, not knowing he was there, swooped in and took them all off. He was in jail and saw for himself what was happening. (Adriance 1986: 143)

These conversions helped shape the social and political consciousness of the Brazilian Church:

Without the repression Brazilian bishops may not have taken the lead. The Brazilian bishops went through a process not unlike Oscar Romero. Most of the important ones were originally conservative bishops who were forced to take stands on human rights issues in defense of their own priests and lay people who were being imprisoned and killed. (Shaull 1987)

One month before the Medellín conference, a letter carrying the signature of 350 Brazilian priests was sent to many of the bishops scheduled to attend Medellín; it described the Brazilian people as "an assassinated people" and asked the bishops to take decisive action (Antoine 1973: 132–33; Dussel 1981: 154). All of this had a notable effect: "When the Brazilian bishops came to Medellín in 1968, their experience of repression pushed them even further to support and accept the Medellín documents" (Bonino 1987).[21]

Shift to the Poor

During the 1960s, and especially after Vatican II, many Catholic pastoral workers shifted the focus of their ministry away from national elites and toward the poor:

In the 1960s, there was a large movement of pastoral workers to live and work with the poor—especially the sisters, the nuns. Hundreds, thousands in Latin America left schools for the rich to go to the poor. (Torres 1988)

The causes of this shift to the poor were many. One was Vatican II:

There was clearly a move toward the poor and away from traditional teaching roles. That was true in many countries after Vatican II, with the emphasis on the church *in* the world. People began to get the sense that what they had been doing was sort of airy-fairy and disconnected. Vatican II was the catalyst, especially the final document "The Church in the Modern World." So there was clearly a rediscovery of the poor, even of finding God in the poor. (Quigley 1987)

Another cause of this shift was renewals in religious orders:

The traditional vows of poverty, chastity, and obedience were front and center of religious order identity. But religious orders started becoming honest about rationalizing their ties to elites and wealth. When, as a member of a religious order, you see that all your needs are cared for in a way that is not true for the people in your country, you have to question whether you are really practicing poverty. So, the new attention to the vow of poverty, reinforced by the Bible, provoked questions about what to do about it. That was important. I remember a large exodus out of elite institutions to the poor—that was the thing—especially Chilean priests. That was what was happening: leaving comfortable circumstances in schools and moving out into the countryside and barrios. (Berryman 1987b)

A third motivation was fear of Marxism:

After Vatican II, more and more clergy and laity began to go to work among the poor, to counterbalance the inroads of Marxist (and sometimes Protestant) organizations among the poor. Nobody made this decision at the top; it came about in many ways— in some countries whole religious orders would make this shift. But mostly only individuals would do it because often their bishops would take absolutely no initiative in this. There was no single decision. It was a myriad of individual and collective decisions all across Latin America. (Maduro 1987)

This shift represented a major change in the demographics of Catholic pastoral workers. In the mid-1960s, the majority of pastoral workers worked with elites, especially in the education of elite children. By the late 1970s, 60 percent of all members of religious orders worked with the poor (Cleary 1985: 141). Even in dioceses or countries "where the numbers who worked with the poor were not large, the impact was significant" (Berryman 1987b).

There were two major impacts, that were mutually reinforcing.

First, clergy working with the poor contributed significantly to the education, organization, and mobilization of the masses (CLAR 1969). Pastoral workers began BECs, trained lay leaders, worked in literacy programs, started development projects, and worked for conscientization. Thus, this shift dramatically increased the number of potential movement organizers out "in the field."

Perhaps more important than the education of the poor was the education of the pastoral workers. Living and working with the poor opened their eyes to a whole new reality. The experience itself had a powerful radicalizing effect (Klaiber 1977: 184–85; Dodson 1979: 120; Bouvier 1983: 27). Quigley (1987) explains:

> Pastoral workers are often more conscientized by the people they work with than the people themselves are by the pastoral workers. The pastoral workers start off doing basic organizing and development projects, like drilling a well—something the World Bank would approve of. Then they begin to ask some probing questions. Gradually, they come to have more radical thoughts and work with more radical groups. I had a missionary friend who went to Guatemala absolutely apolitical and ended up being expelled for working with communists. That helps to give you a picture of where liberation theology came from.

As in Quigley's example, foreign priests were more likely than national clergy to choose to work with the poor and to be radicalized by that experience. For some, part of this may have been the impact of their training at Ivan Illich's Center for Intercultural Formation in Cuernavaca, Mexico. In addition, most foreign clergy came with the desire to have a positive impact on their new environments. Part of this propensity to work with the poor, too, was because most foreign priests had never experienced such massive poverty. Latin poverty came as a tremendous shock to them, and their efforts to understand and do something about it caused them to become more and more radical. Pablo Richard (1988) notes the consequence of their experience:

> Progressive movements have a lot of foreign priests. Why? Priests came from Europe and the United States and were not accustomed to poverty, whereas native priests often were. So, foreign priests played a great role. For example, 65 percent of the members of Christians for Socialism were foreign priests.[22]

Pastoral workers from religious orders, too, were very likely to shift to the poor and become radicalized as a result. This was due, in part, to renewal in their orders. It was also the consequence of a greater independence among religious clergy within the Church. Bonino (1987) explains:

> Religious orders have a certain autonomy. They are not so directly dependent on Rome or on the local hierarchy. So, ferment could go on within the order without being disturbed by the religious authorities.

A Peruvian Carmelite brother illustrates this from his personal experience:

> In Peru, most of us in religious orders are sympathetic to liberation theology. But for diocesan priests, it depends. Religious are by nature more educated and open, closer to the people. Diocesan priests are too involved in diocese politics. In my opinion, religious priests should always be on the cutting edge, like the shock troops. Religious are not directly under the bishop's authority. He can call you on the carpet but he can't really do anything. If he says I can't function in his diocese, then I go to another one—I don't lose. (Anonymous interviewee, 1988)

The shift of pastoral workers to the poor played a major role in breeding an insurgent consciousness in both the poor they worked with and the pastoral workers themselves (Berryman 1987; Maduro 1987; Cleary 1987; Richard 1988). But even for those who did not have a *firsthand* experience of poverty, new, documented reports from Catholic Social Research Centers made the reality of poverty less distant and more pressing.

Catholic Research Centers

Many Latin American Catholics had recognized for years the need for a revitalized social strategy. Many of them also saw the need for accurate data about their social and religious situations which could be used to help make that strategy relevant to the realities of Latin America. In response, research centers were organized in almost every country.

The Chilean Church pioneered the way, organizing the Belarmino Center and OSORE (Office of Religious Sociology) in the late 1950s (Smith 1982: 113–14; Dodson 1979: 122). In the early 1960s, François Houtart, of Louvain, and the French Dominican Louis J. Lebret organized research centers in Bogotá and Rio de Janeiro. In 1961, a Belgian Jesuit, Roger Vekemans, founded DESAL (Center of Economic and Social Development in Latin America) in Santiago, Chile (Dussel 1978: 181). In 1962, the Brazilian bishops' "Emergency Plan," written under the leadership of Hélder Camera, created CERIS (Center for Religious Statistics and Social Research) (Adriance 1986: 99).

The Jesuit order also played a major role:

> The Jesuits . . . began in the 1960s to emphasize social study and action centers on a typically comprehensive basis. Word came down through the ranks that the Jesuits should establish in each Latin American country a CIAS (Center for Social Investigation and Action). This general directive took on some variation from country to country but the commitment to social study and action was clear and steady. (Cleary 1985: 29)

In 1967, for example, the Colombian Jesuits founded IDES, the Institute of Social and Economic Development (Levine 1981: 221).[23]

As the number of Catholic research centers grew through the 1960s, Houtart created a Latin American FERES (Federation of Religious and Social Studies), an organization transported from Europe to bring the Latin American centers into a formal network (Cleary 1985: 27). So, by the late 1960s Catholic social research centers, with communication links across the entire continent and throughout the world, were collecting and publishing data about the socioeconomic reality of Latin America and their relevance for the Church (Bonino 1987; see also Houtart 1963).

These Catholic research centers were important for three reasons. First, they encouraged many talented, young Latin Americans to travel overseas for education in sociology and economics. Many later assumed major roles in the development of liberation theology. Second, the centers switched the attention of many Jesuits away from merely academic or theological concerns to a focus on social problems (Cleary 1985: 30).[24] For many this change caused a radicalization of their social and political views. Finally, the more systematic picture of Latin American poverty and inequity which these research centers documented provoked a more profound set of questions:

> A clearer and clearer view of the human and religious situation in Latin America emerged. But the description of the region from the accumulation of statistics led to more and deeper questions. Why was Latin America underdeveloped? Why were so many millions pushed to or kept at the margins of society? (Cleary 1985: 30)

These research centers helped to create the conditions that forced concerned Catholics all over Latin America to wrestle more deeply than ever before with the causes of poverty and injustice. The facts of poverty were now clear, having been systematically researched and documented. Now what was needed was an explanation for poverty, and a solution.

Two years before Medellín, a powerful and appealing explanation for Latin America's poverty and underdevelopment swept through academic, intellectual, and religious circles. It was called dependency theory, and, in it, Catholic progressives found the key to unlocking their new strategy.[25]

Dependency Theory

After World War II, the question of Latin American development focused on modernization, since the problem of poverty was thought to be one of underdevelopment and backwardness. Modernization theories were based on the assumption that development could be achieved by following the path—albeit with shortcuts—already taken by the "advanced" countries. It was thought that through education and training, and with the infusion of foreign capital investment, Latin American economies would "take off" toward full, industrial modernization (Rostow 1960; H. Muñoz 1981: 1–2; Valenzuela and Valenzuela 1981: 17–24).

But in the late 1950s and 1960s, a new generation of Latin American economists, many of whom worked in Santiago, Chile, began to analyze their problems on a continental and international level, from a distinctively Latin American perspective. Working away from the Prebisch-ECLA thesis they developed more critical economic analyses, the most important being the Marxist-influenced dependency theory (Valenzuela and Valenzuela 1981: 24–25; H. Muñoz 1981: 2).

Dependency theory was written by a number of authors, the most influential of which in Latin America were Fernando Cardoso, Enzo Faletto, Osvaldo Sunkel, Pedro Paz, Thentonio Dos Santos, Fernando Danel Janet, and Andre Gunder Frank (Valenzuela and Valenzuela 1981: 16, 35; Carroll 1987: 11; Richard 1979: 9). Their works ranged from rather sophisticated analyses (e.g., Cardoso and Faletto) to more simplistic works (e.g., Gunder Frank). Although these writers conceptualized "dependency" and its consequences somewhat differently (H. Muñoz 1981: 3; Caporaso and Zare 1981: 52), together their works formed a single, "general and comprehensive conceptual framework" (Valenzuela and Valenzuela 1981: 16).

Osvaldo Sunkel and Pedro Paz (1970) describe the dependency approach:

Both underdevelopment and development are aspects of the same phenomenon, both are historically simultaneous, both are linked functionally and, therefore, interact and condition each other mutually. This results . . . in the division of the world between industrial, advanced or 'central' countries, and underdeveloped, backward or "peripheral" countries

In the words of Theotonio Dos Santos (1971: 180),

Dependency is a situation in which certain groups of countries have their economies conditioned by the development and expansion of another country's economy. . . . [It occurs] when some countries (the dominant) can expand and be self-starting, while at the same time the others (the dependent ones) can only act as a reflection of this expansion, an expansion that can have positive or negative influence on the dependent countries' development. In whatever form, the basic situation of dependency produces a global situation in which the dependent countries are placed in a backward situation and under the exploitation of the dominant countries. The dominant countries thus impose a dominant technology, commerce, capital, and socio-political values on the dependent countries . . . that permits them to impose conditions of exploitation. [26]

Some theorists, such as Frank, contended that dependency actually impedes the economic growth of the periphery; others, such as Cardoso, argued that dependency and growth are compatible (Caporaso and Zare 1981: 52). In either case, however, in this view, "the interdependent nature of the world capitalist system and the qualitative transformations in that system over time make it inconceivable to think that individual nations on the periphery could somehow replicate the evolutionary experience of the now developed nations" (Valenzuela and Valenzuela 1981: 26).

Dependency theory was—and is—controversial. As a theory, it represented a major paradigm shift in economics that rejected modernization theory. Many analysts in and outside of Latin America criticized and rejected dependency theory (e.g., O'Brien 1975; Chilcote 1974; Lall 1975; Weisskopf 1976; Ray 1973; Packenham 1974, n.d.; Bath and Dilmus 1976; T. Smith 1979; Novak and Jackson 1985; Berger and Novak 1985; Novak 1982). But, others, including many Latin American Catholic progressives, quickly adopted it and used it as a lens to understand and interpret their world (Berryman 1987a: 20; Galilea 1971: 172).[27] According to Valenzuela and Valenzuela (1981: 16), "the 'dependency perspective' became the dominant approach in most Latin American intellectual circles by the mid- to late 1960s."[28]

Regardless of dependency theory's merits and demerits, the diffusion of dependency theory was rapid within the Church, taking a little more than a year to be understood and adopted by many interested Catholics.

Phillip Berryman remembers his own mentality at the time:

There was a great and rapid diffusion of dependency theory. When I first heard it, it clicked right away—once you see it, it clicks. Cultural dependency is especially obvious. One year after I first read it, I was back in Orange County, California giving a missionary slide show. People in the audience wanted to know what they could do to help Latin America. I told them to look into United States foreign policy. Then I launched into an explanation of dependency theory, clearly explaining the boom-and-bust cycles of mono-exports. Even I, a gringo, had grasped dependency enough to raise the hostility level in that room a lot. (Berryman 1987b)

Cleary (1987) says:

It was just incredible how the communication of these ideas spread so quickly. The progressives were looking to economics and soaking up ideas. There was an easy communication between theology and the social sciences. The world of the closed seminary was over and people were getting in touch with the modern world.[29]

Some Catholics learned of dependency theory by reading the original works; many others learned by word of mouth: "the realization of dependency in the Church came through very close personal contacts of people working in the Church" (Bonino 1987). Berryman (1987b) recalls the often informal nature of the spread of dependency theory:

Among pastoral workers, dependency theory was diffused more through workshops, conferences, and meetings than through publications. There was a kind of networking and groups of people traveling around different countries, gathering people to discuss issues, to spread new ideas. It was horizontal, not from above.

Julio de Santa Ana (1988) recounts his own experience:

I first came into contact with dependency theory in 1966. Some of us were reading it then. I received articles from my friends who were teaching at the Catholic University. By July of 1967, I had already organized a two-day meeting with university students in Arequipa on "The Theory of Dependency."

And Pablo Richard (1988) remembers:

I first read dependency theory in 1965: Cardoso, Frank, Faletto. Theologians were reading social science because we wanted to understand poverty and death. We saw that the Alliance for Progress and United States interventions were part of the crisis of dependence. We realized that the struggle was not East-West but North-South. We learned about neocolonialism and imperialism.

The version of dependency theory adopted by many progressive Catholics was often a simplified version of the original theories, due in part to the rapid, grass-roots, often word-of-mouth nature of the diffusion of the theory. This streamlined view understood Latin American underdevelopment as a simple result of its historical exploitation and domination by Europe and, later, North America. Latin America's development was entirely dominated, dependent, and distorted. It clearly operated in the interests of foreign powers and national elites, against the interests of the majority of Latin Americans. According to this view, Latin America could never catch up with the advanced countries by following in their path, because that would clash with the interests of the dominant countries (Gutiérrez 1978: 236–37).

In this simplified view, the theory of modernization was in reality only an ideological cloak to justify exploitation. Thus, with dependency theory, modernization theory's development *(desarrollo)* was soon called "developmentalism" *(desarrollismo)*, and used as a dirty word. The appropriate conceptual terms were thought to be not "advanced" and "backward," "modernized" and "underdeveloped," but "dominant" and "dependent," "exploiter" and "exploited." Consequently, the logic went, if Latin America was to experience true development, it would need to break the relationship of dependence with Europe and North America: it would need to throw off the hands of the exploiters.

For many Catholic progressives, dependency theory caused everything to fall into place. In their thinking, frustrations now met their causes; questions now found their answers. The reasons for poverty no longer seemed a mystery to them. Nor did the means to overcome it. For these Catholic progressives and radicals, armed now with dependency theory, the strategic road that the Church had to take seemed to them to be obvious (Goulet 1971; Jaworski 1971; see also McGovern 1987: 113–15).[30]

Other progressive Catholics remained unconvinced, and did not join in the popular acceptance of dependency theory. They held fast to the modernization approach to development, and argued that the world was more complex than dependency theory allowed.[31] This put them at odds with those who adopted dependency theory, and helped set the stage for later conflicts between liberation theologians and more moderate and traditional Catholics.

But the many progressive Catholics in Latin America who did seize upon dependency theory, decided that what was needed was not reform or development or patience. What was clearly needed, they thought, was liberation (Ramirez 1971; Nuñez 1985: 28–30). As Gustavo Gutiérrez (1973: 81) wrote: "Dependence and liberation are correlative terms. An analysis of the situation of dependence leads one to attempt to escape from it."

With that perception, the thing that remained to to be done, for these progressive-cum-radical Catholics, was to break officially all ties of the Catholic Church with wealth and power, and to commit the Church publicly and irrevocably to structural change toward the total liberation of the poor and oppressed. The upcoming Medellín conference— prompted by Vatican II to renew the Church—was, in their thinking, the obvious time and place for that to happen.

7

Making Medellín

The key historical turning point for the liberation theology movement was the Medellín conference. Most importantly, Medellín provided a opening of political opportunity that Catholic progressives and radicals exploited in the years after 1968. Medellín also fueled insurgent consciousness in the movement, increasing the sense among Catholics that the Church and society not only must be, but could be changed.

Medellín was organized by the progressives, many of whom were becoming increasingly radical. CELAM's progressive bishops organized the event, setting the meeting's agenda and hand-picking the conference's staff advisers. This select group of theologians and social scientists wrote the preparatory documents, held high-profile positions on key committees, and wrote the final documents. Although the Medellín conclusions contained a mix of liberationist, reformist, and traditional elements, the key themes of liberation were established clearly enough for radicals later to interpret the concluding documents from a liberationist perspective.[1]

Preparations

The idea of Medellín was initiated by Manuel Larraín at the end of Vatican II, where Larraín was given the authority to apply Vatican II to Latin America. Marcos McGrath, a progressive leader said in a 1988 interview, "Larraín put his mind and heart into CELAM and immediately organized his team."

First, Larraín brought together, from all over Latin America, the progressive bishops who formed the core of his team: "Hélder Cam-

era, Pironio, Lorscheider, Proaño, Sales, McGrath were all important, more or less the fathers of Medellín" (Richard 1988). Second,
Larraín chose progressive advisers to help prepare Medellín.

> The list of experts was chosen in the Larraín style, which was es-
> sentially an inside affair between friends, without the formality
> that later developed in CELAM. The naming and choosing of
> theologians was done by the presidency. (McGrath 1988).[2]

Consequently, the progressive perspective was dominant in the preparations:

> When CELAM began preparing for Medellín, they were very con-
> scious of the need for change, for a new orientation. So, they
> specifically chose people to prepare Medellín with that orienta-
> tion. It's not that Medellín was a run-of-the-mill meeting that was
> then "taken over" by progressives. It was all set up. The leadership
> of CELAM was terribly important. They chose experts who they
> saw had these progressive ideas, who were very much into Vatican
> II. (Cleary 1987)

Central to the process of preparation was a series of informal,
CELAM-sponsored consultations, held over a period of two years:

> In preparation of Medellín, there were informal meetings where
> CELAM began to identify themes. They met in quiet Catholic re-
> treat centers—bishops, theologians, and pastoral workers, also
> some lay people. And they came up with working documents. (Cle-
> ary 1987)

McGrath (1988) recounts:

> Between the Council and Medellin, with this new setup of CELAM
> departments and commissions, there began to be in the whole of
> Latin America specialized sessions, seminars, meetings on issues at
> the Latin American level. These were sponsored by CELAM, which
> brought together the top people from all over Latin America,
> which was not being done before the Council and the renovation.
> This went on for several years.

There were six major meetings in all, each focused on a specific
theme. The consultations were as follows (Prada 1975: 35; CELAM
1967a, 1967b, 1968a, 1968b):

—June 5–8, 1966: Baños, Ecuador; on "Education, Ministry, and
   Social Action"

—October 11–16, 1966: Mar del Plata, Argentina; on "Develop-
ment and Integration in Latin America"
—February 12–25, 1967: Buga, Colombia; on "The Mission of
Catholic Universities in Latin America"
—April 20–27, 1968: Melgar, Colombia: on "The Pastoral of Mis-
sions"
—May 12–19, 1968: Itapoan, Brazil; on "The Church and Social
Change"
—August 11–18, 1968: Medellín, Colombia; on "Catechesis."[3]

Participation in these consultations was by invitation only, and the
invitations came from the progressive bishops in the CELAM leadership. Some of the regular participants included the progressives
Manuel Larraín, Hélder Camera, Eduardo Pironio, Candido Padin,
Marcos McGrath, Gustavo Gutiérrez, Juan Luis Segundo, José Comblin, Lucio Gera, José Marins, Raimundo Camuru, Cecilio de Lora,
and Renato Poblete (Gutiérrez 1988; Cleary 1985: 34; Poblete 1988;
CELAM 1968c; Richard 1988). Although the meetings were not *exclusively* attended by progressives, these individuals exerted an especially strong influence.[4]

The effect of these informal consultations on the final shape of
Medellín was substantial. Cleary (1985: 34) explains:

> Experts were drawn from all over Latin America to produce *ponen-
> cias* (working papers) or to react to *ponencias* and then rewrite
> them into fuller working papers. Many of the experts were mem-
> bers of the new leadership networks mentioned earlier. To their
> numbers were added new members, experts in one field or an-
> other who had been working in their own national context some-
> what isolated from the transnational networks. Thus those net-
> works expanded and reshaped themselves for the purpose of
> influencing the outcome of the Medellín conference. . . . The
> dynamics of their meetings were such that advances in theological
> and practical thinking were made rather easily . . . [leading] to
> conclusions that were later taken for granted by Medellín partici-
> pants who had taken part in preliminary consultations. In effect,
> the conference outcome was being determined even before the
> conference began.

Specifically, it was at these meetings that the experts began to
move in their collective thinking beyond the social reformism of
Vatican II and the modernization model of development. It was precisely during this time that dependency theory was becoming popular, that BECs were spreading like wildfire, that pastoral workers were

TABLE 7.1
INCOME DISTRIBUTION IN LATIN AMERICA, 1968

Country		Percentage Share of Total Income by Groups			
	Poorest 20%	30% Below Median	30% Above Median	15% Below Maximum	Richest 5%
Argentina	5.2	15.3	25.4	22.9	31.2
Brazil	4.2	12.6	24.2	26.0	33.0
Chile	3.5	12.5	25.6	27.8	30.6
Colombia	5.9	14.3	23.1	26.3	30.4
Costa Rica	5.5	12.5	22.0	25.0	35.0
El Salvador	5.5	10.5	22.6	28.4	33.0
Mexico	3.6	11.8	26.1	29.5	29.0
Panama	4.9	15.6	22.9	22.1	34.5
Venezuela	3.0	11.3	27.7	31.5	26.5
Average	4.5	12.9	24.4	26.6	31.4

Source: *Statistical Abstract of Latin America* (Los Angeles, 1968); *Statistical Abstract of Latin America*, vol. 25 (1987).

moving to the poor, and that Marxism was showing an increase in influence among university students, with whom many of these experts worked.[5] The perspectives of these experts, whose job it was to understand and respond to these kinds of realities, were being transformed.[6]

The conference participants were particularly disturbed by the facts about inequality and poverty that had been established in recent years by the research of the United Nations, ECLA, Catholic research centers, and other research organizations. "The CELAM technicians who prepared the documents for Medellín came armed with statistical surveys, theological treatises, and sociological arguments" (Lernoux 1982: 37). Studying this information, they had become acutely aware of the enormous disparity in the incomes of the rich and the poor (see tables 7.1 and 7.2), of the extraordinarily high percentage of Latin Americans living in poverty (table 7.3), and of the gross inequity in land distribution (table 7.4). These research data were made all the more painfully real for the many who personally lived and worked among the poor.

The single most important person in this process was the Peruvian theologian Gustavo Gutiérrez, who had for years been concerned to formulate a pastoral strategy appropriate for Latin America. Gutiérrez was educated in Lima and received graduate training in psychology and theology at the Universities of Lyons and Louvain.

TABLE 7.2

INCOME DISTRIBUTION IN LATIN AMERICA: RICHEST AND POOREST

Country	Year	Percent Share of Total Income by Groups	
		Poorest 40%	Richest 10%
Argentina	1970	14.1	35.2
Brazil	1972	7.0	50.6
Chile	1968	13.4	34.8
Colombia	1970	10.0	44.4
Costa Rica	1971	12.0	39.5
Ecuador	1970	5.2	56.6
El Salvador	1969	12.4	33.0
Honduras	1967	7.3	50.0
Mexico	1968	9.1	46.7
Panama	1976	7.2	44.2
Peru	1970	7.0	42.9
Uruguay	1967	14.2	30.4
Venezuela	1970	10.3	35.7
Average	1970	9.9	41.8

Source: *World Labor Report* (Geneva: World Labor Organization, 1984).

His major pastoral work was among university students, primarily as national adviser to the National Union of Peruvian Catholic Students (UNEC).

While studying in Lyons, Gutiérrez first became acquainted with the polemics against Maritain's "Social Christianity." His first published work, *The Mission of the Church and the University Apostolate* (1960), reflects doubts about "New Christendom." By Illich's Petrópolis meeting of 1964, Gutiérrez had begun to formulate a new method of theological inquiry. And, increasingly, through the influence of progressive conciliar theologians such as Yves Congar, Gutiérrez became more oriented toward finding God in one's neighbor.

Gutiérrez's work with UNEC at one of the most Marxist-influenced universities in Latin America—the National University of San Marcos—led him to engage with Marxism (Mottesi 1985: 74). Gutiérrez also made contacts with radical Brazilian students involved in the political party "Popular Action" (Santa Ana 1988; Torres 1988), and through this involvement, Gutiérrez had become friends with the Brazilian educator, Paulo Freire (Mottesi 1985: 82). Furthermore, Gutiérrez became involved with pastoral work among the poor in a slum of Lima. All of this provoked him to confront political and

TABLE 7.3
PERCENTAGES OF LATIN AMERICAN HOUSEHOLDS IN POVERTY

Country	Year	Households in Absolute Poverty (%)[a]	Households in Relative Poverty (%)[b]
Brazil	1972	49	54
Colombia	1972	45	48
Costa Rica	1971	24	36
Chile	1968	17	39
Honduras	1967	65	58
Mexico	1967	34	48
Panama	1970	39	47
Peru	1972	50	48
Venezuela	1971	25	38
Average	1970	39	46

Source: *Statistical Yearbook for Latin America* (New York: United Nations, 1981), 84.
[a]Below nationally defined poverty line.
[b]Defined as below half the average family income.

TABLE 7.4
LAND DISTRIBUTION IN LATIN AMERICA, 1950

Country	Small Land Owners		Large Land Owners	
	% of population	% of land possessed	% of population	% of land possessed
Argentina	34.4	0.87	1.2	41.43
Bolivia	59.3	0.2	8.1	95.1
Brazil	34.43	1.3	14.58	64.0
Chile	23.0	1.7	2.1	40.5
Colombia	60.5	6.88	0.87	40.22
Ecuador	73.13	7.2	10.7	56.62
Mexico	76.16	1.42	1.42	89.43
Uruguay	25.89	0.62	1.34	34.0

Source: Houtart 1963.

economic issues in his search for an appropriate Christian pastoral strategy.

Gutiérrez's thought continued to develop, and was especially effected by dependency theory. In July 1967, he gave a course in Montreal, Canada, called "The Church and the Problem of the Poor," in which he taught the necessity for solidarity with the poor toward the abolition of poverty. On July 21–25, 1968, one month before Medellín, the priest group ONIS held its second national meeting.

There Gutiérrez delivered a paper entitled, "Toward a Theology of Liberation." It was the first formulation of what would become his ground-breaking work, *Notes on a Theology of Liberation* (1971), and also contained the germ of much of his later thought (Mottesi 1985: 79–87).

Gutiérrez recalled in a 1988 interview: "I was called in July 1968, to speak at a national meeting in Chimbote about the theology of development. When I arrived I said, 'No, I'm going to speak about the theology of liberation.' I remember revising a famous French statement: 'War is too important to leave to military people.' I said, 'Development is too important to leave to economists, we need to take a more global view.' That was not sudden with me. The title of liberation came from that time, but the content was as far back as Petrópolis, with the methodology of liberation."

Thus, through reckoning with European theological innovations, Vatican II, Marxism, popular political movements, the problem of poverty, and dependency theory over eight years, Gutiérrez's thinking had developed from a mild criticism of Maritain's Social Christianity to a commitment to socialism and anti-imperialist liberation. The CELAM consultations in preparation for Medellín offered Gutiérrez a forum to test his thoughts with others who were going through similar processes. By 1967, "liberation" had become for many staff experts *the* key concept. At the eleventh regular meeting of CELAM on November 19–26, 1967, for example, the group discussions began to abandon developmentalist rhetoric and to focus on the idea of liberation (Dussel 1981: 143).

Meanwhile, on June 22, 1966, bishop Manuel Larraín, co-founder of CELAM and initiator of Medellín, had died. The most important progressive Latin American bishop was gone, and the loss was felt severely in CELAM (Dussel 1981: 143). Nevertheless, the cadre of progressive bishops pressed on toward Medellín, postponing the date of that conference for a year.[7] First vice-president, Dom Avelar Brandão Vilela, assumed Larraín's office of president. Second Vice-President Pablo Muñoz Vega assumed Brandão's position, Secretary General Marcos McGrath became second vice-president, and Eduardo Pironio of Argentina became secretary general. Functionally, however, it was Dom Hélder Camera who would be the new leader of the bishops and the most important figure at Medellín.

The Preliminary Documents

On January 19–26, 1968, forty-three CELAM staff members met together at the Cristo Rey retreat center in Bogotá, Colombia, to write the preliminary documents for Medellín (Cleary 1985: 38).[8] Three documents were written, one by Gustavo Gutiérrez on the social structure of the Church, one by Raimundo Camuru on Church unity and coordination, and one by Renato Poblete on the role of the Church in social advancement (Prada 1975: 47; Poblete 1988). Each document had three parts: descriptions of the Latin American reality, theological reflection on that reality, and possible pastoral responses (Dussel 1981: 143).

These preliminary statements were not intended to be used as the conclusions of Medellín. Officially, they were intended to be the basis for a common focusing of the preconference discussion of the various national episcopates. However, the documents did act to map out the major concerns of the forthcoming conference, and did, in fact, contain many of the basic ideas of the Medellín conclusions (Cleary 1985: 38–39).[9]

Copies of the preliminary documents were sent out to the bishops of each country, who responded to CELAM through their national episcopates.[10]

Some of the responses were critical, especially those of the bishops of Colombia and Argentina (Camps 1969: 12–15). Many Latin American bishops and Vatican officials felt that the views portrayed in the document were overly negative and critical (Mutchler 1971: 101–12). Others disagreed. For example,

> Bishop Botero Salazar of Medellín stated that [the document] had to be negative in view of the fact that a true diagnosis of the Latin American situation could hardly have been positive. The president of CELAM, bishop Brandão Vilela, also believed that "a false optimism would be even more dangerous [than negativity]." (Dussel 1981: 143)

The reactions of the Roman Congregations were largely critical. A private CELAM document, prepared for the organizers of Medellín, summarized the appraisals from Rome:

> The Roman Congregations (of the Vatican) found the section of the working document on "Latin American Reality" too long. They observed that the section was "fairly close to reality," but that it tended to "reduce the explanation of everything, religion included, to socioeconomic causes." . . . They considered the entire first section "too pessimistic." They also objected to the criticisms of the Church made at the end of the chapter. . . . The Congregation for the Clergy found the first part too "reductionistic" and "lacking a treatment of the Marxist presence and its danger." The Congregation for the doctrine of the faith found nothing heretical but also criticized

the document for excessive concern with the temporal and not enough for the "eschatalogical." The Congregation for the Clergy also insisted in its commentary on the second and third parts of the working document that "the mission of the Church would be more pure and authentic insofar as it made social action a necessary condition for the spread of the Gospel" (rather than an end in itself). It mentioned especially the need for a "competition with Marxism for the attention of the people, especially for the attention of workers and university students." The Congregation for Catholic Teaching faulted the working document in all of its sections for failing to refer to the "social doctrine of the Church, except for references to the Second Vatican Council and to Progress of Peoples." . . . The Congregation also criticized what it called "an underestimation of the supernatural, a tone of discontent and a lack of confidence in the Church." It warned that "structural changes in the Church that would follow from this posture could well deprive the Church of its means of influence." (Mutchler 1971: 103–5)

However, interestingly, the Vatican Curia's response did not change any of the signals from the highest authority in Rome. McGrath (1988) recalls:

> The Pope was very insistent with us that we feel free to act on our own responsibility. As Medellín approached, in May or June 1968, he called us all [the CELAM leadership] to Rome. We didn't know what it was all about, but all he had to say was, "I approve of what you're doing, go right ahead." He told us that the documents we approved would have his approval. So, it was a real carte blanche.

Second drafts of the preliminary documents were written and sent out to the bishops. However, the negative responses to the first draft—which typically came from more conservative bishops—were largely ignored in the rewriting process:

> There were many confidential criticisms of the CELAM working document. The major episcopal conferences and the Vatican congregations all sent private appraisals to CELAM. . . . It is a measure of the relatively high autonomy of the CELAM organization . . . that none of the criticisms were acted upon. The criticisms were received before the preparatory commission of CELAM met on June 2–8, 1968; they were read and then filed. The working document was released to the press on July 16, substantially unchanged. (Mutchler 1971: 103)

In effect, a small group of CELAM officers and advisers forged ahead with their own conclusions. This lack of collegiality and attention to criticism would later backfire against the liberationists.

The Conference

The Medellín conference ran from August 26 to September 8, 1968. Unlike Vatican II, which every bishop attended, only 146 Latin American bishops participated, representing the more than 600 bishops of Latin America. In addition, 14 religious brothers, 6 nuns, and 15 lay people took part, for a total of 181 official participants (Dussel 1981: 145). In addition to that group, almost 120 staff experts attended with their bishops to help with the writing.[11]

Many of the bishops in attendance understood the gravity of the moment and the need for decisive action. The Bolivian bishops, for example, received a letter signed by eighty of their priests criticizing the bishops' political conservatism and imploring them to "take sufficient cognizance of the cry for justice that motivates the [national movement of revolutionary] guerrillas" (Houtart and Rousseau 1971: 214). There was also a letter presented by all of the Latin American provincial superiors of the Jesuit order, lamenting the fact that the majority of Latin Americans live in conditions of destitution "which cry to heaven for vengeance" and calling for appropriate changes (ibid.). In addition, a letter signed by a thousand priests from all over Latin America, entitled *Latin America: Continent of Violence,* was addressed to the Medellín participants (Oviedo and Mamontov 1986: 85; Carroll 1987: 15). Houtart writes:

Describing the situation, the letter declares: "Because the privileged few use their power of repression to block this process of liberation, many see the use of force as the only solution open to the people. . . . This light [of the Gospel] shows us clearly that one cannot condemn oppressed people when they feel obliged to use force for their own liberation; to do so would be to commit a new injustice." This letter calls for an unequivocal condemnation of unjust violence and the recognition of the right of an oppressed people to legitimate self defense (Houtart and Rousseau 1971: 214). The bishops had both the pressure and the support to make bold—even radical—decisions and directives.

By most accounts, the atmosphere of the conference itself was very open; there was room for free discussion (Gutiérrez 1988; Bandeira 1988).[12] Seven progressive bishops—McGrath, Pironio, Sales, Ruiz García, Muñoz Vega, Henriquez, and Proaño—began the conference by reading "well conceived and elegantly phrased" position papers on the preparatory documents (Dussel 1981: 145; Cleary 1985: 41).[13] The entire group then broke down into sixteen committees and subcommittees and proceeded to work on the conference conclusions ("Hace 5 Años . . . en Medellín," 1973: 6).[14]

The originality of what they produced was mixed:

> The Medellín participants did not write universally strong statements. Of the sixteen sections of the *Conclusions*, only three made a strong impact. The rest of the sections were mostly throwaways—unimaginative statements typical of international meetings. But the three on justice, peace, and poverty acquired a life of their own in the years to come. (Cleary 1985: 42–43)

Although Medellín as a whole was under the progressives' control, it was on those three documents—"Justice," "Peace," and "Poverty"—that this group focused, taking the lead in the committees and writing the documents.[15] Gustavo Gutiérrez and Pierre Bigo wrote the drafts on Peace (Poblete 1988). Gutiérrez wrote the draft on Poverty (Gutiérrez 1988).[16] And, Hélder Camera, Renato Poblete, and Samuel Ruiz García wrote the draft on Justice (Poblete 1988).[17]

As in the Latin American leadership generally, the progressives did not dominate numerically. However, they had enthusiasm and took the initiative to direct the conference and to head off opposition. Bonino (1987) explains:

> The idea that the whole Latin American episcopacy was radicalized and inclined to liberation theology and dependency theory is a misunderstanding. Really you had a few key people moving into a few key positions, having as consultants the new intellectual leadership and theologians.[18]

For example, during the proceedings of the Committee on Justice and the Subcommittee on Peace,

both Eugenio Sales and Carlos Parteli described their respective sees as characterized by revolutionary ferment, unrest among young workers and students. Both were anxious to meet the expectations of these groups, which meant clear denunciation of capitalism and imperialism. The documents that issued from the Committee on Justice and Peace reflect this preoccupation. (Mutchler 1971: 122)

Berryman (1987b) argues:

> That the progressives were in control wasn't really a political thing. The fact is that anyone who would do the work could have

the job and anyone who was concerned with the issues would end up heading the committees. Also, at Medellín, the staff people who were willing to stay up writing documents until 3:00 in the morning got to write them. That's the way it was done—it wasn't really devious or anything.

Nevertheless, some bishops would look back on Medellín with the feeling of having been manipulated by an opportunistic minority. This fact is crucial in understanding the withdrawal of support by the majority of bishops in 1972.

Why did the majority of moderate bishops at Medellín accept the work of this handful of progressives? They did so because the progressives were not, at the time, perceived by most to be a threat. Indeed, for most they seemed to represent the best option for the Church's future. Until the conference actually got under way, Gutiérrez himself was not sure whether there would be serious opposition to the progressive agenda (Gutiérrez 1988). Maduro (1987) explains:

> The articulate, progressive bishops of CELAM in the 1960s were the only ones in Latin America who had a certain esprit de corps. The bishops at the political center were quite open to the left and didn't have many fears yet. The right-wing bishops were scattered, not organized and not yet feeling the threat from the progressive side of the church. So, there was an implicit alliance of the center and the left which allowed the most articulate group to channel the orientation of the Medellín documents.

Bonino (1987) confirms this view:

> Some of bishops in Latin America are ideologically conservative and never change. But not many. The great majority of bishops are very pragmatic, trained to administer a diocese. They knew that the only strength they had before was the alliance with the conservatives, but that didn't work anymore; they were looking for something else. They came back from Vatican II looking for something to do with it. So, they were carried by this small, progressive minority, the articulate visionaries. And that really won the day at Medellín.

Mutchler (1971: 112) also states:

> Within the episcopal conferences, there were many bishops who were not truly represented by the official position of the national

conference [in response to the preliminary document] because the latter tended to reflect the views of the Archbishop or Cardinal of the capital city. These "underrepresented" bishops would later support the working document during the egalitarian meetings at Medellín.

The documents on peace, justice, and poverty together provide an analysis of the Latin American social situation. They charge that Latin America suffers under "neocolonialism," "internal colonialism," "external colonialism," "the international imperialism of money," "a dependence on a center of economic power," and "a marked bi-classism" (Gremillion 1976: 451, 455, 456). These exploitative structures constitute "serious sins," "a sinful situation," and "a situation of injustice that can be called institutionalized violence" (446, 455, 460). The documents claim that poverty "is in itself evil," that the "growing distortion of international commerce [is] . . . a permanent menace against peace," and that "those who have the greater share of wealth, culture, and power [by retaining their privilege] are responsible to history for provoking explosive revolutions of despair" (457, 460–461). In response, the documents call for "all-embracing, courageous, urgent, and profoundly renovating transformations" (460).[19]

Claiming that "to create a just social order . . . is an eminently Christian task," the documents commit the Church to a project of radical social change toward "authentic liberation" (462, 446). Condemning both "liberal capitalism" and "the Marxist system" as "militating against the dignity of the human person," the documents devote the church to a "solidarity with the poor" which "gives preference to the poorest and most needy sectors" (449, 474). What is necessary, claim the documents, is "a global organization, where all of the peoples, but especially the lower classes, have, by means of territorial and functional structures, an active and receptive, creative and decisive participation in the construction of a new society" in which man is "an agent of his own history" (448, 459). This will require the "task of 'conscientization' and social education" which "ought to be integrated into joint Pastoral Action at various levels" (452). "The Church—the People of God—will lend its support to the downtrodden," states the document on Justice, "so that they might come to know their rights and how to make use of them" (453). Reflecting a commitment to the development of BECs and to ecumenism, the documents encourage the formation of "small communities," "grass-roots organizations," and "collaboration . . . with non-Catholic Christian churches and institutions dedicated to the task of restoring justice in human relations" (475, 462, 454).[20]

The results, then, though mixed in political orientation, clearly contained many elements supporting the progressive agenda:

> The hierarchy officially approved things that some individual bishops would not necessarily agree with or didn't know the implications of what they were agreeing to. There were code words or sleepers in the documents, for example: "conscientization" or "people should be the subjects of their own development." It sounds sort of harmless, but if you take it seriously they have implications. The people that wrote these things had more in mind than the people who approved them. It's not conspiratorial, really, just the kind of thing that operates in any organization. (Berryman 1987b)

Problems did arise with the conservative Colombian bishops, however, as they had over the preliminary documents. They essentially rejected the final documents of Medellín and published their own report on September 5, the day before the Medellín documents were formally voted on (Mutchler 1971: 133). They rejected the negative picture of Latin America as a frustrated continent embroiled in prerevolutionary turmoil and rejected any criticism of the Church. "The rationalization made was that the deliberations at Medellín had been meant for Latin America as a whole, and that the sweeping generalizations they had produced were to be qualified by local interpretations and revision" (Multcher 1971: 133).

In the end, however, the Colombian bishops' actions backfired:

> The Medellín Conference witnessed the defection of the Colombian bishops from the CELAM consensus, but this public demonstration of division served to bring the other bishops closer together. The votes on conference documents treating the delicate issues of "imperialism," "violent revolution," "tyranny," and "class conflict" were always overwhelmingly in favor of acceptance of the "Brazilian" position as evidenced in the working documents. (Mutchler 1971: 130)

The CELAM leadership—perhaps because of the pope's earlier signals of confidence—broke protocol by distributing the conclusions of Medellín to the press, to be published before the reaction of Rome was received (MacEoin and Riley 1980: 79; Dussel 1981: 145).

Thus, by September 1968, the work of the progressives had paid off. It was true that many bishops did not support Medellín's *Conclusions* and still others did not really understand what they were getting the Church into—a fact that would later come back to haunt the liberation theology movement. Nevertheless, the basis for a new, liberationist strategy was, for the moment, formally and publicly endorsed—wittingly or unwittingly—by the bishops of the Latin American Church.

8

From Medellín to Sucre, 1968–1972

Medellín provided the final push for liberation theology to emerge in full force. It was "*the* event which opened the way to legitimately communicate and act on liberation theology" (Santa Ana 1988). In the four years after Medellín, from 1968 to 1972, the liberation theology movement, which had been gaining momentum, took off. During this "honeymoon" period, political opportunity was virtually unrestricted, organizational strength was at a maximum, and insurgent consciousness was burgeoning. The same period saw in the Church the beginnings of a reaction against liberation theology that eventually came to a head in 1972. Nevertheless, during this time prior to organized opposition, the movement spread rapidly through the Latin American Church, gaining a strength that would sustain it through the backlash of the years thereafter.

Open Political Opportunity

The most important factor in expanding political opportunity at this time was Medellín. What Vatican II had done for progressives after 1965, Medellín did for radicals after 1968.[1] Catholic radicals now had Medellín as an inspiration and authority (Adriance 1984: 505). To put it more accurately, Catholic radicals *appropriated* Medellín as their authority.

The Medellín documents were not unambiguously liberationist in orientation, but contained a mix of conservative, moderate, and liberationist elements (Salazar 1973: 25–26). That the Medellín *Conclusions* championed liberation theology was not, at the time, entirely

165

self-evident in the documents themselves. As Marcos McGrath (1988) observes:

> It was only *after* Medellín that liberation was very much spelled out and became the bone of contention. Of what liberation theology was to later develop into, we were quite unaware in 1968.

But, opportunity and authority fell to those who took the initiative. And, the initiative was taken, for the moment, by the radicals. Liberationists took the somewhat ambiguous documents and interpreted them as unambiguous declarations of support for their strategy.[2] Otto Maduro (1987) explains:

> The struggle for the interpretation of the Medellín documents was as or more important than the struggle for the production of the documents. If the documents are seen today as progressive documents, it is because those who were the most active in appropriating, knowing, spreading, and interpreting the documents were the most progressive groups in the Church.

Pablo Richard (1988) agrees:

> Medellín was a great legitimation of liberation theology. But the real battle was interpreting Medellín, because the documents themselves were not so powerful. A large part of the documents was completely confused, a small part was conservative, and a small part was liberation theology. What we did was interpret the large confused part in light of the small liberation theology part. So, today Medellín is liberation theology because we won the battle of interpretation. And, we did the very same thing with the Puebla document.[3]

For years, the Latin American Church had been searching—sometimes desperately—for a more adequate pastoral and social strategy, an alternative to the one which seemed to be failing. For those currently in power, Medellín was a major step in the resolution of that search (Metzinger 1973). With Medellín, the bishops formally articulated, adopted, and publicized a new strategy—one that the progressives and radicals then skillfully defined as liberationist. For many, the answer to the Church's problem seemed to have been found; what was needed was only to implement it.

On November 24–28, 1968, CELAM held its twelfth regular assembly in São Paulo, Brazil. The bishops there reaffirmed the Medellín *Conclusions,* declaring them "the norm for inspiration and action for the coming years" (Dussel 1981: 147).

On October 4, 1968, the Chilean bishops met as a national synod and called for that county's Church to unite around the challenge of Medellín. The other national bishops' conferences met in the following months to formulate specific strategies for implementing Medellín. These included the Brazilian bishops soon after the Chileans, the Argentine bishops between April 21 and 26, 1969, the Mexican bishops on August 19 and 20, 1969, the Paraguayan and Venezuelan bishops in August 1969, and the entire Episcopal Council of Central America and Panama between August 17 and 22, 1969. "Within a year of Medellín, [almost] all of the Latin American episcopacies had reaffirmed the *Conclusions* of Medellín" (Dussel 1979: 78–79; 1981: 147).

Furthermore, Dussel (1981: 147) writes,

> The new spirit prompted a joint meeting between CELAM and the National Catholic Conference of Bishops of the United States, which took place June 3–5, 1969, in Caracas [Venezuela]. In the final communique of this inter-American meeting the bishops declared their support of "the principal outline of the pastoral contained in the Conclusions of the II General Conference of Latin American Bishops." A second meeting followed in Miami in February 1970.

Individually, there were certainly many bishops who were not at all convinced of or invested in Medellín's new strategy. For example, during these years a Mexican bishop stated, "Medellín is more a matter of what people say about it than of what really happened there. Read carefully, the commitments of Medellín do not oblige the church to side with the poor" (quoted in Ferm 1986: 54).

Nevertheless, the majority of bishops were, for the time being, supportive of Medellín. And, as important, *institutionally*, the Latin American Church was committed to implementing the strategy of Medellín. This was true at the national level of many countries but also at the continental level, through the progressively controlled organization of CELAM. With this combination of support, temporary as it may have been, the political opportunity available to the liberation theology movement could hardly have been greater.

Powerful Organizational Strength

The political opportunity of the years 1968 to 1972 offered the liberation theology movement a chance to strengthen itself organizationally. The leaders of the movement seized that chance.

Central to this increase in organizational strength was CELAM. Perhaps no other Church organization worked as aggressively as

CELAM to implement the vision of Medellín, and probably no other official Church organization was as insistent on clearly defining the vision of Medellín as liberationist. As Dussel (1988) states, "From 1968 to 1972, liberation theology became the theology of CELAM." For these few years, CELAM provided support and protection for the leadership, membership, and communication channels of the liberation theology movement to form and grow strong.

Leadership

In the early-to-mid 1960s, only a handful of Latin American theologians looked beyond imported European theologies, to explore the possibilities of a distinctively Latin American theology and pastoral strategy. These included those who met in Ivan Illich's Petrópolis meeting in 1964: Illich himself, Gustavo Gutiérrez, Juan Luis Segundo, Segundo Galilea, and Lucio Gera.

Between 1965 and 1968 that group began to expand. Through the CELAM-sponsored consultations in preparation for Medellín, theologians and social scientists were brought together to analyze the Latin American situation, the key features of which they believed were underdevelopment and poverty. Their interactions provoked new questions and established important communication channels. Meanwhile, a group of radicalized Protestants were publishing numerous works on a "theology of revolution."

By 1968, many Latin American Catholics had rejected the modernization model of development and embraced dependency theory. Consequently, they sought for a new theological paradigm to help make sense of the Christian faith in light of Latin America's perceived dependency. The most important among these thinkers were Gustavo Gutiérrez, Juan Luis Segundo, Enrique Dussel, José Comblin, Rubem Alves, and Hugo Assman.[4] And of this core group, it was Gutiérrez who first elaborated the theological paradigm which built on the concept of liberation, took hold, and spread throughout the Church in Latin America.

In the next few years, distinct networks of theologians formed. Often grouped along national or regional lines, they elaborated the theology of liberation. By 1970, the theologians in all of these networks probably numbered no more than thirty. They held low-profile conferences in various cities on liberation theology, most of which were attended by no more than thirty people (Santa Ana 1988; Dussel 1988).

By 1972, all of these networks had come together for the first time at the April 1972 meeting of Christians for Socialism. Out of this, a single network of radical theological elites emerged with a core

TABLE 8.1

FIRST GENERATION OF LIBERATION THEOLOGIANS

Rubem Alves	Julio de Santa Ana	Camilo Moncada
Richard Antoncich	Gomez de Souza	Alex Morelli
Gonzalo Arroyo	Luis del Valle	Ronaldo Muñoz
Hugo Assman	Enrique Dussel	Noel Olaya
Rafael Avila	Segundo Galilea	Pablo Richard
Edgar Beltran	Rene Garcia	Juan Carlos Scannone
Paul Blanquart	Lucio Gera	Juan Luis Segundo
José Míguez Bonino	Gustavo Gutiérrez	Sergio Torres
Aldo Buntig	Franz Hinkelammert	Luis Ugalde
José Comblin	Jorge Larraín	Raul Vidales
J. Servino Croatto	José Marins	

Sources: Torres 1988; Richard 1988.

TABLE 8.2

AGE COHORT OF KEY THEOLOGIANS

Theologian	Born	Age in 1968
José Comblin	1923	45
José Míguez Bonino	1924	44
Juan Luis Segundo	1925	43
Gustavo Gutiérrez	1928	40
Segundo Galilea	1928	40
Juan Carlos Scannone	1931	37
Ronaldo Muñoz	1933	35
Rubem Alves	1933	35
Hugo Assman	1933	35
Enrique Dussel	1934	34

Source: Dussel 1978.

group that was working to elaborate and propagate the theology of liberation. This group represented the first generation of liberation theologians (see table 8.1). With it, the organized leadership of the liberation theology movement was formed.

Although the boundaries of this group were never perfectly defined, from the beginning a clear set of characteristics marked its members. First, the key members of this group were similar in age (see table 8.2). Two consequences of this age distribution were significant. First, membership in one age cohort helped facilitate similar life experiences for these theologians, increasing the likelihood of in-group cohesion. Second, the specific age of these theologians placed them, at the right time in history, at the "prime" of their professional lives: at Medellín they were all in their late 30s and early 40s— old enough to be experienced and respected and young enough to be highly energetic and aggressive.

In addition, according to Cleary (1985: 16–17) and my own research, almost all of these leaders were:

1. Internationally educated, usually in Europe or the United States;
2. Ordained priests, ministers, or bishops;
3. Associated with some historic public event, such as Vatican II, Medellín, or the publishing of a controversial book;
4. Ecumenically—rather than confessionally—oriented;[5]
5. Cosmopolitan, deeply involved in the urban world;
6. Involved in international activities and organizations;
7. Sociologically minded;[6]
8. Engaged in many institutional roles, such as pastor, teacher, writer, organizer, research, at the same time;
9. Members of or consultants to high-level church committees, such as institutes of CELAM, commissions carrying on the work of Vatican II, key departments of the World and National Council of Churches (Geneva and New York), or the Confederation of Evangelical Churches in Latin America;
10. Driven by a concern with the poor and oppressed.

As a result of the formation of this theological elite, the liberation theology movement acquired a nucleus of interconnected leaders who would articulate its vision, inspire its members, legitimate its strategy, and plot out its future.

Membership

From 1968 to 1972, the membership of the liberation theology movement mushroomed, due in part to the integration of preexisting, activated groups and individuals—such as national priest groups, Catholic Action movements, radical pastoral workers—into the newly emerging movement. It was also due to the individual and "block" conversion of new members, largely through the extensive, aggressive educational work of CELAM.

CELAM organized and sponsored training courses and seminars taught by theologians such as Gustavo Gutiérrez, Enrique Dussel, Juan Luis Segundo, José Comblin, Segundo Galilea, José Marins, and Edgar Beltran. For example:

In the late 1960s, CELAM gathered steam and its departments set up institutes on various topics to retrain priests and sisters. The typical style was that someone, like Enrique Dussel or Juan Luis Segundo, came in for a week or two and taught their particular thing. It was a hodgepodge, without heavy-handed control, that continued until 1972. (Berryman 1987b)

CELAM also organized training conferences for bishops. Renato Poblete, a regular teacher, recalls in a 1988 interview:

> In the time between Medellín and Puebla, CELAM sponsored conferences for bishops—more than four hundred of them. I gave three hundred myself. Their purpose was to educate bishops on social problems. In my opinion, they were the most important thing done during that period.

In these years, CELAM also sponsored a program to further propagate BECs:

> CELAM training institutes spread the ideas and methodology of BECs. Two priests, José Marins, a Brazilian, and Edgar Beltran, a Colombian, traveled full time giving courses on BECs throughout Latin America. (Berryman 1987a: 67)

The most important of CELAM's educational works, however, took place through the Pastoral Institute of Latin America (IPLA) of Quito, Ecuador, the Catechetical Institute of Santiago, Chile, and the Liturgical Institute of Medellín, Colombia.[7] The progressive bishops from Ecuador and Panama, Lionidas Proaño and Marcos McGrath, organized and directed these operations; IPLA thus reflected their interests. According to McGrath (1988):

> I personally set up IPLA in Quito. It was set up at the time of Medellín and was expressive of Medellín. Bishop Proaño also had a large part in the direction of IPLA, which became more and more oriented toward a commitment to the poor and liberation.

One of IPLA's professors, Enrique Dussel (1988), describes its widespread influence:

> There were a number of IPLA professors—myself, Gustavo Gutiérrez, José Comblin, and Juan Luis Segundo. We shocked the students. For example, I shocked them with a liberationist interpretation of Latin American Church history. For five years, 1967 to 1972, we were the professors for all types of CELAM meetings throughout Latin America. I crossed Latin America thirty times. We gave courses in every country, often invited by IPLA institutes. Many times we had three to four hundred people attending.

Once, in Buenos Aires, in 1967, I gave six talks to seven hundred religious school directors in an opera house. But there were many meetings organized by CELAM, universities, and religious orders beside the big ones; there were smaller, low-level meetings everywhere. The big meetings were just the tip of the iceberg.

Through IPLA, then, over a period of five years, Roman Catholics all over Latin America were being exposed to the message of liberation theology. Besides the traveling work of IPLA, more than five hundred pastoral workers were trained in-house at the IPLA headquarters in Quito, Ecuador (Dussel 1978: 182). Julio de Santa Ana (1988) observes: "IPLA was a very important instrument in the communication of liberation theology to the churches. Gutiérrez, Segundo, Dussel, and Galilea were all theologians of IPLA."[8] Gutiérrez (1988) recalls:

> IPLA was a very important place for pastoral and theological reflection for all of Latin America. Quickly after the birth of liberation theology, liberation theology ideas were present in IPLA. So, IPLA was very, very important in disseminating liberation ideas. Bishop Proaño took the lead in that.

Through the retraining seminars for priests and sisters, the social education conferences for bishops, the work of Marins and Beltran in promoting BECs, and the itinerant programs of IPLA, the membership of the liberation theology movement was rapidly expanding.

Communication Networks

From 1968 to 1972, there were many channels of communication that facilitated the development and diffusion of liberation theology. The seminars and conferences of CELAM and IPLA and the formation of an elite network of liberation theologians served this purpose. In addition, a number of religious and theological journals, magazines, and newsletters helped to promote and spread liberation theology throughout Latin America. Some were existing periodicals that began to carry works on liberation theology; others were new journals devoted almost entirely to liberation theology. Among these, the most important were periodicals from Mexico, Colombia, Peru, and Brazil (see table 8.3). Other important periodicals included *Medellín* and *Tierra Nueva* of Colombia, *Mensaje, Christianismo y Revolución*, and *Teología y Vida* of Chile, *Revista Brasileira de Teología* and *Popular Pastoral* of Brazil, *Noticias Aliadas* of Peru, *Stromata* of Argentina, *Dialogo* of Panama, *SIC* of Venezuela, and *ECA* of El Salvador (Lernoux 1980, 208–9; Richard 1981: 427; Gotay 1983: 67; Santa

TABLE 8.3

PERIODICALS PUBLISHING WORKS ON LIBERATION THEOLOGY

Periodical	Number of Regular Liberation Theology Authors (1970–82)
Sirvir (Mexico)	21
Christus (Mexico)	20
Puebla (Brazil)	16
Ediciones C.R.T. (Mexico)	14
Contacto (Mexico)	10
Popular Pastoral (Peru)	9
Meic-Jeci (Peru)	9
Solidaridad (Colombia)	9
Iglesia Nueva (Colombia)	8
Christianismo y Sociedad (Dom. Rep.)	8
CLAR (Colombia)	6
Estudios Ecumenicos (Mexico)	5
Paginas (Peru)	4

Source: Jimenez et al. 1984, 41.

Ana 1988; Dussel 1978: 184; Oliveros 1977: 390). Most liberation theologians published articles in a number of periodicals (see table 8.4).

In addition to religious and theological journals, the ideas of liberation theology were diffused through informal newsletters and writing-exchange networks which circulated through the liberation theology network and beyond. For example, Julio de Santa Ana (1988) tells of a newsletter, produced by Hugo Assman, that reached thousands of interested Catholics:

> By the early 1970s, when someone wrote something, it got out everywhere. That was a very fertile period and there was very good communication. One of the crafters of this process of circulation was Hugo Assman, who had the capacity to be in contact with many people and to put them in contact with each other. When he was study secretary of ISAL, he started a project which went on for more than one year called *Pasos*, which means "steps." From early 1972 until the coup against [Chile's Salvador] Allende, each week he found something that was written by someone, even if it was unfinished, and circulated it to over *two or three thousand people*. There were a total of 54 issues of *Pasos* published. That was fantastic, because people were sending Hugo many manuscripts and he

TABLE 8.4

NUMBER OF PERIODICALS IN WHICH LIBERATION THEOLOGIANS PUBLISHED, 1966–1977

Theologian	No. of Journals	Theologian	No. of Journals
Leonardo Boff	13	Ricardo Antoncich	5
Gustavo Gutiérrez	11	Jesus García	5
Segundo Galilea	10	Juan Luis Segundo	5
Raul Vidales	10	Franz Vanderhoff	5
Enrique Dussel	8	Clodovis Boff	4
Jon Sobrino	8	Miguel Concha	4
Hugo Assman	6	Luis Alberto Gomez de Souza	4
José Comblin	6	Jose Ignacio Gonzalez Faus	4
Ignacio Ellacuría	6	José Míguez Bonino	4
Ronaldo Muñoz	6	Manuel Valesquez	4
Pablo Richard	6	Other	1–3[a]

Source: Jimenez et al. 1984, 41.
[a]The following theologians published articles in three or less periodicals: Gonsalo Arroyo, Teofilo Cabestrero, Pedro Casaldáliga, Georges Casalis, Vincent Cosmão, Alejandro Cussianovich, Luis del Valle, Julio de Santa Ana, Alfredo Fierro, Pablo Fontaine, Gilberto Giminez, Guilo Girardi, José Maria Gonzalez Ruiz, Otto Maduro, bishop Sergio Méndez Arceo, Carlos Mesters, Lionidas Proaño, Juan Carlos Scannone, and Arnaldo Zenteno (Jimenez, et al., 1984: 41).

immediately reproduced them and put them into circulation. In this way the theology of liberation was reproduced like the multiplication of bacteria, through the creation of links and networks.

Another important channel of communication was the religious orders. Maduro (1987) explains:

Religious orders are international organizations. They are constantly in contact with people from other countries and continents. As a result, the orders serve as networks of ideas, books, experiences, articles, authors, and so on. For example, they publish newsletters which carry the news from other regions of their same order. So, if there were a renewal or set of new ideas in another place, the religious orders would serve as channels to carry this information to and around Latin America.

Phillip Berryman (1987b) confirms this point:

Religious orders are network kinds of things. A diocesan priest is much more localized and immobile than a religious order priest. Religious orders encourage travel and thinking that is broad-ranging. Also, there is a kind of mystique to being a Jesuit. Anytime I ever wanted a clear idea of what was going on in a place, I did and

TABLE 8.5

TIES OF THE THEOLOGICAL ELITE TO PRIEST GROUPS

Theologian	Member of Priest Group
Rubem Alves	ISAL
Ricardo Antoncich	ONIS
Gonzalo Arroyo	The Eighty
Hugo Assman	ISAL
Paul Blanquart	The Eighty
José Míguez Bonino	ISAL
Julio de Santa Ana	ISAL
Luis del Valle	Priests for the People
Enrique Dussel	Priests for the Third World
Rene Garcia	Golconda
Lucio Gera	Priests for the Third World
Gustavo Gutiérrez	ONIS; The Eighty
Camilo Moncada	Golconda
Ronaldo Muñoz	The Eighty
Noel Olaya	Golconda
Pablo Richard	The Eighty
Juan Carlos Scannone	Priests for the Third World
Sergio Torres	The Eighty
Raul Vidales	Priests for the People

Sources: Jimenez et al. 1984; Jimenez 1987; Torres 1988; Santa Ana 1988; Richard 1988; Klaiber 1977.

still do ask a Jesuit. They are extremely good at giving a clear, crisp overview of what is happening.

Finally, priests groups, which continued to meet during this time, were important for the formulation and diffusion of liberation theology. The priest groups themselves were trying to articulate a new Church strategy in light of dependency theory. As the theology of liberation was introduced and elaborated, priest-group leaders—who were in touch with innovative theological developments—diffused these ideas to the members of their groups. This diffusion of liberationist ideas among priest groups was helped by the fact that every important group had at least one member who belonged to the core group of theological elites described above (see table 8.5).[9]

In January 1970, the members of all of the priest groups gathered together in Lima, Peru, to share their experiences and discuss strategies for the future (Torres 1988). This meeting strengthened the networks of communication not only within groups, but between them.[10]

Growing Insurgent Consciousness

As important as the communication networks were the ideas and feelings that were being shared. "The new magazines, research institutes, priest movements were, in effect, primitive think tanks" (Cleary 1987). What emerged from these networks was an urgent sense that the social order had to and could, in fact, be changed by Christians working in popular movements to break the oppressive ties of dependency and injustice.

Naming Liberation Theology

As a result of the preparations for Medellín and the widespread acceptance of dependency theory the thinking of many progressive Catholics (and Protestants) became more and more radical. Gustavo Gutiérrez's theological reflection began to make increasing use of the concept of liberation. One month before the Medellín conference, Gutiérrez delivered to the second national meeting of the priest group, ONIS, a paper entitled "Toward a Theology of Liberation,"representing the first formulation of what would become his ground-breaking book. In June 1969, this paper was published in pamphlet form under the same title (Mottesi 1985: 79). Gutiérrez spent the next year expanding it into a fully formed theology of liberation.

Meanwhile, the exiled Brazilian Protestant and ISAL member, Rubem Alves, was studying theology at Princeton Theological Seminary under the direction of Richard Shaull. Alves' thinking, too, was coming to focus more and more on the idea of "liberation," and his doctoral dissertation at Princeton was a first attempt to articulate a theology of liberation.

In November of 1969—fourteen months after Medellín—both Gutiérrez and Alves were invited to Campine, Switzerland to present papers at a WCC-sponsored SODEPAX (Committee on Society, Development, and Peace) Consultation on Theology and Development (Mottesi 1985: 87). Many European and North American theologians were present as well. The two Latin Americans met there for the first time, neither having read any of the other's work . They immediately recognized, however, that "their thinking was on the exact same wavelength" (Santa Ana 1988). The consultation's organizers had originally entitled Gutiérrez's presentation "The Meaning of Development"; on the plane to Switzerland, however, Gutiérrez renamed it "Notes on Theology of Liberation" (Mottesi 1985: 87). Realizing their common mind, Gutiérrez and Alves gave a joint presentation at that meeting, arguing that "the question is not development, but how to break dependency and create conditions for radical social transformation" (Santa Ana 1988). Their unity had a tremendous impact on that conference and Alves' contribution helped stimulate and refine Gutiérrez's theological reflection (Santa Ana 1988; Bonino 1987).

By the beginning of 1970, the idea that Gutiérrez and Alves were suggesting, of formulating a Latin American "theology of liberation," had spread throughout the entire network of progressive and radical theologians and beyond. In a short time, consensus developed that this was the task that needed to be carried out. The next two years saw an eruption of meetings and conferences, and a first wave of writings elaborating the theology of liberation.

Conferences on Liberation Theology

Having become convinced of the need for a theology of liberation, many of Latin America's theologians proceeded to work toward that end in the way most familiar to them: by holding invitation-only conferences. Most of the meetings were small—never more than thirty people—and organized by region (Dussel 1988).[11] Some Protestant theologians took part in these discussions.

The first meetings were low-profile, but those held later became more formal and publicized. Berryman (1987b) recalls:

> In 1970, in Bogotá, there was a meeting on liberation theology I attended. It was almost clandestine, let's say a very discreet meeting. Yet within a year, the very things we were talking about then were discussed openly in other meetings sponsored by the official bureaucratic establishment. People were then kicking around ideas that only a few months before I had heard in a very different kind of atmosphere. There was a rapid pace of development.

ISAL, having abandoned Shaull's rhetoric of revolution, organized a number of these meetings on liberation:

> In 1970, ISAL meetings were organized in Bogotá and Buenos Aires, where fewer than 30 people would meet. We came with papers, shared our views, and a common body of thought started to emerge. Gustavo Gutiérrez was the one who best articulated these ideas. (Santa Ana 1988)

Although the total number of conferences on liberation theology in 1970 and 1971 is unknown, the following eleven were very important (Hennelly 1978: 10–11; 1979: 25; Assman 1976: 53; Richard 1979, 13; 1987a, 151; Santa Ana 1988):

—March 2–7, 1970: "Liberation: Option for the Church in the Decade of the 1970s," Bogotá, Colombia;

—March 1970: "Second Symposium on Liberation Theology," Bogotá, Colombia;

—July, 1970: "Exodus and Liberation," Buenos Aires, Argentina;

—July 24–26, 1970: "Symposium: Underdevelopment as Dependence," Bogotá, Colombia;

—August 3–6, 1970: "Symposium: on Liberation Theology" (ISAL) Buenos Aires, Argentina;

—October 16–18, 1970: "Seminar on Liberation Theology," Ciudad Juarez, Mexico;

—December 1970: "Liberation Theology and Pastoral Work," Oruro, Bolivia;

—June 1971: "The Theological Reality" (ISAL) Buenos Aires, Argentina;

—July 3, 1971: "Popular Motivation and the Christian Faith" (ISAL), Nana, Peru;

—July 7–10, 1971: "Methodology of Liberation" (ISAL), Bogotá, Colombia;

—July 26–31, 1971: "Liberation in Latin America" (ISAL), Bogotá, Colombia.

Participants in most—though not all—of these conferences were almost entirely members of the core of theological elites, the first generation of liberation theologians. For example, the 1970 ISAL conferences in Bogotá and Buenos Aires were attended by Rubem Alvez, Gustavo Gutiérrez, Juan Luis Segundo, Hugo Assman, Julio de Santa Ana, Emilio Castro, Rene Padilla, Brenon Schumann, Antonio Chequin, Pedro Negre, and others (Santa Ana 1988; LADOC 2:52). The lists of those who presented papers at other conferences shows the same pattern (see, for example, table 8.6).

As a result of these conferences, liberation theology received widespread attention, and many of Latin America's most active theologians wrote works to develop it. Between 1969 and 1973, the first liberation theology books were published (see table 8.7). Liberation theology had become the new project of many progressive Latin American Catholics. A critic of liberation theology, Belgian Jesuit sociologist-priest Roger Vekemans, antagonistically described the state of affairs in a December 1971 letter to a German Catholic funding agency (LADOC 2:57):

TABLE 8.6

PRESENTERS AT TWO LIBERATION THEOLOGY CONFERENCES

Liberation in Latin America (Bogotá, July, 1971)

Hugo Assman, "Theological Reflection on a Strategic-Tactical Level"

Juan Luis Segundo, "Instruments of Latin American Theology"

Luis G. del Valle, "The Role of Theology in Latin America"

Noel Olaya, "Social Sciences and Theology"

Luis Ugalde, "The Ambiguity of the Hope of Christians, Utopia, and the Transformation of the Latin American Reality"

Rafael Avila, "Prophecy, Interpretation, and Re-Interpretation"

Alex Morelli, "A Theological Essay on Violence"

Arnaldo Zenteno, "Liberation and the Teaching Profession"

The Theological Reality (Buenos Aires, June, 1971)

Hugo Assman, "Theological Reflection on a Strategic-Tactical Level" & "Socioanalytical and Ideological Implications of the Language of Liberation"

José Míguez Bonino, "New Theological Perspectives"

Emilio Castro, "The Growing Presence of Standards of Historical Interpretation in the Evolution of Biblical Hermeneutics"

Julio de Santa Ana, "Revolutionary Reflection, Reflection at the Strategic-Tactical Level" & "Reflection on the Faith as Praxis for Liberation"

Noel Olaya, "Faith and Social Praxis"

Luis N. Rivera Pagan, "Theology and the Praxis of Liberation " & "Contributions from Marxism"

J. Servino Croatto, "Liberation and Liberty"

Pedro Negre, "The Methodological Way of the Social Sciences and Theological Interpretation"

Sources: SCCS 1971; Tierra Nueva 1972.

[Liberation theology] has now solidified into a movement and has succeeded in penetrating some of the institutional Church's nerve centers. Not only theologians highly regarded for their specialties, but many priests and Christian militants are, like real agitators, making full use of ecclesiastical structures, with the naive acquiescence of weak authorities and sometimes with logistical, intellectual, and financial support from abroad. The saddest part is that to combat this brutal and unscrupulous attack we see only scattered and intermittent reactions that seem to acknowledge beforehand their inevitable defeat.

Christians for Socialism

The most important conference of the early 1970s for the development of the liberation theology movement was the April 1972 meeting of Christians for Socialism.[12] It was at this meeting that the net-

TABLE 8.7

EARLY PUBLISHED BOOKS ON LIBERATION THEOLOGY

Date	Theologian	Title
1969	Gutiérrez	*Toward a Theology of Liberation*
1969	Alves	*Religion: Opium or Instrument of Liberation?*
1969	Alves	*A Theology of Human Hope*
1968–72	Segundo	*Open Theology for Adult Laity* (series)
1970	Bonino	*Theology of Liberation*
1971	Assman	*Oppression-Liberation: Challenge to Christians*
1971	Gutiérrez	*Liberation Theology: Perspectives*
1971	Dussel	*History of the Church in Latin America*
1971	Miranda	*Marx and the Bible*
1972	Boff, L.	*Jesus Christ Liberator*

Sources: Richard 1979, 13–14; Mottesi 1985, 79.

work of theological elites that constituted the first generation of liberation theologians first met together as a whole and were unified around a consensus declaration (Torres 1988).

In 1969, the Marxist Salvador Allende ran for the Chilean presidency, with the backing of the Popular Unity party. A number of progressive Chilean priests, who were becoming increasingly disenchanted with President Eduardo Frei's Christian Democratic party, began to discuss informally the possibility of responding positively as a group to the Allende program (Torres 1988).[13] On September 4, 1970, Allende was elected president—the first democratically elected Marxist president in the West.

At the December 1970 international seminar for Latin American priests—sponsored by Santiago's Jesuit research center, ILADES—one of these disenchanted priests, Gonsalo Arroyo, proposed to the seminar participants a meeting to assess the meaning of Allende's victory. Some in the group decided to hold the meeting in Santiago in April 1971. Many of the priests at the ILADES seminar went back to their dioceses and countries and conveyed Arroyo's proposal to others (Torres 1988).

Eighty priests showed up for the 1971 meeting. They consequently called themselves *Los Ochenta*—The Eighty.[14] One of them, Sergio Torres, describes in a 1988 interview those who attended:

> Most of us already knew each other, had similar life experiences, and thought similarly. Chile is a small country, with not too many priests, and many of us were classmates in seminary. We knew each other for several years through different meetings and confer-

ences. Many foreign priests who were very active and progressive came too. Almost all of us had supported Frei in 1964, but we were disappointed with the results of his administration. We all believed that an alternative to Christian Democracy was needed, something more radical. Marxism was very appealing.

On April 16, The Eighty issued a public declaration called "Christian Participation in the Construction of Socialism in Chile." It declared that Chile's poverty and exploitation were the result of "the capitalist system, which is produced by the domination of a foreign imperialism and abetted by our own country's ruling classes." Finding "no incongruity between Christianity and socialism," the document declared a total commitment of these priests to the realization of socialism in Chile (LADOC 6:25–26; Donoso Loero 1975: 129–30; Vekemans 1976: 336–44).

Within a week of the declaration by the Eighty, the Chilean hierarchy responded with a public warning about Church involvement in politics. A month later, the Chilean bishops responded in greater depth with the pastoral letter "Gospel, Politics, and Various Types of Socialism." In it they warned against Church identification with specific economic or political strategies and against the public involvement of priests in politics (Vekemans 1976: 345–50; Smith 1982: 235; see also Donoso Loero 1975, 138–42; Smith 1982, 162).

In response, in July and October of 1971, The Eighty published two analyses of the bishops' pastoral letter (the second written by the Uruguayan theologian Juan Luis Segundo), critical of the bishops' lack of structural analysis of capitalism, abstract language, oversimplification of Marxism, and hope for a politically neutral Church. According to Brian Smith (1982: 235–36), "aside from publicly disagreeing with the bishops, the two critiques by 'the 80' misrepresented positions of the hierarchy. They claimed that the bishops in their letter ruled out all forms of socialism. . . . They also accused the hierarchy of tacitly endorsing Christian democracy." That neither claim was accurate undoubtedly served to fuel the conflicts between the group and the bishops that were to come.

In November 1971, the Eighty formed the organization Christians for Socialism. The core of this group consisted of the secretariat of the Eighty, but it also included religious, lay, and Protestant leaders from Chile and other countries, including Peru, Argentina, Bolivia, and Brazil (Richard 1975). It thus brought together much of the core leadership of the liberation theology movement. "Leaders of radical priest movements in other Latin American countries (ONIS in Peru, Golconda in Colombia, Priests for the Third World in Argentina) assisted those in Chile who inaugurated Christians for Socialism, and provided them with much of their inspiration and organization" (Smith 1982: 249).

Sergio Torres (1988), then secretary general of Christians for Socialism, describes the reasoning behind that organization:

> The rationale of Christians for Socialism was that, in the past, the Church had always opposed socialist revolutions—in Russia, China, Cuba. In Cuba, religious were expelled from the country for the Church's opposition. We had that in mind with Allende: we did not want to repeat the same mistake, to have the same thing to happen in Chile. We wanted to support the positive in Allende's program and criticize the negative *from the inside*. We desired to work *with* the programs, to not automatically be opposed to socialism.

Christians for Socialism intended to become directly involved in political activities.[15] Among its more publicized events, two separate groups of priests from Christians for Socialism visited Cuba in 1971 and 1972 at the invitation of Fidel Castro; then Castro, while on a trip to see Allende in 1972, met with Christians for Socialism in Santiago (Richard 1976: 63–69; 1975: 60; Torres 1988; Donoso Loero 1975: 155–60).

According to Brian Smith (1982: 232–33), Christians for Socialism,

> drew heavily upon the writings and the advice of liberation theologians (such as Gustavo Gutiérrez of Peru, Juan Luis Segundo of Uruguay, and Hugo Assman of Brazil). They established local chapters in almost every province of [Chile], and published monthly bulletins, articles, and pamphlets (with a circulation of over 500 copies) commenting on aspects of Chile's transition to socialism. . . . In their pastoral work they also made efforts to raise the social awareness of their parishioners in small base communities and so enhanced the mobilization of workers and peasants for the Left. Christians for Socialism also established close connection with radical priest movements in other parts of Latin America.

From April 23 to 30, 1972, four hundred members of Christians for Socialism converged on Santiago for an international conference.[16] "Most of the significant Latin American theologians [i.e., liberation theologians] . . . were active participants" (Bonino 1975: xxi) (for a list of papers presented at the meeting, see table 8.8).[17] According to Smith (1982: 237),

TABLE 8.8

<small>CHRISTIANS FOR SOCIALISM PAPERS PRESENTED</small>

Gonsalo Arroyo, "Latin American Thought in Sub-development and Dependency," and "Considerations on Sub-development in Latin America"

José Comblin, "The Catholic Church and its Three Religious Types"

Gustavo Gutiérrez, "Christian Fraternity and Class Struggle"

José Míguez Bonino, "New Theological Perspectives"

Julio de Santa Ana, "Revolutionary Theory: Reflection on Strategical-Tactical Level and Reflection on Faith as Praxis of Liberation," and "The Middle Classes: Agents of Change for a New Society?"

Pablo Richard, "Socialist Rationality and Historical Verification of Christianity"

Franz Hinkelammert, "Christian Institutions and Society"

Noel Olaya, "Christian Unity and Class Struggle'

Paul Blanquart, "Christian Faith and Marxism in the Revolution"

Fernando Castillo and Jorge Larrain, "Worker-Peasant Power and the Transition to Socialism in Chile"

Julio Girardi, "Christian Liberation and Social Liberation"

Pedro Negre, "The Significance of Methodological Changes of the Social Sciences for Theological Interpretation"

Cesar Aguiar, "Christians and the Process of Liberation in Latin America"

Sergio Vuskovic, "Ideological Pluralism"

R. Viola, "Surpassing the Marxist-Christian Dialogue"

J. M. Flamment, "What does China's Cultural Revolution Propose?"

Henrique de Lima Vaz, "Humanism and Antihumanism in the Face of the Social Teachings of the Church"

Lucio Margi, "Problems of the Marxist Theory of Political Participation"

Gerrit Huizer, "Summary of Peasant Movements in Latin America"

Rodolfo Stavenhagen, "Marginality and Participation in the Mexican Agrarian Reform"

V. Bambirra, "Liberation of Women and Class Struggle"

J. Tamayo, "The Middle Strata and the Power of the Workers"

Catholic Action Youth, Lima, "New Society and Popular Motivation"

Women's Commission of the Encounter, "Integration of Women in the Chilean Revolutionary Process"

Source: Eagleson 1975.

At the end of the week-long exchange, the participants issued a consensus document which spelled out in more detail the basic position prefigured by "the 80" a year before: the necessity of socialism as the only legitimate Christian option, the religious obligation to involve oneself in a revolutionary process and to identify with working-class parties, the impossibility of eventual unity in the Church without first endorsing class struggle, and the requirement that priests form political movements. They stated that there is "no middle ground between capitalism and socialism" as proposed by the Christian Democratic Party. The "Cuban revolution and the Chilean transition toward socialism" are the best and most hopeful models available to achieve socialism, they said, since these "propose a return to the wellsprings of Marxism and a criticism of traditional Marxist dogmatism."

Torres (1988) recalls of the 1972 conference: "Christians for Socialism was at its peak then. The Allende government gave us much media attention in Chile. So, we were relatively small in number, but had an enormous impact." At its peak, approximately 300, or 12 percent of Chile's 2,500 priests, were members of Christians for Socialism (Smith 1982: 232). The experience of convergence and interaction at this meeting was as important as the substance of the final declarations in generating insurgent consciousness among Latin American Catholics. The April 1972 meeting of Christians for Socialism united on a continental level most of the participants of the national and regional meetings of 1970 and 1971, bringing together for the first time virtually all of those devoted to constructing a Latin American theology of liberation. Consequently, the identity of the network of theological elites that constituted the first generation of liberation theologians was established and unified around a consensus declaration for the first time at this meeting.

However, Christians for Socialism also set in motion powerful forces of opposition. To begin, although the Chilean bishops, acting moderately and prudently, did not actually publicly condemn the group until September 1973 (Smith 1982: 254), they presented opposition to Christians for Socialism at every stage. This opposition came in the form of increasingly critical pastoral letters and public statements, beginning with the initial response to the Eighty's original declaration and ending with the bishops' official condemnation in 1973 (Smith 1982: 241–47; Donoso Loero 1975: 199–205). Noting the heavy involvement of foreign priests in Christians for Socialism, in 1972 the Chilean bishops asked foreign priests "to remain on the margins of [Chile's] political affairs" since "they were in a country . . . not their own" (Smith 1982: 248). Criticisms also came from Chilean priests and theologians (LADOC 6:27–34).

In addition, Christians for Socialism provoked a strong reaction from Catholics outside of Chile who began to organize countermovement activities. Smith (1982: 247, 249) argues:

Paralleling the tensions that emerged within the Chilean Church over CpS [Christians for Socialism], there developed significant criticisms of liberation theology and Christians for Socialism both in Rome and in the Latin American Episcopal Conference (CELAM) in 1972 and 1973. Those opposed to efforts to assimilate Marxist theories and strategies within the Church also mobilized key resources of international Catholicism to block such a synthesis. . . . Those who were concerned about CpS's implications for the universal Church . . . also began to use the network of the Church to discredit it and mobilize resources to stop it. . . . The stronger the Christians for Socialism movement became . . . the more there arose criticisms both from the Vatican and from groups closely identified with the Latin American Bishops' Conference (CELAM) headquartered in Bogotá.

For example, the Belgian-turned-Chilean Jesuit Roger Vekemans, who had left Chile for Colombia a few days after Allende's victory, began to organize European resources to oppose Christians for Socialism and liberation theology (Sigmund 1988: 32; Smith 1982: 250; Lernoux 1980: 305–7).

Vekemans amassed considerable documentation on "the 80" and the new Christians for Socialism movement in Chile, and as early as July 1972 began to publish these materials in a new quarterly journal, *Tierra Nueva,* launched that year to offset the influence of what he considered extremely radical tendencies in the Latin American Church. . . . As a result a critical voice (and that of a powerful international Church figure) began to be heard throughout Latin America by mid-1972 regarding liberation theology and Christians for Socialism, and the Chilean case was singled out as his primary target to be discredited and destroyed. (Smith 1982: 251)[18]

Vekemans published and helped others publish a number of books criticizing the Christians for Socialism movement (Vekemans 1971, 1972, 1976; Donoso Loero 1975).

CELAM's Department of Social Action, headed by the increasingly conservative Cardinal Eugenio Sales of Brazil, began to react against Christians for Socialism and liberation theology:

In June 1972 the Episcopal Commission of the Department of Social Action in CELAM issued a strong criticism of the growing "political instrumentalization of the Church in Latin America." . . . The statement specifically criticized the documents for the April 1972 international convention of Christians for Socialism in Chile for purportedly justifying Marxist ideological and tactical infiltra-

tion of the Church. It concluded by suggesting that all the episcopal conferences throughout Latin America promote investigations
of where and how such methods were being employed in their own
countries to "destroy or weaken the institutional Church" or to
manipulate "small base communities, popular religiosity, and
Church organizations." (Smith 1982: 251)

Finally, Rome began to react against liberation theology:

> A document from the Holy See was sent to bishops and papal
> nuncios in 1972 warning against the implications of liberation
> theology. In December 1972 the Sacred Congregation for Catholic
> Education in Rome also sent a letter to the Latin American hierar-
> chy criticizing the "increased politicization of Catholic education"
> and the tendencies in CELAM-sponsored projects of "being ori-
> ented consciously or unconsciously in many cases toward ques-
> tioning, criticism, and flirting with negative ideologies." In early
> 1973, an apostolic visitor was sent from Rome to investigate criti-
> cisms against Bishop Leonidas Proaño of Riobamba, Ecuador, for
> purportedly moving too far in establishing socially committed
> base communities in his diocese. (Ibid., 252)

In short, liberation theology and Christians for Socialism,

> were encountering powerful opposing forces also operating
> through the transnational network of the Church. Money from
> West Germany, theological expertise from other parts of Latin
> America, and disciplinary warnings from Rome against leftist ten-
> dencies in the Church all combined to mount a major campaign
> against liberation theology and Christians for Socialism by the last
> year of Allende's presidency. Such an international Church con-
> text reinforced the growing antipathy of the Chilean bishops for
> these trends, and paved the way for their own strong condemna-
> tion of Christians for Socialism written during Allende's last
> months in office. (Ibid., 253)

Escorial

The first international, public exposition of liberation theology
was at the November 1969 SODEPAX conference in Campine, Switzerland. There Gustavo Gutiérrez and Rubem Alves gave their joint
presentation to Europeans and North Americans. Through their presentations, non–Latin Americans caught the first glimpse of the new
theological movement taking place in Latin America.

TABLE 8.9

PAPERS PRESENTED AT THE ESCORIAL CONFERENCE

Gustavo Gutiérrez, "Evangelism and the Praxis of Liberation"

Hugo Assman, "Christian Conscience and Extreme Situations in Social Change"

Juan Luis Segundo, "Theology and the Social Sciences," and "The Latin American Elites: a Human and Christian Problematic in the Presence of Social Change"

Enrique Dussel, "History of the Christian Faith and Social Change in Latin America," and "Present Features of Latin American Catholicism: a Consideration of its Historical Genesis"

José Comblin, "Movements and Ideologies in Latin America"

Segundo Galilea, "The Faith as the Critical Principle of Promotion of Popular Religiosity"

José Míguez Bonino, "Vision of Social Change and Their Theories of the Non-Catholic Christian Church"

Cándido Padín, "The Human Transformation of the Third World: Demand for Conversion"

Cecilio de Lorra, "Some Forces Concerning Liberating Education"

Gonzalo Arroyo, "Latin American Thought About Under-Development and External Dependency," and "Considerations on Under-Development in Latin America"

Juan Carlos Scannone, "The Necessity and Possibilities of a Socio-Culturally Latin American Theology," and "Theology and Politics: The Present Challenge Established For the Latin American Language of Liberation"

Renato Poblete, "Specific Forms of the Process of Secularization in Latin America"

Aldo J. Buntig, "Dimensions of Latin American Popular Catholicism and its Insertion in the Process of Liberation: Diagnosis and Pastoral Reflections"

Hector Borrat, "The Beatitudes and Social Change"

Noe Zevallos, "New Forms of Religious Life and Religious Communities in Latin America: I"

Manuel Edwards-Maria Aqudelo, "New Forms of Religious Life and Religious Communities in Latin America: II"

Ronaldo Ames Cobian, "Economic Factors and Political Forces in the Process of Liberation"

Source: Ediciones Sigueme 1973.

Liberation theology also made a public appearance at the CICOP (Catholic Inter-American Cooperation Program) meetings, sponsored by the United States Catholic Conference, which ran from 1964 through 1972. The purpose of CICOP was to bring together Latin Americans and important North Americans—"people from the Senate, the State Department, bishops, Rabbis, and so on, very important people"—to facilitate mutual understanding and dialogue (Poblete 1988). Under the direction of Michael Colonese, a progressive North American priest heading the Latin American Bureau of the USCC, many progressive and radical Latin Americans were included in the program. Among these were Gustavo Gutiérrez, Juan Luis Segundo, Paulo Freire, Julio de Santa Ana, Dom Hélder Camera, José Míguez Bonino, Luiz Alberto Gomez de Souza, Leo Mahon,

Samuel Ruiz García, Marina Bandeira, Gustavo Perez, Marcos Mc-Grath, Cecilio de Lora, Renato Poblete, Edmund Leising, and Rubem Alves (CICOP 1964–72). However, while papers on liberation theology were presented, for the liberation theology movement, not many important connections were made, communication networks built, or resources obtained (Poblete 1988; Gutiérrez 1988).

The first international event that did make a significant impact for the liberation theology movement was the theological conference, "Christian Faith and Social Change in Latin America," held between July 8 and 15, 1972, in Escorial, Spain. (For a list of some of the more important papers presented at Escorial, see table 8.9). This conference was sponsored by the Institute of Faith and Secularization, and was designed specifically to introduce European theologians to Latin American liberation theology (Poblete 1988). It was a major event: all of the Latin American liberation theologians were brought in and more than four hundred European theologians attended (Dussel 1988).

Escorial was the first of several international conferences that presented liberation theology outside of Latin America. These conferences were important because they gave the liberation theology movement important international recognition, linkages, and support.

Sucre

The political opportunity and organizational strength that the liberation theology movement enjoyed during the four years after 1968 were greatly curtailed in 1972. At the 1972 meeting of CELAM in Sucre, Bolivia, the conservative bishops organized for the first time significant opposition to the progressives and radicals. In elections, most of the CELAM officers associated with liberation theology were removed from their positions and replaced with moderate and conservative bishops. Alfonso López Trujillo, the bishop elected secretary general of CELAM, then purged almost all liberationist elements from all levels of the CELAM organization.

9

From Sucre to Puebla, 1972–1979

For liberation theology, 1972 to 1979 was a time of great opposition. Consequently, this period offers a chance to study the dynamics of a social movement facing attempts to control the effects of its earlier success.

The political process model maintains that the response of elites to the actions of challenger groups is likely to be negative, because it is typically not in the interest of elites for the challenger to succeed. According to the model, the effects of social control on a movement may vary. Depending on the situation, measures of control may either crush or strengthen a movement. It is of importance, therefore, to explore how and why forces of opposition affect the three conditions which shape the life of any social movement: political opportuity, organizational strength, and insurgent consciousness.

Sucre and the Conservative and Moderate Catholic Backlash

Sucre—the Fourteenth Ordinary Assembly of CELAM held on November 15–23, 1972, at Sucre, Bolivia—was a major turning point for the liberation theology movement. After Sucre, access to the organizational and doctrinal resources of CELAM was denied proponents of liberation theology.

Four issues were placed on the agenda for Sucre: (1) the general restructuring of CELAM; (2) the reelection of CELAM officers; (3) the future of CELAM's specialized institutes, such as IPLA, especially their financing; and (4) guidelines for pastoral practice (Dussel 1981: 223). These were issues fundamental to the future character and mission of CELAM.

189

Many conservative Catholics in Latin America were increasingly distressed about CELAM's support for liberation theology (Smith 1982: 247). Some began to organize responses.

In 1971, the Belgian Jesuit Roger Vekemans— previously an outspoken advocate of progressive social change (see Vekemans 1964)— set up an institute in Colombia, called the Research Center for the Development and Integration of Latin America (CEDIAL), to analyze liberation theology and groups like Christians for Socialism. CEDIAL was funded largely by foreign Catholic agencies, including Adveniat and the DeRance Foundation (Lernoux 1982, 421; German Theologians 1978; Quigley 1978).[1] CEDIAL began to publish its own journal, *Tierra Nueva,* which severely criticized liberation theology (Dussel 1981: 224; Berryman 1984b: 30).

In 1972, even some within CELAM had started to resist the overall direction of that organization. The June 23–25 meeting of the Department of Social Action, held in Rio de Janeiro, produced a letter that circulated among all of the social action committees of the national bishop's conferences warning about liberationist tendencies (Richard 1987: 151; SCCS 1973). *La Nación* of Buenos Aires (November 15, 1972), sensing this shift in temper, predicted that,

> after the Sucre assembly, CELAM will run on a more conservative track since bishops in several countries have been questioning the activities and pastoral approaches in some of the CELAM departments. Bishops here [in Argentina] and in Colombia, among others, have not disguised their displeasure with initiatives taken by that organization. (Quoted in Dussel 1981: 223)

Similarly, Catholic journalist, Hector Borrat, wrote:

> For the right wing, [Sucre] is the opportunity they have been waiting for and working towards to defeat the followers of Medellín. Will they, by electing new officers, succeed in effecting the shift that would turn Latin American bishops aside from the road opened up in 1968? (Dussel 1981: 223)

These predictions were well founded. At Sucre, Bishops Brandão Vilela and Marcos McGrath were voted out of office and other, more conservative, officers were elected to replace them. Archbishop Alfonso López Trujillo, of Colombia, became the secretary general of CELAM, bishop Luciano Duarte became president of the Department of Social Action, and bishop Antonio Quarracino became president of the Department of the Laity (Carroll 1987: 18).

López "lost no time in closing CELAM training institutes [i.e., IPLA], which had been giving courses to several hundred pastoral agents a year in the spirit of Medellín, and collapsing them down to one location in Colombia where it could be carefully watched" (Berryman 1984b: 30). He also replaced the progressive theologians, teachers, and staff of CELAM with more conservative counterparts (Medina 1980: 21). In effect, liberation theology was ousted from CELAM.[2]

The changes at Sucre do not simply reflect the personal politicking of López Trujillo, but a genuine backlash from the majority of Latin American bishops. López Trujillo represented a widespread desire among Latin American bishops at the time to retreat from Medellín.

The key to this shift at Sucre was the majority of moderate bishops. The moderates had backed the progressive bishops at Medellín. Afterwards, however, some of them began to suspect that they had been hoodwinked by the progressive organizers of Medellín, who appeared to have railroaded their agenda through. More importantly, many moderate bishops became disturbed by the radical consequences that Medellín produced among clergy and laity, especially Christians for Socialism, and so began to back away from Medellín.

Archbishop Eduardo Pironio, for example, once a supporter of the progressives, complained:

> Medellín is distorted because it is not interpreted in a context definitely evangelical . . . [but] is read in a context essentially sociological. . . . Some people are interested in presenting it as a nonexplainable temporalization or as an absurd incitement to violence. . . . The concept of liberation is quite distorted and also its demands are changed when it is purposely identified with violent revolution or guerrilla justice. (Quoted in López Trujillo 1977: 47–48)

Lernoux (1982: 44) explains this shift in attitude among the moderate bishops:

> The religious rebellion [after Medellín] gave the bishops a sharp jolt, and, under the influence of the conservatives among them (particularly the Colombians, who had raised the lone dissenting voice at Medellín), they began to worry about what they had wrought. The idea that Marxist analysis had been used by CELAM theologians and sociologists to reach some of the Medellín Conclusions was particularly galling—and confusing. While by now the bishops had no love for capitalism . . . [they were] wary of anything with socialist connotations. And then, of course, everyone could see what trouble . . . Cardinal Silva was having in Chile with Chris-

tians for Socialism. There was no telling where the Church would find itself if such shenanigans were allowed to continue.

In short, most moderate bishops had backed Medellín because they believed it would strengthen the Church. As they began to perceive that Medellín was actually threatening the Church, they started to withdraw their support for the Medellín strategy. Adriance (1984: 500) explains the underlying principle: "Innovations which were begun as a means of preserving the influence of the Church over society will not be permitted to go so far as to raise questions about the structure of the Church itself or the authority of the bishops."

Consequently, "after 1972 the progressive direction of the *Celamistas* [CELAM officers] largely ended and new personnel began to pursue a more cautious, spiritualizing tendency. . . . CELAM became increasingly less important to the spearheading groups that were guiding the church in the direction of change" (Cleary 1985: 45). For liberation theology this meant a significant, but temporary, contraction of political opportunity and weakening of organizational strength.

Military Repression

Opposition within the Church was matched by a backlash from outside. In the 1970s, Latin American military regimes repressed not only political organizations such as political parties, labor unions, and student groups, but also many Catholics engaged in progressive and radical pastoral activities.[3]

Ironically, this military reaction did not deal a death blow to liberation theology. Rather, it helped to save the movement from dissolution and to relegitimate its strategy.

> By 1972 many of the bishops were in hurried retreat. The progressive prelates who had engineered Medellín were voted out of their CELAM posts, and the think tanks that had nourished the theology of liberation were either closed or restaffed. The retreat might easily have become a rout had the region's armed forces not intervened in the nick of time, swinging the balance back in favor of Church progressives by unleashing a reign of terror unequaled in Latin American history. . . . [Consequently] many bishops came to the conclusion that they had been right after all to take a hard line at Medellín; only it now appeared that the Medellín documents had not been tough enough. (Lernoux 1982: 44–45, 47)

In this experience, the Brazilian Church had been the forerunner, encountering first the military repression that would later spread to many of the Latin American Churches. Beeson and Pearce (1984:90–91) describe the Brazilian experience:

Following the [1964 Brazilian] coup, the Church gradually discovered that it was impossible to remain in alliance with a regime whose ideology gave priority to a narrowly defined concept of national security rather than the goals of democracy, social justice and freedom. . . . The Church began to seek a new relationship with those who had been excluded from power. . . . There was an immediate reaction from the government—churches were invaded, Catholic radio stations and newspapers were censored, bishops, nuns, priests, as well as laymen and laywomen, were arrested, tortured and even killed. The Church was accused of subversion and of interfering in politics, instead of concerning itself exclusively with souls. . . . When the National Congress, trade unions and student organizations were closed, banned or placed under restriction, and the press censored, the Church found that it alone had the power to denounce violations of human rights, including police violence, torture, land evictions, neglect of urban housing and all the abuses carried out in the name of national security. Thus, and at times reluctantly, the Church became the mouthpiece of oppressed groups.

Jether Pereira Ramalho recalls (1988):

Repression was generalized in society, so the Catholic Church became a refuge. Political parties and trade unions were abolished. The press was censored. The only institution that had the moral position to fight was the Catholic Church. It became the only space for many people. Later, after the amnesty in Brazil, people moved back into trade unions; but then they were influenced by their time in the Church.

This experience of the Brazilian Church became the experience of the Catholic Church in much of Latin America in the 1970s. The first military coup was in Bolivia on August 21, 1971. Next came the Pinochet coup against Allende in Chile on September 11, 1973, and the coup in Argentina on March 24, 1976. In addition, existing military governments shifted rightward in Peru (August 28, 1975) and Ecuador (January 13, 1976). These came in addition to the previously existing repressive dictatorships of Somoza in Nicaragua (which ended in 1979), Stroessner in Paraguay, and Duvalier in Haiti (Dussel 1981: 222). "Only in Mexico, Colombia, Venezuela, and

Costa Rica did the mechanisms of formal democracy remain" (Berry-man 1987a: 97).

In some countries, the repression was fierce. Thousands of Catholics were threatened, arrested, tortured, kidnapped, exiled, and murdered (Lernoux 1982: 463). For example, in Argentina, "by the end of 1977 seventeen priests and nuns had been murdered, thirty were in prison, and the country's most outspoken bishop was dead, killed by security forces in a fake automobile accident" (Lernoux 1982: 345). Quigley (1987) recalls the atmosphere then:

> I remember talking with an Argentine seminarian in 1976 just after the killing of six people. He said that the word "Medellín" couldn't be mentioned, that the word itself had taken on so much political significance that "the Kremlin" was a more neutral term than "Medellín." Medellín had become the symbol of subversion, of communist infiltration.

In August 1976, forty-eight bishops and priests attending a Vatican-approved international pastoral meeting in Ecuador were arrested at gunpoint, abused, and interrogated for subversion. One of the bishops, Mariano Parra León, of Venezuela, collapsed with a heart attack (Lernoux 1982: 137–40). When the Chilean delegates later arrived home, they were detained and manhandled by the secret police in the Santiago airport (Cleary 1985: 147). Afterward, one of the bishops exclaimed about the event, "If this can happen to us, what happens to peasants, workers, and Indians when they are arrested?" (Dussel 1981: 225).[4]

According to an anonymous informant, for a number of years, in Guatemala, police seized the Bibles of Christians, shooting dead on the spot owners of those found with underlined passages from the book of Exodus or the Old Testament prophets—important passages in liberation theology.

In Chile, after the 1973 military coup, 140 Chilean priests were harassed, tortured, or expelled, and the organization Christians for Socialism was crushed (Gotay 1983: 71; Bouvier 1983: 61–63).[5] The military then launched a smear campaign against Santiago's moderate Cardinal Raul Silva (Lernoux 1982: 46; Escobar 1987).

According to Berryman (1987a: 101):

> How systematic and deliberate these attacks could be became clear in the leaked 1975 document of the Bolivian government under General Hugo Banzer. The "Banzer Plan" laid down procedures for discrediting progressive Church leaders and dividing the Church. Archbishop Jorge Manrique of La Paz was one of the

targets. Suggested tactics included planting subversive documents on church premises. Censoring or closing church papers and radio stations was suggested. This plan was later endorsed by some ten Latin American governments that sent delegations to the meetings of the Latin American Anti-Communist Confederation at its 1977 meeting.

A number of the leaders of the liberation theology movement were persecuted. In 1973, Enrique Dussel was placed second on the Argentine military's "death list" and his home was firebombed; he narrowly escaped to Mexico (Dussel 1988). Fifteen attempts were made to assassinate Dom Hélder Camera—all unsuccessful (Cox and Sand 1979: 57). In Brazil, Hugo Assman's life was threatened, so he fled to Chile. After the 1973 Pinochet coup in Chile, Assman, Pablo Richard, Sergio Torres, and many others involved with Christians for Socialism had to flee for their lives to Canada, Costa Rica, and Europe (Torres 1988; Richard 1988).

Comprehensive data on the extent of repression against the Church are unavailable because of censorship and poor communication (Lernoux 1982: 463). Nevertheless, more than a thousand *documented* cases of repression of well-known Christian leaders have been recorded (see table 9.1). And, while the repression against the Church that was widespread after 1968 subsided in 1972, it began again after Sucre, and increased in mid-1973 (see table 9.2).

These brutal military actions actually produced a positive outcome for the liberation theology movement. At Sucre, conservative and moderate bishops had begun to reverse the direction taken at Medellín, hoping to return the Church's strategy and external relations to a more moderate state. But the repression of military regimes against Catholics blocked that effort. The backlash against liberation theology from outside the Church neutralized that from inside the Church, and thereby opened new political opportunities.

The key to this reopening of political opportunity lay with the moderate bishops. Most of them were unsettled by the militant Catholic activists, socialist priests, and revolutionary rhetoric that Medellín seemed to produce. Christians for Socialism was particularly disturbing. However, these problems paled to insignificance in the face of ever increasing arrests, torture, murders, and expulsions of Catholic bishops, priests, nuns, and laity. Repression shifted their attention from control within the Church to the protection of pastoral workers in their countries.

Repression put the bishops on the defensive, generating an antagonism between Church and government that created a deep rift be-

TABLE 9.1

DOCUMENTED REPRESSION AGAINST THE CATHOLIC CHURCH: 1964–78

	Threatened/ Defamed	Arrested	Tortured	Killed	Kidnapped/ Disappeared	Exiled/ Expelled
Bishops	60	35	2	2	2	3
Priests	118	485	46	41	11	253
Religious	18	44	7	3	3	26
Laity	12	371	18	33	21	6
Groups	64	—	—	—	—	—
TOTAL	314	935	73	79	37	288

Source: Lernoux 1982, 466.

tween the two (Medina 1980: 25). Lernoux (1982: 45–46) explains this effect in the case of Chile:

> The Chilean experience . . . forced the Catholic Church in Latin America to take a good look at what was happening in its midst. Unlike Hélder Camera and the other bishops of northeastern Brazil who made no secret of their radical leanings, Chile's Cardinal Silva has always opposed Marxism. . . . Chile's military junta committed a terrible blunder when it launched a smear campaign against this aging but resolute man. The suggestion that Silva was unpatriotic . . . merely because he defended human rights focused the Latin American Church's attention on political realities as no amount of persecution of Hélder Camera had done. Camera was the "Red Bishop" of Brazil; Silva, a man of the middle. By attacking the political center of the Church, the military forced the moderates back into the ranks of the progressives.

In many cases, a radicalizing, escalating cycle of protest and repression—illustrated in the life of Oscar Romero—worked to push moderate bishops back to the side of progressives (Welna 1983: 253). Typically, military forces would arrest and possibly abuse or torture a radical priest or BEC leader. The local bishop, even if he was unsympathetic to the activities of that individual, would feel compelled to protect his own, and would register an official protest against the abuses. Military and government officials would take the bishop's protest as a sign of support for subversive activities and increase their repression. The bishop would protest more strongly and the military would respond in kind, sometimes threatening the bishop himself.

The bishop, now more personally involved and more offended than ever, would step up his protest, possibly enlisting the help of his fellow bishops to support him. Progressive and radical pastoral work-

TABLE 9.2

PERIODS OF INTENSE REPRESSION AGAINST THE CHURCH IN THE 1970s

	YEARS														
	1964	1965	1966	1967	1968	1969	1970	1971	1972	1973	1974	1975	1976	1977	1978
Argentina							■	■	■		■	■	■	■	■
Bolivia							■	■			■	■	■	■	
Brazil	■				■	■	■	■	■	■	■	■	■	■	
Chile											■	■	■	■	
Colombia				■				■		■	■	■			
Dominican Republic							■	■							
Ecuador								■	■		■		■		
El Salvador						■	■	■			■	■	■	■	■
Guatemala							■		■						■
Haiti							■								
Honduras									■		■	■	■		
Mexico								■	■			■	■		
Nicaragua						■	■	■			■	■	■	■	■
Panama									■						
Paraguay						■	■	■	■			■	■		
Peru						■	■	■	■						
Uruguay						■	■	■	■	■	■	■	■		
Venezuela							■	■	■						

Source: Lernoux 1982, 463–70. This table is based on data compiled by the Paris-based Bureau of Information on Latin America (DIAL) from human rights groups, Church social action groups, and Latin American and European publications.

ers would organize demonstrations of solidarity with their bishop. This would be interpreted by military governments as confirmation that the Church as a whole was dangerously subversive. Consequently, they would continue or expand their repression.

In the end, the bishop, who may originally have preferred closer alliances with government and military powers, would have become totally alienated from the military and government. Meanwhile, the bishop would have become an outspoken social critic, defender of the poor and oppressed, and leading champion of human rights and social justice.

Thus, many bishops concluded that the strategy of Medellín was right and justified after all. In this way, by reopening political opportunity, military regimes unintentionally saved the liberation theology movement from the conservatives within the Church. Alexander

Wilde (1979: 301) argues that the Church's commitment to the poor is, in part, "due . . . to the context of authoritarian military regimes. . . . The depth of the Church's new social commitments in different countries closely parallels the harshness of their regimes."

Social Control and Insurgent Consciousness

How did opposition from inside and repression from outside of the Church affect the insurgent consciousness of those in the liberation theology movement? One might assume that these forces of social control would have decreased such consciousness, but that was not the case.

Insurgent consciousness—the conviction that change is both imperative and possible—remained strong during the 1970s. The effect of opposition was not to extinguish it, but to change its form. The leaders and members of the liberation theology movement became more sober and persistent (Assman 1974). Without giving up hope, they realized that the struggle would be a longer and more difficult one than they had originally expected (see, for example, Peruvian Theologians 1978). Sergio Torres (1988) recalls: "In 1970, we thought that revolution led by the vanguard was imminent; after 1973 we became more realistic and changed our strategy."[6]

Forces of social control exercised by opponents can sometimes strengthen a social movement. This can happen in a number of ways. Excessive social control measures, if publicized, can shift the weight of moderate public opinion against the movement's opponents; repression may elicit increased support from the constituencies favoring the social movement and sympathetic audiences; and social control can convince activists that their movement is a genuine threat to their opponents and, therefore, that their actions stand a chance of success (Marx 1979). All three possibilities occurred in the case of the liberation theology movement.

When moderate bishops experienced the brutal repression of the Church by military and government powers, many of them shifted their support back to the liberation theology movement. Latin American bishops began issuing documents and pastoral letters of protest, many using the language of "liberation" (see table 9.3). Moreover, argues Cleary (1985: 156),

> The bishops did not stop with simply calling for an end to repression and torture. More importantly, they urged secular leaders to make more radical changes: to effect a more equitable distribution of land and other resources, to respect workers organizations,

TABLE 9.3

SELECTED BISHOPS' DOCUMENTS AGAINST REPRESSION

Condemnation of Violence (Argentina, 1971)
Declaration Against Torture (Argentina, 1971)
Violence Breeds Violence (Uruguay, 1972)
I Have Heard the Cry of My People (Brazil, 1973)
Exhortation for Liberty, Justice, and Peace (Bolivia, 1973)
Marginalization of the People, Cry of the Churches (Brazil, 1973)
The Indian: Those Who Are Dying (Brazil, 1973)
Declaration of the Episcopal Conference (Paraguay, 1975)
Do Not Oppress Your Brother (Brazil, 1975)
Socio-Political Conflict in Latin America (Brazil, 1975)
Communiqué on the Expulsion of Priests (Bolivia, 1975)
The Bishops and Repression (Ecuador, 1976)
Mass for the Murder of John Bosco (Brazil, 1976)
United in Hope (Guatemala, 1976)
Amidst Persecutions and Consolations (Paraguay, 1976)
Open the Path of the Good Samaritan (Chile, 1976)
A Christian Reflection for the People (Argentina, 1977)
The Hope That Unites Us (Chile, 1977)
The Call to End Violence and Promote Justice (El Salvador, 1977)
Christian Requirements for a Political Order (Brazil, 1977)
Renewing Christian Hope (Nicaragua, 1977)
Declaration of Machala (Ecuador, 1977)
Gathering the Clamor (Peru, 1977)
Injustice in the Barrios (Venezuela, 1977)
On the Anniversary of the Death of Tupaj Katari (Bolivia, 1977)
Christian Celebration of Oppressed People (El Salvador, 1977)
Communiqué of the Archbishop of San Salvador (El Salvador, 1978)

Sources: Dussel 1981, 225; CEP 1978; LADOC 15; LADOC 16; Marins et al. 1978.

to allow greater participation in the social order for the rural and urban poor, and to enforce laws impartially. This vision led the way to the setting up of a whole new series of social and pastoral programs at the grass-roots level and the establishment of church-sponsored organizations for the defense of human rights.

Hence it is clear that the opinion of moderate bishops shifted against the movement's opponents.

Repression also brought increased resources from constituencies sympathetic to the movement. We will see below that the movement was able to survive organizationally, in part through the support of sympathetic external agencies, such as the World Council of Churches.

Finally, repression convinced the leaders of the liberation theology movement that they were on to something important. To be ignored means one is irrelevant. To be repressed means one is threatening. To be repressed so extensively and brutally means that one represents a serious threat to one's opponent, who must perceive that the movement actually stands a chance of success. Such a realization can be heartening to the repressed.

Enrique Dussel (1988) conveys the determination—or from a critic's point of view, stubbornness—of liberation theologians after Sucre:

> After 1972, liberation theologians began to suffer repression not only from governments but also from within the Church. The effect of this, however, was to make the theologians more able to identify with the poor of Latin America. Later, Rome believed it could criticize one theologian to hurt us. It was a mistake. This type of condemnation only gives us publicity. Liberation theologians are repressed, poorly paid, threatened, and so on—all of our biographies are the same in this way. But we are happy because we know that history is on our side. We are like a group of close brothers; there is a special, strong bond among us. So, we refuse to allow ourselves to be thrown out of the Church—it is our Church and we'll stay there.

Santa Ana speaks simlarly of this strong fraternal bond among liberation theologians:

> Our close relationships are even now [1988] helping to write a massive, coordinated collection of books on liberation theology. Today a group of about 100 theologians come together every year from all over Latin America, and there is a power of convocation. This is very important. In Europe this had only happened once, for a short time, between Barth, Brunner, and so on. However, very quickly that group broke. But we liberation theologians have been working closely together for almost twenty years.

One indicator of the continuation of insurgent consciousness among liberation theologians is increased development of the movement's ideology. Repression did not curtail the writing of liberation theology. Rather, in the 1970s, the theology of liberation grew in volume, scope, and maturity (Berryman 1987a: 101–2; Richard 1987a: 152–54; Cleary 1985: 49; McGovern 1980: 203).

As part of this growth, a second generation of liberation theolo-

TABLE 9.4
SECOND GENERATION LIBERATION THEOLOGIANS

Julio Barriero	Noel Leo Erskine	Antonio Perez-Esclarin
Clodovis Boff	Antonio Fragroso	Hernandez Pico
Leonardo Boff	Gilberto Gorgulho	George Pixley
José Oscar Beozzo	Tom Hanks	Jon Sobrino
Christian Brecht	João B. Libanio	Elsa Tamez
Ernesto Cardinal	Otto Maduro	
Beatriz M. Couch	Carlos Mesters	
Ignacio Ellacuría	José P. Miranda	

Source: Ferm 1986; Comblin, n.d.; Gibellini 1979.

gians joined the ranks of the first, and helped continue the work of reformulating the Christian gospel in the light of Latin America's poverty and oppression (see table 9.4). With this near doubling of the size of the movement's leadership network, the liberation theology movement's organizational capacity and insurgent consciousness were sustained, if not increased.

Pastoral Diffusion of Liberation Theology

Part of the reason for the sustained insurgent consciousness was the ever-growing spread of the movement at the grass-roots level. As Dussel (1988) remarks: "After 1972, liberation theology was able to survive because in every country, there were BECs, there were bishops with us, priests, nuns, religious, lay people—all on our side." The conservative reaction ousted progressive bishops and staff from CELAM; but it did not stop the spread of liberation theology among priests, brothers, nuns, and laity.

Many pastoral workers were, like the theologians, shaken by the opposition to Medellín. But, also like the theologians, their insurgent consciousness stayed alive. They, too, became more sober and realistic about their work. Berryman (1984b: 30) explains:

> As the meaning of [Sucre, and Pinochet's coup] sank in, the mood among pastoral agents shifted. It was clear that before "liberation" came there would be a long period of "captivity." One frequently heard remarks like "We may not see it, but we're working for our grandchildren." Characteristic of this new phase was a concentration on quiet, steady work on the local level, especially with basic Christian communities.

In the four years after Medellín, largely through the institutes of

CELAM, movement leaders spread the basic ideas of liberation theology to thousands of pastoral workers all over Latin America. Many
of these workers embraced liberation theology and helped to diffuse
it to the Catholic laity of their parishes. Cleary (1987) explains how
this often happened:

> A great many of the pastoral workers involved in base communi-
> ties began reading liberation theology and realized that this is
> where they were headed, that it fit the kind of people they were
> dealing with. They had previously used foreign catechetical mate-
> rials which didn't have much appeal: filmstrips with all white faces,
> for example, which had nothing to do with Latin cultures. They
> began to want Latin American material. Then liberation theology
> came along at just the right time and they said "if only I had a
> catechism made out of this; I would much rather use this libera-
> tion stuff." So they translated liberation theology into catechisms.
> In this way, pastoral workers were mediators between liberation
> theology and local catechism and liturgy. There was a great deal of
> activity back and forth; the energy in the field was incredible.
> Before they said, "Oh yeah, let's just use this European manual."
> But when liberation theology came out, it really resonated with
> the pastoral workers. And even though they may have perceived
> inadequacies in it, they were still willing to use it.

By the early 1970s, the liberation theology movement was well
established at the grass-roots level. Many pastoral workers and laity by
then understood its basic ideology and were committed to implementing its strategy for social change. For example, in a 1975 opinion poll taken in Chile, 34.8 percent of priests, 36.4 percent of nuns,
and 36 percent of laity surveyed indicated unqualified agreement
with the statement "the theology of liberation offers a valid image of
the Catholic faith of the Latin American people." Only 16.7 percent
of the bishops surveyed agreed with that statement (see table 9.5).

This development, in addition to the military repression, put
those in the Church hierarchy who wanted to back away from
Medellín in a difficult position. In 1968 they had officially validated
a movement which, in 1972, could not be stopped with a simple
"changing of the guard" at CELAM. The liberationist genie, so to
speak, was out of the bottle.

Thus many moderate bishops came to realize that, "to renounce
that commitment [to social justice] would be akin to institutional
suicide, particularly since so many priests and nuns—those responsible for the day-to-day functioning of the Church—had chosen to

TABLE 9.5

VALIDITY OF THE THEOLOGY OF LIBERATION (CHILE, 1975): "DO YOU FEEL THAT THE THE-
OLOGY OF LIBERATION OFFERS A VALID IMAGE OF THE CATHOLIC FAITH OF THE LATIN AMER-
ICAN PEOPLE?" (N = 176)

	% Bishops (N = 24)	% Priests (N = 69)	% Nuns (N = 33)	% Laity (N = 50)
Yes	16.7	34.8	36.4	36.0
Yes but only for an elite or sector of the people	20.8	11.6	12.1	4.0
No	45.8	30.4	18.2	20.0
In the sense of liber-ation from sin, yes; in a political or social science sense, no	16.7	17.4	9.1	2.0
Don't know, no answer	—	5.8	24.2	38.0

Source: Smith 1982.

work with the poor" (Lernoux 1982: 50). The observation of a Carmelite priest working in a massive slum outside of Lima, Peru, who
asked to remain anonymous, illustrates this predicament:

> They can't stop liberation theology; it's too late. They can make all
> the bishops Opus Dei, but we're the ones with the people and
> we're not going to change. Still, it's helpful to have a sympathetic
> bishop to serve as a protection. But ultimately, if we want to obey,
> fine, if not, fine. Basically, there's a lot of room to work because
> there are too many people and too few of us clergy. They [the
> bishops] can't screw around with us, they need us. If I leave, there
> will be forty thousand people without a pastor. So, often they can't
> officially agree with us, but they let us go anyway.

Once again, the shortage of clergy had worked to perpetuate the
momentum of the liberation theology movement.

Further remarks of this priest reveal how much influence these
pastoral workers had with the people because of their work among
them:

> Some Marxists came to our shanty during elections and began
> mouthing all this garbage, like "The Church is the opium of the
> people!" I just asked: "Where were you before the elections? Did

you bring water to the people? Did you organize a kitchen to feed the poor? Did you bring lawyers in to defend human rights? Where the hell were you?" We ran them out of the shanty.

Military repression, we have seen, had a strange way of bolstering the commitment of the liberation theology movement's leaders. Similarly, external repression was an ingredient in the mix of forces which caused BECs to spread so rapidly in the 1970s (Libanio 1985). When authoritarian governments closed or censored opposition political movements, student groups, the press, and labor unions, the Church was often the only institution left capable of voicing opposition. It then became a refuge for persecuted progressives and leftists—Christian and non-Christian alike (Poblete 1988). BECs played a key role in providing this space for dissidents, and offered an atmosphere of hope for poor Catholic laity. Berryman (1987a: 99–100) explains:

> The most important development within the church during this period was the quiet, steady growth of base communities. They provided a space in which people could meet in an atmosphere of respect and reaffirm their own faith and hope. Where the media were censored and intimidated and where governments and armies imposed their ideology of national security, the base communities provided a small space where the truth could be spoken, even if guardedly. In a situation that seemed to offer no human reason for believing things could be different, their message was that things could change. They became a space where poor people could "speak their word" and where they heard that God was in their side.

Because they met this need so well, the number of BECs swelled in the 1970s to almost 200,000.

Reorganizing and Internationalizing the Movement

Secretary General López Trujillo's restructuring of CELAM after Sucre left the liberation theology movement significantly weakened in its organization. With the consequent loss of institutional resources, communication channels, and enterprise tools, movement leaders had to re-group and generate other means of maintaining organizational strength. While few other arrangements could offer the abundant resources that CELAM did from 1968 to 1972, liberation theologians were able to create alternatives to sustain the movement's organization through the 1970s.

This transition was greatly aided by the fact that most of the movement's leaders had never relied on CELAM as their sole source of financial support. Had it been otherwise, it is doubtful that the movement could have survived such a drastic loss. For the liberation leaders, Sucre did not mean expulsion from the Church institution, a cutting off of the means of livelihood. Rather, it meant having to shift to another place in the same institution.

Pironio, Brandão, and McGrath were still bishops; they simply returned to the duties of their diocese. Gutiérrez, Dussel, Segundo, and other liberation theologians were still priests; they returned to working in their parishes and as staff advisers to their bishops. Many liberation theologians held teaching positions in universities. Others worked in research centers or international church organizations. The few who did lose jobs in the CELAM shake-up were quickly employed by the sympathetic organization CLAR, the Latin American Confederation of Religious (Lernoux 1979: 420).

The problem, then, was not how to provide financial support for the leaders, but rather how to organize the tasks of national and international communication and education necessary to maintain the movement's momentum. In time, the liberation theologians were able to solve that problem.

First, they continued to use existing religious periodicals and journals to publish new articles. In this way, theologians were able to communicate developments in their own thinking to other theologians and to pastoral workers.

Second, some liberation theologians founded their own publishing companies. For example, the Brazilian Franciscan Leonardo Boff, who came from a wealthy family, founded *Editora Vozes, Ltda.* in Petrópolis, Brazil, to publish and distribute new works of liberation theology. Also, the *Centro de Estudios y Publicaciones* of Lima, Peru, and Pablo Richard and Franz Hinkelammert's *Departmento Ecumenico de Investigaciones* in San Jose, Costa Rica published numerous titles in liberation theology.

Third, some religious orders offered a sympathetic organizational infrastructure for liberation theology. Because of the semiautonomous status of religious orders vis-à-vis the Vatican and bishops, they provided especially good protection against opposition and good communication channels for liberation theologians. Dussel (1988) explains:

> Rome can dominate bishops, but they can't do a coup d'etat of the Jesuits. The religious orders for us liberation theologians in Latin America are very important, and CLAR is important too. Religious

TABLE 9.6
LIBERATION THEOLOGY RESEARCH & TRAINING INSTITUTES

Founder/Director	Institute Name	Location
Enrique Dussel	CEHILA	Quito
Gustavo Gutiérrez	Bartolome de Las Casas Center	Lima
Juan Luis Segundo	Peter Faber Center	Montevideo
Julio de Santa Ana	CECEP	São Paulo
Pablo Richard	DEI	San José
Jether Ramalho	CEDI	Rio de Janeiro
Uriel Molina	Antonio Valdevieso Center	Managua

orders made the Church a complex institution which gave us many places to reside and survive.

Fourth, liberation theologians founded their own research and training institutes (Compton 1984: 36–37; see table 9.6). Dussel (1988) comments, "We liberation theologians were excluded after 1972. But we learned. We founded new Centers, gave many courses, and began new institutes. We developed our own institutes like IPLA, a number of them."

Fifth, movement leaders began to internationalize the movement. They set up international communication and resource ties that worked to support the movement. For example, they began publishing their work overseas. A major publisher was Orbis Books, operated by the Catholic Maryknoll Order, of Maryknoll, New York. In the 1970s, Orbis published more than one hundred works of liberation theology in English. Works in this field were translated into many other languages as well. Gustavo Gutiérrez's book, *A Theology of Liberation,* for example, was translated and published in twelve different languages.

Movement leaders also received financial support from foreign agencies to fund their research centers and educational work. Liberation theologians obtained support from the World Council of Churches, the National Council of Churches (U.S.A.), the United States Catholic Conference, North American Protestant denominations—especially the Methodists and Lutherans—the Maryknollers, German Catholic funding agencies, and others (Torres 1988). Pablo Richard (1988) explains the rationale: "Sure there are lots of agencies that finance our work. The third world dialogue is financed by the first world. But that is an obligation: they financed colonialization, they must finance decolonialization."[7]

Finally, movement leaders organized a number of international

TABLE 9.7

MAJOR INTERNATIONAL LIBERATION THEOLOGY CONFERENCES

Year	Place
1975	Mexico City, Mexico
1975	Detroit, Michigan
1976	Dar es Salaam, Tanzania
1977	Mexico City, Mexico
1977	Accra, Ghana
1977	Detroit, Michigan
1979	Wennappuwa, Sri Lanka
1980	São Paulo, Brazil
1981	New Delhi, India
1986	Oaxtepec, Mexico

Sources: DEI 1982; Torres and Fabella 1978; Dussel 1981, 432.

theological conferences on liberation theology in North America, Africa, Latin America, and Asia, which were atttended by major theologians from around the world (see table 9.7). According to Sergio Torres (1988), "many, though not all, of the leaders of Latin American liberation theology attended these conferences." These conferences were organized by the Ecumenical Association of Third World Theologians, of which Sergio Torres became the general secretary. Torres (1988) states that, because of the external financial support, "unlike earlier meetings on liberation theology, in 1971 and 1972, this time no theologians wanting to attend had to beg for money from their bishops, it was all provided for."

The August 10–15, 1975 Mexico City conference, "Liberation and Captivity," was organized by Enrique Dussel, who was in exile there from Argentina. It was attended by 700 people, including European theologians. Almost every Latin American liberation theologian participated, including José Comblin, Enrique Dussel, Juan Luis Segundo, Leonardo Boff, Jon Sobrino, Edgar Beltran, Cándido Padin, Sergio Méndez Arceo, Samuel Ruiz García, Alberto Gomez de Souza, Luis del Valle, Miguel Concha, Raul Vidales, Vincente Cosmão, Luis Fernandez, J. M. Vargas, and Javier Lozano (Ediciones Paulinas 1984: 447).

The Detroit Conference, held in August 1975, was called "Theology in the Americas." It followed immediately after the Mexico City conference and was organized by Sergio Torres, who was in exile in Maryknoll, New York, from Chile.[8] Again, the majority of the Latin American liberation theologians attended, and presentations were given by José Miguez Bonino, Juan Luis Segundo, Gustavo Gutiérrez,

Enrique Dussel, José Porfirio Miranda, Sergio Torres, Hugo Assman, Leonardo Boff, Javier Iguíñiz, and Beatriz Melano Couch (Torres and Eagleson 1976). The conference was attended by North American mainline, black, feminist, and Hispanic theologians, including Avery Dulles, Gregory Baum, Fredrick Herzog, John Coleman, Joseph Holland, Rosemary Ruether, James Cone, Sheila Collins, Beverly Harrison, and Manuel Febres (Torres and Eagleson 1976).

The Detroit conference challenged the Latin Americans to stretch their thinking. Robert McAfee Brown (1988) remembers their interaction with North American feminists:

> In Detroit, the Latin Americans were as macho as anyone, not aware of the problem of the liberation of women. It was the North American women who really put that question to them for the first time. So they learned something about a whole arena of oppression in their own societies that hadn't occurred to them before. And, if you look at where they stand today on this issue, the change is unbelievable. So the conscientization was not only one-way.

The Latin Americans challenged the North Americans as well. Again, Brown remembers:

> In Detroit, the North American blacks said clearly that they weren't interested in economic analysis because the real issue was not economics but racism. However, as a result of the feedback from the Latin Americans, in a short time the blacks began to take the economic analysis more seriously. Today economic analysis is very important to them.

After Mexico City and Detroit, Enrique Dussel and a student from Zaire had the idea of expanding these conferences to include Africans and Asians. They explored this possibility with Belgian sociologist François Houtart and later proposed the idea to Sergio Torres, who by then was very experienced at organizing these kinds of events (Gibellini 1988: 61–62). Torres liked the idea, and created the Ecumenical Association of Third World Theologians. Under the sponsorship of that organization, he organized the international conferences in Tanzania, Ghana, Sri Lanka, Brazil, and India .

These international conferences served to broaden and deepen the theological reflection of the Latin Americans. They provided the Latin Americans with new international contacts, and strengthened insurgent consciousness when the Latin Americans came to believe that the struggle they initiated at home was part of a much broader struggle around the world. Through these conferences they came to perceive that they were not only fighting for Latin America, but for

TABLE 9.8

AFRICAN AND ASIAN LIBERATION-ORIENTED THEOLOGIANS

Carlos H. Abesamis (Philippines)	Jean-Marc Ela (Cameroun)
Samuel Amirtham (India)	Sebastian Kappen (India)
C. G. Arevalo (Philippines)	Kosuke Koyama (Thailand)
Charles Avila (Philippines)	Ting Kuang-Hsun (China)
Tissa Balasuriya (Sri Lanka)	Geevarghese Mar Osthathios (India)
Allan Boesak (South Africa)	Samuel Rayan (India)
Manas Buthelezi (South Africa)	Choan-Seng Song (Taiwan)
Kim Chung-Choon (South Korea)	Desmond Tutu (South Africa)
Edicio de la Torre (Philippines)	Kim Yong-Bok (South Korea)

Sources: Ferm 1986; Gibellini 1988.

the whole of the Third World, a thought which strengthened their sense of mission.

Through the influence of the Latin Americans at these conferences, liberation theology began to spread to other Third World theologians. A number of Africans and Asians began writing theology in response to their particular social contexts—such as the Marcos Regime in the Philippines and Apartheid in South Africa—with a general liberationist orientation (see table 9.8).[9] Liberation theology did not take these regions by storm. Indeed, liberation theology remained a primarily Latin American phenomenon. Still, within a decade of Medellín, the liberation theology movement had established important international support and communication channels.

The Battle for Puebla

At the end of the 1970s, CELAM scheduled a meeting which opened the possibility that Medellín might be officially and permanently reversed, and the liberation theology movement terminated. This was the Third General Conference of the Latin American Bishops, CELAM III, held in Puebla, Mexico, from January 27 to February 13, 1979. The meeting's title was "Evangelization in the Present and the Future of Latin America." Medellín had been called to apply Vatican II to Latin America; Puebla was similarly convened to apply Pope Paul VI's 1974 apostolic exhortation *Evangelii Nuntiandi* to Latin American reality (Berryman 1979: 60; Galilea 1978: 72).[10]

However, unlike Medellín, control over the organization of Puebla was in the hands of three powerful opponents of liberation theology: Belgian Jesuit and CELAM staff member Roger Vekemans, the president of the Roman Curia's Pontifical Commission for Latin America,

Cardinal Sebastiano Baggio, and CELAM General Secretary Alfonso López Trujillo (Lernoux 1982: 413).[11] Representing a more conservative perspective, these three hoped to undercut, if not terminate, the liberation theology movement at Puebla (Sandoval 1979: 28–31; Lernoux 1979: 23; 1982: 422).[12] Alberto Methol Ferre, one of the advisors who helped write Puebla's preliminary document (MacEoin and Riley 1980: 56), expressed the post-1972 CELAM view on liberation:

> Liberation without evangelization is the breech through which secularism penetrates. . . . The secularists [i.e., some liberation theologians] want to talk about a liberation without evangelization. Those of them who are still priests want to leave evangelization as a second concern. And, when evangelization is made a primary concern, they automatically claim that "the liberation of the poor is forgotten" and that one is "over-spiritualizing." Puebla, which specifically concerns evangelization, should properly put evangelization as a first concern, without diminishing the secondary importance of liberation. Evangelization is the source of liberation—and not the inverse. Rather, the inverse corrupts true liberation. (Methol Ferre 1979: 114–15)

The strategy, then, was not to oppose and condemn overtly the idea of liberation, but to reshape the meaning of liberation according to their view, and to subordinate it to the work of evangelization.

Conservatives saw themselves as correcting serious theological and political errors and distortions in the Church. Liberation theologians, however, viewed the conservatives as attempting to co-opt and mutilate the central Christian imperative of liberation. The progressive bishops and liberation theologians recognized their vulnerability, and strove to prevent the liberation theology movement from being undermined. Thus, the preparations for Puebla, and Puebla itself, reflected the ongoing struggle within the Church over the liberation theology movement (Bouvier 1983: 20; Berryman 1979: 82).

Phillip Berryman (1987a: 103–4), who attended Puebla, describes the dynamics among bishops:

> The Puebla conference may be seen as a clash between three mind-sets among the bishops. On the one side were conservatives who stressed hierarchical authority and doctrinal orthodoxy and were consciously combatting liberation theology for what they saw as its Marxism. At the other extreme was a group that might be called liberationists. . . . The largest group might be called centrists and was most concerned with church unity. . . . These cen-

trists played a leading role in leading the conference itself while conservatives and liberationists lobbied, changing wording, adding to some passages, objecting to others.

Using a strategy similar to that of the progressives who organized Medellín, López orchestrated Puebla to increase his chances of success (Costa Rican Ecumenical Council 1978). His specific tactics, however, more closely resembled those typically used by the Vatican bureaucracy. The organizers of Medellín had worked somewhat surreptitiously before, during, and after the conference to acquire and act upon authorization from bishops for a program the implications of which many of the bishops did not entirely understand and may not have endorsed had they understood. López's tactics were more straightforward: at Puebla, he simply loaded the meeting, excluded opposition, and pushed ahead with orthodoxy. According to Cleary (1985: 47), "Medellin was a conference controlled in large part by experts; Puebla was a conference controlled by the bishops." The liberation theologians, not to be outmaneuvered, devised countertactics to try to make an impact on the conference.[13]

Many countries had offered to host the meeting, including Brazil, Mexico, Puerto Rico, and Italy. López choose Puebla for its huge seminary, set within an eighty-acre campus surrounded by a stone wall over ten feet high which served to isolate the bishops from outsiders. Passage in and out was tightly controlled by guards (Sandoval 1979: 29; Kirby 1981: 101).

According to Sandoval (1979: 30), "if nothing had been left to chance in selecting Puebla and the Palafoxiano seminary, the delegates were chosen with equal care. . . . [López and Baggio] made sure that the delegate-selecting processes they controlled brought in mainly conservatives." López and Baggio requested and obtained papal approval for an additional 181 nonvoting delegates, to be selected by themselves. Thus, "of the 365 delegates, only 175 were elected by the national bishops' conferences. The majority of the other 181 . . . were chosen by López Trujillo; most were conservatives" (Lernoux 1982: 422; see also MacEoin and Riley 1980: 54–57; Ferm 1986: 55).[14]

Many of Latin America's leading progressive bishops were not invited or elected to participate, including Pedro Casaldáliga, Arturo Rivera y Damas, Jaime Francisco, Samuel Ruiz García, José Parra León, Sergio Mendez Arceo, Antonio Batista Fragoso, Marcelo Pinto Carvcalhiera, José Maria Pires, Alberto Devoto, and Tomas Balduino (Sandoval 1979: 31). And, all of the twenty-five or thirty progressive bishops that did attend "were placed in groups with carefully picked conservative counterparts so as to neutralize their effect on the process" (Cox and Sand 1979: 58; MacEoin and Riley 1980: 58).[15]

Furthermore, López decided to not invite representatives from the Latin American Confederation of Religious (CLAR), which backed the theology of liberation by employing theologians and social scientists expelled from CELAM after Sucre. However, on this action, the President of CELAM, Cardinal Aloisio Lorscheider, protested, threatening to resign his post if CLAR was not invited. Conceding, Baggio sent a belated invitation to CLAR to send seventeen representatives (Lernoux 1982: 420–21).

Finally, all of the liberation theologians were excluded. In a reversal of the tactics used to make Medellín, of the *periti* appointed by Trujillo, "all but one of the theologians and sociologists were hostile to the theology of liberation" (Lernoux 1979: 422; see also Berryman 1979: 62). Renato Poblete—a progressive—remarks (1988): "At Puebla, many bishops were wary about staff advisers because the saying was that Medellín was not written by bishops. They were afraid—afraid of confrontation. So, people like Gutiérrez were not there, even though he should have been." Dussel (1988) states: "Of course, the exclusion of the totality of liberation theologians was an injustice. How can a church exclude its theologians?"

In July and August of 1977, CELAM held four regional meetings of various national episcopates.[16] The concerns and perspectives of the attending bishops were discussed and recorded, and were later integrated into a working document for Puebla (Poblete 1979: 50; CELAM 1978). In November 1977 CELAM wrote and in December 1977, it released this 214-page preliminary document of CELAM III, which came to be known as the "Green Book" (Monni and Grieco 1978). This statement contained an analysis of the Latin American situation that was unsympathetic to the liberationist perspective. The Green Book evoked some support and much criticism from bishops, theologians, and laity throughout Latin America (Cleary 1985: 47; Levine, ed. 1986: 194–95; Kirby 1981: 99–101; MacEoin and Riley 1980: 34–53; Lernoux 1979: 417).[17]

On the one hand, the Columbian hierarchy, for example, responded favorably to the CELAM document. In a report detailing their own situation and position, they argued that the very existence of the Church is threatened by attempts "to question the age-old structures of the Church, and to begin only from the people, from their values, struggles, and contradictions; to rethink faith only from the perspective of the commitment to liberation of the poor and oppressed; to revive prophetic charisms in the very heart of existing ecclesiastical institutions, in order then to condemn anything not in line with these premises" (quoted from Levine, ed. 1986: 194–95).

On the other hand, many other bishops and national bishops' conferences criticized the Green Book as "weak," "confusing," and "superficial," and failing to deal with the principal challenges of the Church (Rosales 1979: 60; Lernoux 1979: 23). Progressive bishop Dom Pedro Casaldáliga called it "an encyclopedia of everything and nothing." Bishop Pinera, speaking for the Chilean bishops, said, "It does not reflect the Church's immediate historical perspective and fails to analyze the development of the continent over the past several years" (Rosales 1979: 62). The Brazilian bishops drafted an alternative document containing 128 specific recommendations for changes and additions (Lernoux 1979: 417). Liberation theologians met in Venezuela in early 1978 and published two communiqués criticizing the Green Book from a liberationist point of view, arguing that it ignored the poor and the need for a new society (Berryman 1979: 62).

In response to criticisms, López Trujillo published an article defending the Green Book, entitled "On The Poor: Neglect or Redemption?" (López Trujillo 1980: 263). In it he contended that the document could be understood as neglecting the poor only by revolutionary Marxists:

> The document obviously emphasizes a new society, justice, and solidarity, penetrated by the values of a *loving civilization*. But clearly, the document does ignore the poor, especially in the area of evangelization, if one's main concern is the revolutionary power of the proletariate. And, it does ignore the new society, but only if one views the kingdom of God as the promise of Marxist socialism. Isn't this the crux of the difference [between the document and its critics]? (López Trujillo 1980, 273)

Because of the controversy it stirred, the Green Book became a best seller in Latin America. And, the issues it raised were hotly discussed in BECs, university groups, labor unions, peasant federations, women's movements, and so on (Lernoux 1982: 418; 1979: 23–24).

In response to the feedback received on the Green Book, a small group of bishops met at CELAM headquarters in Bogotá in mid-1978 to rewrite the working document for Puebla. This group wrote under the direction of CELAM's president, Cardinal Lorscheider. The rewritten version was shorter and emphasized more heavily the Church's commitment to social justice in the spirit of Medellín (Lernoux 1979: 24; 1982: 419).

Understanding the threat and opportunity of Puebla, liberation theologians worked to prepare for it as well. According to Dussel (1988):

We liberation theologians started to organize for Puebla in 1976, three years ahead. Puebla was a fantastic opportunity for us, so we worked very hard for this meeting. We organized sessions for each of the sections of the document. In each section, there was at least one bishop working with us. It was very fluid and authentic.

As Puebla drew near, tension and suspicion between the conservatives and liberationists increased (Libanio 1978; Nuñez 1985: 110). Liberation theologian Sergio Torres, still feeling underprepared, took steps to ensure the influence of liberation theology at Puebla. Lernoux (1982: 423) explains:

As fears and distrust mounted, Sergio Torres . . . set off on a ten-nation tour of Latin America to consult with the progressive bishops. Torres believed that the liberation theologians could contribute to Puebla, even though they had been officially excluded, by becoming personal advisors to bishops who would be attending the conference. . . . The plan found favor with a number of bishops in Brazil, Uruguay, Chile, Peru, Ecuador, Venezuela, Panama, and Guatemala, and twenty-two theologians and eight social scientists, comprising the continent's leading spokesmen for liberation theology, were unofficially invited to Puebla. Each had the personal protection of a bishop, as well as direct lines of communication into the conference through the progressive bishops.[18]

Puebla itself was a major event. Between two and three thousand journalists came to report on the conference. Pope John Paul II arrived to inaugurate the meeting. And an estimated twenty million people turned out to see the Pope during his five-day visit (Cleary 1985: 50; Berryman 1979: 55; Sandoval 1979: 32).[19]

Many priests and laity, including representatives of BECs, demonstrated outside the seminary walls in support of liberation theology (MacEoin and Riley 1980: 15, 82–87). Others demonstrated against liberation theology:

There were demonstrations by young people in the city streets chanting slogans like "Christianismo, si. Socialismo, no," and handing out leaflets saying: "Communism is a mask: it hides hunger, misery, crime, destruction, robbery, and death." One of these demonstrations called itself a "Popular Catholic Demonstration against the Marxist Theology of Liberation." Two different press conferences were held, one by a group called The Movement of Fathers of Families, and the other by the Chamber of Commerce, whose main aim was to denounce by naming cardinals, bishops, theologians, and priests accusing them of being Marxist and in "open rebellion against the pope." (Kirby 1981: 102; see also Sandoval 1979: 38)

In his addresses, the Pope tried to steer a conciliatory, middle course amid the conflict within the Latin American Church, calling for unity and faithfulness to the Church's true mission (Ferm 1986: 55). On the one hand, he expressed support for many of the concerns and aspirations of liberation theology (MacEoin and Riley 1980: 74). Calling for the bishops to "reflect seriously on the relationships and implications existing between evangelization and human promotion or liberation," the Pope affirmed the need for Christians "to serve the least of their brothers and sisters, the poor, the needy, the marginalized" and to participate in "humanizing systems and structures" (John Paul II 1979: 60, 66). He charged the bishops: "Do not be afraid. . . . To [Christ's] saving power open the boundaries of the State, economic and political systems, the vast fields of culture, civilization, and development" (61). And, he recognized that "an indispensable part of [the Church's] evangelizing mission is made up of works on behalf of justice and human promotion" (66).

Furthermore, the Pope expressed concern over the "materialistic" mechanisms of the global "ties of interdependence" which lead to "the ever increasing wealth of the rich at the expense of the ever increasing poverty of the poor," charging that "the growing affluence of a few people parallels the growing poverty of the masses" (67). John Paul II also affirmed the social obligations of private property, arguing that this principle "must lead to a more just and equitable distribution of goods" and that "if the common good demands it, there is no need to hesitate at expropriation itself, done in the right way" (67, 82).

Finally, the Pope condemned abuses of human rights, imploring the bishops to give attention to the many violations of human dignity in Latin America (65–66). He affirmed that the Church must act "in favor of brotherhood, justice and peace; and against all forms of domination, slavery, discrimination, violence, attacks on religious liberty, and aggression against human beings and whatever attacks life" (66).

However, on the other hand, the Pope issued clear and strong warnings against the dangers of the liberation theology movement (Schall 1982: 90–103; Sigmund 1988: 33; Novak 1986: 65–69). John

Paul (1979: 74) stated that Puebla's point of departure was Medellín, but noted that "there have been interpretations [of Medellín] that are sometimes contradictory, not always correct, and not always beneficial for the Church."

The Pope criticized "'re-readings' of the Gospel that are the product of theoretical speculations" (59). Some people, he noted,

> depict Jesus as a political activist, as a fighter against Roman domination and the authorities, and even as someone involved in class struggle. This conception of Christ as a political figure, a revolutionary, as the subversive from Nazareth, does not tally with the Church's catechesis. (60)

The Pope also criticized those for whom, "the Kingdom of God is understood in a rather secular sense: i.e., we do not arrive at the Kingdom through faith and membership in the Church but rather merely by structural change and sociopolitical involvement" (62). Against these views, the Pope declared: "it is a mistake to state that political, economic, and social liberation coincide with salvation in Jesus Christ; that the *regnum Dei* is identified with the *regnum hominis*" (ibid.).

The Pope affirmed the need for human liberation, but only "liberation" in its fullest, deepest sense. In his opening address at the conference, he stated:

> Pastoral commitments in this field must be nurtured with a correct Christian conception of liberation. The Church . . . has the duty of proclaiming the liberation of millions of human beings, . . . the duty of helping to bring about this liberation. But it also has the corresponding duty of proclaiming liberation in its deeper, fuller sense, the sense proclaimed and realized by Jesus. That fuller liberation is liberation from everything that oppresses human beings, but especially liberation from sin and the evil one. . . . It is a liberation that . . . cannot be reduced simply to the restricted domain of economics, politics, society, and culture. . . . [It] can never be sacrificed to the requirements of some political strategy, some short-term praxis or gain. . . . We must at all costs avoid reductionism and ambiguity. (68)

Alan Riding, of the *New York Times*, quoted the Pope as saying in an informal discussion:

> You know that liberation theology is a true theology. But perhaps it is also a false theology because if it starts to politicize theology, apply doctrines to political systems, ways of analysis which are not

Christian, then this is no longer theology. That is the problem. Theology of liberation, yes, but which one? (Quoted in Sandoval 1979: 33; see also MacEoin and Riley 1980: 70)

Finally, the Pope rejected the idea of "a people's Church, one which 'is born of the people' and is fleshed out in the poor" and "parallel magisteria, which are ecclesially unacceptable and pastorally sterile" (John Paul II 1979: 63, 65).

These warnings were clearly directed against liberation theology. Thus, Pope John Paul II attempted to rein in the radicals but, at the same time, where possible, express support for their cause, so as not to alienate them entirely, and further polarize the contentious situation (Schall 1982: 102).[20]

None of this was lost on the liberation theologians, all of whom came to Puebla. Along with supporters from Europe and North America, they took up residence at a convent three blocks away from the seminary (Torres 1988; Sandoval 1979: 35).[21] Dussel (1988) reports: "All the liberation theologians were there—perfect attendance! We considered it a duty to be there."

But even as the Pope spoke and the conference began, the liberationists were not sure exactly what their strategy should be. Sergio Torres later admitted, "We were very worried" (Lernoux 1982: 423).[22] There was talk of holding an "alternative Puebla," of publicly opposing what went on inside the seminary. But, after discussion, that option was rejected. The group chose, instead, to interpret the Pope's messages in the most favorable light and to press on and try to infiltrate, with the help of sympathetic bishops, the process inside the walls.[23]

> Breaching the "wall of freedom," as López Trujillo called it, proved simple.[24] Though the outsiders could not go into the compound, the bishops could not be denied exit and entry by the . . . security guards. So, as soon as the document became available it was quickly taken by one of the progressive bishops to a convent three blocks away from the Palafoxiano, where it was analyzed by the liberation group; their position papers were soon circulated in the assembly. . . . Four hours after the pope gave his opening talk to the bishops . . . forty bishops had a twenty-page analysis written and duplicated by the outsiders. (Sandoval 1979: 35)

López had advised the bishops to avoid contact with outsiders . However,

> on the morning of the second day of the conference . . . [Brazilian Bishop Alano Pena] came out from the seminary to meet with the

liberation theologians and carry their analysis of the Pope's Puebla speech back to the . . . bishops. At the same time, Gustavo Gutiérrez sent a note to Archbishop Marcos McGrath, stating that the group had come to Puebla only to be of service to the bishops and that it was in no way attempting to set itself up as a parallel church. Within a week of the opening, the liberation group's papers were freely circulating throughout the conference, and were even officially recognized by the CELAM staff. (Lernoux 1982: 434)

Pablo Richard (1988), one of the theologians outside the gate, describes the experience:

At Puebla, there were one hundred uninvited liberation theologians and sociologists together outside of the seminary. We were waiting, not protesting.[25] At the beginning there were eight bishops working with us. At the end, there were eighty! It was really a work of infiltration. It was the most beautiful thing because when the bishops began to ask Trujillo's theologians about Latin America's problems, about our history, about using the documents of the magisterium, these theologians had nothing impressive to say. We outside had written little papers, 2–3 pages, which we published. When the bishops read our papers, many of them said: "this is beautiful, this is correct." So more and more the bishops in Puebla started to listen to what came from outside the seminary.[26]

According to one insider observer,

By working day and night (at one point Gustavo Gutiérrez went twenty-four hours with only one hour of sleep) the outsider theologians and social scientists were able to prepare eighty-four position papers for the twenty-one commissions as the document went through four drafts. As a result, according to several delegates, at least 25 percent of the final document was written directly by these uninvited assistants. (Sandoval 1979: 36)[27]

In the end, the final Puebla document, reflecting the disagreements among the bishops, was a mix of conservative, moderate, and liberationist elements (Rosales 1979: 61).[28] "On virtually every page, and sometimes in the same paragraph or sentence, there are diverse catagories and languages which reflect divergent—ultimately contradictory—visions of Church and society" (Berryman 1979: 65).[29]

Thus, neither side can be said to have won a resounding victory, although both claimed that they did (Kirby 1981: 105).[30] Liberation theology did not dominate Puebla, but the progressive bishops were not silenced and liberation theology was not repudiated (Carroll 1987: 21). In other words, from a progressive perspective, the final Puebla document was one that "did not betray Medellín even if it made no great advances" (Cox and Sand 1979: 58–59).[31]

Rather than criticize the final document for its weaknesses, the liberation theologians decided to appropriate the document by publicly embracing it, interpreting it from a liberationist point of view, and praising it. Robert McAfee Brown (1988) argues:

> It was clear that the liberation theologians decided to affirm Puebla. I was at a conference with some of them a few months after Puebla and one of them came in with a stack of documents and said, "Hey, there are fifty phrases we can use! We can quote the bishops fifty times!" That's the way the Catholic Church is—I've seen it again and again. That happened with Vatican II. One bishop at Vatican II told me: "As long as we can get our two paragraphs in the document, we're happy." That's not cheating. That's the way advances come in the Catholic Church: new things are always encased in the past. And, since the Puebla documents are so long, people aren't going to read the whole document—they'll read only what is supposed to be important. So, what Puebla means is what the subsequent interpreters say it means.

As with Medellín, liberation theologians took the initiative to interpret and publicize Puebla as a victory for their cause.[32] Thus, they claimed: "The groups that attempted to condemn the popular Christian movements, the base communities, the 'popular church,' the Latin American theology of liberation, and the so-called parallel magisterium failed in their objective and were completely defeated" (Dussel 1981: 232), and "Puebla was a great triumph for the BECs and the people" (Richard 1988).[33]

However, opponents of liberation theology also interpreted Puebla as a success for their cause. For example, López Trujillo (1980: 306, 326) claimed:

> There is an old struggle of the Church in our countries for human dignity, but it should never confused with an ambiguous and reductionistic "liberationism." . . . It remains clear that, while Puebla advances an authentic, integral, truthful *Christian liberation,* it rejects other types of liberation. Concretely, it rejects those that march in pursuit of ideologies; more clearly, it rejects the liberation that is inspired by Marxist analysis.[34]

And, Catholic priest Francisco Interdonato, also a critic of libera-

TABLE 9.9
Important Liberationist Influences in Puebla Document

Sections	Subject
3–14	Historical overview of Latin America
28–30	Latin American poverty and its causes
31–39	Presence of Christ among the poor
87–89	The cry of the poor for justice
90	Poverty and evangelization
96–97	Positive assessment of Christian BECs
263	Positive definition of the "popular church"
385–96	Evangelization and popular religiosity
470–506	Liberating evangelization
507–62	Evangelization, ideologies, and politics
1134–65	Preferential option for the poor
1166–1205	Preferential option for the young
1207–20	Collaboration with building pluralistic societies
1308	The new person
1309	Signs of hope and joy

Sources: Henriot et al. 1988, 110–13; Richard 1987a, 154–55; Berryman 1979, 65–78; MacEoin and Riley 1980, 90–92; Wilde 1979, 272–77.

tion theology, interpreted Puebla as a gracious correction of the fallacies of liberation theology by those who hold a more complete and authentic view: "Puebla has not wanted to point out directly the positive mistakes of the theology (or theologies) of liberation, but [only to point out] the negative imperfections, that is, what it lacks, with the goal of perfecting or completing the concept of liberation" (quoted in Nuñez 1985: 112).

Perhaps the most accurate account was written by Daniel H. Levine:

> Puebla . . . was less a high-water mark of commitment than a compromise, an uneasy standoff between those advancing further identification with the cause and condition of the poor and others pursuing consolidation, reaffirmation of hierarchy, and a withdrawal from exposed and politically risky positions. (Levine, ed. 1986: 12)

Nevertheless, because of the work of the progressive bishops and the theologians outside the walls, a number of key liberationist passages are situated within this "compromise" document (see table 9.9).

What was ultimately important about the outcome of Puebla for the liberation theology movement was not that certain passages were included nor that neither side completely won, but that neither side was completely defeated (Sigmund 1988: 33; Ferm 1986: 56; Berryman 1979: 78–79; MacEoin and Riley 1980: 101).

On the one hand, the fact that neither side was completely defeated meant that liberation theology's critics were still in a position to advance criticism and opposition. They had partially accomplished their goal at Puebla. And, they still held power in CELAM, since, soon after Puebla, López Trujillo was reelected by the bishops as secretary general of CELAM. Thus, liberation theology continued to face opposition and social control throughout the 1980s.

On the other hand, it was clear that the liberation theology movement had more than survived the best, most organized effort of Latin American conservatives to end it. This indicated that, as far as the majority of bishops were concerned, for the time being, the liberation theology movement was a tolerable, if not acceptable, expression of Christian faith and practice for Catholics in Latin America (Cleary 1985: 50).35 Thus, Dussel (1981: 232) argued, "in the last analysis, Medellín was the point of departure and inspiration, and Puebla can be regarded as a continuation. . . . The door remains open, therefore, for Christians to continue supporting the interests of the people, the poor, and the oppressed."

10

Liberation Theology since Puebla

Briefly, how has liberation theology fared since Puebla? The movement has survived, matured, and made what in its view are some significant advances. However, liberation theology has also seen increasing Church opposition and a change in the Latin American political environment that, in the 1970s, had helped it persist. The most important changes have been a shrinkage in the movement's political opportunity, and new challenges to maintaining its insurgent consciousness. Hence, there is some reason to question whether the liberation theology movement will continue to endure and significantly influence the Latin American experience in the future.

Contracting Political Opportunity

Pope John Paul II and a Renewed Vatican Conservativism

Liberation theology has experienced a significant reduction of political opportunity within the Catholic Church, as Rome has sought to undercut the institutional supports of liberation theology. Pope John Paul II has proven to be more conservative than his major predecessors, John XXIII and Paul VI (Novak 1986: 65–74). And, the Vatican's prefect of the Congregation for the Doctrine of the Faith, Cardinal Joseph Ratzinger, appointed by John Paul II, has proven to be quite active in criticizing liberation theology (Sigmund 1988: 36).[1]

Since Puebla, there have been a number of actions taken by the Vatican to curtail and, in some cases, to combat the influence of liberation theology in Latin America. For example, "on each of Pope John Paul II's major trips to Latin America (Mexico, 1979; Brazil,

1980; Central America, 1983; Andean countries of South America, 1985), he has issued warnings . . . aimed at [liberation] theologians" (Berryman 1987a: 3). Indeed, according to Novak (1986: 26), "from the beginning of his pontificate, step by step, piece by piece, Pope John Paul II has built a theological case against liberation theology."[2]

In addition, one of the most important ways that Rome has sought to curb the influence of the liberation theology movement has been to appoint conservative bishops in Latin America (Riding 1990: 529–30; Berryman 1987a: 109; Brooke 1989a). Arthur F. McGovern (1989a: 589) observes:

> An apparent trend in the appointment of new bishops raises doubts about the church's role in any new social transformations. Priorities about maintaining orthodoxy and reasserting church authority appear to outweigh social concerns. Since Pope John Paul II has come to office, he has replaced progressives with conservatives in nine of Brazil's thirty-six archdioceses, with only three progressive bishops appointed during the same period. The diocese of Recife and Olinda, for years one of the most progressive dioceses in Brazil, now has a conservative bishop. Peru . . . now has seven *Opus Dei* bishops. The bishop of Cusco has dismantled social centers once looked upon as models of work for change. The new head of the bishops conference in Peru, Bishop Ricardo Durand, is one of the fiercest critics of liberation theology.

Likewise, James Brooke notes (1989b: 14):

> In the 1970s and 1980s, Brazil's church was watched the world over as it decisively embraced social action in the name of the poor. Today, members of the church's long dominant social action wing charge that Pope John Paul II is quietly but steadily curbing their influence by appointing conservatives to key positions, censoring liberal [liberation] theologians, and trimming the territory of liberal prelates.

For example, when Dom Hélder Camera, Archbishop of Recife and a prime mover of the liberation theology movement, retired from his post in 1985, he was replaced by the conservative Dom José Cardoso Sobrinho, Vatican official for 26 years.

> Archbishop Cardoso is now dismantling the work of his predecessor. . . . In the last 18 months, the human rights office of the archdiocese has been closed, the land rights office has been purged of militants, the church's Commission of Peace and Justice has been ordered not to speak in the name of the archdiocese,

and two liberation theology seminaries founded here by Archbishop Camera have been ordered to close their doors. Priests
associated with liberation theology are no longer invited to celebrate Masses on television. (Brooke 1989b: 14)

Brooke (ibid.) cites another Brazilian example of Rome's curtailing
the power of liberationist bishops:

> This year, the Vatican cut in half the archdiocese of São Paulo,
> headed by Paulo Evaristo Cardinal Arns, an energetic proponent
> of liberation theology. . . . Cardinal Arns' influence may be fur-
> ther diluted by the creation of a new archdiocese in Mogi das
> Cruzes, an area adjacent to São Paulo. . . . The conservative
> cardinals of Rio de Janeiro, Brasilia, and Salvador now hold 22
> offices in the Vatican, while Cardinal Arns no longer has any.

These conservative appointments could significantly damage the liberation theology movement, since the movement needs committed
bishops for protection and support. Mainwaring and Wilde (1989:
15) explain:

> Change at the grass roots in single dioceses, or in national
> churches as a whole, ultimately requires at least the acquiescence
> of institutional authority. . . . Bishops need not actually sponsor
> progressive grass-roots activities, since all over Latin America pas-
> toral agents are anxious to do so. But where the bishops are hostile
> to autonomous grass-roots groups, their dissemination is next to
> impossible. In this context, progressive Church sectors are easily
> isolated. . . . All over Latin America, progressive innovators have
> emerged, but in many countries they have been consistently iso-
> lated by conservative prelates.

McGovern (1989a: 589) concurs:

> Attitudes and decisions in the institutional church will greatly af-
> fect the future of both liberation theology and the base communi-
> ties. Movements cut off from support of the church are unlikely to
> have great impact. Moreover, leaders in such movements may well
> become targets of government repression and even elimination, if
> government officials see that they have no support from the insti-
> tutional church.

Hence, "this trend in the hierarchy, combined with the worsening of
economic conditions in most Latin American countries, does not

presage a very promising future for the hopes expressed in liberation theology" (ibid.).

The Silencing of Leonardo Boff

The Vatican's appointment of conservative bishops as a long-term means to control liberation theology has been matched by the more immediate tactic of criticizing and censuring specific liberation theologians. For example, in 1983, Rome attempted to have Gustavo Gutiérrez condemned (Sigmund 1988: 36; Richard 1987a: 158; Cox 1988: 4):

> In 1983 Cardinal Joseph Ratzinger, the head of the Vatican's Sacred Congregation of the Doctrine of the Faith, sent the Peruvian bishops a letter listing objections to Gustavo Gutiérrez's theology. . . . Gutiérrez was even called to Rome for private consultation with Vatican officials. . . . [But] even under Vatican urging the Peruvian bishops were deadlocked over whether they could condemn Gutiérrez. (Berryman 1987a: 108–9).[3]

The Vatican also censured liberationist bishop Pedro Casaldáliga of São Felix, Brazil, in September 1988 (Hennelly 1990: 532).

In a more dramatic case, the Vatican disciplined the Brazilian liberation theologian Leonardo Boff for questionable doctrines found in his 1981 book, *Church: Charism and Power*.[4] In this book, Boff had sharply criticized the way the hierarchy often exercises its authority in the Catholic Church (Cox 1988: 3). The Vatican official in charge of guarding doctrinal orthodoxy, Cardinal Joseph Ratzinger, decided to respond. According to Berryman (1987a: 109),

> rather than going through the Brazilian bishops, who would have supported [Boff], Ratzinger first called Boff to Rome for a discussion in September 1984. Two Brazilian cardinals accompanied him to show the hierarchy's support.

On September 3, 1984, four days before Boff's meeting with Ratzinger, the Vatican published the document *Instruction on Certain Aspects of the Theology of Liberation*, which came to be known as the "Ratzinger Report" (Gibellini 1987: 43–44). In it, Ratzinger made two major criticisms of liberation theology:

> first, that it takes over the Marxist analysis of society, thus running the risk of turning Christian faith into an ideology; second, that it favors the formation of a parallel church, the *Iglesia popular*, in opposition to the official church represented by the bishops. (Gibellini 1987: 46)

These errors, the report argued, make some kinds of liberation theology "a fundamental threat to the faith of the Church" (Ratzinger and Messori 1986: 175).

On September 7, 1984, Ratzinger examined Boff, after which Boff returned to Brazil. In March 1985 the Vatican issued a document answering and condemning some of Boff's theology (Berryman 1987a: 109). Then, on May 9, 1985, Boff received an official notice from the Vatican ordering him to observe an "obsequious silence for a period of time" (Sigmund 1988: 36). Boff chose to obey, and remained silenced for ten months (Cox 1988: 6).[5]

Ironically, the Vatican's disciplining of Boff helped to spread further the ideas of liberation theology in Latin America. "The net result was that the theology of liberation became more widely known and studied" (Richard 1987a: 159). In Enrique Dussel's words (1988): "Rome believed it could criticize one theologian to hurt us. It was a mistake. This type of condemnation only gives us publicity." Harvey Cox (1988: 5) explains:

> [Boff] became something of an unwilling celebrity. His . . . face . . . appeared in newspapers and magazines all over the world. Letters, cards, and telegrams of support arrived daily at the monastery [where he resided]. Many Brazilians looked upon the Franciscan friar as a religious version of Pele, a champion of Latin American religion and Brazilian national spirit against outside intruders. Ten Brazilian Catholic bishops took the highly unusual step of publicly criticizing the Vatican's treatment of Boff. Various Catholic groups and some Protestant religious bodies issued statements of support for Boff. Labor unions organized public demonstrations protesting the silencing. T-shirts and posters appeared for sale in Brazil picturing Boff with his mouth gagged. Bishop Pedro Casaldáliga . . . of Mato Grosso, published a poem called "The Blessing of St. Francis on Friar Leonardo Boff."

Thus, Otto Maduro claims, "When Boff was condemned, liberation theology became a hot thing everywhere in Latin America. Many Catholics had never heard of liberation theology until then. After, millions were exposed to the claims of liberation theology. Millions!"

Despite the helpful publicity liberation theology received, by condemning and silencing Leonardo Boff the Vatican demonstrated its increased willingness to take forceful action to maintain its authority and control over liberation theology. And, the limits of just how far Rome would go to censure liberation theology was and is still unknown.

Challenges to Insurgent Consciousness

Central American Revolutions

Beside problems with contracting political opportunity, during the years since Puebla liberation theology has had to face a set of social changes that pose considerable challenges for maintaining the movement's insurgent consciousness.

Soon after the end of the Puebla conference, in July 1979, the Sandinista Front of National Liberation (FSLN) overthrew the Somoza regime in Nicaragua. Then, in January 1981, the Farabundo Martí National Liberation Front (FMLN) launched a major revolutionary offensive in El Salvador. With these events, much of the focus of the liberation theology movement shifted to Central America . It is widely recognized that both the nearly successful FMLN offensive in El Salvador and the Sandinista victory in Nicaragua depended on the critical support and participation of radical Christians (Montgomery 1982; Dodson 1986; Belli 1988). Michael Dodson (1986: 85) notes that, in Nicaragua, the zones where fighting was most intense and resistance most effective during the popular insurrection were exactly those towns and neighborhoods were BECs tended to be most concentrated. And, he continues:

> The FSLN . . . found the work of organizing people in the insurrection to be much easier in areas where [BECs] were firmly rooted. These institutions of religious inspiration were, in short, effective vehicles of grass-roots political action in the revolutionary setting of the popular insurrection.

Tommie Sue Montgomery (1982: 220–21) likewise observes:

> The rapid growth of popular organizations of the left in El Salvador cannot be explained without taking into account the role of the [BECs] in organizing and conscienticizing the people. . . . The churches in both countries [El Salvador and Nicaragua] have contributed leaders to the top levels of revolutionary organizations. . . . Given the involvement of laity, nuns, and priests in the revolutionary process of each country . . . there has been a dialectical relationship between Christian theology and revolutionary ideology.[6]

Liberation theology leaders viewed these events as major breakthroughs for their movement. In particular, they viewed the Sandinista victory as the opportunity to fulfill their aspirations to begin a popular reconstruction of Latin American society. McGovern (1989b: 189) confirmed: "A poll of liberation theologians would almost certainly show strong, if not unanimous, support for the 'revolutionary process' in Nicaragua. It has represented the kind of hope for liberation of the poor that we associate with liberation theology." Indeed, four liberation-oriented priests—Miguel d'Escoto, Ernesto Cardenal, Edgar Paralles, and Fernando Cardenal—assumed high-level positions in the Sandinista regime in an attempt to maintain an internal Christian influence on the revolution.

However, the Sandinista revolution quickly encountered difficulties and setbacks. Led by the newly elected Ronald Reagan, the United States began actively to oppose the Sandinista regime through a cut-off of foreign aid, an economic embargo, and the United States–funded, counterrevolutionary, military operations of the "Contras." The Sandinistas faced a growing loss of popular support at home, as the Nicaraguan economy increasingly deteriorated throughout the 1980s. Furthermore, Managua's Archbishop Obando y Bravo—who during the insurrection had helped to undermine the Somoza regime—began to oppose and criticize the Sandinista government. And, the Nicaraguan priests with political positions were forced by the hierarchy and Rome to leave the priesthood (Berryman 1987a: 108).

Many observers interpreted the Sandinista's inability in the 1980s to achieve many of their key goals as concrete evidence that a Marxist-Leninist revolution must inevitably fail. However, liberationists claimed that the cause of these difficulties was often external imperialism and oppression. Hence, Sandinista Nicaragua has represented both a hope and a frustration to liberation theologians.

Events in Nicaragua took a surprising and dramatic turn when in February 1990 the Sandinistas were defeated by a coalition opposition led by Violetta Chamorro in a fair, democratic presidential election. This popular rejection of the Sandinista regime has raised serious questions for liberation theologians.[7] Where did the Sandinista program go wrong? Do the Latin American people really want socialism? Are democratic elections and parliamentary politics reliable means to achieve liberationist goals? As of this writing, the full effect on liberation theologians of the Sandinista defeat by the Nicaraguan people has yet to be seen. However, it could prove to be an event troubling enough to force liberation theologians to reconsider some of their assumptions and strategies.

Developments in Latin American Economics

In addition to problems in revolutionary Central America, liberation theology in the 1980s and into the 1990s has faced the development of a more problematic economic and political climate in Latin America and the world. This changed climate may, in the long run, work to undermine the strength and legitimacy of the liberation theology movement.

Most importantly, Latin America's economic situation has deteriorated badly. Howard Wiarda (1990: 31) observes:

> The per capita income for Latin America . . . has fallen 7 percent between 1980 and 1988. There has also been a sharp decline in capital inflows and investment rates; foreign exchange reserves are down; and private banks no longer wish to lend to the area. Unemployment and inflation are rampant.

Theoretically, such a situation could bolster the standard liberationist economic worldview. These problems could be interpreted as continued signs of an external exploitation and subjugation that needs to be overcome. Probably some liberation theologians will continue in this line of thought.

However, certain experiences could also make such an interpretation difficult. Important among them is the fact that many Latin American experiments in nationalization and other similar policy recommendations suggested by dependency theory have proven unsuccessful. In the case of Peru, for example, it appears that it was specifically the military government's reforms of the 1970s, inspired by dependency theory, that helped to lay the foundation for the economic disaster Peru now faces (Palmer 1990: 5).[8]

Also important are the popular anticommunist movements that erupted in Eastern Europe, China, and the Soviet Union in 1989. In most of these cases, liberation of the people meant the dismantling of socialist and communist systems. Few liberation theologians, however, interpret these events as the final triumph of capitalism and the inevitable end of socialism itself. They only see here the demise of *centralized, authoritarian* socialism, a form of socialism they never admired or embraced. With the end of repressive, top-down socialism, they argue, the ground is now cleared for the growth of authentic, democratic forms of socialism. Still, one wonders how credible calls for *any* form of socialism in Latin America will now be in light of the apparent failure of these socialist experiments in Eastern Europe and the Soviet Union.

With more than two decades of social experience since their original embrace of dependency theory, some liberation theologians are beginning to back away from the theory and its implications (McGovern 1989b: 135–38, 164, 180–81). Indeed, "socialism no longer remains an unqualified paradigm for liberation aspirations" (McGovern 1989a: 589). Leonardo Boff (1979: 66) was one of the first to express doubts about dependency theory. In the mid-1970s he wrote:

> [Dependency theory] is only a theory, not an established truth. It is one stage in an ongoing investigation and has its own intrinsic limitations. It offers a good diagnosis of the structure of underdevelopment, but it does not do much to offer any viable way out.

However, as Arthur McGovern points out, more recently, in his introduction to the 1988 revised English edition of his *A Theology of Liberation*, Gustavo Gutiérrez has virtually repudiated dependency theory:

> It is clear that the theory of dependency, which was so extensively used in the early years of our encounter with the Latin American world, is now an inadequate tool, because it does not take sufficient account of the internal dynamics of each country or of the vast dimensions of the world of the poor. (Quoted in McGovern 1989b: 136)

Similarly, in a recent interview with McGovern, Gutiérrez also distanced himself from socialism: "Socialism is not an essential of liberation theology; one can support liberation theology or do liberation theology without espousing socialism" (McGovern 1989b: 148).

Gutiérrez was always a relative moderate among liberation theologians when it came to social analysis. Hence, these remarks are not as astounding as the recent, radical change José Porfirio Miranda has made in his views on Marxism. According to McGovern (146), "in a more recent essay [Miranda] simply rejects Marxism, arguing that Marxist analysis is based on a false reductionism." Given Miranda's previous radical position, this is a dramatic conversion.

Despite claims to the contrary, when dependency theory is removed from liberation theology, something essential in the spirit and logic of that theology is altered.[9] The question then arises, if liberation theologians continue to abandon dependency theory and distance themselves from socialism, will not their developing theology, de facto, increasingly resemble the progressive, reformist theology they repudiated in the late 1960s?

The Resurgence of Democracy

Another important social change for liberation theology has been that, throughout the 1980s, repressive military dictatorships in many nations of Latin America have given way to civilian democracies. Wiarda and Kline (1985: 639) observe:

At the end of 1977, thirteen . . . Latin American countries . . .
were under military rule. . . . But in the early 1980s the pendu-
lum began to swing back the other way. Several military regimes
had been thoroughly discredited by their mismanagement of their
nation's economic accounts and their indiscriminate use of repression. A number of new democratically elected governments
were inaugurated.

Specifically, moves away from military rule toward elected civilian
governments took place in Peru in 1980, Honduras in 1982, Argentina in 1983, Brazil and Guatemala in 1985, Chile in 1988, and
Paraguay and Panama in 1989.

In the 1970s, military repression served to strengthen the liberation theology movement. In that light, the effects of this recent re-de-
mocratization on the liberation theology movement could prove interesting. For, the more open and responsive Latin American
governments appear, the more positive, reformist change seems possible, and the less compelling and plausible the radical liberationist
vision appears. Popular control of politics is a major element of liberation theology's vision for a new society. Yet, ironically, moves toward that goal could actually marginalize the liberation theology
movement.

Like the problems with dependency theory and socialism, this
resurgence of Latin American democracy has had an effect in re-
shaping liberation theology. In the early 1970s, many liberation theologians viewed electoral democracy as a fraudulent mechanism of
bourgeois rule (Sigmund 1988: 41; McGovern 1989b: 186). Today,
however, "an evolution toward more cautious political positions is
visible among Church progressives" (Mainwaring and Wilde 1989:
27). McGovern (1989a: 589) notes:

Liberation theologians have . . . modified their politico-economic
views in recent years. The new political context in many parts of
Latin America has led liberation theologians to talk about building a "participatory democracy" from within civil society.

Hugo Assman, for example, "long considered the most Marxist of the
liberation theologians, . . . spoke in the mid-1980s of the 're-
democratization of Latin American' as an essential priority" (ibid.,
186). According to Sigmund (1988: 40), "Assman seems now to
equate revolution with democracy." And, Roth (1988: 239) observes
that "Assman has apparently become much more concerned to consider how democracy can work on behalf of the poor."

It seems likely that most liberation theologians will eventually follow Assman's lead in affirming some form of liberal democracy. But again, the question arises, if liberation theologians fully embrace the liberal democratic process in Latin America, will not their theology, de facto, increasingly resemble the progressive, reformist theology which they repudiated in the late 1960s?

An Uncertain Future

In 1988, liberation theology leaders met in Maryknoll, New York, to celebrate the twenty-fifth anniversary of the publication of Gustavo Gutiérrez's *A Theology of Liberation*. At that meeting, they confidently discussed the future of their movement. But, in light of the many changes mentioned above, is such confidence warranted?

Liberation theology emerged in the context of an open Church environment and an open Latin American political climate. Then, liberation theology established itself and expanded in the context of a partially open Church environment and a repressive Latin American political climate. The question for the years ahead is, will the liberation theology movement be able to survive and succeed in the relatively closed Church environment, problematic Latin American economic situation, and open Latin American political climate that began to develop in the 1980s?

A number of future scenarios are possible. On the one hand, it is possible that social conditions in Latin America and the world could develop in a way that increases political opportunity and insurgent consciousness for the liberation theology movement: democracy could falter and military repression could easily return to Latin America. Wiarda and Kline (1985: 639) warn: "The military remains in the wings, and as the economic and political crisis intensifies [the military] seems in several countries prepared to return to center stage." The popular political process in Eastern Europe and the Soviet Union could develop in such a way that, after initially flirting with market economies, they do not fully embrace Western capitalism but rather establish a more moderate, genuinely *democratic* form of socialism. It is possible, too, that the Vatican, if pleased with the changes in liberation theology mentioned above, would abandon a strategy of control and condemnation for a strategy of mutual acceptance and support. Pentecostalism and Protestant fundamentalism is still spreading rapidly in Latin America, a very important continent to Rome (Lernoux 1989: 153–64).[10] And, in the face of this religious competition, Catholic authorities still need to find strategies to maintain popular commitment to Catholicism. If the liberation theology movement appears able to deliver this popular commitment and if it is able to assuage the Vatican's concerns about Marxism and a rebellious "popular church," perhaps liberation theology will win back the support of Rome and of the majority of moderate Latin American bishops.[11] With these kinds of developments, it would be possible for liberation theology survive and grow in influence in the future.

On the other extreme, conditions could develop that would further undermine and marginalize liberation theology: new Latin American democracies could prove effective and resilient enough to ward off a return to repressive military rule. Socialist regimes in Latin America and the world could be increasingly discredited and rejected by popular movements. Dependency theories could become increasingly implausible in Latin American academic and theological circles. And, the Vatican could judge that it does not need liberation theology to maintain its ability to carry out its mission in Latin America. Those conditions would greatly curtail the political opportunity and insurgent consciousness of liberation theologians, undermining and marginalizing the movement.

However, a third scenario is that liberation theology will continue to adapt and struggle ahead, finding support and success in some areas and setbacks and frustrations in others. This less clear-cut experience is probably the most likely future of liberation theology.

Conclusion

Grass-roots social movements of the powerless and excluded have received considerable attention from sociologists. But liberation theology represents a different kind of social movement: a revitalization movement. We have seen that before the liberation theology movement was able to become a mass-based movement of excluded peasants and workers, the movement's leaders had to gain control over the Church's institutional authority and resources through a task logically akin to an organizational takeover. Before it could mobilize its members to exert pressure to transform society, it had to institutionalize its ideology and action strategy in the Church. And this first, critical step of the movement was carried out not by powerless, excluded masses using nonconventional means, but by theological elites in the context of a powerful, well-established organization using largely institutionalized means.

Hence, the liberation theology movement should be understood as one of many elite-initiated revitalization movements that aim to force drastic redirections in the strategies and resources of established institutions. Other examples of revitalization movements that come to mind are Jesse Jackson's "Rainbow Coalition" within the Democratic party, the collective action of scientists in political groups such as the Union of Concerned Scientists, and Mikhail Gorbachev's program of *perestroika* and *glasnost* within the Communist party of the Soviet Union. These revitalization movements are often very interesting, important types of social movements. Yet they are largely unexamined in the literature on social movements. The case of liberation theology examined here has offered one opportunity to correct that imbalance.

I have argued that Doug McAdam's political process model, although originally conceived to analyze grass-roots movements of politically excluded challengers, nevertheless offers the most useful theoretical tool for analyzing revitalization movements such as liberation theology. Throughout this study I have used that model's three key variables—political opportunity, organizational strength, and insurgent consciousness—as major interpretive, analytical tools.

Especially important in the emergence of liberation theology, yet often misunderstood or ignored in other theoretical accounts of social movements, was the social-psychological variable of insurgent consciousness. Grievances were not stable and ubiquitous; they developed with changing circumstances. Human deprivations did not automatically provoke mass reaction; they had to be interpreted and reinterpreted through the formation of new, experience-organizing frames. And, the insurgent consciousness of a group of elites alone could not mobilize a mass movement; that insurgent consciousness had to find expression in a context of organizational strength and political opportunity.

With these theoretical considerations in mind, we return to the empirical question, why and how did the liberation theology movement emerge where and when it did? The answer, in short, is that a small cadre of young, aggressive, radicalized theologians outraged by Latin America's poverty and dependency gained access to positions of influence in the Latin American Catholic Church. They did so at a critical time when, because of a growing organizational crisis and an increased ideological openness, the Church was searching for a new organizational strategy that would strengthen its ability to achieve its mission in society.

The strategy of this cadre was to abandon alliances with Latin America's political, economic, and military elites, and establish ties instead with Latin America's poor masses. They wanted to redefine the Church as an advocate of social justice, economic equality, human rights, anti-imperialism, and popular political participation. The bishops of Latin America accepted key aspects of this view in their conference at Medellín in 1968. It appeared to them that the direction, if not the detail, of this theological perspective was right and necessary.

For the next four years, the liberation theologians diffused this new strategy to thousands of Catholics at all levels of the Church throughout the entire continent. The movement caught on at the grass-roots level. By the time enough critical bishops realized what had happened, it was too late to stop it. The movement by then had, for the time being, generated enough momentum and support to continue. It had also drawn brutal repression from military governments—repression that often alienated moderate Catholic bishops from the governments. By then, the movement was entrenched and direct actions against it by conservative bishops, Rome, and Latin American governments could not remove it.[1] That is the basic story.

The key factors in the generation of this movement were the same as those associated with the emergence of many other social movements: an expansion of political opportunity, increasing organizational strength, and the formation of insurgent consciousness.

A significant expansion in political opportunity was the first necessary factor in the emergence of liberation theology. The Roman Catholic Church, with Europe's "New Theology," developments in Catholic Social Teachings, and Vatican II, was open to new ideology and organization. In Latin America, with new problems of competition from Protestants, Spiritists, unions, and leftists and the old problem of a shortage of clergy, the Church was facing an organizational crisis. The success of the Cuban revolution and the failure of the Alliance for Progress exacerbated this sense of crisis and increased the pressure for a new approach.

Then, a core of progressive bishops began to apply Vatican II to Latin America. They shared the reins of this process with their staff members—theologians who had recently become convinced of the need to reconstruct the Church so that it could help to reconstruct Latin American societies. Through this series of events, the political opportunities for this group of theological radicals and the radical pastoral workers they represented had, by 1968, been expanded enormously.

A significant increase in organizational strength was a second necessary factor in the emergence of the liberation theology movement. Concurrent with the forces and events expanding political opportunity, organizations that would facilitate the liberation theology movement were being created and strengthened. Hélder Camera and Manuel Larraín organized and expanded the CNBB and CELAM. Young, European-trained theologians established a relational network. New, foreign pastoral workers streamed into Latin America and, disturbed by its poverty, began working in slums and shantytowns. Bishops and pastoral workers created conscientizing BECs. Religious orders, such as the Jesuits, Maryknollers, and Dominicans, underwent renewals that led them to work with the poor, and groups of radical priests proliferated.

When the liberation theology movement appeared, other facilitating organizations emerged. They included Christians for Socialism, the theological conferences of 1970 and 1971, liberation theology journals, publishing houses, and institutes, and the Ecumenical Association of Third World Theologians. Thus, not only did the protagonists of liberation theology enjoy an open political environment, but they also had the organizational capacity to capitalize on that political opportunity.

Finally, the formation of a driving insurgent consciousness was the third necessary factor in the emergence of the liberation theology movement. The "New Theology" of Europe, developments in Catholic Social Teachings, and the innovations of Vatican II provoked a generation of Latin American theologians to begin to think progressively. The experience of Camilo Torres, the revolutionary theology of ISAL, and the radical statements of the bishops of Brazil's northeast challenged their thinking still further. Then, the Cuban revolution, the 1964 Brazilian coup, and the failure of the Alliance for Progress created an intellectual crisis. The old beliefs and teachings seemed inadequate, but an alternative was still unformed. Catholic social research centers had exposed religious leaders to data on the dismal religious and socioeconomic conditions of Latin America. The problems were becoming clear. What was less clear was their cause and solution.

Then, a radical interpretation of Latin America's situation, dependency theory, took many concerned Catholics by storm. They came to believe that Latin America's dependence on and domination by capitalist oppressors was the problem. The answer to that problem was not development but liberation, not a new Christendom but an option for the poor. With that insight, Catholic progressives shifted to an "injustice frame" and formed the shared conviction that radical change was both necessary and possible. Insurgent consciousness erupted.

This combination of conditions—a band of Catholic radicals with a driving insurgent consciousness who had access to organizations capable of generating and sustaining a major social movement and who were situated in a political environment of great openness and little opposition—was the mix of key factors that produced the liberation theology movement. It was a sufficiently favorable combination of political opportunity, organizational strength, and insurgent consciousness that enabled the movement to survive and grow during the 1970s.

In the 1980s, liberation theology came upon difficult times. And it appears that liberation theology, facing a complex of changing social conditions, will have some difficult years ahead, as well. Exactly how well liberation theology adapts to these changing conditions will depend largely on the insight, flexibility, and skill of its theologians. Exactly what conditions the liberation theologians will have to adapt to will depend largely on the uncontrollable social forces that make history.

Notes

Introduction

1. See, for example, Brockman 1982: 21, 93, 115–17, 120, 151–52, 197, 203, 219.

2. "With his penchant for conciliation, his clearly conservative outlook, the links he had with the Salvadoran oligarchy and with traditionalist groups within the church (with Opus Dei, even!), Romero appeared to be the perfect man to return the church to the sheepfold, the priest to the sacristy, and Catholic teaching back to the Council of Trent and Vatican I. For their part, a good number of clergy of the archdiocese received the news of his appointment with dejection and apprehension" (Martin-Baro 1985: 4).

3. Martin-Baro (1985: 4) states, "Before Chavez's resignation of archbishop of San Salvador, both the government and the Salvadoran oligarchy pressured the Vatican to choose as his successor someone who would have the complete confidence of those in power. . . . When news came from Rome that Bishop Romero had been chosen to succeed Archbishop Chavez, the Salvadoran government and the oligarchy were jubilant. They were certain they had won a great victory for the conservative cause. As far as right-wing forces were concerned, Bishop Romero was, from every point of view, the ideal candidate."

4. See, for example, McGurn 1987; Shepherd 1979; Kansteiner 1988; West 1984; Baum 1978; Arokiasamy and Gispert-Sauch 1987; Bolasco 1986; Murickan 1985; Garrett 1988; McElvaney 1980; Carroll 1987: 8.

5. See Kissinger 1984; Einaudi et al. 1969; Rockefeller Report 1969; Carroll 1987: 15.

6. Furthermore, the liberation theology movement has generated much controversy, criticism, and opposition; see, for example, Vekemans 1971, 1976; López Trujillo 1977, 1978, 1980; Novak 1979, 1986; Novak, ed., 1987; Berger and Novak 1985; Novak and Jackson 1985; Ratzinger and Bovone 1984; Nash 1986; Francis 1985; Geld 1987; Grenz 1987; Haight 1985; Henry, n.d.; J. Schall 1982, 1986; Tunnerman 1987; Shea 1987; Conyers 1983; McCann, n.d.; Min 1984; Perry 1985; Correspondents for the Economist 1977, 1980, 1981, 1983a, 1983b, 1984, 1986a–c.

239

1. A Brief History of the Liberation Theology Movement

1. For example, the Bartolomé de Las Casas Institute in Lima, Peru and the Antonio de Valdivieso Center in Managua, Nicaragua.

2. Jacques Maritain, *True Humanism* (New York: Charles Scribner's Sons, 1938); Maritain, *Christianity and Democracy*, translated by Doris C. Anson (New York: Charles Scribner's Sons, 1950).

3. Latin American Documentation Service (hereafter abbreviated as LADOC) 5:1–10.

4. For greater detail on ISAL and the "theology of revolution," see chapter 5.

5. For a more detailed exploration of the importance of Vatican II on Latin America, see chapter 5.

6. The first plenary session had been held in Rio de Janeiro, Brazil in 1955.

7. The Medellín document quotes in the following two paragraphs are taken from the final documents on "Peace," "Justice," and "Poverty" in Gremillion 1976: 445–76. The entire final document is translated into English in *The Church in the Present-Day Transformation of Latin America in the Light of the Council: Conclusions*, vol. 2, United States Catholic Conference (hereafter USCC), Latin American Bureau, 1970.

8. See chapter 7 for details on the process of making Medellín and its outcomes.

9. These include (for Latin American publication dates) Enrique Dussel's *History of the Church in Latin America* (1971), José Miranda's *Marx and the Bible* (1971), Hugo Assman's *Oppression—Liberation: Challenge to Christians* (1972) and *Theology for the Praxis of Liberation* (1973), Juan Luis Segundo's *Open Theology for Adult Laity* (1968–1972), Leonardo Boff's *Jesus Christ Liberator* (1972), Rubem Alvez's *A Theology of Human Hope* (1969), and Míguez Bonino's *Theology of Liberation* (1970).

10. For an in-depth exploration of the making of Puebla and its outcomes, see chapter 9.

2. What Is Liberation Theology?

1. Gutiérrez (1983: 94) writes: "We usually find the theology of the poor emanating from spiritual movements of the poor, which are frequently social movements as well."

2. Similarly, Clodovis Boff argues: "Before the emergence of liberation theology at the close of the 1960s, a full-fledged liberation praxis was already under way in Latin America. . . . A life *practice* was well under way even in the early 1960s. The *theology* of liberation, then, came in a 'second moment.' It came as the *expression* of this liberation praxis on the part of the Church" (Boff and Boff 1986: 9). In addition, see Segundo 1976: 71–90; Boff and Boff 1987: 4–9.

3. Leonardo and Clodovis Boff (1987: 19) write: "Where is liberation theology to be found? You will find it at the base. It is linked with a specific community and forms a vital part of it. Its service is one of theological enlight-

enment of the community on its pilgrim way. You can find it any weekend in any slum, shantytown, or rural parish. It is there alongside the people, speaking, listening, asking questions, and being asked questions. It will not take shape in the form of an 'ivory tower' theologian."

4. According to Gutiérrez (1973: 135), two fundamental questions of liberation theology are: "What is the *meaning of faith* in a life committed to the struggle against injustice and alienation? How do we relate the work of building a just society to the absolute value of the kingdom?"

5. Leonardo Boff writes: "Thus one can reread, using liberation as one's hermeneutical key, the mystery of God, of Christ, of the church, of grace and sin, the sacraments, eschatology, anthropology, and mariology . . . to rethink, in systematic fashion, the traditional themes of theology in the interest of the liberation of the oppressed" (Boff and Boff 1984: 26–27).

6. Other theologians cited are José Miranda, Hugo Assman, Ignacio Ellacuría, Ronaldo Muñoz, Francis O'Gorman, Franz Hinkelammert, Alvaro Barreiro, Alex Morelli, and Segundo Galilea.

It ought to be noted that liberation theology is replete with ambiguities and inconsistencies, rhetorical overstatements, exegetical flaws, epistemological difficulties, and a certain political and historical naiveté. Even Segundo (1990: 353) admits: "It would be naive and unrealistic to deny that within what is labeled Latin American liberation theology there could be and surely often are superficial, boastful, and excessive features."

7. The Boff brothers maintain: "'Liberation' means liberation from oppression. Therefore, liberation theology has to begin by informing itself about the actual conditions in which the oppressed live, the various forms of oppression they may suffer. Obviously, the prime object of theology is God. Nevertheless, before asking what oppression means in God's eyes, theologians have to ask more basic questions about the nature of actual oppression and its causes. The fact is that understanding God is not a substitute for or alternative to knowledge of the real world. As Thomas Aquinas said: 'An error about the world redounds in error about God'" (1987: 24–25). Segundo, in his chapter "In Search of Sociology," writes: "The hermeneutical circle . . . summons us to a task in which we cannot prescind from sociology, that is, the study of the human attitudes that are bound up with social structures" (1976: 47). Also see Boff and Boff 1984: 13.

8. Segundo also criticizes "positivist and behaviorist sociology" (1976: 48).

9. Gutiérrez notes: "We Christians are not used to thinking in conflictual and historical terms. We prefer peaceful conciliation to antagonism and an evasive eternity to a provisional arrangement. We must learn to live and think of peace in conflict and of what is definitive in what is historical. Very important in this regard are collaboration and dialogue with those who from different vantage points are also struggling for the liberation of oppressed peoples" (1973: 137). Ellacuría assumes that any theology written after Marx must deal with the challenges of Marxism; in this way, Marxism actually transforms theology (1976: 17–18).

10. Bonino (1975: 111) writes similarly: "The Christian will, therefore, understand and fully join the Marxist protest against the capitalist demonic

circle of work-commodity-salary. But out of the justification by faith alone, he will have to ask whether alienation does not have deeper roots than the distortions of the capitalist society, even in the mysterious original alienation, in man's denial of his humanity which we call sin."

11. Gutiérrez, 1973: 152. Elsewhere (1973: 172), Gutiérrez refers to sin as "a human, social, and historical reality."

12. Gutiérrez (1973: 175–76) argues: "Sin is evident in oppressive structures, in the exploitation of man by man, in the domination and slavery of peoples, races, and social classes. . . . It cannot be encountered in itself, but only in concrete instances, in particular alienations." And again (1983: 18), "Love and its antithesis, sin, are historical realities. They are experienced and lived in concrete circumstances."

13. Earlier in this work, Galilea writes: "The proclamation of the kingdom constitutes the implantation in history, once and for all, of a principle of freedom and social critique, both as promise and denunciation. As promise, it is the leaven of nonconformism. As denunciation, it demands the removal of everything in society that assaults the nature and destiny of the human being as revealed at the heart of the gospel" (1984: 96).

14. Gutiérrez, too, writes (1973: 154): "Biblical faith is, above all, faith in a God who reveals himself through historical events, a God who saves in history."

15. Elsewhere, the Boff brothers write: "Because the kingdom is the absolute, it embraces all things: sacred and profane history, the church and the world, human beings and the cosmos. Under different sacred and profane signs, the kingdom is always present where persons bring about justice, seek comradeship, forgive each other, and promote life. . . . The kingdom of God is something more than historical liberations, which are always limited and open to further perfectioning, but it is anticipated and incarnated in them in time, in preparation for its full realization with the coming of the new heaven and new earth" (Boff and Boff 1987: 53). Gutiérrez (1973: 168) writes: "The struggle for a just world in which there is no oppression, servitude, or alienated work will signify the coming of the Kingdom."

16. Elsewhere, Gutiérrez writes: "The denunciation of injustice implies the rejection of the use of Christianity to legitimize the established order. It likewise implies, in fact, that the Church has entered into conflict with those who wield power" (1973: 115).

17. Gutiérrez (1973: 278) argues: "The unity of the Church is not truly achieved without the unity of the world. In a radically divided world, the function of the ecclesial community is to struggle against the profound causes of social division among men. It is only this commitment that can make of it an authentic sign of unity. Today, in Latin America especially, this unity implies the option for the oppressed; to opt for them is the honest, resolute way to combat that which gives rise to this social division. The Church itself will become more and more unified in this historical process and commitment to the liberation of the marginated and exploited."

18. For other arguments for "a church of the poor," see Gutiérrez 1983: 21, 22, 71, 34, 212; Gutiérrez 1973: 301–2; Boff and Boff 1987: 59.

19. For Gutiérrez's comments on the sign of preaching against oppression and for liberation, see his 1973: 115, 223, 262, 265.

20. See also Muñoz 1981: 157–58.

21. Gutiérrez (1973: 46) sees this realization of utopia as both consistent with the social aspirations of "contemporary man" and, through faith, possible (ibid., 237).

22. This expectation of total transformation is rooted in Boff's theology of resurrection: "To the question: What is to become of humankind? Christian faith joyfully answers: resurrection, as total transfiguration of the human reality, both corporal and spiritual" (L. Boff 1978: 135).

23. Gutiérrez's view here is very much influenced by Hegel (whom he cites eight times in his 1973 work) and the "cosmic-evolutionary," Catholic philosopher Teilhard de Chardin. Writes Gutierrez (1973: 32–33): "Teilhard de Chardin has remarked that man has taken hold of the reins of evolution. History, contrary to essentialist and static thinking, is not the development of potentialities pre-existent in man; it is rather the conquest of new, qualitatively different ways of being a man in order to achieve an ever more total and complete fulfillment of the individual in solidarity with mankind."

24. The Boffs continue: "These ideals *can* also be realized in the capitalist system, as we see from centuries of Christianity lived by a capitalist society. But the capitalist system is attended by many contradictions that could be overcome in another system—which for its part will present other contradictions, but lesser ones" (Boff and Boff 1984: 10–11).

25. The Boffs write: "Liberation theology longs and fights for a new society in this world: an alternative society to capitalism, but really alternative and therefore going beyond socialism as it exists today, embodying the hopes and needs of the least of all peoples. . . . In Latin America, the one area of the world whose population is both Christian and oppressed, liberation theology has realized that it cannot lose this unique opportunity of saying a new word in history; it cannot just follow the path trodden by other societies: it knows where they lead. Starting from the absolute utopia of the kingdom, faith can contribute by marking out new paths to a new society—an alternative to capitalism and socialism" (Boff and Boff 1987: 92–93). See also Molina and Larraín 1971.

26. The Boff brothers write: "Those committed to integral liberation will keep in their hearts the *little utopia* of at least one meal for everyone every day, the *great utopia* of a society free of exploitation and organized around the participation of all, and finally the *absolute utopia* of communion with God in totally redeemed creation" (Boff and Boff 1987: 94–95).

3. Theoretical Tools for Analysis

1. The typology below synthesizes F. Turner 1971: 96–108, 139–140; Levine 1981: 99–141; Fleet 1988: 166–67; and Berryman 1979: 56.

2. In the Latin American context, the term "popular" does not mean regarded with favor or affection by most persons, but having broad-based

support among and participation from the middle and (especially) lower strata of society.

3. According to Berryman, Juan Luis Segundo has "written of 'Two Theologies of Liberation.' He points out that the initial formulations were the work of theologians involved not so much with the poor as with university groups and intellectuals who were becoming aware of the structural crisis of Latin America. Coming to a new 'ideological suspicion' that existing forms of Christianity were strongly affected by dominant ideologies, they conceived of their work as one of unmasking 'the anti-Christian elements hidden in a so-called Christian society.' He sees a second line of liberation theology as having arisen subsequently in connection with pastoral work among the poor people. Pastoral agents and theologians felt that they should learn from the poor. One sign of this shift was a more positive assessment of popular religiosity" (Berryman 1987a: 86).

4. "Institutionalizing" here means ensuring that a sufficient number of those with power within an institution will defend the relevant ideas, practices, and practitioners against attack.

5. For an excellent summary and critique of both breakdown-deprivation and resource mobilization models of social movements, see McAdam 1982: 5–35.

6. Tilly's contributions (1975, 1978) include his emphasis on the shifting structure of political opportunities, the organizational capacity to mobilize, the role of beliefs and interests, the distinction between challengers and members, understanding elite responses as typically repressive in nature, the indirect effects of broad social change for social movement emergence, and the need to synthesize causal and purposive explanations.

7. McAdam (1982: 41) notes that these processes are similar to the "social strains" which, according to the breakdown-deprivation model, cause social protests. He argues, however, that traditional theorists wrongly posit a direct causal link between those strains and social movements (triggered by felt deprivations). The political process model, in contrast, claims that those broad social changes promote social movements only *indirectly*, through a restructuring of power relations.

8. Robert C. Liebman (1983: 73) identified the key to the mobilizing success of the "Moral Majority" in its ability to draw on preexisting organizations: "Moral Majority outdistanced its competitors by riding the back of a large and growing body of fellowshipped fundamentalists."

9. Whereas McAdam only mentions the latter items in passing, I believe they are of great practical importance and so have chosen to name them "enterprise tools" and to add them to the list of key organizational resources.

10. See case studies on German fascism (Oberschall 1973), the student movement (Flacks 1967), the Social Credit party movement in Quebec (Pinard 1971), the civil rights movement (Morris 1981), sit-in movements (Von Eschen et al. 1971), black protests (Marx 1967), the union movement (Moore 1975), political protest movements (Marsh 1977; Barnes and Kaase 1979), riot participation (Paige 1971), leftist radicalism (Portes 1971), the feminist movement (Freeman 1973, 1979), the Pentecostal movement

(Gerlach and Hine 1970; Heirich 1977), the anti-pornography movement (Curtis and Zurcher 1983), the Boston anti-busing movement (Useem 1980), and the environmental, anti-abortion, and anti-nuclear movements (Leahy and Mazur 1978).

11. See Fireman and Gamson (1979: 21–26) for a helpful discussion of solidary incentives and group interests.

12. McAdam (1982: 40, 48–51) labels this component of the model "Cognitive Liberation" and only speaks of "insurgent consciousness" in passing. I, however, think that "insurgent consciousness" is a more appropriate name for this process, because "cognitive" carries an overly *cerebral* connotation, neglecting the important volitional and emotive aspects of this process, and "liberation" stresses the negative release *from* a condition but fails to capture the positive reality of *coming into* a new condition, of *coming to* a new realization. Insurgent consciousness, in contrast, implies both the substantive outcome of this process (insurgency) and a more holistic sense of the subjective realm (consciousness) in which human interpretation of the meaning of social experience is formed and transformed.

13. Alejandro Portes (1971: 829) identified the growth of what I am calling insurgent consciousness among lower-class, urban Chilean radicals as a socialization process in which the personal problems of living in a lower-class situation come to be seen within the general imperative framework of a coherent theory of classes, class interests, and class conflict.

14. Ennis and Schreuer (1983: 395) identify "a sense of efficacy . . . interacting with grievances such as fear" as an important "purposive incentive" necessary to generate mass mobilization. On the negative side, Downs (1972) identifies the difficulty and cost of achieving social change—the realization of powerlessness—as the cause of escape from and discouragement and boredom with a social problem previously defined as necessary to solve.

15. Ferree and Miller (1985: 44) write: "Movement recruiting provides people with a basis for seeing their outcomes as the result of controllable forces external to themselves. This recognition delegitimates the system; we argue that a perception of stable external causality is a prerequisite to sustained action for change."

16. Fireman and Gamson (1979: 8) argue: "Utilitarian assumptions and the conceptual imagery of economics are most useful when the relevant interests are given, concrete, and selfish. . . . But the mobilization of social movements often hinges on changing interests, changing opportunities and threats to interests, and changing inclinations to act on group interests rather than individual ones. Such matters tend to be ignored by utilitarian models, if not ignored altogether."

17. In contrast to some evidence against deprivation as a factor in social movement emergence, the grievances of deprivation have been found, in other cases to play a central role in generating social movements. See, for example, cases of poor people's movements (Piven and Cloward 1977), riot participation (Crawford and Naditch 1970; Caplan and Paige 1968; Bowen et al. 1968), peace groups (Bolton 1972), the early Quaker movement (Kent 1982), and anti-nuclear movements (Opp 1988). The concept of insurgent

consciousness, as conceived in the political process model, helps to reconcile this conflicting evidence.

18. Charles Bolton (1972: 556) represents an early attempt—though one lacking an organizational factor—to formulate a multivariable explanation of social movements: "it seems reasonable to conclude that a high degree of meaninglessness, normlessness, and isolation, in combination with a high sense of being able to influence a social environment . . . predisposes persons toward radical social action." Likewise, Ralph Dahrendorf (1959: 182–93) attempted to formulate a multivariable explanation—including technical, political, social, and psychological conditions—of conflict group formation.

19. In some cases, increased insurgent consciousness may also act to further open political opportunity. For example, the 1933 burning of the Reichstag building by the Nazis—motivated by a growing Nazi insurgent consciousness due to Hitler's appointment as chancellor—served in that situation to expand significantly political opportunity for the Nazi party.

20. This political process model possesses the strength of being both causal and purposive (Tilly 1978: 6). That is, it views social movements as both caused by macrosocial forces and purposefully intended by groups of people. In this way it accounts for both structural determination *and* human agency, which is no small accomplishment.

21. Steedly and Foley (1979: 9) write: "It appears that talk of change is acceptable, even change itself is tolerable, but if that change endangers a member of the polity, then the establishment reacts quickly and with overwhelming strength to end the protest as soon as possible."

22. Ralph Turner, in "The Public Perception of Protest" (1969), explores various factors which determine whether a movement's actions are interpreted by moderates as legitimate protest or illegitimate crime or rebellion.

23. For a few scattered works on revitalization movements that do extist, see Wallace 1956; Zald and Berger 1978; Porterfield 1987; Takayama 1988.

4. The Historical Context

1. Typically caused by situations of instability or threat to one's opponents, which consume their resources and/or diminish their authority that otherwise would have been used to obstruct the realization of one's will.

2. In addition to internal migration, accelerated urbanization was also caused by Latin America's increased natural population growth, through greater life expectancy, taking place among ever-increasing urban populations (Balan 1983: 167; Butterworth and Chance 1981: 42; Beyer 1967: 112). "The decline in mortality was already noticeable after the early 1900s, but it became general and even more significant with the 1930s. . . . The decline in mortality was faster in large cities. . . . The lowering of mortality rates as a whole was unprecedented in world demographic history . . . thus leading to a rapid increase in population growth" (Balan 1983: 167).

3. According to Quijano (1975: 130–31), Argentina, Brazil, Chile, Mexico, and Uruguay "were compelled to find substitutes for the principal consumer goods imported for their urban population. Import substitution had to be

financed almost entirely by national capital. . . . The expansion of industry gave further impetus to urbanization in those countries. . . . The result was that the urban population and the major towns grew far more rapidly than elsewhere in Latin America." In other countries, such as Peru and Ecuador, import substitution industries only developed significantly after World War II (ibid.).

4. Various scholars have conceptualized the Latin American Catholic Church's key interest, and therefore problem, differently. Bouvier (1983) and Einaudi et al. (1969), for example, stress the Church's need for "institutional survival." Vallier (1967, 1970) and Bruneau (1974, 1985) emphasize the Church's interest in exercising "influence." These kinds of reductionistic conceptualizations, however, confuse means and ends. However, if one understands the Church on its own terms (Levine 1981: 13; Sanders 1982: 255), one sees that the Church's key interest is *carrying out, as effectively as possible, its self-defined mission:* to spread and strengthen the Catholic faith and to facilitate the changes in human life that faith demands. While institutional survival and influence are among the necessary conditions for achieving that mission, they are not the mission itself.

5. Most notably, the Assemblies of God, Seventh Day Adventist, Presbyterian, Methodist, and Christian and Missionary Alliance churches.

6. In Salvador, Brazil, in 1950 there were 6,831 professing Spiritists, in 1960 there were 15,330, and in 1965, 19,580. The average increase in Spiritists over a decade for the state of Bahia was 187.3 percent, but in cities and episcopal sees it was 224 percent (Bruneau 1974: 63). Also, studies in 1950 indicated that one in three Brazilians participated in an Afro-Brazilian cult, and that 300,000 Umbanda centers of worship existed in Brazil (Latourette 1962: 164; O'Gorman 1977: 25).

7. By 1975, Brazil alone had a shortage of twenty thousand priests, with only eighty-six new ordinations per year (Della Cava 1976: 21).

8. Hurtado's book was modeled after a book published in France the previous year, titled *France: A Pagan Country?* with whose author Hurtado was in contact (Quigley 1987; Torres 1988).

9. In fact, in most Latin American countries, while census data report that over 90 percent of Latin Americans consider themselves Catholic, most surveys show that less than 10 percent regularly participate in Sunday mass and other important Catholic activities, even in the best-staffed cities (Latourette 1962: 162; Della Cava 1976: 24; see also Bruneau 1974: 60–61).

10. Pablo Richard, a Chilean liberation theologian, recalls Hurtado's book: "It was very important. It opened us up. I read this book and it impressed me a lot; it made us realize that not all Roman Catholics are evangelized people" (interview, 1988).

11. The delegates agreed, though, to maintain a tolerant, rather than hostile, attitude toward Protestants, helping to set the stage for the ecumenical cooperation of liberation theologians (Cleary 1985: 5).

12. For an excellent description of the Cursillo Movement see Cleary 1985: 6–8.

13. The following Catholic theology departments were founded: Bogotá

in 1937, Lima in 1942, Medellín in 1945, São Paulo and Rio de Janeiro in 1947, Porto Alegre in 1950, Campinas and Quito in 1956, Buenos Aires and Cordoba in 1960, and Valparaiso and Guatemala in 1961 (Dussel 1978: 178).

14. Indeed, Ralph Della Cava (1976: 24) characterizes the unsuccessful attempts to bolster the number of priests: "By 1966, the hope of resolving the 'priest-problem south of the border' had come full circle to crashing despair."

15. In 1928, two priests—Caggiano and Miranda—went to Rome to study the relevance of Catholic Action for Latin America. Catholic Action was then founded in Argentina and Chile in 1931, in Uruguay in 1934, in Brazil, Costa Rica, and Peru in 1935, and in Bolivia in 1938 (Dussel 1978: 178; Adriance 1986: 20).

16. A different, though related, strategy of the Brazilian Church to "re-Catholicize" society was the Catholic Electoral League, which operated from 1932 to 1937 as a Catholic political pressure group. The League was founded by Cardinal Leme, who also was responsible for establishing, in 1935, Catholic Action in Brazil (M. Williams 1974; Della Cava 1976).

17. In Chile, Catholic Action had 45,761 members in 1936 and 58,071 in 1945; in 1957, JOC alone had 380 trained leaders and 2,800 militants (Smith 1982: 95–96). In Brazil, JOC had 15,000 members by 1953 and 120,000 by the mid-1960s (Cleary 1985: 4).

18. For example, Eduardo Frei, was introduced to Social Christianity by bishop Manuel Larraín of Talca, Chile and, in 1964, became President of Chile with the Christian Democratic Party (Torres 1988).

19. As of 1953 (Gibbons et al. 1958: iv).

20. Despite the fact that, "nowhere in canon law . . . and Roman practice had there been any precedent for creating a *permanent* structure of the likes of the CNBB and its secretariat" (Della Cava 1976: 32).

21. The CNBB received the official approval of Pope Pius XII in 1958.

22. Explaining this effect of national bishops' conferences, Cleary (1985: 12) writes, "It is one thing for the President of Bolivia to deny the request of Jorge Manrique, archbishop of La Paz, that a foreign priest not be expelled; it is quite another thing for the President to face the 'demand' of the national council of bishops to keep hands off."

23. The CNBB was a pioneer organization, instituted ten years before *Lumen Gentium,* the Vatican II document that provided the official basis for national bishops' conferences in countries around the world (Adriance 1986: 25).

24. The following national councils were approved by Rome: Mexico in 1955, Bolivia in 1956, Peru, Columbia, Chile, and Ecuador in 1957, Paraguay and Venezuela in 1958, Haiti and Argentina in 1959 (CELAM 1982: 77).

25. Larraín actually had the idea of trying to help form a political restructuring of Latin America, modeled after the United States, a "United States of Latin America" (Torres 1988).

26. Departments of Preservation and Diffusion of the Catholic Faith, Clergy and Religious Institutes, Education and Youth, Apostolates of the Laity, and Social Action and Assistance (CELAM 1982: 365).

27. According to Marina Bandeira, it was commonly assumed that Hélder Camera would function as secretary general of CELAM. However, the CNBB did not have the funds to headquarter CELAM in Rio (where Hélder Camera was newly appointed as auxiliary bishop), so the post was give to Msgr. Julian Mendoza of Columbia. Hélder Camera served as vice president of CELAM from 1959 to 1965 (Bandeira 1988; CELAM 1982: 365–66).

28. The two Popes between Leo XIII and Pius XI—Pius X and Benedict XV—contributed little to the Church's social teachings (Dorr 1983: 52–56).

29. See also Cleary 1985: 58.

30. Henri de Lubac had been an inspiration for the resistance movement, developing a theory of the lawfulness of resistance to an unjust power (Martina 1988: 31). On the other hand, many French Catholic priests had discovered, to their deep concern, during the war, that French prisoners of war and members of the underground resistance with whom they attempted to establish contacts were totally estranged from the Church—practical atheists (Praamsma 1981: 188).

31. Speaking critically about the use of the New Theology by liberation theologians, Praamsma (1981: 190) continues: "The New Theology tried to build bridges everywhere, but in its extremist form it came out in favor of dynamiting bridges, for leftist adherents of the New Theology joined with the Marxists in preaching the gospel of liberation."

32. For example, Fernando Cardoso and Enzo Faletto wrote the first draft of their book, *Dependency and Development in Latin America,* in 1965–67, while still working for the United Nations' Latin American Institute for Economic and Social Planning, an organizational offshoot of ECLA (Cardoso and Faletto 1979: vii).

5. From the Creation of CELAM to Vatican II

1. According to Adriance (1984: 502), for example, by the late 1950s, "some observers were going so far as to say that the Brazilian Catholic Church was dying."

2. For an exploration of the effects of the Cuban revolution on the Cuban Church, see Crahan 1985.

3. According to interviewees, the Cuban Revolution was an event that "scared some bishops to death, in Venezuela, Puerto Rica, Dominican Republic, where many Cubans fled to" (Quigley 1987), that "provoked terror" in many Catholics (Bonino 1987), that was *"the* event which really made an impact on Latin America" (Torres 1988).

4. It was, according to Berryman, a "kick in the behind for reformism" (Berryman 1987b).

5. Vatican II convened every Autumn in Rome for three and one-half months (Cleary 1985: 19). It was covered by 3,000 approved journalists, produced 16 documents, 27,000 pages of records, and about 138 miles of audio recording tape (Nichols 1968: 290, 292).

6. Indeed, Cleary (1985: 168) calls it "the greatest event in the last four

centuries of Catholicism." Liberation theologian José Comblin states, "Vatican II was an event of utmost importance, for Catholics everywher ›. By creating an atmosphere of freedom and inviting people to critically rethink their ideas, it encouraged fresh avenues of thought, awoke a spirit of discovery, and dared people to undertake great, new things" (LADOC no. 2: 3).

7. The documents of Vatican II can be found in Abbott 1966.

8. Martina argues that there was a "continuity between various preconciliar theological trends and the basic ideas of the documents of Vatican II. The Ecumenical Council does not represent a break with the past, but a development and fulfillment of aspirations that were already widespread, even if not at the center [Rome] but only in the outlying areas [France, Belgium, Germany, the Netherlands]" (Martina 1988: 42; see also Mutchler 1971: 26).

9. The six hundred Latin American bishops represented 22 percent of those attending the Council (CELAM 1982: 91).

10. McGrath (1988) recalls: "In the Council we learned to consult much more and to work things out together."

11. See also Mutchler 1971: 29.

12. Even at Vatican II, there were 319 approved Latin American advisers. "Many of them were young priests who had recently completed their studies, often in Europe. They acted as intellectual bridges for the Latin American church, interpreting what was taking place in Council discussions and eventually reinterpreting for Latin America the ideological thrust of the Council" (Cleary 1985: 19).

13. Other observers support this observation: "The Latin American bishops discovered advisers at Vatican II" (Bonino 1987); "Some of the bishops and some of the hierarchies in Latin America began to use staff advisers after the example of the Council" (McGrath 1988); "Latin American bishops started using advisers and staff people much more after Vatican II than previously; the Council demonstrated the need for advisers, that nobody had all the answers" (Poblete 1988); "The decision to expand staff sectors came at precisely the time when these positions were being given international attention. It was the Second Vatican Council that, in spectacular fashion, elevated . . . *periti* to a level of prominence" (Mutchler 1971: 25).

14. Indeed, for this and other reasons, Lernoux argues that liberation theology would have never come into existence without Vatican II (Lernoux 1982: 31). Otto Maduro (1987) argues that Vatican II cut ten years off the time it would have taken for liberation theology to emerge.

15. According to Quigley (1987), "The official story is that they sensed with one voice the need to meet again, but I have no idea how true that is. So, people like Hélder Camera, Larraín, Proaño, and McGrath put things together."

16. A few of these bishops were not actually progressives themselves, but were willing to listen to and support progressives: "Pablo Muñoz Vega was a moderate, but a very good thinker. He was quite open-minded" (Dussel 1988). Also, eventually, some of these bishops who *were* progressives in early

years abandoned the liberation theology movement, such as Eugenio Sales, who became a major opponent in later years. Other bishops who would later use their positions to facilitate and protect what eventually became the liberation theology movement included Cardinal Arns, Aloisio Lorscheider, Oscar Romero, Pedro Casaldáliga, Antonio Batista Fragoso, José Maria Pires, Tomas Balduino, José Parra León, and Arturo Rivera y Damas.

17. Quigley (1987), likewise, describes Larraín as "a bridge person and an organizer who knew how to put things together."

18. Robert MacAfee Brown (1988) recalls of Hélder Camera: "At Vatican II, Hélder Camera never spoke once. He preferred to work behind the scenes."

19. Furthermore, there was an absolute increase during this time of progressive bishops through new appointments. In Chile, for example, "between 1955 and 1964, fourteen of the twenty-eight bishops in the country retired or died and their replacements tended to be social progressives" (Smith 1982: 112).

20. According to Einaudi et al. (1969), it was part of Rome's plans for "shoring up Church structures in Latin America" that "promising Latin American priests were to be sent abroad, particularly to Louvain (Belgium) for training in socially useful disciplines like sociology." Nuñez states: "At that time there was great concern in Europe for the state of poverty in Latin America and for the threat of communism. Scholarships were provided for Latin American students with the hope that they would help to counter that threat, eliminating poverty and establishing a 'just and Christian order'" (1985: 115–16).

21. Nuñez states: "Father Gerardo Alarco, principle professor of the Catholic University in Peru, discovered that [Gustavo] Gutiérrez was extremely intelligent and encouraged him to continue his studies in Chile, Louvain, and Lyons. Alarco had been influenced by the Catholic 'New Theology' during his studies in Europe and came to be known in Lima as a 'renovating rebel'" (Nuñez 1985: 115).

22. Bonino explains: "The Latin American bishops brought some of their advisers and were using some of their people who were already studying in Europe, who were beginning to relate to the European advisers, too. When these advisers came back [to Latin America], they became very, very influential, because now they had to do in their own situation what the Europeans had done in theirs" (Bonino 1987).

23. For detailed explorations of the phenomenon of BECs, see Levine and Mainwaring 1989; Barreiro 1982; L. Boff 1986; Cook 1985; LADOC no. 14; O'Gorman 1983; Torres and Eagleson 1982; Berryman 1984a; Lernoux 1987; Ramalho 1977; Santa Ana 1986; Fragoso 1987; Hewitt 1986, 1987.

24. The antecedents of BECs were the cell groups of the Young Christian Workers (JOC) in Brazil; the community life of rural *campesinos;* lay renewal movements (such as the *Cursillos de Cristiandad*); the pastoral innovations of bishop José Delgado in Sao Lui, Brazil; the "Natal Movement" (initiated by bishop Eugenio Sales in the 1940s); and the Nizia Floresta parish "nuns only"

experiment (Berryman 1987b; O'Gorman 1988; Adriance 1984: 504; idem. 1986: 54).

25. This proposal grew out of the experience of the Natal Movement, which was inspired by bishop Eugenio Sales (Adriance 1986: 25–28).

26. Radios were set up by MEB to tune into one station only (Adriance 1986: 44).

27. Conscientization (consciousness raising) is a pedagogical method, popularized by Brazilian educator Paulo Freire in the late 1950s, which used the daily life experiences of the poor to promote literacy and foster a critical awareness of social reality (Freire 1972). Three reading lessons from the MEB primer reflect this method of conscientization: (Lesson One) "I live and struggle. Pedro lives and struggles. The people live and struggle. I, Pedro and the people live. I, Pedro and the people struggle. We struggle to live. To live is to struggle." (Lesson Sixteen) "The peasant is a man of the land. He works the land. He gathers the fruit of the land. Does the peasant have land? Does he have all that he needs to cultivate the land? Does he have a guarantee of the harvest? Does the peasant have any guarantee of work?" (Lesson Twenty-One) "The peasants feel the need for unity. They feel that united they can take action. Their right to unity is lawful. Pedro and his fellow workers want to start a union. A union is unity. A union is strength. Unity creates strength in the union" (Adriance 1986: 50–51).

28. By the mid-1980s, according to Rene Padilla (1987: 12), that number had grown to 200,000.

29. 175,000 BECs multiplied by an average of 30 members equals 8,250,000 people.

30. Gutiérrez also met and became friends with Camilo Torres at Louvain in the 1950s (Mottesi 1985: 74).

31. Gutiérrez and the Protestant Alves, however, did not meet until 1969, in Campine, Switzerland; Gutiérrez and Assman did not meet until 1970, at an early conference on liberation theology (Gutiérrez 1988). But by 1972, most of the relational network of the leadership of liberation theology was formed.

32. By 1970, the number of CELAM departments, not counting the Economics Committee, had been expanded to thirteen (CELAM 1982: 372–73).

33. Jerome Levinson, deputy director of the Office of Capital Development of AID's Latin American Bureau, and Juan de Onis, a Latin American journalist who covered the Alliance, in 1970 described the Alliance's outcome thus: "A decade of the Alliance for Progress has yielded more shattered hopes than solid accomplishments, more discord than harmony, more disillusionment than satisfaction. The progress has been halting, painful, and uneven, and the nations allied are discontented, restless, and tense. Without the Alliance the Latin American experience in the 1960s might have been even more turbulent. But the Alliance was unable to impose reconciliation on the fundamental conflicts it sought to overcome. It was a dramatic and noble crusade deriving from excessive idealism and overoptimism a momentum that was slowly but indisputably dissipated in encounters with harsh realities—economic, political, social. . . . As [its proponents] conceived it, the

Alliance could counteract the appeal of Castroism to Latin America's once docile masses of workers and peasants by offering them economic benefits and social reform within a democratic political framework. In retrospect, the program designed to kill two birds with one stone has hit neither squarely. It has not removed the danger of revolution and it has not brought significant economic, social, and political advancement to the poor of Latin America" (Levinson and Onis 1970: 307).

34. Levinson and Onis (1973: 13) comment: "The targets themselves reflect not only the projections of the Latin American development experts but also the optimism with which the Kennedy administration (intentionally, although not cynically) had infused inter-American relations. But hindsight shows that the problems of development are more difficult, and the political consequences of unfulfilled expectations more disastrous, than the authors of the charter ever anticipated."

35. The Spanish word "para" in *Alianza para el Progreso* can mean either "for" or "stop."

36. Incidently, Marina Bandeira (1988) reports that the beginning of the public downfall and (later) repression, of Dom Hélder Camera in Brazil was connected with the failure of the AFP: "First, everyone had hope about Kennedy. Later on, he was viewed as a sort of interference. There was a reaction against that. In the early 1960s, Dom Hélder criticized some aspects of the Alliance for Progress, that it was intervention, not cooperation. The U.S. representative to Brazil for this program asked Dom Hélder if he would repeat that for the U.S. television. Hélder agreed and it was recorded and broadcast all over the United States. A few days later came the first criticism against Dom Hélder in Brazil. Up to then, the man was untouchable, everything he said was perfect, no one could criticize the man for anything. Suddenly, because of that television program, there was an article criticizing the "Red Bishop." Dom Hélder answered back. This began to create an atmosphere against Dom Hélder. By 1964, it was forbidden to mention the name Hélder Camera in the newspapers. The man could have been dead."

37. For documents on the Church and State in Brazil after the coup, see LADOC no. 8, "Brazil."

38. As evidenced by the CNBB, the Natal Movement, MEB, the social criticisms of the bishops of the Northeast, the development of BECs, and so on.

39. See the comments on the "theology of revolution" in chapter 1, p. 17

40. Bonino (1987) rightly observes, "Usually in the history of liberation theology, the Protestant side is neglected." Actually, Protestants played a very important role in the emergence and development of liberation theology. One work which explores this history in depth is: Alan Preston Neely, *Protestant Antecedents of the Latin American Theology of Liberation* (1977). See also Emilio Nuñez 1985: 53–82.

41. Neely (1977: 253) argues that, "it is doubtful if any theologian has more consistently and directly contributed to the shaping of the thought of the contemporary Protestant theologians of liberation than Richard Shaull."

While some (Roger Vekemans) contend that Shaull first introduced the liberation theme into Latin American theological discussions, others (José Míguez Bonino) regard Shaull as only a precursor or forerunner to liberation theology (ibid., 256).

42. Of the SCM, Neely says (1977: 155–56): "A decade before the organization of ISAL, the SCM was functioning as a Protestant ecumenical force of no mean proportion and [as] a veritable pipeline for dispersing throughout Latin America the sociopolitical emphases, insights, perspectives, and concepts of the WCC. Those concepts clearly related to the theology of liberation. . . . It was these [SCM] groups that acted as ideological incubators for the production of young Protestant Christians who were sensitive to the social and political implications of the Christian Gospel and who subsequently became the foremost spokesmen of the ISAL movement in the 1960s."

43. What Shaull meant by "guerrilla warfare" is ambiguous—it is not clear how guerrilla warfare could be carried out from Princeton University. Probably Shaull used the phrase figuratively, meaning an approach in which Christian organizations with inferior resources used noninstitutionalized political tactics in attempts to achieve social-structural change by force.

44. For example, Rubem Alves, an ISAL member and student at Princeton (in exile from Brazil), in 1969, wrote and had published his dissertation entitled, "Toward a Theology of Liberation." This technically would have been the first publication of a work of "liberation theology," had not Alves' publisher disliked the word "liberation" and changed the title to *A Theology of Human Hope* (Alves 1988).

45. As early as 1959, Shaull held dialogues with Brazilian Dominicans on the issue of Marxism. By 1962, ISAL in Brazil began including Catholics in their organization, such as Alberto Gomez de Souza, who worked with Paulo Freire and MEB (Shaull 1987). Between 1963 and 1967, ISAL developed ties with Catholic organizations, such as Pax Romana and Brazilian Catholic Action. This resulted in dialogues with Gustavo Gutiérrez, Juan Luis Segundo, and others, through which they began to realize that, despite their differences in backgrounds, they had common perspectives and interests (Santa Ana 1988).

46. In this sense, through providing leadership, ISAL functioned as much to increase organizational strength as it did to contribute to the generation of insurgent consciousness.

47. Dom Hélder Camera was named archbishop of Recife-Olinda on April 12, 1964, eleven days after the military coup (Kemper and Engel 1987).

48. According to Marina Bandeira (1988), the bishops of the Northeast developed such a reputation in the CNBB that eventually *any* bishop in Brazil, no matter where they were from, who began agitating for social change was identified as "a bishop from the Northeast."

49. In this document, Bishop Dom Inocencio Engelke argued: "We have already lost the workers of the cities. We cannot commit the stupidity of also losing the workers in the fields." Statements of this sort were common during this period (Bruneau 1974: 66).

50. The article caused a considerable uproar among those who were work-

ing to increase foreign support, as did his 1967 article, "The Vanishing Clergyman," predicting the imminent extinction of the role of clergy in Latin America (Dussel 1976: 130).

51. The Bogotá meeting was held June 14–July 9; Cuernavaca was July 4–August 14; Havana was July 14–16 (Mottesi 1985, 32–33; Oliveros 1990: 44).

6. From Vatican II to Medellín

1. A 56-member revolutionary priest group, formed in Panama in January 1968 by Father Herrera, even called themselves the "*Populorum Progressio Movement*" (Gheerbrant 1974: 282).

2. "Priests everywhere . . . felt frustrated; they were having grave doubts about the very value of their priestly life. They could see that the traditional priestly role . . . made little sense in 1967. They couldn't see how they fitted into today's world" (LADOC 5:45).

3. In one attitude survey of seven hundred Chilean priests by ILADES of Santiago, Chile, when asked whether "the Church should ordain married men," 43 percent answered that it was "a possibility to be seriously studied," 43 percent answered that it was "one of the changes most necessary for the future of the Chilean Church" (Mutchler 1971: 423–24). According to Lernoux, more priests and nuns left the Church to marry than did the religious of any other continent (Lernoux 1982: 43).

4. Maduro (1987) remarks: "Arrupe had a very profound sensitivity for the plight of the oppressed in the world. He had personally experienced oppression being a Basque in Spain, which caused in him a repugnance of dictatorship. After Vatican II, he became more and more open to hearing the voices of the oppressed coming from Latin America."

5. Bonino (1987) comments: "I suspect the renewal of Jesuits has its roots in Northern Spain, the Basque and Catalonian area, at the end of Franco's dictatorship—they were the most anti-Franco. And, Jon Sobrino, Ignacio Ellacuría, and probably twelve other important Jesuits in Latin American liberation theology come from Spain."

6. Arrupe's energy is reflected in the fact that he was the first Order General to hold regular press conferences (Hollis 1968: 253).

7. "No organization has occupied itself so intensively with the study of Marxism since the days of the old Socialist First International, and certainly no Catholic order has a more legitimate right to concern itself with social issues—and the problem of socialism—than the Society of Jesus" (Barthel 1984: 293).

8. See, for example, the Peruvian Bishops' Commission for Social Action's, *Between Honesty and Hope* (Maryknoll Documentation Series 1970) for an excellent collection of progressive and radical Church documents from this period (1966–69).

9. Torres had proclaimed: "I took off my cassock to be more truly a priest," "the duty of every Catholic is to be a revolutionary, the duty of every revolutionary is to make the revolution," and "the Catholic who is not a revolutionary is living in mortal sin" (Gerassi 1971: xiii). After his death, we have seen,

hundreds of "Camilista groups" sprung up in Columbia, Venezuela, Ecuador, Peru, and Bolivia (Maduro 1987; Gotay 1983: 55) and questions about the futility of reformist strategies and the justification of violent revolution were forced to the center of Christian debates.

10. The one exception was ONIS, of Peru, which was supportive of and was supported by the Peruvian hierarchy.

11. Cleary (1987) states: "By 1967 and '68, Vatican II was activating a large number of priests and pastoral workers, many of whom were foreign. Then activist groups got started in places where the bishops weren't going fast enough."

12. In 1975, 250 priests, representing 19 percent of priests in Peru, were members of ONIS (Bonino 1975: 52).

13. The signers were archbishops Dom Hélder Camera, João da Mota e Albuquerque and bishops Luiz Gonzaga Fernandes, Severino Mariano de Aguiar, Fransisco Austregesilo, Manuel Pereira da Costa, and Antonio Batista Fragoso of Brazil, bishops Angelo Cuniberti of Columbia, George Mercier of Algeria, Amand Hubert of Egypt, Etienne Loosdregt of Laos, Charles Joseph van Melckebeke of China, Gregori Haddad of Lebanon, Franx Franic of Yugoslavia, and Michel Darmancier of Oceania (LADOC 5:10).

14. All quotes taken from LADOC 5:2–10.

15. The bishop of Buenaventura, Gerardo Valencia Cano, was one of the few progressive Columbian bishops; he signed "The Golconda Declaration" and publicly proclaimed: "Definitely, I proclaim myself, with the companions of Golconda, revolutionary and socialist because we cannot remain indifferent to the capitalist structure which is producing among the Colombian people the most tremendous frustration and injustices" (Cabal 1978: 173).

16. This declaration created an uproar throughout the Colombian Church; the group was repressed by the hierarchy and interests outside of the Church (Torres 1988). Golconda met again in Bogotá, in February 1970, and in July 1970, at which time they chose to disband themselves (LADOC 5:40–41). According to Cabal, "many of them became tired of meditating about a theology of liberation, and some, fretfully, hung up their soutanes while others guided by the spirit of Camilo Torres joined the guerrillas" (Cabal 1978: 173).

17. An exception was Peru's ONIS, which chose to work with rather than against the Peruvian hierarchy. The emergence of the Chilean priest group, "The Eighty," will be examined in chapter 8.

18. For example, Gustavo Gutiérrez of ONIS, Pablo Richard, Sergio Torres, and Gonzalo Arroyo of The Eighty, Enrique Dussel of Priests for the Third World, and Otto Maduro of Camilista groups (Maduro 1987; Torres 1988). For an extended list, see table 8.5, p. 175).

19. The government campaigned intensively (though unsuccessfully) to persuade Rome to remove Hélder Camera from office (Dussel 1981: 154) and made numerous death threats and actual attempts on his life (Kemper and Engel 1987).

20. "Eventually," reports Bandeira (1988), "in the 1970s, the anticommunist propaganda became unbelievable, so the Church began to consider social-

ism as an alternative." Berryman (1987a: 113) agrees: "At the official level bishops did not immediately respond to the shift to repressive governments. Some Brazilian bishops welcomed the 1964 coup, for example. Gradually, however, often spurred by the arrest, torture, expulsion, or murder of Church personnel, bishops began to take stands."

21. For more detailed explorations of the Brazilian Church's response to the military regime, see José Comblin's, *The Church and the National Security State* (Orbis Books, 1979); Luiz Gonzaga de Souza Lima's *Political Evolution of the Catholic Church in Brazil* (1979); Ulisse Floridi's *Brazilian Catholic Radicalism* (1973).

22. Protopapas (1974: 99) confirms this figure: at the time when Christians for Socialism had 225 members, 175 of them were foreign priest.

23. Mitchell (1981: 295) claims that the research of Jesuit sociologists Emile Pin (who worked with Houtart) had an important influence on the thinking and orientation of Ivan Illich.

24. And, they provided forums for systematically and creatively dealing with those problems: "The new magazines, the research institutes, priest movements, and CIAS were, in effect, primitive think tanks" (Cleary 1987).

25. Though the term was and is used in the singular, there were many dependency theories.

26. Cardoso writes: "Capitalist accumulation in dependent economies does not complete its cycle. Lacking autonomous technology, as vulgar parlance has it, and compelled therefore to utilize imported technology, dependent capitalism is crippled. . . . It is crippled because it lacks a fully developed capital goods sector. The accumulation, expansion, and self-realization of local capital requires and depends on a dynamic compliment outside itself" (quoted in Caporaso and Zare 1981: 45).

27. For example, titles in a series of studies on dependency published in Argentina between 1970 and 1975—which included some Catholic radical authors, such as Gustavo Gutiérrez, Hector Borrat, and Aldo Buntig—illustrate the extent to which dependency theory was used to interpret almost all aspects of social realities: *The Law in a Dependent Society, The Cyultural Sciences and Dependency, Religion: Alienation in a Dependent Society, Economic and Political Analysis of Dependency, Sociological and Psychosocial Analysis of Dependency, The Experience of Science and Technology and Dependency, The University and Dependency, Theology, Pastoral Action, and Dependency, International Politics and Dependency, Historical Analysis of Argentine Dependency, Imperialism and the Church, Internal Neocolonialism* (Argentine Dependency in the Latin American Context [Argentina: Editorial Guadalupe, 1970–1975]).

28. Critics have pointed out that many implications of dependency theory—for example, freedom from responsibility for one's own failures by laying blame on the exploitation of Europe and North America—make it inherently attractive to Third World leaders and intellectuals (Novak 1982: 272–73; idem. 1986: 127–42; Berger 1985: 4–20).

29. The Jesuit Order's traditional concern with academic excellence naturally put them in contact with developments in the social sciences: "Previously [before the shift to the poor] Jesuits had always worked with the elites

which gave them an intellectual respectability. This enabled them to spot first the developments in sociology and economics" (Bonino 1987).

30. This early and strong identification with dependency theory and the use of it as a major foundation for liberation theology would later become problematic to some theologians who, as significant criticisms of and doubts about the theory mounted, had to revise their theological system in a way less dependent on dependency theory. For attempts to do this, see Gutiérrez 1984; Haight 1985; see also McGovern 1987: 115–16; idem. 1989a: 589).

31. Bonino (1987) observes, "The major historical shift was the rise of dependency theory. It was a dividing of the waters. When people influenced by the Catholic renewal were confronted with the dependency theory crisis, there was a parting of the ways. Some remained in modern Eurpean renewal theology and others left to pursue liberation."

7. Making Medellín

1. For a detailed study of Medellín, see Prada 1975.

2. "The presidency" meant the president, first vice-president, second vice-president, and the presidents of the commissions; specifically, this meant the cadre of progressive bishops: Larraín, Brandão, Muñoz Vega, McGrath, Padin, Proaño, Sales, Mendoza, Baccino, Henriquez, and Dammert Bellido (CELAM 1982: 368–69).

3. In addition to these CELAM-sponsored informal consultations, the network of progressive theologians organized meetings of their own. For example, they gathered in Santiago, Chile in July 1966 to reflect on the theme "Word and Evangelization." Participants included Gustavo Gutiérrez, José Comblin, Juan Luis Segundo, and Severino Croatto (Mottesi 1985: 36).

4. Cleary (1987) describes the kinds of interactions: "You get a guy like Gustavo Gutiérrez, who comes along just at the right time in his life when he's really thinking and being creative, and he says, 'Oh yes, we can't go on with this idea of lay people simply being in submission to bishops.' And they look at him and ask why not. And he says, 'well, because of the priesthood of all believers.' And he's mouthing the slogans from Vatican II, which was really heady stuff. A lot of us felt light-headed, it's wild stuff."

5. Sergio Torres (1988) explains the unsettling effect on progressive theologians of working with radicalized university students: "Many of the questions which preceded the liberation theology movement started with university students in Brazil. Others came from Uruguay, with lay thinkers interacting with European thought about Marxism. Gustavo went several times to Brazil to attend meetings and listen to others. He and others knew something was wrong, that something needed to be done. But nobody knew what. We had been trained to be afraid of Marxism. It was very difficult at the time to imagine remaining faithful to Catholic teachings, yet being open to Marxism. Many lay people left the church because they could not figure out how to be revolutionary and Catholic—there was not yet a sympathetic response from the church, as there is today in liberation theology. Liberation theology was a response, then—in addition to grinding poverty—to middle-

class students who were finding Christianity to be irrelevant. There was a real drama for us, a real crisis, many conversations and nights without sleep during 1965 to 1967. Then, in 1968, there came some clarity."

6. Richard (1988) argues: "Buga, Baños, Mar del Plata, and the rest were very important because they were exactly the break with development and the Vatican II mentality. In these conferences was a break with a concern with atheism to a concern with idolatry."

7. The original projected date for Medellín was 1967.

8. Participating bishops included McGrath, Brandão, Pironio, Metzinger, Proaño, and Padin (Cleary 1985: 38).

9. Cleary (1985: 38) argues: "Because of their experience with Vatican Council II, [the CELAM insiders] believed the bulk of the work of the conference had to be expressed in the preparatory documents if there were to be any breakthroughs, given the relatively short duration of the conference. Conference participants thus would ratify what had been prepared for them by the core group." McGrath's (1988) perspective is somewhat different: "In Medellín, the preliminary documents were not used. Instead, we had several new working papers which were used to clear the air, to get us organized around a central idea in the conciliar line of thought."

10. For accounts of the reactions of various bishops, national episcopal conferences, and of Rome, see Prada 1975: 51–64, 69–72.

11. Mutchler (1971: 128) writes: "At the beginning of the conference, a large number of staff experts startled most of the bishops by requesting the right to vote. Had they been given voting rights, the documents on justice, peace, masses, and elites would doubtless have been very different, and the conflicts over their resolution much more bitter."

12. Gutiérrez (1988) recalls: "We had the atmosphere of Vatican II: rather open dialogue. Some of the people were more or less afraid but the atmosphere in general was good, open, friendly."

13. Poblete (1988) states: "Eugenio Sales gave a very good talk. Sales was the most advanced there, and he inspired the whole committee on Peace later on. Today he is very conservative, but at that time he was the most advanced, together with Hélder Camera and McGrath."

14. According to Mutchler (1971: 122): "The formal meetings of the conference saw the early rejection of Vatican Cardinal Zamore's directives and hegemony in favor of the Brazilian model. The bishops elected their own heads of committees and determined to open full debate on the working document[s] rather than merely endorse the papal positions on violence, reforms, and cooperative development outlined in papal encyclicals and in Bogotá [where the Pope himself had just visited]."

15. Eugenio Sales was president of the Commission on Justice and Peace and president of the subcommission on Justice; Carlos Parteli was president of, and Pierre Bigo, Gustavo Gutiérrez, and Hélder Camera were members of, the subcommission on Peace; Lionidas Proaño was a member of the commission on Poverty (Prada 1975: 261–62, 267).

16. Gutiérrez was not even a formal member of the Commission on Poverty (Prada 1975: 267).

17. Gutiérrez (1988) recalls: "We often did the writing. I was on the commission for Peace but also wrote several texts for other commissions, for Poverty, for example. The theological text on Poverty was my draft. I gave many suggestions for other documents as well."

18. One of the most important was Dom Hélder Camera: "Dom Hélder Camera was perhaps the most important person at Medellín. Dom Hélder brought together these young theologians, like Gutiérrez, and so on, and they drafted the documents" (Bonino 1987). "Hélder was more the prophet; he was a constructor, he organized Medellín. He and McGrath worked together very closely, very well" (Poblete 1988). Marina Bandeira (1988) argues, on the other hand, that the success of the progressive agenda was inevitable: "There were groups of people organizing to pull strings, but the outcome of the meeting was unavoidable."

19. The latter statement is reminiscent of *Populorum Progressio.*

20. For the documents on justice, peace, poverty, and family and demography, see Gremillion 1976: 445ff.

8. From Medellín to Sucre

1. Because of the widespread process of radicalization that many progressives experienced during the period 1966 through 1968, many of those whom I previously referred to as "progressives" became a distinct group which, in this and the next chapters, I refer to as "radicals."

2. An excerpt from a 1972 article by liberation theologian José Comblin illustrates this point: "Latin American Christian thought has made a choice among three visions of the world and of the Church that it found offered. It rejected the vision of the 'conservatives' and that of the 'developmentalists.' It adopted the vision of the 'revolutionaries.' That is immediately obvious from chapter 7 of the Medellín *Conclusions,* on the 'Pastoral Concern for the Elite,' and it is implicit all through the other chapters" (LADOC 2:4). On the question of interpreting and reinterpreting Medellín, see Comblin 1973.

3. That is, the conclusions of the third plenary session of CELAM at Puebla, Mexico, in 1979.

4. According to Enrique Dussel (1988), in the late 1960s, small groups of five or six theologians would frequently meet together for informal exchanges of ideas. Dussel met with Gutiérrez in this way thirty separate times and with Juan Luis Segundo seven times.

5. "Their field is the whole Christian enterprise—and beyond that, the universe. They do not attempt to promote Roman Catholicism, Lutheranism, or Methodism. Instead, they focus on the universal church and the modern world" (Cleary 1985: 17). Míguez Bonino is fond of saying: "there is nothing more ecumenical than liberation" (Santa Anna 1988).

6. "They use either sociological concepts and research findings or sociological metaphors in their theological reasoning" (Cleary 1985: 17).

7. These three Institutes worked closely together and were focused on similar concerns. Gutiérrez (1988) argues, "The Liturgical Institute in Medellín was very important. 'Liturgical' was the name but it was really about

pastoral issues. Likewise with the Catechetics Institute in Santiago, Chile." For this reason, many refer to them collectively as IPLA, as I do in this chapter.

8. Other IPLA professors included Ivan Illich, José Comblin, and Lucio Gera (Nuñez 1985: 117).

9. In table 8.5 I treat the organization ISAL as a kind of "Protestant priest group," since it served a similar function within Protestant denominations to that served by priest groups.

10. Sergio Torres (1988) recalls of that meeting: "There were disagreements between ONIS and all of the other groups about whether to work within the Church. The rest of us were very critical of the Church, but ONIS advocated working within the Church structures."

11. One exception was the March 2–7, 1970, "First Symposium on Liberation Theology," organized by Golconda's Camilo Moncada, in Bogotá, Columbia, and attended by thirteen hundred Colombians (Moncada 1971; LADOC 5:41).

12. The following provide in-depth histories and documents of the Christians for Socialism movement. For sources sympathetic to the movement see Richard 1976, and Eagleson 1975. For sources critical of the movement, see Donoso Loero 1975, and Vekemans 1976. See also LADOC 6.

13. In 1968, a small group of Christian Democrats had broken away from the Christian Democratic party, and formed a new, more radical political organization called Movement of Unitary Popular Action (MAPU). Later another group broke and called itself The Christian Left. Sergio Torres (1988) recalls: "That ended the automatic identification of Catholics and the Christian Democrats. 1968 was a very important year—Christians with the same tradition and the same education separated ways. All over Latin America, there was disillusionment with the reforms of the capitalist system. Marxism became an option and many people wanted a more radical change of the system. In 1968, in Chile, church people—priests, nuns, pastors—divided among themselves. The symbol in Chile was the split in ILADES: Renato Poblete and Pierre Bigo stayed and Gonsalo Arroyo left." For a review of the ILADES controversy, see LADOC 5:9–18.

14. Members of the Eighty included Rodrigo Ambrosio, Gonzalo Arroyo, Pablo Fontaine, Martin Garate, Esteban Gumucio, Diego Irarrazaval, Antonio Mondelaers, Mariano Puga, Ignacio Pujadas, Roberto Quevillon, Guillermo Redington, Pablo Richard, Santiago Thijssen, and Sergio Torres (Donoso Loero 1975: 295–305).

15. Another group, devoted more to internal renewal and reforms of the church, was organized, and called "The 200" (Torres 1988).

16. Two hundred were priests, 40 were Protestant leaders, and 160 were Catholic lay men and women (Smith, ibid.). According to Bonino (1975: xxii): "One North American Board of Missions silently underwrote a large portion of the [conference's] expenses." Sergio Torres (1988) reports that a European Mission Agency also financed many of the conference's expenses. Torres, Christians for Socialism's secretary general, organized the meeting. According to Santa Ana (1988), "Torres was the organizer; he is the kind of

person who could be a very first-class, high executive in a transnational corporation: you get something to Sergio and it will be done, no problem with the results."

17. According to Julio de Santa Ana and Pablo Richard (who was Christians for Socialism's main ideologue, according to Santa Ana) these included—directly and indirectly—Gustavo Gutiérrez, Hugo Assman, Enrique Dussel, José Comblin, Rubem Alves, José Míguez Bonino, Sergio Torres, Pedro Negre, Gonzalo Arroyo, Luis G. del Valle, Franz Hinkelammert, Ronaldo Muñoz, Raul Vidales, Gomez de Souza, Alex Morelli, Rafael Avila, Luis Ugalde, Paul Blanquart, J. Servino Croatto, Jorge Larraín, Rene García, Juan Luis Segundo, Juan Carlos Scannone, Segundo Galilea, José Marins, Emilio Castro, Camilo Moncada, Aldo Buntig, and Lucio Gera (Santa Anna 1988; Richard 1988).

18. In Berryman's (1987a: 98) words: "In Bogotá Vekemans set up a research center and in collaboration with the young, shrewd, and ambitious Bishop Alfonso Lopez Trujillo began to publish a journal, *Tierra Nueva,* whose clear purpose was not only to attack liberation theology but to propose an alternative kind of social analysis and theology."

9. From Sucre to Puebla

1. Vekemans was a skilled international fund raiser. He sparked a major controversy in the 1960s when it became known that he, working at Santiago's Jesuit Bellarmino Center, had solicited and received five million dollars of covert aid from the United States Central Intelligence Agency to help fund Christian Democrat Eduardo Frei's 1964 run for the Chilean presidency (H. Torres 1978; Berryman 1987a: 98; Smith 1982: 150–51).

2. In June 1973, López Trujillo organized a conference on liberation theology in Toledo, Spain, perhaps as the new CELAM administration's answer to the pro–liberation theology conference in Escorial. The Toledo conference was attended mostly by critics of liberation theology, including Jimenez Urresti, Cardinal Raul Silva Henriquez, López Trujillo, and Yves Congar (Ediciones Aldecoa 1973). In 1975, López Trujillo published his own forceful critique of political priest groups and of liberation theology (López Trujillo 1977).

3. For in-depth accounts of this repression, see Lernoux 1982; Beeson and Pearce 1984; Lange and Iblacker 1981; Comblin 1979.

4. Archbishop Proaño, who had organized the conference, wrote later that year: "I am honored when called a subversive. I hope we are permanently subversive. . . . If we are living within a state or a system that is evidently not in accord with the designs of God, we must oppose it. In this sense, Christ, too, was subversive" (Lernoux 1982: 153).

5. As were most other priest groups in Latin America. According to Secretary General Sergio Torres (1988): "The records of Christians for Socialism were destroyed in 1973—we were in an irrational panic because of the repression."

6. According to Berryman (1984b: 30), "The Chilean coup dashed hopes throughout the continent that electoral politics offered a peaceful path to social transformation." However, rather than give up altogether on social transformation, liberation theologians began to consider other strategies and tactics.

7. An interesting development, in light of liberation theology's use of dependency theory.

8. Torres (1988) reported: "I organized the 'Theology in the Americas' conference in Detroit in 1975. After the Pinochet coup, I went to Maryknoll because the general superior was a friend of mine whom I had met several years earlier. Orbis was interested in publishing Latin American sources. Someone there suggested, 'why not invite the Latin America theologians to come dialogue with North Americans?' So, they asked me to organize this. These two conferences [Mexico City and Detroit] were financially supported by Maryknoll, the United States Catholic Conference, the National Council of Churches, and some Methodist and Lutheran Denominations." Robert McAfee Brown, a North American theologian in attendance, said (1988): "Sergio was the one without whom this wouldn't have happened. Of course, he had all of the Latin American contacts, so they all trusted him to come up here."

9. Interestingly, theologians from the Philippines, with its strong Spanish cultural tradition, seemed especially receptive to liberation theology.

10. For in-depth descriptions and analyses of Puebla, see: Eagleson and Scharper 1979; Berryman 1979: 55–86; Lernoux 1982: 407–48.

11. Each authored works against liberation theology (e.g., Vekemans 1971, 1972, 1976; Vekemans and Silva 1976; López Trujillo 1977, 1978, 1980; Ediciones Aldecoa 1973). Lernoux (1982: 414) comments: "Of the two, Vekemans is more polished, but they have both [Vekemans and Trujillo] been notoriously outspoken in their disdain for 'those bastards' in the progressive wing of the Church." Moises Sandoval noted: "No one seemed in a more advantageous position than Archbishop Alfonso López Trujillo. . . . Everything said and done seemed to favor the secretary general's side" (Eagleson and Scharper 1979: 28).

12. According to Sigmund (1988: 33), "during the meeting a leftist newspaper in Mexico published the contents of a cassette dictaphone tape that had been inadvertently given to a journalist by the secretary of Archbishop López Trujillo. It complained of the leftism of the Jesuits and other religious orders in Latin America and urged it recipient to 'prepare your bombers for Puebla and get into training before entering the ring for the world match'" (see also Kirby 1981: 103; MacEoin and Riley 1980: 59–60; Sandoval 1979: 37).

13. I am grateful to Donald Warwick, of the Harvard Institute for International Development, for suggesting this distinction in the tactics used by the organizers of Medellín and Puebla.

14. By another account, of the voting delegates, about 11 percent were progressive, 18 percent were conservatives, and 71 percent were moderates (Sandoval 1979: 30).

15. Actually, López planned to have the CELAM staff appoint a steering committee to oversee the work of Puebla's twenty-one commissions. But when the time arrived, the attending bishops rejected this idea and elected the committee themselves, choosing Panama's Archbishop Marcos McGrath as chairman. (Lernoux 1982: 433).

16. Specifically, Colombia, Venezuela, Ecuador, Peru, and Bolivia met in Bogotá, Colombia between July 1 and 3; the Southern Cone countries in Rio de Janeiro, Brazil between July 26 and 28; the Central American countries, Mexico, and Panama in San Jose, Costa Rica between July 30 and August 1; and the Caribbean countries in San Juan, Puerto Rico between August 22 and 24 (López Trujillo 1980: 278).

17. For conservative views of the process of preparing for Puebla, see Methol Ferre 1979; López Trujillo 1980: 275–86. For a summary of the preliminary document, see Poblete 1979: 50–54.

Poblete (1979: 50–51) contends that the diagnosis of the Green Book "attempts to avoid comprehensive theories on the problems of underdevelopment and prostration in Latin America. Since the injustices are so evident in themselves and with different theories still not proven, the bishops did not want to set forth any one theory. . . . Economic dependence is pointed out as one of the most serious factors, but not the only one."

Lernoux (1982: 417) more antagonistically describes the Green Book as follows: "The document avoided the central issue of poverty by resurrecting the colonial church's fatalistic message of resignation: the poor were once again to accept misery in the hope of a better hereafter, because 'even when they are deprived of everything, they posses the richness of having a God and faith that will enable them to live with fortitude and the joy of the Kingdom which no human pain can take away.' The 'development' models of the 1960s that had been rejected by Medellin were once again presented as the only solution to Latin America's economic and social problems. . . . Similarly, the wealthy elites trained at the continent's universities would continue to be the leaders of Latin America and the Church's 'chosen few.'"

18. "Gustavo Gutiérrez, for example, was personal adviser to eight bishops, including Brazil's Dom Hélder Camera and Ecuador's Bishop Leonidas Proaño; José Comblin, the adviser of Cardinal Arns; Segundo Galilea, of Chile's Bishops Enrique Alvear and Fernando Ariztia" (Lernoux 1982: 423).

19. For a chronicle of the daily activities and politics of Puebla, see Hernando 1979.

20. According to Nuñez (1985: 111), "The discourses of John Paul II in Puebla . . . lend themselves to more than one interpretation. . . . For more than a few observers the pope gave the impression of rejecting completely the theology of liberation and condemning all political activism of priests. But it was also reported that upon his return to Rome John Paul II declared that liberation theology is necessary not only for Latin America, but for the whole world" (see also Sandoval 1979: 36–37). After Puebla, John Paul, in a number of addresses, reaffirmed the position he took at Puebla (Quade 1982: 97–138).

21. According to Cleary (1985: 15), the theologians at Puebla were almost

the exact group that met for the 1975 "Liberation and Captivity" conference in Mexico City.

22. On the eve of Puebla, progressive Bishop Proaño remarked: "I strongly hope that Puebla will be a step forward, an expression of closer fidelity to the Word of God and to the cry of the Latin American people. But there are some who want to move backwards to a pyramidal church, a church without conflict, to the construction of a Christendom-type church. Thus I believe there will be a confrontation at Puebla, and no one can predict which of the two tendencies will triumph" (quoted in Kirby 1981, 101).

23. McGovern (1980, 202) comments: "Liberation theologians themselves made a decision which may turn out to be as important as anything they have written. They decided to work with the bishops at the conference rather than waiting to criticize Puebla documents or to write their own alternative documents."

24. According to MacEoin and Riley (1980, 78), it was Bishop Dario Castrillon, president of CELAM's Department of Communication, that coined the phrase "wall of freedom."

25. Cox and Sand (1979, 59) note: "Puebla marked a certain maturation in their [the liberation theologian's] style. They consistently avoided confrontation and sloganeering. They worked quietly and patiently, often in the small hours of the night, with bishops who sought their counsel. They gave the Pope the benefit of the doubt, insisting (correctly, we think) that he never actually condemned liberation theology (despite a badly translated, widely reported casual remark)."

26. Dussel confirms Richard's argument about the inadequacy of López's people: "At Puebla, there were twenty three commissions and seven Cardinals. Five Cardinals joined one commission—five in one! It was on BECs. Five cardinals so controlled this commission. But when they began to speak, nobody had any experience, they were so institutional that they knew nothing. So, they had to call José Marins in."

27. This twenty-five percent figure is confirmed by Cox and Sand 1979, 58.

28. A translation of the final Puebla document and commentary on it can be found in Eagleson and Scharper 1979. For an exploration of the contents of the document in terms of liberation theology see Berryman 1979, 64–82.

29. Berryman (1979: 65) argues, "The two languages are not on equal footing. The basic framework was set up by the conservative group and could only be modified by adding some elements and diminishing others. The conservatives laid down the basic harmony and melody, to which the liberationists could add some dissonances and counterpoint melodies, which at some moments became the main theme."

30. According to Berryman (1979: 65): "As the meeting was closing, I asked one theologian what he thought of the final documents. 'Quite good,' he said. 'We could compile a "Little Red Book" of good quotations.' He paused. 'Of course *they* could put together their own "Little Black Book."'"

31. One liberation theologian, who asked to go unnamed, did tell me in an interview that, on balance, in his judgement, Puebla was a defeat for the liberation theology movement.

32. According to Dussel (1988), immediately following Puebla, forty liberation theologians met together in Petrópolis, Brazil to assess their situation and begin planning a coordinated, fifty-volume series of books on liberation theology. Later, Lionidas Proaño, bishop of Riobamba, Ecuador, sponsored a conference in May, 1979 to assess Puebla, whose attendees included José Comblin, Gustavo Gutiérrez, Segundo Galilea, Enrique Dussel, José Marins,' Edgar Beltran (CEP 1980). Presenters there claimed—in papers entitled, for example, "Liberation Theology in Puebla," "The Poor and Liberation in Puebla," "The Prophetic Mission of the Church in Puebla, "Base Ecclesial Communities in Puebla"—that "Puebla signifies a continuity with Medellín" (Comblin, in CEP 1980: 24) and "Puebla reiterates and deepens the great lines of liberating evangelization in Latin America" (Gutiérrez, in CEP 1980: 106; see also the collection of essays in Editorial Laia 1980).

33. Archbishop Oscar Romero concluded: Puebla contains "sufficient elements to be used in our pastoral work. I speak especially of the denunciation of injustices and the abuses of power, the dangers of idolatries, as they call them, of money and materialism. There are plenty of phrases and sentences which fit in well with our priorities here. So I'm content because of the validity which Puebla gives our work" (quoted in Kirby, 1981: 105).

Soon after Puebla, Dussel wrote of the need to value the Puebla "quarry" for its "gems": "The apparent intention [of CELAM] was to bury Medellín and to consign to limbo many of the questions related to the Church committed to the poor. But this attempt failed. The 'text' of Puebla, the *quarry-text*, contains many precious stones and an abundance of marble. We should avoid the historical mistake of allowing Puebla to be appropriated by the dominant classes, by the national security governments, or by those elements in the Church that are not committed to the poor. It would be a crime to surrender the Puebla 'text' for which so many in the Christian community have struggled and labored with their hundreds of meetings, demonstrations, writings, and sufferings" (Dussel 1981: 239).

34. For López Trujillo's extended reflection on the meaning of Puebla, see López Trujillo 1980: 295–332.

35. Hence, Cox and Sand (1979: 59) claimed: "Puebla made it clear that this reality [popular, participatory Christianity which is the social basis for liberation theology] is here to stay."

10. Liberation Theology since Puebla

1. There is actually some disagreement about exactly who in the Vatican is the key source of opposition to liberation theology. Both Berryman 1987a and Novak 1986, for example, despite their different ideological perspectives, tend to view John Paul II as the main source of resistance to liberation theology, because of his Polish background which predisposes him to a negative view of Marxism. Cox 1988, on the other hand, portrays the Pope as more supportive of liberation theology, and Joseph Ratzinger as the real advocate of opposition to liberation theology; for evidence to support the later view, see John Paul II 1990b: 526; and see n. 5 below.

2. This is an exaggeration. For example, in a letter to the Brazilian bishops' conference, Pope John Paul II declared: "We are convinced, we and you, that the theology of liberation in not only timely but useful and necessary. It should constitute a new state . . . of the theological reflection initiated with the apostolic tradition and continued by the great fathers and doctors. . . . The poor of this nation, the poor of this continent, are the first to feel the urgent need for this gospel of radical and integral liberation. To deny them would be to defraud and disillusion them" (John Paul II 1990a: 503–4).

3. For a translation of the Sacred Congregation's letter, see Hennelly 1990: 348–50. For a translation of a letter by influential Catholic theologian Karl Rahner to Gutiérrez's bishop, Landazuri Ricketts, in defense and support of Gutiérrez, see ibid. 351–52.

4. See Boff 1985. For an excellent account and interpretation of "the Boff affair," see Cox 1988.

5. On April 5, 1986, the Vatican issued a second, more conciliatory document called *Instruction of Christian Freedom and Liberation,* which held a more favorable view of liberation theology (Berryman 1987a: 110).

6. Indeed, a post-victory communique of the FSLN recognized that Christians had taken part in the revolution "to a degree unprecedented in any other revolutionary movement in Latin America and perhaps the world. This fact opens new and interesting possibilities for the participation of Christians in revolutions elsewhere" (Belli 1988: 213).

7. Indeed, only months after the election, liberation theology conferences were already being scheduled in Nicaragua on the subject "Where Do We Go From Here?"

8. In 1988, inflation in Peru, at 1,722 percent, more than quintupled its previous record high. In 1989, inflation rose to 2,775 percent. The legal economy shrank by 8.5 percent in 1988 and contracted another 22.8 percent in the first five months of 1989. Real wages fell 60 percent during the twelve months after February, 1990 (Palmer 1990: 5; Gallagher 1990).

9. Thus, Garrett argues: "While liberation theologians have attempted of late to establish a degree of social distance between their own perspective and Marxist social theory, they have been hampered in that effort by constraints imposed on their theological reflection by the potent ramifications originating from the dependency frame of reference. . . . Should subsequent research on Third World economic-political dynamics or a paradigm shift among sociological theorists discredit dependency theory, then liberation theology would almost certainly be impossible to sustain, or at the very least it would require such drastic alterations that little of its former substance would remain in evidence. . . . Few schools of thought have a larger investment in the enduring cogency of dependency theory than the liberation theologians of Latin America" (Garrett 1988: 182, 186–87).

10. Indeed, Lernoux links the growth of protestant sects and Rome's opposition to liberation theology and BECs: "Ironically, the Vatican's refusal to countenance a more pluralistic, lay-oriented church has contributed to the growth of U.S.-sponsored Protestant fundamentalist churches in Latin America. . . . The communities are the best hope to counter the spread of generally

anti-Catholic, born-again churches. . . . Surveys by Catholic institutions showed that wherever base communities flourished, fundamentalist churches were unlikely to gain recruits. But because Rome feared the loss of its institutional power to a democratic base, it discouraged the growth of the communities. Encapsulated in its own small world, the Curia could not see that it was aiding Catholicism's avowed enemies in the fundamentalist churches by opposing a lay-directed renewal" (Lernoux 1989: 153).

11. According to Sigmund, in the 1980s, "once their revolutionism was tempered, it was easier for the liberation theologians to become part of the mainstream of Catholicism, which has always had an anti-capitalist strain and from early Christian times has thought of itself . . . as a church of the poor" (Sigmund 1988: 40).

Conclusion

1. This explanation incorporates two important motivational elements: (1) the Church preserving its institutional interests and (2) the Church attempting to realize its religious values (McNamara 1979).

References

Abbott, Walter M., ed. 1966. *The Documents of Vatican II*. New York: Herder and Herder.

Adriance, Madeleine. 1984. "Whence the Option For the Poor?" *Cross Currents* 34 (Winter): 500–507.

———. 1986. *Opting for the Poor*. Kansas City, Mo.: Sheed and Ward.

Alvez, Rubem. 1969. *A Theology of Human Hope*. St. Meinard, Ind.: Abbey Press.

———. 1988. Personal communication to Christian Smith, February 8.

Aman, Kenneth. 1984. "Marxism(s) in Liberation Theology." *Cross Currents* 34 (Winter): 427–38.

Antoine, Charles. 1973. *Church and Power in Brazil*. Maryknoll, N.Y.: Orbis Books.

Arokiasamy, S., and G. Gispert-Sauch. 1987. *Liberation in Asia: Theological Perspectives*. Delhi: Vidyajoyotin Faculty of Theology.

Assman, Hugo. 1974. "Medellín: La Desilusión que nos Hizo Madurar." *Cristianismo y Sociedad* 12(40–41):137–43.

———. 1976. *Theology for a Nomad Church*. Maryknoll, N.Y.: Orbis Books.

———. 1984. "The Actualization of the Power of Christ in History: Notes on the Discernment of Christological Contradictions." In *Faces of Jesus: Latin American Christologies*, ed. José Míguez Bonino. Maryknoll: Orbis Books.

Aveni, Adrian F. 1978. "Organizational Linkages and Resource Mobilization: The Significance of Linkage Strength and Breadth." *The Sociological Quarterly* 19 (Spring): 185–202.

Balan, Jorge. 1983. "Agrarian Structures and Internal Migration in a Historical Perspective: Latin American Case Studies." In *Population Movements*, ed. *Peter Morrison*. Liege, Belgium: Ordina Editions.

Bandeira, Marina. 1988. Interview, July 28, Rio de Janeiro, Brazil.

Bandera, Armando. 1975. *La Iglesia Ante el Proceso de Liberación*. Madrid: La Editorial Catolica.

Barbé, Dominique. 1987. *Grace and Power: Base Communities and Nonviolence in Brazil*. Maryknoll, N.Y.: Orbis Books.

Barnes, Samuel and Max Kaase. 1979. *Political Action*. Beverly Hills, Calif.: Sage Publications.

Barreiro, Alvaro. 1982. *Basic Ecclesial Communities: The Evangelization of the Poor.* Maryknoll, N.Y.: Orbis Books.

Barthel, Manfred. 1984. *The Jesuits: Hisotry and Legend of the Society of Jesus.* New York: William Morrow and Company, Inc.

Bastos, Irany. 1966. "Sisters in the Climate of Vatican II." Pp. 140–47 in *The Religious Dimension in the New Latin America,* ed. John Considine. Notre Dame: Fides Publishers.

Bath, C. Richard, and James D. Dilmus. 1976. "Dependency Analysis of Latin America: Some Criticisms, Some Suggestions." *Latin American Research Review* 9 (Fall): 3–54.

Bauer, Arnold J. 1983. "The Church in the Economy of Spanish America." *Hispanic American Historical Review* 6(34):707–33.

Baum, Gregory. 1978. "Canadian Bishops Adapt Liberation Theology." *Cross Currents* 28 (Spring): 97–103.

Beeson, Trevor, and Jenny Pearce. 1984. *A Vision of Hope: The Churches and Change in Latin America.* Philadelphia, Pa.: Fortress Press.

Belli, Humberto. 1988. "Liberation Theology and the Latin American Revolutions." In *The Politics of Latin American Liberation Theology.* Washington, D.C.: The Washington Institute Press.

Berger, Peter L. 1985. "Speaking to the Third World." In *Speaking to the Third World: Essays on Democracy and Development,* ed. Peter L. Berger and Michael Novak. Washington, D.C.: American Enterprise Institute.

Berger, Peter L. and Michael Novak, eds. 1985. *Speaking to the Third World: Essays on Democracy and Development.* Washington, D.C.: American Enterprise Institute.

Berryman, Phillip. 1979. "What Happened at Puebla." In *Churches and Politics in Latin America,* ed. Daniel H. Levine. Beverly Hills, Calif.: Sage Publications.

———. 1984a. "Basic Christian Communities and the Future of Latin America." *Monthly Review,* no. 36 (July-August): 27–40.

———. 1984b. *The Religious Roots of Rebellion: Christians in Central American Revolutions.* Maryknoll, N.Y.: Orbis Books.

———. 1987a. *Liberation Theology: The Essential Facts About the Revolutionary Movement in Latin America and Beyond.* N.Y.: Pantheon Books.

———. 1987b. Interview, December 29, Philadelphia, Pa.

Betto, Frei. 1987. *Fidel and Religion.* New York: Simon and Schuster.

Beyer, Glenn H., ed. 1967. *The Urban Explosion in Latin America.* Ithica, N.Y.: Cornell University Press.

Bittencourt Filho, José. 1988. *Por uma Eclesiologia Militante: Isal como Nascedouro de uma Nova Eclesiologia para a América Latina.* São Bernardo de Campo, Brazil: Instituto Metodista de Ensino Superior.

Boff, Clodovis. 1987. *Feet on the Ground Theology: A Brazilian Journey.* Maryknoll, N.Y.: Orbis Books.

Boff, Leonardo. 1978. *Jesus Christ Liberator: A Critical Christology for Our Time.* Maryknoll, N.Y.: Orbis Books.

———. 1979. *Liberating Grace.* Maryknoll, N.Y.: Orbis Books.

———. 1985. *Church, Charism and Power: Liberation Theology and the Insitutional Church.* New York: Crossroad.

———. 1986. *Ecclesiogenesis: The Base Communities Reinvent the Church.* Maryknoll, N.Y.: Orbis Press.

Boff, Leonardo, and Clodovis Boff. 1984. *Salvation and Liberation: In Search of a Balance between Faith and Politics.* Maryknoll, N.Y.: Orbis Books.

———. 1986. *Liberation Theology: From Confrontation to Dialogue.* San Fransisco: Harper and Row.

———. 1987. *Introducing Liberation Theology.* Maryknoll, N.Y.: Orbis Books.

Bolasco, Mario. 1986. "The Church and National Liberation." *Kasarinlan,* 3d quarter, pp. 3–8. Univ. of Philippines, Third World Studies Center, Manila.

Bolton, Charles D. 1972. "Alienation and Action: A Study of Peace-Group Members." *American Journal of Sociology* 78(3):537–61.

Bonino, José. 1975. *Doing Theology in a Revolutionary Situation.* Maryknoll, N.Y.: Orbis Press.

———. 1985. "The Reception of Vatican II in Latin America." *Ecumenical Review,* no. 37, 266–74.

———. 1987. Interview, December 5, Atlanta, Ga.

Bonino, José, ed. 1984. *Faces of Jesus: Latin American Christologies.* Maryknoll, N.Y.: Orbis Books.

Bonpane, Blase. 1985. *Guerrillas of Peace: Liberation Theology and the Central American Revolution,* Boston: South End Press.

Bouvier, Virginia Marie. 1983. *Alliance or Compliance: Implication of the Chilean Experience for the Catholic Church in Latin America.* Syracuse, N.Y.: Maxwell School of Citizenship and Public Affairs Publications, Syracuse University.

Bowen, D., E. Bowen, S. Gawiser, and L. Masotti. 1968. "Deprivaiton, Mobility, and Orientation toward Protest of the Urban Poor." In *Riots and Rebellion: Civil Violence in the Urban Community,* ed. L. Masotti and D. Bowen. Beverly Hills, Calif.: Sage Publications.

Boyer, Richard E. and Keith Davies. 1973. *Urbanization in Nineteenth-Century Latin America: Statistics and Sources.* Los Angeles: University of California.

Brockman, James R. 1982. *The Word Remains: A Life of Oscar Romero.* Maryknoll, N.Y.: Orbis Books.

Bronx, Humberto. 1978. *Golconda y Origen de Ideas Marxistas en Minorias del Clero Colombiano y Templos de Medellín.* Medellín: Editorias Argenmiro Salazar y Cia.

Brooke, James. 1989a. "Vatican Undercuts Leftist Theology in Brazil." *New York Times,* Monday, April 23, Sec. I, p. 8.

———. 1989b. "Two Archbishops, Old and New, Symbolize Conflict in the Brazilian Church." *New York Times,* Sunday, November 12, sec. I, p. 14.

Brown, Robert McAfee. 1966. "The Church Today: A Response." In *The Documents of Vatican II,* ed. Walter M. Abbott. New York: Herder and Herder.

———. 1988. Interview, July 18. Maryknoll, N.Y.

Bruneau, Thomas C. 1974. *The Political Transformation of the Brazilian Catholic Church,* New York: Cambridge University Press.

————. 1985. "Church and Politics in Brazil: The Genesis of Change" *Journal of Latin American Studies,* no. 17, 271–93.

Buhle, Paul, and Thomas Fiehrer. 1985. "Socialism and Spirituality." *Monthly Review,* November.

Burns, E. Bradford. 1980. *The Poverty of Progress: Latin America in the Nineteenth Century.* Berkeley: University of California Press.

Butterworth, Douglas, and John Chance. 1981. *Latin American Urbanization* Cambridge: Cambridge University Press.

Cabal, Hugo Latorre. 1978. *The Revolution of the Latin American Church.* Norman: University of Oklahoma Press.

Cabestrero, Teofilo. 1983. *Ministers of God, Ministers of the People: Testimonies of Faith From Nicaragua.* Maryknoll, N.Y.: Orbis Books.

Callahan, Daniel. 1966. *The New Church: Essays in Catholic Reform.* New York: Charles Scribner's Sons.

Camps, José. 1969. *Iglesia y Liberación Humana.* Barcelona, Spain: Nova Terra.

Caplan, Nathan, and Jeffery Paige. 1968. "A Study of Ghetto Rioters." *Scientific American* 219:15–21.

Caporaso, James A., and Behrouz Zare. 1981. "An Interpretation and Evaluation of Dependency Theory." In *From Dependency to Development,* ed. Heraldo Muñoz. Boulder, Colo.: Westview Press.

Cardenal, Ernesto. 1982. *The Gospel in Solentiname.* Maryknoll, N.Y.: Orbis Books.

Cardoso, Fernando Henrique, and Enzo Faletto. 1979. *Dependency and Development in Latin America.* Berkeley: University of California Press.

Carroll, Denis. 1987. *What is Liberation Theology?* Dublin: The Mercier Press.

Castro, Emilo. 1971. "A Call to Action." Pp. 38–48 in *Freedom and Unfreedom in the Americas,* ed. Thomas Quigley. New York: IDOC Books.

Castro, Mary García, Eugenio Neto, Mario Duayer de Souza, Giselia Grabios, and Leda Fraenkel. 1978. *Migration in Brazil.* Liège, Belgium: Ordina Editions.

CELAM. 1967a. *Mision de la Universidad Católica en América Latina.* Departamento de Educación, 12–18 February.

————. 1967b. *Presencia Activa de la Iglesia en el Desarrollo y en la integración de América Latina.* Departamento de Acción Social.

————. 1968a. *Presencia de la Iglesia en el Proceso de Cambio de América Latina.* Comisiones Episcopales de Acción Social, 12–19 May.

————. 1968b. *Primer Encuentro Sobre Pastoral de Misiones en América Latina.* Departamento de Misiones Pastoral, 20–27 April.

————. 1968c. *Igreja América Latina: Desenvolvimento e Integracao.* Petrópolis: Editoria Vozes, Ltd.

————. 1978. *Aportes de las Conferencias Episcopales.* Bogotá, Columbia: CELAM.

————. 1982. *Elementos para su Historia.* Bogotá, Colombia: Consejo Episcopal Latinoamericano.

CEP. 1978. *Signos de Lucha y Esperanza.* Lima, Peru: Centro de Estudios y Publicaciones.

————. 1980. *Encuentro de Riobamba: Estudios Sobre Puebla.* Lima: Centro de Estudios y Publicaciones.

Chilcote, Ronald H. 1974. "A Critical Synthesis of the Dependency Literature." *Latin American Perspectives* 1 (Spring).

CICOP. 1964–72. Annual Catholic Inter-American Cooperation Program conference schedules. Chicago: CICOP.

CLAR. 1969. "El Evangelio de los Pobres Ante el Sub-Desarrollo de América Latina." In *Signos de Liberación.* Lima: Centro de Estudios y Publicaciones.

Cleary, Edward L. 1985. *Crisis and Change: The Church in Latin America Today.* Maryknoll, N.Y.: Orbis Books.

————. 1987. Interview, November 27, Middletown, Pa.

Cloin, Tiago G. 1966. "Bishops on the March in Brazil." Pp. 105–16 in *The Religious Dimension in the New Latin America,* ed. John Considine. Notre Dame: Fides Publishers.

Collier, David, ed. 1979. *The New Authoritarianism in Latin America.* Princeton, N.J.: Princeton University Press.

Comblin, José. 1973. "Medellín: Problemas de Interpretación." *Pasos* (August): 1–5.

————. 1979. *The Church and the National Security.* Maryknoll, N.Y.: Orbis Books.

————. N.d. "Theologie der Befreiung in Lateinameika." Pp. 13–25 in *Lateinamerika: Gesellschaft Kirche Theologie.* Göttingen: Vanderhoek and Ruprecht.

Compton, Roberto. 1984. *La Teología de la Liberación.* El Paso: Casa Bautista de Publicaciones.

Considine, John. 1966. *The Religious Dimension in the New Latin America.* Notre Dame: Fides Publishers.

Conyers, A. J. 1983. "Liberation Theology: Whom Does it Liberate?" *Modern Age,* no. 27 (Summer/Fall): 303–8.

Cook, Guillermo. 1985. *The Expectation of the Poor: Latin American Basic Ecclesial Communities in Protestant Perspective.* Mayknoll, N.Y.: Orbis Books.

Correspondants for *The Economist.* 1977. "El Salvador: Go or Die." *The Economist,* July 23.

————. 1980. "Brazil: Priests Unrestrained." *The Economist,* June 28, p. 35.

————. 1981. "Nicaragua: The Bishops Draw a Line." *The Economist,* June 13.

————. 1983a. "They Shoot Priests, Don't They?" *The Economist,* March 5, pp. 31–32.

————. 1983b. "Pastor Among Wolves: Should the Pope Have Gone to Central America?" *The Economist,* March 12, pp. 13–14.

————. 1984. "Liberation Theology: Thy Kingdom Come, Here and Now." *The Economist,* October 13, pp. 31–33.

————. 1986a. "Nicaragua: The Enemy From Within," *The Economist,* March 15, p. 36.

————. 1986b. "Roman Catholics: A Blessing For Some Rebels." *The Economist,* April 12, pp. 43.

———. 1986c. "Nicaragua: The Cross Gets Hammered." *The Economist,* July 26, pp. 33–34.

Costa Rican Ecumenical Council. 1978. "The Manipulation of CELAM." *Cross Currents* 28 (Spring): 60–70.

Costas, Orlando. 1976. *Theology of the Crossroads in Contemporary Latin America.* Amsterdam: Rodopi.

Cox, Harvey. 1984. *Religion in the Secular City: Toward a Post-Modern Theology.* New York: Simon and Schuster.

———. 1988. *The Silencing of Leonardo Boff.* Oak Park, Ill.: Meyer-Stone Books.

Cox, Harvey, and Faith Annette Sand. 1979. "What Happened at Puebla?" *Christianity and Crisis,* no. 39 (March): 57–60.

Crahan, Margaret E. 1985. "Cuba: Religion and Revolutionary In-stitutionalizaton." *Journal of Latin American Studies,* no. 17, 319–40.

Crawford, T. J., and M. Naditch. 1970. "Relative Deprivation, Powerlessness, and Militancy: The Psychology of Social Protest." *Psychiatry* 33:208–23.

Curtis, Russel, and Louis Zurcher. 1983. "Social Movements: An Analytical Exploration of Organizational Form." *Social Problems* 21(3):356–70.

Dahrendorf, Ralph. 1959. *Class and Class Conflict in Industrial Society.* Stanford, Calif.: Stanford University Press.

Damboriena, Prudencio. 1963. *El Protestantismo en América Latina.* Bogotá, Colombia: FERES.

Damico, Linda. 1987. *The Anarchist Dimension of Liberation Theology.* New York: Peter Lang.

David, Rene. 1985. "A New Voice from Cuba Proclaims Role for Church in Socialist State." *National Catholic Reporter,* September 20, pp.10–11.

DEASAPAU. 1967. *The Alliance for Progress and Latin American Development Prospects: A Five-Year Review, 1961–1965,* prepared by the Departments of Economic Affairs and Social Affairs of the Pan American Union. Balti-more: The John Hopkins Press.

DEI. 1982. *Teología Desde el Tercer Mundo.* San Jose, Costa Rica: Departmento Ecuménico de Investigaciones.

Deiner, John T. 1975. "Radicalism in the Argentine Catholic Church." *Govern-ment and Opposition* 10, no. 1 (Winter): 70–89.

Della Cava, Ralph. 1976. "Catholicism and Society in Twentieth-Century Bra-zil." *Latin American Research Review* 2(2):7–50.

Dodson, Michael. 1979. "The Christian Left in Latin American Politics." In *Churches and Politics in Latin America,* ed. Daniel H. Levine. Beverly Hills, Calif.: Sage Publications.

———. 1984. "Comparing the 'Popular Church' in Nicaragua and Brazil." *Journal of Interamerican Studies and World Affairs* 26, no. 1 (February): 131–36.

———. 1986. "Nicaragua: The Struggle for the Church." In *Religion and Polit-ical Conflict in Latin America,* ed. Daniel H. Levine. Chapel Hill: University of North Carolina Press.

Donoso Loero, Teresa. 1975. *Los Cristianos por el Socialismo en Chile.* Santiago: Editorial Vaitea.

Dorr, Donald. 1983. *Option for the Poor: A Hundred Years of Vatican Social Teaching*. Maryknoll, N.Y.: Orbis Books.

Dos Santos, Theotonio. 1971. "La crisis de la teoría del desorrollo y la relaciones de dependencia en América Latina." In Helio Jagvoribe, Aldo Ferrer, Miguel S. Wionczek, and Theotonio Dos Santos, eds., *La dependencia político-económica de América Latina*. 3d ed. Mexico: Siglo Veintiuno.

Downs, Anthony. 1972. "Up and Down With Ecology: The 'Issue-Attention Cycle'." *The Public Interest* 28 (Summer): 38–50.

Dreier, John C. 1962. *The Alliance for Progress: Problems and Perspectives*. Baltimore: The Johns Hopkins Press.

Dulles, Avery C. 1966. "The Church." In *The Documents of Vatican II*, ed. Walter M. Abbott. New York: Herder and Herder.

Dussel, Enrique. 1976. *History and Theology of Liberation*. Maryknoll, N.Y.: Orbis Books.

———. 1978. "The Political and Ecclesial Context of Liberation Theology in Latin America." Pp. 175–92 in *The Emergent Gospel: Theology from the Developing Third World*, ed. Sergio Torres and Virginia Fabella. London: Geoffrey Chapman.

———. 1979. *De Medellín a Puebla*. Yosemite, Mexico: Centro de Estudios Ecumenicos.

———. 1981. *A History of the Church in Latin America: Colonialism to Liberation*. Grand Rapids, Mich.: William. B. Eerdmans.

———. 1988. Interview, July 18. Maryknoll, N.Y.

Eagleson, John, ed. 1975. *Christians and Socialism: Documentation of the Christians for Socialism Movement in Latin America*. Maryknoll, N.Y.: Orbis Books.

Eagleson, John, and Phillip Scharper. 1979. *Puebla and Beyond*. Maryknoll, N.Y.: Orbis Books.

Ediciones Aldecoa. 1973. *Teología de la Liberación: Conversaciones de Toledo*, Burgos: Ediciones Aldecoa.

Ediciones Paulinas. 1984. *Historia General de la Iglesia en América Latina*, vol. 5. Coyoacon, Mexico: Ediciones Paulinas.

Ediciones Sigueme. 1973. *Fe Cristiana y Cambio Social en América Latina*. Salamanca, Spain: Instituto Fe y Secularidad.

Editorial Laia. 1980. *La Batalla de Puebla*. Barcelona: Editorial Laia.

Einaudi, Luigi, Richard Maulin, Alfred Stepan, and Michael Fleet. 1969. "Latin American Institutional Development: The Changing Catholic Church." Santa Monica, Calif.: The Rand Corperation.

Ellacuría, Ignacio. 1976. *Freedom Made Flesh: The Mission of Christ and His Church*. Maryknoll, N.Y.: Orbis Books.

Ennis, James G., and Richard Schreuer. 1987. "Mobilizing Weak Support for Social Movements: The Role of Grievance, Efficacy, and Cost." *Social Forces* 66:390–409.

Escobar, Jaime. 1987. *Persecucion a la Iglesia en Chile: 1973–1986.*, Santiago: Terranova Editores.

Ferm, Deane William. 1986. *Third World Liberation Theologies: A Reader.* Maryknoll, N.Y.: Orbis Books.

Ferree, Myra Marx, and Frederick D. Miller. 1985. "Mobilization and Meaning: Toward an Integration of Social Psychological and Resource Mobilization Perspectives of Social Movements." *Sociological Inquiry* 55:38–51.

Fireman, Bruce, and William Gamson. 1979. "Utilitarian Logic in the Resource Mobilization Perspective." In *The Dynamics of Social Movements,* ed. Mayer Zald and John McCarthy. Lanham: University Press of America.

Flacks, Richard. 1967. "The Liberated Generation: An Exploration of the Roots of Student Protest." *Journal of Social Issues* 23 (July): 52–75.

Fleet, Michael. 1988. "Catholics and Marxist Leftists in Latin America." In *The Politics of Latin American Liberation Theology,* ed. Richard Rubenstein and John Roth. Washington, D.C.: The Washington Institute Press.

Floridi, Ulisse Alessio. 1973. *O Radicalismo Católico Brasiliero.* São Paulo: Hora Presente.

Fragoso, Dom Antonio B. 1987. *Face of a Church.* Maryknoll, N.Y.: Orbis Books.

Francis, Michael J. 1985. "Dependency: Ideology, Fad, and Fact." In *Latin America: Dependency or Interdependence?* ed. Michael Novak and Michael P. Jackson. Washington, D.C.: American Enterprise Institute.

Frank, Andre Gunder. 1967. *Capitalism and Underdevelopment in Latin America.* New York: Monthly Review Press.

Freeman, Jo. 1973. "The Origins of the Women's Liberation Movement." *American Journal of Sociology* 78:792–811.

———. 1979. "Resource Mobilization and Strategy: A Model for Analyzing Social Movement Organization Actions." In *The Dynamics of Social Movements,* ed. Mayer Zald and John McCarthy. Lanham: University Press of America.

Freire, Paulo. 1972. *Pedagogy of the Oppressed.* New York: Herder and Herder.

Galilea, Segundo. 1971. "Situación Pastoral de América Latina." *Mensaje,* no. 198 (May): 170–74.

———. 1978. "Between Medellín and Puebla." *Cross Currents* 28 (Spring): 71–78.

———. 1984. "Jesus' Attitude Toward Politics: Some Working Hypothises." In *Faces of Jesus: Latin American Christologies,* ed. José Míguez Bonino. Maryknoll, N.Y.: Orbis Books.

Gallagher, David. 1990. "Peru, in Its Darkest Hour, May Be Close to Dawn." *The Wall Street Journal,* Friday, February 23, p. A11.

Gamson, William. 1988. "Political Discourse and Collective Action." In *From Structure to Action: Social Movement Participation across Cultures,* ed. Bert Klandermans, Hanspeter Kreisi, and Sidney Tarrow. Greenwich, Conn.: JAI Press.

———. 1989. "Media Discourse and Public Opinion on Nuclear Power: A Constructionist Approach." American Journal of Sociology 95(1):1–37.

———. 1990. *Strategy of Social Protest.* Homewood, Ill.: Dorsey Press.

Gamson, William, and André Modigliani. 1989. "Media Discourse and Public Opinion on Nuclear Power: A Constructionist Approach." *American Journal of Sociology* 95, no. 1 (July): 1–37.

Garrett, William R. 1988. "Liberation Theology and Dependency Theory." In

The Politics of Latin American Liberation Theology, ed. Richard Rubenstein and John Roth. Washington, D.C.: The Washington Institute Press.

Geld, Ellen B. 1987. "Brazil's Liberation Theologians Look for a Quick Fix," *The Wall Street Journal*, Friday, July 31, p. 15.

Gerassi, John. 1971. *Revolutionary Priest: The Complete Writings and Messages of Camilo Torres.* New York: Random House.

Gerlach, Luther P., and Virginia Hine. 1970. *People, Power, Change: Movements of Social Transformation.* New York: Bobbs-Merrill.

German Theologians. 1978. "We Must Protest." *Cross Currents* 28 (Spring).

Germani, Gino. 1981. *The Sociology of Modernization.* New Brunswick: Transaction Press.

Gheerbrant, Alain. 1974. *The Rebel Church in Latin America.* Baltimore: Penguin Books.

Gibbons, William, et al. 1958. *World Horizons Report 24: Basic Ecclesiastical Statistics for Latin America.* Maryknoll: Maryknoll Publications.

Gibellini, Rosino. 1988. *The Liberation Theology Debate.* Maryknoll, N.Y.: Orbis Books.

Gibellini, Rosino, ed. 1979. *Frontiers of Theology in Latin America.* Maryknoll, N.Y.: Orbis Books.

Goldstone, Jack A. 1979. "The Weakness of Organization: A New Look at Gamson's *The Strategy of Social Protest*," *American Journal of Sociology* 85:1017–1042.

Gomez de Souza, Luiz Alberto. 1982. "Church and Society in Brazil: The Basic Elements for an Analytical Framework." *Journal of International Affairs*, 36, no. 2 (Fall-Winter): 285–95.

Gordon, Lincoln. 1963. *A New Deal for Latin America: The Alliance for Progress,* Cambridge, Mass.: Harvard University Press.

Gotay, Samuel Silva. 1983. *El Pensamiento Cristiano Revolucionario en América Latina y el Caribe.* Cordillera: Ediciones Sigueme.

Goulet, Denis. 1971. "Development . . . Or Liberation." Pp. 1–15 in *Freedom and Unfreedom in the Americas*, ed. Thomas Quigley. New York: IDOC Books.

Gremillion, Joseph, ed. 1976. *The Gospel of Peace and Justice: Catholic Social Teaching Since Pope John.* Maryknoll, N.Y.: Orbis Books.

Grenz, Stanley J. 1987. "German Scholar Faults Marxism as Liberation Theology's Basis." *Christianity Today* 31, no. 8 (May 15).

Gutierrez, Gustavo. 1960. *Misión de la Iglesia y Apostolado Universitario.* Lima: UNEC.

———. 1971. "Iglesia y Mundo: Crisis de un Sistema Teológico." *Mensaje*, no. 199 (June): 203–9.

———. 1973. *A Theology of Liberation.* Maryknoll, N.Y.: Orbis Books.

———. 1978. "Two Theological Perspectives: Liberation Theology and Progressivist Theology." In *The Emergent Gospel: Theology From the Developing Third World*, ed. Sergio Torres and Virginia Fabella. London: Geoffrey Chapman.

———. 1979. "Liberation Praxis and Christian Faith," In *Frontiers of Theology in Latin America*, ed. Rosino Gibellini. Maryknoll, N.Y.: Orbis Books.

———. 1983. *The Power of the Poor in History.* Maryknoll, N.Y.: Orbis Books.

———. 1984, "Teología y Ciencias Sociales." *Christus,* nos. 579-580 (October-November): 9–20.

———. 1987. *On Job: God-Talk and the Suffering of the Innocent.* Maryknoll, N.Y.: Orbis Books.

———. 1988. Interview, July 18. Maryknoll, N.Y.

———. 1990. "Criticism Will Deepen, Clarify Liberation Theology." In *Liberation Theology: A Documentary History,* ed. Alfred Hennelly. Maryknoll, N.Y.: Orbis Books.

"Hace 5 Años . . . en Medellín." 1973. *Pasos, un Documento de Reflexion por Semana,* no. 59 (16 July).

Haight, Roger. 1985. *An Alternative Vision: An Interpretation of Liberation Theology.* Mahwah, N.J.: Paulist Press.

Hardoy, Jorge. 1975. "Two Thousand Years of Latin American Urbanization." In *Urbanization in Latin America: Approaches and Issues,* ed. Jorge Hardoy. Garden City: Doubleday.

Hauser, Philip M., ed. 1961. *Urbanization in Latin America.* New York: International Documents Service.

Hebblethwaithe, Peter. 1975. *The Runaway Church: Post-Conciliar Growth or Decline.* New York: Seabury Press.

Heirich, Max. 1977. "Change of Heart: A Test of Some Widely Held Theories About Religious Conversion." *American Journal of Sociology* 83:653–80.

Hennelly, Alfred T. 1978. "Courage With Primitive Weapons." *Cross Currents* 28 (Spring): 8–19.

———. 1979. *Theologies in Conflict.* Maryknoll N.Y.: Orbis Books.

Hennelly, Alfred T., ed. 1990. *Liberation Theology: A Documentary History.* Maryknoll, N.Y.: Orbis Books.

Henriot, Peter, Edward DeBerri, and Michael Schultheis. 1988. *Catholic Social Teaching.* Maryknoll, N.Y.: Orbis Books.

Henry, Carl. N.d. "An Evangelical Apprasial of Liberation Theology." *This World,* pp. 99–107.

Hernando, Bernardino M. 1979. *Los Pasillos de Puebla.* Madrid: Editorial PPC.

Hewitt, W. E. 1986. "Strategies for Social Change Employed by Comunidades Eclesiais de Base (CEBs) in the Archdiocese of Sao Paulo." *Journal for the Scientific Study of Religion* 25(1):16–30.

———. 1987. "Basic Christian Communities of the Middle-Classes in the Archdiocese of Sao Paulo." *Sociological Analysis* 48(2):158–66.

———. 1988. "Myths and Realities of Liberation Theology: The Case of Base Christian Communities in Brazil." In *The Politics of Latin American Liberation Theology,* ed. Richard Rubenstein and John Roth. Washington, D.C.: The Washington Institute Press.

Hinkelammert, Franz J. 1986. *The Ideological Weapons of Death: A Theological Critique of Capitalism.* Maryknoll, N.Y.: Orbis Books.

Hollis, Christopher. 1968. *The Jesuits: A History,* New York: The Macmillan Company.

Houtart, François. 1963. *The Latin American Church and the Council.* Bogotá, Colombia: FERES.

Houtart, François, and Andre Rousseau. 1971. *The Church and Revolution.* Maryknoll, N.Y.: Orbis Books.

Hundley, Raymond, C. 1987. *Radical Liberation Theology: An Evangelical Response.* Wilmore, Ky.: Bristol Books.

ISAL. 1971. *América Latina: Movilización Popular y Fe Cristiana.* Montevideo, Uruguay.

Jaworski, Helan. 1971. "The Integrated Structures of Dependence and Domination in the Americas." In *Freedom and Unfreedom in the Americas,* ed. Thomas Quigley. New York: IDOC Books.

Jerez, Cesar. 1984. "The Church and the Nicaraguan Revolution." *Cross Currents* 34 (Spring): 5–42.

Jimenez, Roberto. 1987. *Teología Latino Américana.* Bogotá, Colombia: CEDIAL.

Jimenez, Roberto, Joaquin Lepeley, Roger Vekemans, and Juan Cordero. 1984. *Teología de la Liberación,* Bogotá, Colombia: CEDIAL.

John XXIII. 1961. *Mater et Magistra.* In *The Gospel of Peace and Justice,* ed. Joseph Gremillion. Maryknoll, N.Y.: Orbis Books.

————. 1963. *Pacem in Terris.* In *The Gospel of Peace and Justice,* ed. Joseph Gremillion. Maryknoll, N.Y.: Orbis Books.

John Paul II. 1979. "Addresses and Homilies at Puebla." In *Puebla and Beyond,* ed. John Eagleson and Phillip Scharper. Maryknoll, N.Y.: Orbis Books.

————. 1990a. "Letter to Brazilian Episcopal Conference." In *Liberation Theology: A Documentary History,* ed. Alfred Hennelly. Maryknoll, N.Y.: Orbis Books.

————. 1990b. "Excerpts from 'On Social Concern'." In *Liberation Theology: A Documentary History,* ed. Alfred Hennelly. Maryknoll, N.Y.: Orbis Books.

Johnson, Hank and Jozeff Figa. 1988. "The Church and Political Opposition: Comparative Perspectives on Mobilization Against Authoritarian Regimes." *Journal for the Scientific Study of Religion* 21(1):32–47.

Kahl, Joseph. 1976. *Modernization Exploitation and Dependency in Latin America.* New Brunswick, N.J.: Transaction Books.

Kansteiner, Walter. 1988. "Zimbabwe's Churches and the New Order." *The Wall Street Journal,* January 5.

Kemper, Vicki, and Larry Engel. 1987. "A Prophet's Vision and Grace." *Sojourners,* December, 12–15.

Kennison, Kenneth. 1968. *Young Radicals.* New York: Harcourt, Brace and World.

Kent, Stephen A. 1982. "Relative Deprivation and Resource Mobilization: A Study of Early Quakerism." *British Journal of Sociology* 33 (December): 529–44.

Kirby, Peadar. 1981. *Lessons in Liberation.* Dublin: Dominican Publications.

Kirk, Andrew. 1980. *Theology Encounters Revolution,* Downers Grove, Ill.: Inter Varsity Press.

Kissinger, Henry. 1984."Report to the National Bipartisan Commission on Central America." Washington, D.C.: U.S. Government Printing Office, January.

Klaiber, Jeffrey L. 1977. *Religion and Revolution in Peru, 1824–1976.* Notre Dame, Ind.: University of Notre Dame Press.

Klandermans, Bert. 1984. "Mobilization and Participation: Social Psychological Expansions of Resource Mobilization Theory." *American Sociological Review* 49 (October): 583–600.

Kselman, Thomas A. 1986. "Ambivalence and Assumption in the Concept of Popular Religion." In *Religion and Political Conflict in Latin America,* ed. Daniel H. Levine. Chapel Hill: University of North Carolina Press.

Lacy, Hugh. 1985. "Liberation: Philosophy and Politics." *Cross Currents* 35 (Summer-Fall): 219–41.

LADOC, vol. 2. "The Theology of Liberation." Washington, D.C.: Latin American Documentation Service.

_____, vol. 4. "Sisters and Priests for Latin America." Washington, D.C.: Latin American Documentation Service.

_____, vol. 5. "Social Activist Priests: Chile." Washington, D.C.: Latin American Documentation Service.

_____, vol. 6. "Social Activist Preists: Columbia, Argentina." Washington, D.C.: Latin American Documentation Service.

_____, vol. 8. "Brazil." Washington, D.C.: Latin American Documentation Service.

_____, vol. 14. "Basic Christian Communities (BCC's)." Washington, D.C.: Latin American Documentation Service.

_____, vol. 15. "Latin American Bishops Discuss Human Rights." Washington, D.C.: Latin American Documentation Service.

_____, vol. 16. "Latin American Bishops Discuss Human Rights." Washington, D.C.: Latin American Documentation Service.

_____, vol. 18. "Repression Against the Church in Brazil 1968–1978." Washington, D.C.: Latin American Documentation Service.

———. 1986. *Liberation Theology.* Lima: LADOC.

Lall, Sanjaya. 1975. "Is Dependency a Useful Concept in Analyzing Underdevelopment?" *World Development* 3 (November).

Landsberger, Henry A. 1970. *The Church and Social Change in Latin America.* Notre Dame, Ind.: University of Notre Dame Press.

Lange, Martin, and Reinhold Iblacker. 1981. *Witness of Hope: The Persecution of Christians in Latin America.* Maryknoll, N.Y.: Orbis Books.

Langton, Kenneth P., and Ronald Rapoport. 1976. "Religion and Leftist Mobilization in Chile." *Comparative Political Studies* 9, no. 3 (October): 277–308.

Latourette, Kenneth Scott. 1962. *Christianity in a Revolutionary Age.* Vol. 5. New York: Harper and Row.

Lattes, Alfredo. 1981. "The Dynamics of the Rural Population in Argentina between 1870–1970." In Jorge Balan, *Why People Move.* Paris: Unesco Press.

Leahey, Peter, and Allen Mazur. 1978. "A Comparison of Movements Opposed to Nuclear Power, Floridation, and Abortion." *Research on Social Movements, Conflict, and Change,* vol. 1, pp. 121–39.

Leo XIII. 1903. *Rerum Novarum.* In *The Great Encyclical Letters of Pope Leo XIII,* ed. John J. Wynne. New York: Benziger Brothers.

Lernoux, Penny. 1979. "The Long Path to Puebla." In *Puebla and Beyond,* ed. John Eagleson and Phillip Scharper. Maryknoll, N.Y.: Orbis Books.

———. 1980. "The Latin American Church." *Latin American Research Review* 15(2):201–11.

———. 1982. *Cry of the People: Then Struggle for Human Rights in Latin America— the Catholic Church in Conflict with U.S. Policy.* New York: Penguin Books.

———. 1987. "In Common Suffering and Hope." *Sojourners Magazine,* December.

———. 1989. *People of God: The Struggle for World Catholicism.* New York: Penguin Books.

Levine, Daniel H. 1979. "Church Elites in Venezuela and Columbia: Context, Background, and Beliefs." *Latin American Review* 14(1):51–79.

———. 1981. *Religion and Politics in Latin America: The Catholic Church in Venezuela and Columbia.* Princeton, N.J.: Princeton Univeristy Press.

———. 1984. "Popular Organizations and the Church: Thoughts From Columbia." *Journal of Interamerican Studies and World Affairs,* 26, no. 1 (February): 137–42.

———. 1985. "Continuities in Columbia." *Journal of Latin American Studies* 17, pt. 2 (November): 295–317.

———. 1986. "Is Religion Being Politicized? and Other Pressing Questions Latin America Poses." *PS,* no. 19 (Fall): 825–31.

Levine, Daniel, ed. 1979. *Churches and Politics in Latin America.* Beverly Hills, Calif.: Sage Publications.

———. 1986. *Religion and Political Conflict in Latin America.* Chapel Hill: University of North Carolina Press.

Levine, Daniel, and Scott Mainwaring. 1989. "Religion and Popular Protest in Latin America: Contrasting Experiences." In *Power and Popular Protest: Latin American Social Movements,* ed. Susan Eckstein. Berkeley: University of California Press.

Levine, Daniel, and Alexander Wilde. 1977. "The Catholic Church, 'Politics,' and Violence: The Colombian Case." *Review of Politics* 39, no. 2 (April): 220–49.

Levinson, Jerome, and Juan de Onis. 1970. *The Alliance That Lost Its Way: A Critical Report on the Alliance for Progress.* Chicago: Quadrangle Books.

Libanio, João B. 1978. "CELAM III: Fears and Hopes." *Cross Currents* 28 (Spring): 20–33.

———. 1985. Interview, August 7, Oxford, England.

Libby, Ronald. 1983. "Listen to the Bishops." *Foreign Policy,* no. 50-53 (Fall): 78–95.

Liebman, Robert, C. 1983. "Mobilizing the Moral Majority." Pp. 4–73 in *The New Christian Right: Mobilization and Legitemation,* ed. Robert Leibman and Robert Wuthnow. New York: Aldine.

Lima, Luiz Gonzaga de Souza. 1979. *Evolcão Política dos Católicos da Igreja no Brasil.* Petropolis: Vozes.

Littwin, Lawrence. 1974. *Latin America: Catholicism and Class Conflict.* Encino, Calif.: Dickenson Publishing Co.

López Trujillo, Alfonso. 1977. *Liberation or Revolution?* Huntington, Ind.: Our Sunday Visitor.

————. 1978. *Hacia uno Sociedad Nueva, Socialismo: Opción Cristiana?* Bogotá, Colombia: Ediciones Paulinas.

————. 1980. *De Medellín a Puebla.* Madrid: La Editorial Catolica.

McAdam, Doug. 1982. *Political Process and the Development of Black Insurgency, 1930–1970.* Chicago: University of Chicago Press.

McCann, Dennis. N.d. "Liberation and the Multinationals." *Theology Today,* no. 41, pp. 51–60.

McElvaney, William K. 1980. *Good News is Bad News is Good News. . . .* Maryknoll, N.Y.: Orbis Books.

MacEoin, Gary, and Nivita Riley. 1980. *Puebla: A Church Being Born.* New York: Paulist Press.

McGovern, Arthur F. 1980. *Marxism: An American Christian Perspective.* Maryknoll: Orbis Books.

————. 1987. "Latin America and 'Dependency' Theory." In *Liberation Theology and the Liberal Society,* ed. Michael Novak. Washington, D.C.: American Enterprise Institute.

————. 1989a. "Liberation Theology Adapts and Endures, and Keeps a Perspective From Below." *Commonweal,* November 3.

————. 1989b. *Liberation Theology and Its Critics.* Maryknoll, N.Y.: Orbis Books.

McGrath, Archbishop Marcos. 1988. Interview, June 28, Panama City, Panama.

McGurn, William. 1987. "Philippine Church Entangled in Marxist Insurrection." *The Wall Street Journal,* Monday, June 22, p. 27.

McNamara, Patrick H. 1979. "Conscience, Catholicism, and Social Change in Latin America." *Social Research,* no. 46 (Summer): 329–49.

Maduro, Otto. 1982. *Religion and Social Conflicts.* Maryknoll, N.Y.: Orbis Books.

————. 1987. Interview, December 9, Cambridge, Mass.

Mainwaring, Scott. 1984. "The Catholic Church, Popular Education, and Political Change in Brazil." *Journal of Interamerican Studies and World Affairs* 26, no. 1 (February): 97–124.

Mainwaring, Scott, and Alexander Wilde. 1989. "The Progressive Church in Latin America: An Interpretation." In *The Progressive Church in Latin America,* ed. Scott Mainwaring and Alexander Wilde. Notre Dame: The University of Notre Dame Press.

————, eds. 1989. *The Progressive Church in Latin America.* Notre Dame: The University of Notre Dame Press.

Marins, José, et al. 1978. *Praxis de los Padres de América Latina.* Bogotá, Colombia: Ediciones Paulinas.

Marsh, Alan. 1977. *Protest and Political Consciousness,* Beverly Hills, Calif.: Sage Publications.

Martina, Giacomo, S.J. 1988. "The Historical Context of the Ecumenical Council." In *Vatican II: Assessments and Perspectives,* ed. René Latourelle. New York: Paulist Press.

Martin-Baro, Ignacio. 1985. "Oscar Romero: Voice of the Downtrodden." In Oscar Romero, *Voice of the Voiceless*. Maryknoll, N.Y.: Orbis Books.

Maryknoll Documentation Series. 1970. *Between Honesty and Hope: Documents From and about the Church in Latin America*. Peruvian Bishops Commission for Social Action. Maryknoll, N.Y.: Maryknoll Publications.

Marx, Gary T. 1967. *Protest and Prejudice*. New York: Harper and Row.

———. 1979. "External Efforts to Damage or Facilitate Social Movements." In *The Dynamics of Social Movements*, ed. Mayer Zald and John McCarthy. Lanham: University Press of America.

Marzani, Carl. 1982. "The Vatican as a Left Ally?" *Monthly Review* 34, no. 3 (July-August): 1–42.

Medhurst, Kenneth. 1987. "The Church and Politics in Latin America." *South America, Central America and the Caribbean*. London: Europa Publications.

Medina, Augusto Merino. 1980. *Iglesia y Política en América Latina: De Medellín a Puebla*. Santiago: Instituto de Estudios Internacionales Universidad de Chile.

Methol Ferre, Alberto. 1979. *Puebla: Proceso y Tensiones*. N.p.

Metzinger, Luciano. 1973. "Quinto Aniversario de Medellin." *Documentación Latinoamericano*, no. 10 (December): 26–28.

Min, Anselm K. 1984. "The Vatican, Marxism, and Liberation Theology." *Cross Currents* 34 (Winter): 439–55.

Miranda, José. 1974. *Marx and the Bible*. Maryknoll, N.Y.: Orbis Books.

———. 1980. *Marx Against the Marxists*. Maryknoll, N.Y.: Orbis Books.

Mitchell, David. 1981. *The Jesuits: A History*. New York: Franklin Watts.

Molina, Sergio, and Hernan Larraín. 1971. "Democratic Socialism, Not Totalitarian Socialism." *Mensaje*, March-April, pp. 1–9.

Moltmann, Jurgen. 1974. *The Crucified God*. New York: Harper and Row.

Moncada, Camilo, ed. 1971. *Liberación en América Latina*. Bogotá, Colombia: Servicio Colombiano de Communicación Social.

Monni, Piero, and Gianfranco Grieco. 1978. *Puebla '78*. Rome: Edizioni Studium.

Montgomery, Tommie Sue. 1982. "Cross and Rifle: Revolution and the Church in El Salvador and Nicaragua." *Journal of International Affairs* 36, no. 2, (Fall-Winter): 209–21.

Moore, Robert S. 1975. "Religion as a Source of Variation in Working-Class Images of Society." In *Working Class Images of Society*, ed. Martin Blumer. London: Routledge and Kegan Paul.

Morelli, Alex. 1971. "Man Liberated from Sin and Oppression: A Theology of Liberation." Chapter 9 in *Freedom and Unfreedom in the Americas*, ed. Thomas Quigley. New York: IDOC Books.

Morris, Aldon. 1981. "Black Southern Student Sit-In Movements: An Analysis of Internal Organization." *American Sociological Review* 45:744–67.

Mottesi, Osvaldo Luis. 1985. An Historically Mediated "Pastoral" of Liberation: Gustavo Gutierrez's Pilgrimage Towards Socialism. Ph.D. diss., Emory University.

Muñoz, Heraldo. 1981. "Introduction: The Various Roads to Development."

In *From Dependency to Development,* ed. Heraldo Muñoz. Boulder, Colo.: Westview Press.

Muñoz, Ronaldo. 1973. "Nuestra Iglesia Antes y Despues de Medellín." NADOC, no. 324 (18 October), pp. 3–4.

———. 1979. "The Historical Vocation of the Church." In *Frontiers of Theology in Latin America,* ed. Rosario Gibellini. Maryknoll, N.Y.: Orbis Books.

———. 1981. "Ecclesiology in Latin America." In *The Challenge of Basic Christian Communities, ed. Sergio Torres and John Eagleson.* Maryknoll, N.Y.: Orbis Books.

Murickan, Joseph K. 1985. From Development to Liberation: Perspectives in the Emergence of Liberation Theology in India. Ph.D. diss., Duquesne University.

Mutchler, David E. 1971. *The Church as a Political Factor in Latin America, with Particular Reference to Columbia and Chile.* New York: Praeger Publishers.

Nash, Ronald, ed. 1986. *Liberation Theology.* Milford, Mich.: Mott Media.

Neely, Alan Preston. 1977. Protestant Antecedents of the Latin American Theology of Liberation. Ph.D. diss., The American University.

Neuhouser, Kevin. 1989. "The Radicalization of the Brazilian Catholic Church in Comparative Perspective." *American Sociological Review* 54 (April): 233–44.

Nichols, Peter. 1968. *The Politics of the Vatican.* New York: Frederick A. Praeger.

Novak, Michael. 1979. "Liberation Theology and the Pope." *Commentary,* no. 67, (June): 60–64.

———. 1982. *The Spirit of Democratic Capitalism.* New York: Simon and Schuster.

———. 1986. *Will it Liberate? Questions About Liberation Theology.* Mahwah, N.J.: Paulist Press.

Novak, Michael, ed. 1987. *Liberation Theology and the Liberal Society.* Washington, D.C.: American Enterprise Institute.

Novak, Michael, and Michael P. Jackson, eds. 1985. *Latin America: Dependency or Interdependence?* Washington, D.C.: American Enterprise Institute.

Nuñez, Emilio A. 1985. *Liberation Theology.* Chicago: Moody Press.

Oberschall, Anthony. 1973. *Social Conflict and Social Movements.* Englewood Cliffs, N.J.: Prentice Hall.

O'Brien, Philip. 1975. "A Critique of Latin American Theories of Dependence." In *Beyond the Sociology of Development,* ed. I. Oxaal et al. London.

O'Donnell, Guillermo. 1973. *Modernization and Bureaucratic Authoritarianism.* Berkeley: University of California Institute of International Studies.

O'Gorman, Frances. 1977. *Aluanda.* Rio de Janeiro, Brazil: Livraria Francisco Alves Editora S.A.

———. 1983. *Base Communities in Brazil.* Rio de Janeiro, Brazil: Federação de Orgãos para Assistência Social e Educacional.

———. 1988 Interview, April 23, Salem, Mass.

Oliveros Maqueo, Roberto, S.J. 1977. *Liberación y Teología: Genesis y Crecimiento de una Reflexion: 1966–1977.* Lima, Peru: Centro de Estudios y Publicaciones.

———. 1990. "Meeting of Theologians at Petrópolis." In *Liberation Theology: A Documentary History,* ed. Alfred Hennelly. Maryknoll, N.Y.: Orbis Books.

Olson, Marcus. 1965. *The Logic of Collective Action.* Cambridge, Mass.: Harvard University Press.

Opp, Karl-Dieter. 1988. "Grievances and Participation in Social Movements." *American Sociological Review* 53 (December): 853–64.

Oviedo, Alvaro, and Stepan Mamontov. 1986. "Theology of Liberation: A New Heresy?" *World Marxist Review* 29, no. 3 (March): 83–90.

Packenham, Robert. 1974. "Latin American Dependency Theories: Strengths and Weaknesses." Paper presented to the Harvard-MIT Joint Seminar on Political Development, February.

———. N.d. "The New Utopianism: Political Development Ideas in the Dependency Literature." Washington, D.C.: Woodrow Wilson Center, Smithsonian Institute.

Padilla, C. Rene. 1987. "Liberation Theology is Remarkably Protestant." *Christianity Today* 31, no. 8 (May 15).

Paige, Jeffery M. 1971. "Political Orientation and Riot Participation." *American Sociological Review* 36:810–20.

Palmer, David Scott. 1990. "Peru's Persistent Problems." *Current History,* January.

Pastene, Luis Pacheco. 1986. "Aproxicacion Historica a Lost Origenes de la Teología de la Liberación." *Dialogo en Torno a la Teología de la Liberación,* pp. 71–85. Santiago: ILADES, Editorial Salesiana.

Paul VI. 1967. *Populorum Progressio.* In *The Gospel of Peace and Justice,* ed. Joseph Gremillion. Maryknoll, N.Y.: Orbis Books.

Perloff, Harvey S. 1969. Alliance for Progress: A Social Invention in the Making. Baltimore: The John Hopkins Press.

Perry, Nicholas. 1985. "Unliberation Theology." *New Statesman* 109 (March 1): 20–21.

Peruvian Bishops' Commission for Social Action. 1970. *Between Honesty and Hope,* trans. John Drury. Maryknoll, New York: Maryknoll Publications.

Peruvian Theologians. 1978. "Our Martyrs Give Hope of Resurrection: The Church of the Poor." *Cross Currents* 28 (Spring): 47–54.

Pinard, Maurice. 1971. *The Rise of a Third Party: A Study in Crisis Politics.* Englewood Cliffs, N.J.: Prentice Hall.

Pius XI. 1957. *Quadragesimo Anno.* In *The Church and the Reconstruction of the Modern World: The Social Encyclicals of Pope Pius XI,* ed. Terence P. McLaughlin. Garden City, N.Y.: Image Books.

Pius XII. 1949. *Selected Letters and Addresses of Pius XII.* London: CTS Publishers.

Piven, Frances, and Richard Cloward. 1977. *Poor People's Movements.* New York: Pantheon.

Poblete, Renato. 1966. "Vocations—Problems and Promise." Pp. 148–58 in *The Religious Dimension in the New Latin America,* ed. John Considine. Notre Dame: Fides.

———. 1979. "From Medellín to Puebla: Notes for Reflection." In *Churches and Politics in Latin America,* ed. Daniel H. Levine. Beverly Hills, Calif.: Sage Publications.

————. 1986. "Antecedentes y Genesis de la Teología de la Liberación: Antecedentes." Pp. 59–70 in *Dialogo en Torno a la Teología de la Liberación.* Santiago: ILADES, Editorial Salesiana.

————. 1988. Interview, August 16, Santiago, Chile.

Pochet, Rosa Maria. 1988. Interview, June 23, San Jose, Costa Rica.

Pomerleau, Claude. 1983. "Church and State in Latin America." In *Latin America and Carribean Contemporary Record,* ed. Jack Hopkins. New York: Holmes and Meier Publishers.

Portes, Alejandro. 1971. "On the Logic of Post-Facto Explanations: The Hypothesis of Lower-Class Frustration as the Cause of Leftist Radicalism." *Social Forces* 50:26–44.

Porterfield, Amanda. 1987. "Feminist Theology as a Revitalization Movement." *Sociological Analysis* 48(3):234–44.

Prada, Hernan. 1975. *Cronica de Medellín.* Bogotá, Colombia: Indo-American Press Service.

Praamsma, L. 1981. *The Church in the Twentieth Century.* Vol. 7. St. Catharines, Ontario: Paideia Press.

Protopas, Chouinard Jorge. 1974. *Los Cristianos y los Cambios Sociales en Latinoamerica.* Santiago, Chile: Editorial del Pacifico S.A.

Ptacek, Kerry. 1986. "U.S. Protestants and Liberation Theology." *Orbis,* 30, no. 3 (Fall): 433–41.

Quade, Quentin L., ed. 1982. *The Pope and Revolution: John Paul II Confronts Liberation Theology.* Washington, D.C.: Ethics and Public Policy Center.

Quigley, Thomas E. 1978. "Latin America's Church: No Turning Back." *Cross Currents* 28 (Spring): 79–89.

————. 1982. "The Catholic Church and El Salvador." *Cross Currents* 32 (Summer): 179–92.

————. 1984. "The Catholic Church and El Salvador." In *The Church and Society in Latin America,* ed. Jeffrey Cole. New Orleans: Tulane Center for Latin American Studies.

————. 1987. Interview, December 30, Washington, D.C.

Quijano, Anibal. 1975. "The Urbanization of Latin American Society." In *Urbanization in Latin America: Approaches and Issues,* ed. Jorge Hardoy. Garden City: Doubleday.

Ramalho, Jether Pereira. 1977. "Basic Popular Communities in Brazil: Some Notes on Pastoral Activity in Two Types." *Ecumenical Review,* no. 29, 394–401.

————. 1988. Interview, August 1, Rio de Janeiro, Brazil.

Ramirez, Gustavo Perez. 1971. "Liberation: A Recurring Prophetic Cry in the Americas." Chapter 3 in *Freedom and Unfreedom in the Americas,* ed. Thomas Quigley. New York: IDOC Books.

Ramirez, Gustavo Perez, and Yvan Labelle. 1964. *El Problema Sacerdotal en América Latina.* Bogotá, Colombia: Oficina Internacional de Investigaciones Sociales de FERES/Centro de Investigaciones Sociales Departemento Socio-Religioso.

Ratzinger, Joseph, and Alberto Bovone. 1984. "Instruction on Certain Aspects of the 'Theology of Liberation'." *Origins*, 14, no. 13 (13 September): 195–204.

Ratzinger, Joseph, and Vittorio Messori. 1986. *The Ratzinger Report: An Exclusive Interview on the State of the Church*. San Francisco: Ignatius Press.

Ray, David. 1973. "The Dependency Model of Latin American Underdevelopment: Three Basic Fallacies." *Journal of Interamerican Studies and World Affairs* 15 (February).

Read, William, Victor Monterroso, and Harmon Johnson. 1968. *Avance Evangélico en la América Latina*. Translated into Spanish by Manuel Gaxoila. {place?:} Casa Bautista de Publicaciones.

Reding, Andrew. 1987. *Christianity and Revolution: Thomas Borge's Theology of Life*. Maryknoll, N.Y.: Orbis Books.

Richard, Pablo. 1975. *Origen y Desarrollo del Movimiento Cristianos por el Socialismo, Chile: 1970–1973*. Paris: Centre Lebret.

———. 1976. *Cristianos por el Socialismo*. Salamanca, Spain: Ediciones Sigueme.

———. 1978. "The Latin American Church: 1959–1978." *Cross Currents* 28 (Spring): 34–46.

———. 1979. "Desarrollo de la Teología Latinoamericana: 1960–1978." Serie Reflexiva Biblico-Teologica. San Jose, Costa Rica: Seminario Biblico Latinoamericano.

———. 1987a. *Death of Christendoms, Birth of the Church*. Maryknoll, N.Y.: Orbis Books.

———. 1987b. *La Iglesia Latinoamericana entre el Temor y la Esperanza*. San Jose, Costa Rica: Departamento Ecumenico de Investigaciones.

———. 1988. Interview, June 24, San Jose, Costa Rica.

———. N.d. *Political Organizations of Christians in Latin America: From Christian Democracy to a New Model*. San Jose, Costa Rica: Departamento Ecumenico de Investigaciones.

Richard, Pablo, ed. 1981. *Historia de la Teología en América Latina*. San Jose, Costa Rica: Departamento Ecumenico de Investigaciones.

Riding, Alan. 1990 "Pope Shifts Brazilian Church to the Right." In *Liberation Theology: A Documentary History*, ed. Alfred Hennelly. Maryknoll, N.Y.: Orbis Books.

Roberts, Bryan. 1981. "Migration and Industrializing Economies: A Comparative Perspective." In Jorge Balan, *Why People Move*. Paris: Unesco Press.

Rockefeller Report. 1969. *The Rockefeller Report on the Americas*. Chicago: Quadrangle Books.

Rosales, Juan. 1979. "The 'Battle' of Puebla." *World Marxist Review* 22, no. 12 (December): 59–62.

Rostow, W. W. 1960. *The Stages of Economic Growth: A Non-Communist Manifesto*. New York: Cambridge University Press.

Roth, John. 1988. "The Great Enemy? How Latin American Liberation Theology Sees the United States and the USSR." In *The Politics of Latin American Liberation Theology*, ed. Richard Rubenstein and John Roth. Washington, D.C.: The Washington Institute Press.

Rule, James, and Charles Tilly. 1975. "Political Process in Revolutionary France: 1830–1832." In *1830 in France,* ed. John Merrinman. New York: New Viewpoints.

Rynne, Xavier (pseudonym). 1964. *Letters from Vatican City, Vatican Council II (First Session): Background and Debates.* Garden City, N.Y.: Doubleday and Company.

Sabatte, Atilo. 1973. *Crisis Sacerdotal en América Latina.* Buenos Aires, Argentina: Editorial Guadalupe.

Salazar, Botero. 1973. "La Conferencia de Medellín." Documentación Latinoamericano, no. 10 (December): 22–26.

Sanders, Thomas G. 1969. *Catholic Innovation in a Changing Latin America.* Cuernavaca, Mexico: Son Deos, no. 41.

———. 1972. "The Chilean Episcopate: An Institution in Transition." Chapter 5 in *The Roman Catholic Church in Modern Latin America,* ed. Karl M. Schmitt. New York: Alfred A. Knopf.

———. 1982. "The Politics of Catholicism in Latin America." *Journal of Interamerican Studies and World Affairs* 24, no. 2 (May): 241–58.

Santa Ana, Julio de. 1986. "Schools of Sharing: Basic Ecclesial Communities." *The Ecumenical Review* 38, no. 4 (October): 381–85.

———. 1988. Interview, August 2, São Paulo, Brazil.

Sandoval, Moises. 1979. "Report From the Conference." In *Puebla and Beyond,* ed. Eagleson and Scharper. Maryknoll, N.Y.: Orbis Books.

SCCS (Servico Colombiano de Comunicacion Social). 1971. *Liberación en América Latin: Encuentro Teologico, Bogotá, July 1971.* Editorial Americana Latina.

———. 1973. "De Medellín a Sucre. La Reacción Eclesiastica." NADOC, no. 320 (Sept. 1973), pp. 3–6.

Schall, James V. 1982. *Liberation Theology.* San Fransisco: Ignatius Press.

———. 1986. "Counter-Liberation." *Orbis* 30, no. 3 (Fall): 426–32.

Segundo, Juan Luis. 1973. *A Theology for Artisans of a New Humanity: The Community Called Church.* Maryknoll, N.Y.: Orbis Books.

———. 1974. *A Theology for Artisans of a New Humanity: Evolution and Guilt.* Maryknoll, N.Y.: Orbis Books.

———. 1976. *The Liberation of Theology.* Maryknoll, N.Y.: Orbis Books.

———. 1979. "Capitalism Versus Socialism: Crux Theologica." In *Frontiers of Theology in Latin America,* ed. Rosino Gibellini. Maryknoll, N.Y.: Orbis Books.

———. 1990. "Two Theologies of Liberation." In *Liberation Theology: A Documentary History,* ed. Alfred Hennelly. Maryknoll, N.Y.: Orbis Books.

Shaull, Richard. 1970. "The Church and Revolutionary Change: Contrasting Perspectives." Pp. 135–53 in *The Church and Social Change in Latin America,* ed. Henry A. Landsberger. Notre Dame, Ind.: University of Notre Dame Press.

———. 1987. Interview, December 29, Philadelphia, Pa.

Shea, Nina Hope. 1987. "The Systematic Destruction of Faith in Nicaragua." *The Wall Street Journal,* Friday, May 22, p. 19.

Shepherd, George. 1979. "Liberation Theology and Class Struggle in Southern Africa and Latin America." *The Review of Black Political Economy*, no. 9 (Winter): 159–73.

Sigmund, Paul E. 1988. "The Development of Liberation Theology: Continuity or Change." In *The Politics of Latin American Liberation Theology*, ed. Richard Rubenstein and John Roth. Washington, D.C.: The Washington Institute Press.

Sigueme. 1987. *Historia General de la Iglesia en América Latina*, vol. 8, Salamanca: Sigueme.

Skidmore, Thomas E., and Peter H. Smith. 1984. *Modern Latin America*. New York: Oxford University Press.

Smith, Brian. 1982. *The Church and Politics in Chile: Challenges to Modern Catholicism*. Princeton, N.J.: Princeton University Press.

Smith, Tony. 1979. "The Underdevelopment of Development Literature: The Case of Dependency Theory." *World Politics* 31 (January): 247–88.

Snow, David, and Robert Benford. 1988. "Ideology, Frame Resonance, and Participant Mobilization." In *From Structure to Action: Social Movement Participation across Cultures*, ed. Bert Klandermans, Hanspeter Kreisi, and Sidney Tarrow. Greenwich, Conn.: JAI Publishers.

Snow, David, E. Burke Rochford, Steven Worden, and Robert Benford. 1986. "Frame Alignment Processes, Micromobilization, and Movement Participation." *American Sociological Review* 51:464–81.

Snow, David, Louis Zurcher, and Sheldon Ekland-Olson. 1980. "Social Networks and Social Movements: A Microstructural Approach to Differential Recruitment." *American Sociological Review* 45 (October): 787–801.

Solberg, Carl. 1978. "Mass Migration in Argentina: 1870–1970." In *Human Migration: Patterns and Policies*, ed. William McNeil and Ruth Adams. Bloomington, Ind.: University of Indiana Press.

Steedly, Homer R., and John W. Foley. 1979. "The Success of Protest Groups: A Multivariate Analysis." *Social Science Research* 8:1–15.

Sunkel, Osvaldo, and Pedro Paz. 1970. *El subdesarrollo latinoamericano y la teoría del desarrollo*. Mexico: Siglo XXI Editores.

Takayama, K. Peter. 1988. "The Revitalization Movement of Modern Japanese Civil Religion." *Sociological Analysis* 48(4):328–41.

Tierra Nueva. 1971. *De La Iglesia y La Sociedad*. Montevideo, Uruguay.

———. 1972. *Pueblo Oprimido, Señor de la Historia*. Montevideo, Uruguay.

Tilly, Charles. 1978. *From Mobilization to Revolution*. Reading, Mass.: Addison Wesley.

Tilly, Charles, Louise Tilly, and Richard Tilly. 1975. *The Rebellious Century*. Cambridge, Mass.: Harvard University Press.

Tinder, Glenn. 1989. *The Political Meaning of Christianity*. Baton Rouge: University of Louisiana Press.

Torres, Camilo. 1969. *Revolutionary Writings*. New York: Herder and Herder.

Torres, Hector, ed. 1978. *Roger Vekemans: Colaborador de la CIA Presente in Colombia*. Bogotá, Colombia: Privately Published.

Torres, Sergio. 1988. Interview, August 17, Santiago Chile.

Torres, Sergio, and John Eagleson, eds. 1976. *Theology in the Americas*. Maryknoll, N.Y.: Orbis Books.

————. 1982. *The Challenge of Basic Christian Communities*. Maryknoll, N.Y.: Orbis Press.

Torres, Sergio, and Virginia Fabella. 1978. *The Emergent Gospel: Theology from the Developing World*. London: Geoffrey Chapman.

Tunnermann, Carlos. 1987. "Nicaragua and the Church." *The Wall Street Journal*, Tuesday, July 7.

Turner, Frederick. 1971. *Catholicism and Political Development in Latin America*. Chapel Hill: University of North Carolina Press.

Turner, Ralph H. 1969. "The Public Perception of Protest." *American Sociological Review* 34, no. 6 (December): 815–31.

————. 1981. "Collective Behavior and Resource Mobilization as Approaches to Social Movements: Issues and Continuities." *Research in Social Movements, Conflict, and Change* 4:1–24.

UCLA. 1969. *Statistical Abstract of Latin America*. Los Angeles: UCLA Latin American Center Publications.

Urresti, Jimenez. 1973. "La Teología de Liberación: Antecedentes, Causas y Contenidos." Pp. 19–42 in *Teología de la Liberación*, ed. Ediciones Aldecoa. Burgos, Spain: Diego de Siloe.

U.S. House of Representatives, Committee on Foreign Affairs. 1969. *New Directions for the 1970's: Toward a Strategy of Inter-American Development*. Washington, D.C.: U.S. Government Printing Office.

Useem, Bert. 1980. "Solidarity Model, Breakdown Model, and the Boston Anti-Busing Movement." *American Sociological Review* 45:357–69.

Useem, Michael. 1975. *Protest Movements in America*. Indianapolis, Ind.: Bobbs-Merrill.

Valenzuela, J. Samuel, and Arturo Valenzuela. 1981. "Modernization and Dependency: Alternative Perspectives in the Study of Latin American Underdevelopment." In *From Dependency to Development*, ed. Heraldo Muños. Boulder, Colo.: Westview Press.

Vallier, Ivan. 1967. "Religious Elites: Differentiation and Developments in Roman Catholicism." Chapter 6 in *Elites in Latin America*, ed. Seymour Lipset, and Aldo Solari. New York: Oxford University Press.

————. 1970. "Extraction, Insulation, and Re-Entry: Toward a Theory of Religious Change." In *The Church and Social Change in Latin America*, ed. Henry A. Landsberger. Notre Dame, Ind.: University of Notre Dame Press, pp. 9–35.

Verhoeven, Thomas W. 1966. "New Army of Catechists in the Andes." In *The Religious Dimension in the New Latin America*, ed. John Considine. Notre Dame: Fides Publishers, pp. 127–39.

Vekemans, Roger E. 1964. "Economic Development, Social Change, and Cultural Mutation in Latin America." In *Religion, Revolution, and Reform*, ed. William D'Antonio and Fredrick Pike. New York: Frederick A. Praeger Publishers.

————. 1971. *Iglesia y Mundo Politico, Sacerdocio y Política*. Barcelona: Editorial Herder.

————. 1972. *Ceasar and God: The Priesthood and Politics*. Maryknoll, N.Y.: Orbis Books.

———. 1976. *Teología de la Liberación y Cristianos por el Socialismo.* Bogotá, Colombia: CEDIAL.

Vekemans, Roger, and Ismael Silva. 1976. *Marinalidad, Promoción Popular, y Neo-Marxismo.* Bogotá, Colombia: CEDIAL.

Vitalis, Helmut Gnadt. 1968. *The Significance of Changes in Latin American Catholicism since Chimbote.* Cuernavaca: Centro Inter-cultural de Documentación.

Von Eschen, Donald, Jerome Kirk, and Maurice Pinard. 1971. "The Organizational Substructure of Disorderly Politics." *Social Forces* 49(4):529–44.

Wallace, Anthony F. C. 1956. "Revitalization Movements." *American Anthropologist* 58(2):264–65.

Weber, Max. 1978. *Max Weber: Economy and Society,* ed. Gunther Roth and Claus Wittich. Berkeley: University of California Press.

Weisskopf, Theodore. 1976. "Dependency as an Explanation for Underdevelopment: A Critique." Paper presented at the Sixth Annual Latin American Studies Association Meeting, Atlanta, Georgia.

Welna, David. 1983. "Argentina's Bishops and the Disappeared." *Christianity and Crisis,* no. 43, 252–53.

West, Cornel. 1984. "Religion and the Left: An Introduction." *Monthly Review,* July-August.

Wiarda, Howard J. 1990. "United States Policy in Latin America." *Current History,* January.

Wiarda, Howard J., and Harvey F. Kline. 1985. *Latin American Politics and Development,* 2d ed. Boulder, Colo.: Westview Press.

Wilde, Alexander. 1979. "Ten Years of Change in the Church: Puebla and the Future." *Journal of Interamerican Studies and World Affairs* 21(3):299–312.

Williams, Margaret Todaro. 1974. "The Politicalization of the Brazilian Catholic Church: The Catholic Electoral League." *Journal of Interamerican Studies and World Affairs* 16(3):301–25.

Williams, Philip J. 1985. "The Catholic Hierarchy in the Nicaraguan Revolution." *Journal of Latin American Studies,* no. 17, 341–69.

Zald, Mayer N., and Michael A. Berger. 1978. "Social Movements in Organizations: Coup D'Etat Bureaucratic Insurgency and Mass Movement." *American Journal of Sociology* 83(4):823–61.

Index

293